THE
Reader's Digest
TREASURY OF
AMERICAN
HUMOR

★ ★ ★

THE
Reader's Digest
TREASURY OF AMERICAN HUMOR

Selected by the Editors of
Reader's Digest

Introduction and
Casual Commentary by
Clifton Fadiman

A READER'S DIGEST PRESS BOOK
published by
AMERICAN HERITAGE PRESS
a division of McGraw-Hill Book Company

New York   St. Louis   San Francisco
Düsseldorf   Toronto   Mexico

This book has been set in English by University Graphics, Inc.

Library of Congress Cataloging in Publication Data
Main entry under title:
The Reader's digest treasury of American humor.

"A Reader's Digest Press book."
1.   American wit and humor.   I. The Reader's digest.
II.   Title: Treasury of American humor.
PN6162.R3737   818 '.07   72-5323
ISBN 0-07-051290-6

ACKNOWLEDGMENTS

The editors wish to make grateful acknowledgment for permission to reprint the following copyright material: ALL UP IN A HEAVAL, by Joseph Henry Jackson, from
The Atlantic Monthly, copyright 1951 by The Atlantic Monthly Co. AMERICA, FROM
A SAFE DISTANCE, by Alex Atkinson, from *By Rocking Chair Across America,* ©
1959 by Alex Atkinson and Ronald Searle, reprinted by permission of Funk & Wagnalls

from *Please Don't Eat the Daisies,* © 1957 by Jean Kerr, reprinted by permission of Doubleday & Company, Inc., and in Great Britain by permission of A. M. Heath & Co., Ltd.

The editors also wish to acknowledge the following publishers and individuals for material reprinted herein: *American Legion Magazine;* Estate of Bennett Cerf; *Changing Times. The Kiplinger Magazine;* Chicago Sun-Times Syndicate; Chicago Tribune—New York News Syndicate; *Christian Science Monitor; Hollywood Reporter;* King Features Syndicate; *Ladies' Home Journal; Look Magazine; Milwaukee Sentinel;* Newspaper Enterprise Association; *Newsweek;* Publishers Hall Syndicate; *San Francisco Chronicle; The Saturday Evening Post; Saturday Review; This Week Magazine;* Time Inc.; *True Magazine; The Wall Street Journal;* Earl Wilson.

Contents

Foreword

THE EDITORS of *Reader's Digest,* having rummaged through the files of half a century and separated the wit from the chaff, offer the result to all Americans free from paralysis of the cachinnatory muscles, if such muscles exist. Here are some of the masters of laughter, past and present, represented: James Thurber, J. P. McEvoy, Ogden Nash, Frank Moore Colby, Ambrose Bierce, Corey Ford, H. Allen Smith, Don Herold, Cornelia Otis Skinner, Art Buchwald, Robert Benchley, Mark Twain, Leo Rosten, Dorothy Parker, Max Beerbohm, Jean Kerr, Stephen Leacock.

But the bulk of the book is made up of short stuff—jokes, gags, epigrams, anecdotes, fillers—in a variety rich enough to coax a smile, at some point or other, from even the members of Mr. Nixon's cabinet. This is the kind of thing we Americans have found entertaining over the last fifty years. Not immortal humor (I doubt that such a thing exists); just quickly comprehended japery that goes straight for our jocular vein. Not philosophical satire on the high Voltairian level; just stuff that Americans recognize as coming close to their own experience.

Love, the arts, death, sex—all these are universals. But even when our humorists deal with such universals the tone is peculiarly American, and we readers unconsciously detect and enjoy it. Most of the material in the following pages, however, turns on situations and attitudes so imbedded in our national life that one wonders whether those pages could ever force a snicker from a Russian or a Turk. The kidding that goes on here is often kidding of institutions that may not be native to us, but that we have developed into uniquely American forms. Our business behavior, bureaucracy, stock exchange, political parties, modes of travel, criminal tendencies, religious habits, educational techniques, social diversions, regional characteristics, sports, and entertainment—all, good, bad, or indifferent, are here laughed at in a way that has the smack, tang, and flavor of our national character.

Doubtless a good many profound generalizations could be drawn from reflection on this obvious fact. You will be relieved to know that I am not the man to draw them. I have read enough theorists of humor to be awed by their power to kill a joke with the instruments of the dissecting table. The brief comments preceding each of the thirty sections that make up this volume do not pretend to explain the secret of the American sense of humor. They're meant to give you time to draw breath between chuckles.

One serious point, however—it's getting harder and harder to be funny in the America of the seventies. Art Buchwald and a few others still command the secret, but the whole drift of things is clearly not on their side. All the more reason, therefore, to get whatever legitimate amusement is available from collections that, like this one, gather up the scattered laughter of the happier years just behind us. These days we can all use a little innocent merriment, and it is the hope of the editors that their *Treasury* may make a modest and cheerful contribution to that end.

Clifton Fadiman

THE
Reader's Digest
TREASURY OF
AMERICAN
HUMOR

★ ★ ★

Be It Ever So Humble:
DOMESTIC AFFAIRS

MARRIAGE, *n.* The state or condition of a community consisting of a master, a mistress and two slaves, making in all, two. [Ambrose Bierce]." Most American wits and humorists take a somewhat more cheerful view of marriage. But only somewhat. Apparently, marriage offers a challenge that almost all of us are eager to take on and that virtually none of us are completely successful with. The gap between our original enthusiasm and our later acceptance is bridged by humor. And that humor is based largely on one joke. In these pages you'll meet a psychiatrist asking his male patient: "And did this feeling of insignificance come on suddenly or develop normally with marriage and parenthood?" There it is—the Great American Marriage Joke. If the American married male ever came to be generally regarded as better than spineless, unreasonable, and foolish, most American humor about the institution would wither. But apparently we're unwilling to change this stereotype. Of course women's libbers claim that the stereotype is kept alive by men. Me? I'm a women's libber. Of *course* they're more than sexual objects. Yet it's hard not to cheer for male chauvinism when it can produce Ogden Nash's "A little incompatibility is the spice of life, particularly if he has income and she is pattable."

For Better, For Worse

MY OWN RULES FOR A HAPPY MARRIAGE
JAMES THURBER

NOBODY, I hasten to announce, has asked me to formulate a set of rules for the perpetuation of marital bliss. The idea just came to me one day; brooding on the general subject of Husbands and Wives, I found myself compiling my own Rules for a Happy Marriage.

Rule One: Neither party to a sacred union should run down, disparage, or badmouth the other's former girls or beaux, as the case may be. The tendency to attack the character, looks, capability and achievements of one's mate's former friends of the opposite sex is a common cause of domestic discontent.

2

Aspersions, insinuations, reflections or just plain cracks about old boy friends or girl friends should be avoided at all times. Here are some of the expressions that should be especially eschewed: "That waffle-fingered, minor-league third baseman you latched onto at Cornell"; "You know the girl I mean—the one with the hips who couldn't read"; "That old flame of yours with the vocabulary of a hoot owl."

This kind of derogatory remark, if persisted in by one or both parties to a marriage, will surely lead to divorce or, at best, a blow on the head with a glass ash tray.

Rule Two: A man should make an honest effort to get the names of his wife's friends right. This is not easy. The average wife who was graduated from school at any time during the past 30 years keeps in close touch with at least seven old classmates. These ladies, known as "the girls," are named, respectively: Mary Marian, Melissa, Marjorie, Maribel, Madeleine and Miriam; and all of them are called Myrtle by the careless husband we are talking about, Furthermore, he gets their nicknames wrong. This, to be sure, is understandable, since their nicknames are, respectively: Molly, Muffy, Missy, Midge, Mabby, Maddy and Mims. The careless husband, out of thoughtlessness or pure cussedness, calls them all Mugs, or, when he is feeling particularly brutal, Mucky.

All the girls are married, one of them to a Ben Tompkins, and as this is the only one he can remember, our hero calls all the husbands Ben, or Tompkins, adding to the general annoyance and confusion.

Try, then, to get the names of your wife's girl friends and their husbands straight. This will prevent some of those interminable arguments that begin after Midge and Harry (not Mucky and Ben) have said a stiff good night and gone home.

Rule Three: A husband should not insult his wife publicly. Thus, if a man thinks the soufflés his wife makes are as tough as an outfielder's glove, he should tell her so when they are at home, not when they are out at a formal dinner where a perfect soufflé has just been served. The same rule applies to the wife. She should not regale his men friends, or women friends, with hilarious accounts of her husband's clumsiness, remarking that he dances like a 1907 Pope-Hartford, or that he locked himself in the children's rabbit pen and couldn't get out. All parties must end finally, and the husband or wife who has revealed all may find that there is hell to pay in the taxi going home.

Rule Four: The wife who keeps saying, "Isn't that just like a man?" and the husband who keeps saying, "Oh, well, you know how women are," are likely to grow farther and farther apart through the years. These famous generalizations have the effect of reducing an individual to the anonymous status of a mere unit in a mass. The wife who, just in time, comes upon her husband about to fry an egg in a dry skillet should not classify him with all the other males but should give him the accolade of a special distinction. She might say, for example, "George, no other man in the world would try to do a thing like that." Similarly, a husband watching his wife laboring to start the car without turning on the ignition should not say to the gardener or a passer-by, "Oh well, you know, etc." Instead, he should remark to his wife, "I've seen a lot of women in my life, Nellie, but never one who could touch you."

Rule Five: A husband should try to remember where things are around the house so that he does not have to wait for his wife to get home from the hairdresser's before he can put his hands on what he wants. Among the things a husband is usually unable to locate are the iodine, the aspirin, the nail file, the French vermouth, his cuff links, black silk socks and evening shirts, the snapshots taken at Nantucket last summer, the garage key, the poker chips, his new raincoat and the screens for the upstairs windows.

I don't really know the solution to this problem, but one should be found. Perhaps every wife should draw for her husband a detailed map of the house, showing clearly the location of everything he might need. Trouble is, I suppose, he would lay the map down somewhere and not be able to find it until his wife got home.

Rule Six: If a husband is not listening to what his wife is saying, he should not grunt, "Okay" or "Yeah, sure" or make little affirmative noises. A husband lost in thought or worry is likely not to take in the sense of such a statement as this: "We're going to the Gordons' for dinner tonight, John, so don't come home from the office first. Remember, we both have to be at the dentist's at five, and I'll pick you up there with the car." Now, an "Okay" or a "Yeah, sure" at this point can raise havoc if the husband hasn't really been listening. As usual, he goes all the way out to his home in Glenville—13 miles from the dentist's office and 17 miles from the Gordons' house—and he can't find his wife. His wife can't get him on the phone because all she gets is the busy buzz. John is calling everybody he can think of except, of course, the dentist and the Gordons. At last he hangs up, exhausted and enraged. Then the phone rings. It is his wife. And here let us leave them.

Rule Seven: A wife's dressing table should be inviolable. It is the one place in the house a husband should get away from and stay away from, and yet the average husband is drawn to it as by a magnet, especially when he is carrying something wet, oily, greasy or sticky, such as a universal joint, a hub cap or the blades of a lawn mower.

His excuse for bringing these alien objects into his wife's bedroom in the first place is that he is looking for "an old rag" with which to wipe them off. There are no old rags in a lady's boudoir, but husbands never seem to learn this. They search hampers, closets and bureau drawers, expecting to find a suitable piece of cloth, but first they set the greasy object on the dressing table. The aggrieved wife may be tempted, following this kind of vandalism, to lock her bedroom door and kick her husband out for good. I suggest a less stringent punishment. Put a turtle in his bed. The wife who is afraid to pick up a turtle should ask Junior to help her. Junior will love it.

Now I realize, in glancing back over these rules, that some of my solutions to marital problems may seem a little untidy; that I have, indeed, left a number of loose ends here and there. For example, if the husbands are going to mislay their detailed maps of household objects, I have accomplished nothing except to add one item for the distraught gentleman to lose. I can only hope, in conclusion, that this treatise itself will not start, in any household, a widening gap that can never be closed.

———— • ————

Annoyed wife to husband: "Can't you just say we've been married 24 years instead of 'almost a quarter of a century'?"

What the heck's happened to you!" exclaimed my husband one evening when I came into the living room with my head bristling with curlers. "I just set my hair," I replied. "Well," he asked, "what time does it go off?"

Wife to husband: "I don't mind your little half-truths, Bob, but you keep telling me the wrong half."

———— • ————

For 20 years," mused the man at the bar, "my wife and I were ecstatically happy."

"Then what happened?" asked the bartender.

"We met."

Happy Anniversary

A-Day minus 5: "Fred, what ever happened to Harry Bush? I haven't seen him since our wedding ten years ago next week."

A-Day minus 4: "Why, this is the very casserole the girls at the office gave me ten years ago just before our wedding!"

A-Day minus 3: "You don't look almost ten years older than when we were married, Fred. Do I?"

A-Day minus 2: "Look, Fred, I can still get into my wedding dress."

A-Day minus 1: "Remember how nervous you were at our wedding rehearsal ten years ago tonight?"

A-Day: "For me? Why, Fred, darling, you *remembered!*"

Man to florist: "Suppose a man goes home late with a rather poor excuse. What would you recommend to close the credibility gap?"

"THAT'S ALL *I* HOPE!"
J. P. McEVOY

I CAN remember when I was little how my mother used to go on about "the patience of a saint," but it wasn't until I grew up that I learned most saints were never married. So how could they possibly know anything about patience? Then I wondered why Mother never mentioned the patience of a father. Now *there's* patience for you. Oh, yes, Mother was patient. But Father was patient about all the things Mother was patient about—

and in addition he was patient about Mother.

Mother used to say, too, that a soft answer turneth away wrath, but I always thought Father's system—a gay answer—was better. Later I discovered the best system of all, and I don't mean no answer; for you don't get anywhere in married life not having an answer. You only get accused of being an old sourpuss. No, the secret of a happy married life without quarrels is always to have an answer, but be sure it doesn't make any sense. Nothing infuriates a woman as much as to be cornered with Reason or—unforgivable sin—fenced in with Truth.

It was a Chinese traveling in this country who evoked the magic formula which makes quarreling almost impossible for my wife and me. One day, late for his train, he rushed over to the baggage room in Grand Central Station, threw his check on the counter, and demanded his bag. The attendant couldn't find it. As precious minutes went by, the Chinese began jumping up and down with inarticulate rage. Finally he couldn't stand it any longer. His train was going—his bag was nowhere to be found—and he pounded the counter with his fist and yelled: "Pretty damn seldom where my bag go. She no fly. You no more fit run station than godsake. That's all *I* hope!"

Before hearing this, when anything of mine got mislaid around the house, which was every time my wife tidied up, I used to scream like a wounded banshee. But now I merely yell, "Pretty damn seldom where my papers go!" In the old days my wife used to come back snappily with, "If you put your papers where they belong, you'd know where to find them!"—which is sheer nonsense, as any husband knows who has ever tried it.

I found the only answer to such an unreasonable remark was, "You no more fit run house than godsake!"—which put her in her place until she learned to retort, "That's all *I* hope!"—stopping all argument dead in its tracks.

In the silly old days I used to moan, "Why don't you fill out your check stubs properly? What is this—$2.20, or $22, or $220? Why can't you keep your balance straight?" Now I just say, "Pretty damn seldom where my money go. She no fly." And I get just as far as I ever did—which was exactly nowhere.

As for the children, we never quarrel any more about who is spoiling which, and the dreadful things we are doing to their future—as if we knew anything about it. One of us—it doesn't matter who—merely looks at the other and says in a resigned way, "You no more fit run children than godsake!" Which nobody can deny.

7

Well, there it is. Pretty damn seldom where your happiness go. She no fly. But if you don't try this next time instead of quarreling, you no more fit run marriage than godsake. That's all *I* hope.

———— • ————

Wife to husband as tailor measures his waist: "It's quite amazing when you realize it takes an oak tree 200 years to attain that girth!"

There isn't one man in a million—no, not one in *ten* million—who would be so mean to his wife and children as you are!" shrieked a housewife.

"Now that's what I admire in you, dear," rejoined her husband. "You have such a head for figures!"

Irate husband calling upstairs to wife: "How soon will you be ready? Be specific—give me a date."

When my husband's ball-point pen broke, it spread a hideous red stain with a dark center on the pocket of his shirt. I took it to the laundry. The counterman gave it a long look. Then, turning to me, he murmured, "Nice shot."

Wife to lounging husband: "Somehow, I find it a little difficult to envision you as the end product of millions of years of evolution."

Wife to surly-looking husband who is shaving: "What would you like thrown into your cage for breakfast this morning?"

I recently purchased a wig from a mail-order house, and when it arrived the following note was enclosed: "Due to the possibility that this wig may slip off your head, do not wear it to bed. Many husbands have been frightened by the sudden awareness of a strange, furry animal under the blankets and have been known to damage the merchandise."

———— • ————

WEDLOCK DEADLOCK
JANE GOODSELL

I S MY marriage a success? Are my husband and I compatible? Did I marry the right man? Am I a good wife?

No.

My marriage doesn't even qualify as a failure. It's a disaster. But I didn't know it until I became addicted to those "Are You Happily Married?" quizzes.

Now, after 19 years of marriage and three children, it's clear that my husband and I are as mismatched a couple as the Owl and the Pussycat. If I'm honest, I can't answer a single one of the quiz questions right. I can't even answer them if I'm *dis*honest.

Question: Do you have a basic understanding about family finances?

Answer: Well, we both deplore extravagance. He deplores mine, and I deplore his.

Q: Do you share mutual interests?

A: No. His passion in life is fishing. I hate wading in that cold, wet water. He likes movies about airplanes, and I like movies about rich people. We both like to play golf, but not with each other. His Brubeck records give me a headache; I like Gilbert and Sullivan.

Q: Do you take offense easily?

A: What's "easily"? Like when I ask him if he thinks I'm too old to wear a bikini, and he says yes?

Q: Do you frequently nag him?

A: How else can I get him to trim the hedge?

Q: Do you have a common goal in life?

A: We would both like to be very, very rich. But we'll never make it, because we married each other.

Q: Does he do things that get on your nerves?

A: I'll say he does! He steams up the bathroom mirror when he takes a shower. He plays the hi-fi so loud he can't even hear me scream at him to turn it down. He leaves apple cores in ash trays.

Q: Do little things irritate him?

A: The littlest things you ever heard of. Dripping stockings in the bathroom. Lost car keys. A telephone receiver left off the hook. An overdrawn checking account. Things like that.

Q: Do you feel that your role as a mother and homemaker is beneath you?

A: No. I feel it's beyond me.

Q: Do you encourage your husband in his work or profession?

A: I do my best. I keep telling him he ought to ask for a raise.

Q: Do you enjoy talking to each other?

A: Oh, we enjoy *talking* to each other all right. The problem is *listening* to each other.

Q: Do you take pains to make yourself as attractive for him as you do for a party?

A: Oh, come now—let's not be ridiculous.

Q: Do you bolster each other's confidence?

A: I keep telling him that anybody with his brains and ability can learn to fix his own breakfast. He tells me that anybody—even a mechanical moron like me—can change a fuse.

Q: When things go wrong, do you blame each other?

A: Not always. Sometimes we blame the children. Sometimes we blame Congress. Sometimes we just slam doors.

Q: Have you, through mutual patience and understanding over the years, achieved a satisfactory sexual adjustment?

A: Golly, is it *that* difficult?

———— • ————

A marriage counselor began to ask a woman some questions concerning her disposition: "Did you wake up grumpy this morning?"

"No," she replied. "I let him sleep."

Woman, trying on fur coat, to salesgirl: "I wish it were called something besides broadtail. My husband fancies himself a comedian."

Heading the list of the people who try us
Are husbands who blissfully sleep on the bias.

The Duke of Windsor was telling a group of admirers how to keep their wives happy. "Of course," he concluded with a smile, "I do have one slight edge over the rest of you. It helps in a pinch to be able to remind your bride that you gave up a throne for her."

———— • ————

Some like it cold, some like it hot.
Some freeze while others smother.
And by some fiendish, fatal plot
They marry one another.

Grouchy-looking wife to grouchy-looking husband: "Look, I'll make a deal with you. You don't tell me about your day—I won't tell you about mine."

The hostess poured a cup of tea for a middle-aged man at her party and asked him if he took sugar.

"No," he said.

"Yes," said his wife brightly at the same moment. Then she turned accusingly to him. "But I *always* put sugar in your tea!"

"I know," the man said ruefully. "I used to remind you not to. Now I just don't stir."

A DEFINITION
OF MARRIAGE
OGDEN NASH

JUST AS I know there are two Hagens, Walter and Copen,
I know that marriage is a legal and religious alliance entered
into by a man who can't sleep with the window shut and a
woman who can't sleep with the window open,
Also he can't sleep until he has read the last hundred pages to
find out whether his suspicions of the murdered eccentric
recluse's avaricious secretary were right,
Moreover, just as I am unsure of the difference between flora
and fauna, and flotsam and jetsam,
I am quite sure that marriage is the alliance of two people,
one of whom never remembers birthdays and the other never
forgetsam,
And the one refuses to believe there is a leak in the water pipe
or the gas pipe, and the other is convinced she is about to
asphyxiate or drown,

And the other says, "Quick, get up and get my hairbrushes off the window sill; it's raining in," and the one replies, "Oh, they're all right; it's only raining straight down."

That is why marriage is so much more interesting than divorce,

Because it's the only known example of the happy meeting of the immovable object and the irresistible force.

So I hope husbands and wives will continue to debate and combat over everything debatable and combatable,

Because I believe a little incompatibility is the spice of life, particularly if he has income and she is pattable.

Mom's the Word

SEE MOTHER RUN!
JOAN MILLS

S EE Mother. Mother is sleeping. "Jump up, Mother," says Father. "Jump up! Today is the first day of school!"

Oh, see Mother get out of bed! Her eyes are not open. Her slippers are on the wrong feet. She cannot find the bedroom door. Funny Mother!

"Hurry, children," says Mother. "Today is the first day of school!"

See the children go down to the kitchen. They hurry slowly on the first day of school, don't they? Mother hurries to the kitchen, too. Mother has one eye open now.

"I will give you a good breakfast," says Mother. "I will give you juice, porridge, toast, bacon, eggs, and milk from the friendly cow."

"Euchh!" says Laurie.

"Euchh!" says Bobby.

"Euchh!" says Chris.

Laurie wants cottage cheese and tea. Bobby wants Choko-Krunch Korn Krisps and cocoa with marshmallow. Chris wants three bananas.

"Euchh!" says Mother.

Here comes Father. He is wearing his clean white shirt and good brown suit. Father is an executive.

"I am going to work, Mother," says Father. "May I please have a dollar to put in my pocket?"

"I do not have a dollar, Father," says Mother. "Ask the children. The children have many dollars."

The children give Father a dollar. How good they are! "Good-by! Good-by, Father!" call Laurie, Bobby, Chris and Mother. Father waves good-by. Father is glad he is an executive and not a mother.

"Children, children!" says Mother. "Hurry and put on your clothes. Hurry, hurry! Soon the school bus will come!"

See Laurie. Laurie is combing her hair. See Bobby. Bobby is reading about Willie Mays. See Chris. Chris is tattooing his stomach with a ballpoint pen.

See Mother's hair stand up! What is Mother saying? Those words are not in our book, are they? *Run, children, run!*

"Mother, Mother!" says Laurie. "I have lost a shoe!"

"Mother, Mother!" says Bobby. "I think I am sick. I think I may throw up on the yellow school bus!"

"Mother, Mother!" says Chris. "My zipper is stuck, and I have a jelly bean in my ear!"

Oh, see Mother run!

"I am going mad," says Mother. "Here is Laurie's shoe on the stove. Here are other pants for Chris. Here is a thermometer for Bobby, who does not look sick to me."

Now what are the children doing?

Laurie is combing her hair. Bobby is playing the banjo. Chris   *13* is under the bed feeding jelly beans to the cat.

"Oh!" says Mother. "Hurry, hurry! It is time for the yellow school bus!"

Mother is right. (Mother is *always* right.) Here comes the yellow school bus!

See all the children on the bus jump up and down. Jump! Jump! Jump! See the pencil boxes fly out the windows! Listen to the driver of the yellow school bus. He cannot yell as loud as the children, can he? Run, Laurie! Run, Bobby! Run, Chris!

See Mother throw kisses. Why do Laurie, Bobby and Chris pretend that they do not know Mother?

"Good-by! Good-by!" calls Mother.

"Barrooom!" goes the yellow bus.

How quiet it is.

Here is Chris's sweater in the boot box.

Here are Bobby's glasses under the cat.

Here is Laurie's comb in the fruit bowl.

Here is crunchy cereal all over the kitchen floor.

Here is Mother. Crunch, crunch, crunch. Mother is pouring a big cup of coffee. Mother is sitting down.

Mother does not say anything.

Mother does not do anything.

Mother just sits and smiles.

Why is Mother smiling?

———————— • ————————

A friend of mine who had her hands full with four young children was taken aback one day when her husband brought home a gift—a young, frisky puppy. Her children were all excited and asked her what they should name the pup. "Better call it Mother," she said, "because if that dog stays, I'm going!"

After a difficult day with the children," a young mother says, "I like to take the car and go for a drive; I like to have something in my hands I can control."

———————— • ————————

Proud mother, holding infant, tells visitor: "He's eating solids now—keys, newspapers, pencils. . . ."

How to Make a Cake

Light oven; get out utensils and ingredients. Remove blocks and toy autos from table. Grease pan, crack nuts.

Measure 2 cups of flour; remove Johnny's hand from flour; wash flour off him. Remeasure flour.

Put flour, baking powder and salt in sifter. Get dustpan and brush up pieces of bowl Johnny knocked on floor. Get another bowl. Answer doorbell.

Return to kitchen. Remove Johnny's hands from bowl. Wash Johnny. Answer phone. Return. Remove ¼ inch salt from greased pan. Look for Johnny. Grease another pan. Answer telephone.

Return to kitchen and find Johnny. Remove his hands from bowl. Take up greased pan and find layer of nutshells in it. Head for Johnny who flees, knocking bowl off table.

Wash kitchen floor, table, walls, dishes. Call baker. Lie down.

Mother trying to persuade youngster to eat: "Look, dear, make believe it's sand."

A six-year-old was looking at photographs of her parents' wedding. Her father described the ceremony and tried to explain its meaning. Suddenly light dawned. "Oh!" Mary Jane exclaimed. "Is that when you got Mother to come to work for us?"

When Tommy came home from school with a swollen eye and bruised lips, his mother said reproachfully, "Oh, Tommy! Have you been in another fight?"

"I was just keeping a little boy from being beat up by a bigger boy," he replied.

"Well, that was brave of you, dear. Who was the little boy?"

"Me, Mommy."

J unior was one of those little terrors, and Papa was surprised when Mama suggested they buy him a bicycle. "Do you think it will improve his behavior?" Papa asked.

"No," said Mama grimly. "But it'll spread it over a wider area."

W oman, accompanied by husband and six children, to marriage counselor: "Our marriage would have broken up if it weren't for the children. Rosco won't take them, and I won't take them!"

H arried mother of large family: "What gets me is why the nations of the world *want* to live together like one big family."

W ife to husband after peeling layers off small snow-suited figure: "George—he isn't ours!"

A woman telephoned a friend and asked how she was feeling. "Terrible," the other woman said. "My head's splitting and my back and legs are killing me and the house is a mess and the children are simply driving me crazy."

"Listen," the caller said, "go and lie down. I'll come over right away and cook lunch for you and clean the house and take care of the children while you get some rest. By the way, how is Sam?"

"Sam?" the complaining housewife asked.

"Yes, your husband."

"I've got no husband named Sam."

The first woman gasped. "My heavens, I must have dialed the wrong number!"

There was a long pause. "Then you're not coming over?" the other woman said.

DINNER'S ON THE TABLE
ELINOR GOULDING SMITH

GENTLE TINKLE OF SILVER DINNER BELL (LONG SILENCE) Must they all disappear every night exactly at dinnertime?

(LOUD PERSISTENT RINGING OF BELL)

Oh, there you are, dear. Would you call the children? Dinner's ready.

Have you washed your hands, boys? Well, please do. I don't care if you washed them this morning, that doesn't make them clean now. Will you carve, honey, while the children wash? I'll get everything else on the table. What's the matter with that knife? I know it isn't sharp. I asked you to sharpen it for me last week. . . .

Please, darling, the children will hear you.

Oh, there you are boys. Let me see your hands. Joe! Did you wash your hands at all? What *is* all that blue stuff? Well, go wash them again. Dan, let me see yours. I don't care if you washed them in lye, they're still dirty.

What's the matter with the meat, honey? It *isn't* tough. It's that knife. . . . You'll just have to do the best you can. . . .

All right, boys, sit down. Darling, sit down and I'll serve. Everything will get cold if we don't start. Dan your napkin is on the floor, darling, pick it up. Joe, don't put your milk glass so close to the edge of the table, sweetheart.

I know you don't like carrots, darling, but you don't like peas, string beans, spinach, beets or cauliflower either. So it's hard to know what to have. Here, have some celery.

Now let me see. You want it rare, dear, don't you? I know *you* like it well done, Joe. I know, honey, *very* well done. And rare for you, Dan. It *is* rare. If it were any rarer it would be raw. Darling, you want gravy on your meat but not on your potatoes? Dan, you want gravy just on your potatoes? Joe, you want gravy just on your *carrots?* Joe, dear, move the glass back from the edge. There now, I think we're all set.

Oh, I forgot to bring the rolls. . . . Here they are. Yes, I know they're burned. It took you all so long to come to dinner, honey. They're only burned a little. Well, eat the inside. I'll just get my coffee. Darling, do you want your coffee now or later? You want grape juice? Joe, you want grape juice too? Dan, I suppose you . . . oh, you want apple juice. Well, you all go ahead and I'll. . . .

There we are. You're ready for seconds, Dan? I haven't had a first yet. Help yourself from the platter. Watch out for Joe's gla . . . oh! Joe, don't just sit there and let the milk drip in your lap. *Stand up.* Here, I'll get a cloth. . . . Just lift the cream pitcher up for me, Joe. Oh, *Joe!*

Dan, get the cream from the icebox and fill the pitcher again. Right there, dear, on the top shelf. See, right in back of the tomato ju——oh, *no. Danny, step back. Don't just stand there in it.* Here, I'll take care of it. Now everybody sit down and eat your dinner.

What's the matter, Joe? You don't like mixed salad? You'd rather have plain lettuce and Russian dressing? Well, Mommy can't fix all different things for everybody, can she? I *know* I sliced tomatoes for Daddy. *Well, that's different, that's why.*

Joe, don't hit the ketchup bottle so hard, let Daddy do it for . . . yes, I see it got in the sugar, dear. Why can't you eat the meat, Dan? It has a speck of fat on it? Where? Well, for heaven's sake cut it off. No, it *hasn't* spoiled the potatoes. What is it, darling? There's ketchup on the butter? Well, there's a little in my coffee, too, but *I'm* not complaining. There's some on your meat, Joe? Why did you use it if you don't like ketchup? Dan, would you *please* pick up your napkin?

Well. There now. Everybody ready for dessert? I've made a really special dessert tonight. Something good . . . it's *chocolate,* darling. You like chocolate, don't you? It's a sort of mousse. What don't you like about the way it looks? Well, you can't tell how it's going to taste by looking at it. No, you *can't.*

Dan, please get up and *carefully* help clear the table. I know there isn't room there, sweetheart. Put them on the counter by the sink. No, no, not on top of the . . . Dan, couldn't you see that all those plates were going to fall if you put them on top of a tomato?

Now everybody sit down and I'll serve the dessert. What is it, Joe? What don't you like about it? Well, we're not having ice cream tonight. Homemade mousse is better than ice cream. *I* say it is. What is it, Dan? It tastes of egg? Of course, it has egg in it. You don't like eggs? You *love* eggs. Oh. You only like them scrambled. Oh, all right. You can both have ice cream.

Let's see, there's butter pecan, vanilla, pineapple, chocolate-chip mocha. No, there isn't any plain chocolate. All right, Dan, you want half mocha and half pineapple? Joe, you want half vanilla and half butter pecan? Can't you get together on it? Oh, for heaven's sake, all right. Dan, pick up your napkin.

There isn't any chocolate-chip mocha, Dan. Somebody put an empty carton back in the freezer. Who did? A baby-sitter. Oh. Joe, this isn't vanilla, it's coffee. Well somebody put the vanilla top on the coffee carton. Well *I* didn't do it, the baby-sitter did. I know you're not babies, it's just an expression.

Dan, please pick up your napkin, sweetheart. Joe, push your glass back, angel. Where is there gravy on my dress? You wish we had some cake, Dan? I see the ketchup, but I don't see any gravy. (LONG PIERCING SCREAM)

Father's Day

WHO'S IN CHARGE HERE?
JAMES LINCOLN COLLIER

SEVEN or eight hundred years ago, when Millard Fillmore was President and I was a little boy, the word "authority" applied to only two beings in my ken—the Diety, and my father. My father combined the intellect of Einstein, the physique of Man Mountain Dean and the learning of Cardinal Newman, and his word in any matter went unquestioned. If he announced that today was Friday, then Friday it was, even if everyone else in the neighborhood was getting ready for church; and if he said "parrelell" was spelled that way, that was the way it was spelled. That's all there was to it.

But the whole idea of fathers has changed, and today's Dad—at least the one I know best—is bathed in scornful contempt by his children. Let me merely announce, "It looks like a good day to go fishing," and somebody under four feet in height will point out disdainfully that the New York *Times* says it's been too dry recently. No matter what I say, somebody instantly quotes outside authority to the contrary.

Of all the authorities, it is Coach Holloway I dislike most. Maybe I wasn't the best right-fielder that ever came out of Wingdale High, but I wasn't the worst either. Once I hit one from old

19

man Searle's well house, where we had home plate, clear over his barn and into the chicken yard—and not with one of your modern cork-center balls either, but a ten-center filled with Chinese newpaper. You'd think somebody around here would be impressed, but no, every time I get chivied, bat in hand, out on the lawn with my boys, Coach Holloway crops up.

"Dad," the younger asks, "how do you hold the bat when you bunt?"

My voice deepens a trifle. "See, son, you slip your hands down like this, and swing around, and sort of crouch over like this. . . ."

"That isn't the way Coach Holloway says."

A moment of silence. With vast patience I ask, "If you already *knew,* why did you ask?"

"I forgot."

There are only two responses. You can either go into the house and sulk, or you can bawl the child out for something he did earlier—a year earlier, if necessary. What gets me is the automatic assumption that the coach is right and I'm bollixed up.

It works even in the area of my own specialty. If, for example, I point out to the elder boy, "Keep on using the lawn mower for a fan-jet and what are you going to cut the grass with?" I am instantly told, "You shouldn't end a sentence with a preposition."

"Who says so? Coach Holloway?"

"Naw. Miss Dilly says so. She's a teacher."

I recall Miss Dilly as a dainty bit of floss, employed at Lamont Cranston Junior High, who is hardly dry behind the ears. "Miss Dilly is a very nice lady, son, but after all, the English language is my stock in trade. Why, ha, ha, that bicycle of yours comes from my knowledge of English. Syntax is my business."

"It's hers, too. She's a teach—"

My temper begins to fray. "I know that," I snap. "She's also 23 years old. I was ending sentences with prepositions when she was in the sixth grade, and selling them to the magazines that way, too"

"Twenty-three? Wow, she doesn't look *that* old."

And it isn't until dark that I realize the lawn is still unmowed.

But these troubles pale beside an occurrence of last month. It transpired that Brucie Hopkins' father had taken him camping up in Mellor's Woods the previous Saturday night. I have no more desire than the next man to spend a night sleeping on a rock pile, but there's this theory that all American fathers were brought up in the North Woods and love nothing better. On hearing the tale about Brucie, my offspring began to circle around my feet, baying.

"All right, all right," I said. "We'll get up there just before bedtime, and if we all go right to sleep we can be home in time for breakfast."

"That isn't the way you do it," I was told. "Brucie Hopkins' father says that half the fun is cooking over an open fire."

It was an omen, but I missed it. I signed on the dotted line.

As the days dwindled down, however, my appetite for the adventure improved. I may not know much about woodcraft, but presumably I knew more than a pair of people who hardly came up to my belt. I began to see myself deftly fashioning sweet-smelling beds of pine boughs and producing miraculous breakfasts of buckwheat cakes and fried potatoes while two boys stared in open-mouthed admiration.

That I was living in a dream world became apparent on Saturday, in Mellor's Woods. "Now then," I said briskly, "let's just make camp down there in that little hollow where we'll be sheltered from—"

"Mr. Foster says you should camp on the side of a hill, so the rain won't come in."

"Frank Foster is a very good accountant, son," I said kindly. "But when it comes to—"

"Oh, no. When he came to talk to our school he told us about when he was in the forest service."

We set up the tent on the hillside, and Frank Foster's name did not come up again for almost 20 minutes. Then I remarked that we needed plenty of wood for the fire in order to keep warm.

"Mr. Foster says, 'Indian make small fire, sit close to keep warm. White man make big fire, keep warm hauling wood.'"

By the time we finished eating, my good humor was restored, and I was ready to join the boys around the campfire to tell some long, dull lie about my youth. "But first we'll fix up our bedrolls," I said. "See how I do it? You tuck this part under here and this part under here."

In the fractional moment of silence that followed, all three of us knew what would occur next: In helpless fascination, like a robin under the gaze of a cat, I simply stared at the pair as they solemnly intoned in unison, "That isn't the way Mr. Foster said."

It may have been the rainbow hues that played across my face. Whatever it was, Foster's name did not come up again until I was making breakfast, and by that time it didn't matter. When you've spent the night on a rock pile, you don't care what Frank Foster says.

Last week I was up at the Sweet Shoppe magazine rack in search of an obscure quarterly. Engrossed, I did not tune in the conversation on the other side of the rack until I heard myself mentioned. A childish voice, the young Foster boy, was insisting, "That isn't the way Jeff Collier's father says."

"And what," Frank Foster responded in an icy tone, "makes you think Jeff Collier's father knows more about sailing than I do?"

"Didn't you know? Jeff Collier's father used to be in the Coast Guard. He knows *everything* about boats."

There wasn't an iota of truth in the story—but why tell Frank Foster that? I just stayed crouched down behind the magazine rack, reflecting on the axiom that it's a long road that has no turning.

———— • ————

A San Francisco father blew up while trying to mediate the usual family hassle around the dinner table. "Everybody wants his own way around here!" he hollered. "Me, I'm just the poor schnook of a father. When do I get *my* way for once?" Four-year-old Mark tugged at his sleeve and suggested, "Cry a little."

My husband took our five- and eight-year-old children to work with him one day so that they would understand how Daddy earns his money—running a chain of dry-cleaning stores. The children drank in, wide-eyed, his every word and action, apparently tremendously impressed by his executive ability. But on the way home his daughter, looking thoughtful, asked, "Do any of those people working for you know that you can talk like Donald Duck?"

Father calling to daughter, as date waits: "Dreamboat! Your barnacle is here!"

Father greeting daughter's date: "You must be the one who defies description."

———— • ————

Father to daughter's beau: "I'm glad to meet you, Johnny, but I somehow pictured you with a telephone attached to your head.

As a young Frenchman pushed his son's carriage down the street, the youngster howled with rage. "Please, Bernard, control yourself," the father said quietly. "Easy there, Bernard, keep calm!"

"Congratulations, monsieur," said a woman who had been watching. "You know just how to speak to infants—calmly and gently." Then, leaning over the carriage, she said, "So the little fellow's named Bernard?"

"No, madame," corrected the father. "He's named André *I'm* Bernard."

Proud father to mother, as they watch small boy lying on floor studying by light from TV screen: "Reminds you of Abe Lincoln, doesn't it?"

Husband to wife, who is taking a picture of him with college-student son: "Wouldn't it look more natural if he had his hand in my pocket?"

A woman made the mistake of leaving her baby daughter in her husband's care while she closeted herself in the library to pay bills. He buried himself behind his newspaper and forgot about the baby until he heard a series of thumps, followed by a horrendous wail. Clearly, baby had fallen down the stairs.

"Martha," called the father excitedly. "Come quick! Our little girl just took her first 24 steps!"

A Father's Day composition written by an eight-year-old: "He can climb the highest mountain or swim the biggest ocean. He can fly the fastest plane and fight the strongest tiger. My father can do anything. But most of the time he just throws out the garbage."

Father pacing floor with wailing baby as wife lies snug in bed: "Nobody ever asks me how *I* manage to combine marriage and a career!"

My husband was absorbed in his favorite TV program when our young son ventured to ask him about a homework problem. "Dad," he said, "where are the Alps?"

"Ask your mother," came the reply. "She puts everything away."

WHAT ARE LITTLE BOYS MADE OF?

WALT McCASLIN

LITTLE Lad and I were out in the tool shed, building and painting a shelf. He provided the opener: "If dogs chase cats and cats chase birds and birds chase worms, who do worms chase?"

(Explained the order of Life's munificence. Undeniably a dirty deal for the worm, to be the very last catch, but I told Little Lad there wasn't much we could do about it.)

"Poor worm."

"Yes, poor worm. Watch the paint can."

"I heard in school that the earth spins all the time. Like this. . . ."

"Yes, and will you please stand back from the paint can?"

"Do dogs and cats and birds and worms spin?"

"Yes."

"Do houses spin?"

"Yes. You almost kicked it that time."

"Do cars and trucks and bulldozers spin?"

"Yes, everything on earth spins."

"Why don't they fly off the earth?"

(Explained gravity. He didn't get the picture and upset paint can trying to stand on the South Pole upside-down. Opened a new can of paint, gave him the devil, feeling mean and at the same time ashamed. He didn't mean to do it.)

"I had a fight with Billy Barr."

"Oh? How come?"

"He gave me some play money and said he wanted it back and I said no you gave it to me and I won't give it back so he hit me in the stomach and I told him I had milk for breakfast and my mother said milk makes boys strong so I am strong enough to beat you up so I beat him up and he called me a crybaby because I hurt my finger on his head and then he hit me with his baseball bat. His mother saw it and spanked him on his bare bottom and I saw her do it and I saw his underwear, too. Then he went in his house and I stayed for lunch. We had scottish cheese and muscle sprouts cold."

"I see. Extremely interesting."

"What do cats eat?"

"Fish."

"They do not. They eat cat food."

"If you know so much about it, why did you ask me? Anyhow, cat food is made out of fish. Will you please move away from that paint can, boy!"

"Do mother cats have little cats in their tummies?"

"Always, as far as I know."

"Did Aunt Eleanor have little cats in her tummy?"

"Now you're being silly. You know very well it was your cousin Clara."

"*La de da, la de da,* we're going to catch a whale. We'll cut him up and fry him nice and barber-cube his tail."

"Barber-cube?"

"Yes. You do it over a fire. Did they cut a hole in Aunt Eleanor's tummy to get my cousin Clara out?"

(Told him it was a legitimate question but rather difficult with a mouthful of nails. Said to wait until he was six.)

"In kindergarten I'm going to have to be a troll in 'Three Billy Goats Gruff.' But I want to be a dragon."

"There isn't any dragon in 'Three Billy Goats Gruff,' is there?"
"I won't be a troll."
"Oh, I'd be one if I were you. Trolls are far superior to dragons."
"No, dragons do like this. . . ."
"Watch the paint can! No, trolls are better because they live by their wits. A dragon probably has a brain the size of a pea, like a dinosaur. And anyone can stomp around breathing smoke."
(Moppets came. Three little girls, pint-size termagants on the prowl, seeking outlet for natural group-brattishness of the female. The girls danced—"Nyaaa-nyaaa-my-dress-is-so-and-so-than-your-dress." Started pushing each other around. Little Lad cracked under pressure, began showing off. Shot into paint can with his water gun. I snatched the water gun from his hand, gave him six rounds from it full in the face. He looked at me with horror. Girls giggled. Everyone ran to the sand box.)
A few minutes later Little Lad returned alone, sat down on the step.
"Why did you shoot me with the water gun?"
He started to sob. I had embarrassed him. Paternal remorse set in. I tried to comfort him, but he wouldn't talk or let me touch him. I finally proposed: "Make you a deal. Will trade you six rounds full in the face. Fill your gun."
He filled the gun at the hose and summoned the girls. They danced with glee as Little Lad pumped water in his father's grimacing face.
He went to bed an hour ago. As he padded down the hall he turned suddenly, threw me an inscrutable cowboy look and did a quick draw.
"You're dead," he said. "Fall down."

Household Finance

Wife to husband working on budget: "Perhaps we could borrow a little each month and set *that* aside."

Wife with armload of packages to husband: "I hatched our nest egg!"

The young couple going over their monthly bills were finally down to the last two.

"Gosh, honey" said the husband, "we're practically broke. I don't know which to pay—the electric company or the doctor."

"Oh, the electric company, of course," answered the wife. "After all, the doctor can't shut off your blood."

Harried wife, figuring at desk, to husband and children: "Well, I worked out a budget. But one of us will have to go."

Breadwinner, doing accounts: "It's happened! There's a monthly installment due every day!"

Wife to husband brooding over bills: "But remember, dear, you had money troubles under the four previous Presidents, too."

I used to feel guilty about the burden I placed on the checkout clerk at the supermarket as I approached with my massive collection of food to feed a family of ten. Then one day, when I started to voice my usual barely audible apology, the clerk gave me a beaming smile as he called across to the manager, "It's okay, boss, she's here! You can go ahead and make up the payroll now."

Wife to husband: "All right, I admit I like to spend money . . . but name one other extravagance."

Mother to father over bills: "Maybe we can get some kind of book and straighten her teeth ourselves."

Wife, at desk with checkbook, to husband: "Well, it balances. The checks total up to exactly the amount I'm overdrawn."

Father to teen-age daughter's boy friend, who is holding a sandwich in one hand and a pop bottle in the other: "Glad to meet you, Herbie—I've noticed you in our budget for some time."

One month not long ago my wife made a real effort to balance her checkbook. Instead of throwing away her canceled checks as she usually does, she matched them with her stubs. After one whole Sunday morning she handed me four sheets of typewritten figures with items and costs sitting neatly in their respective columns. I checked her total with the bank statement—and it balanced! Then, out of curiosity, I went over her list of items: Milkman—$11.25; Cleaner's—$4.60; and so forth. Everything was clear except for one item reading E.S.P.—$24.56.

"What does E.S.P. mean?" I asked warily.

"Error Some Place," she answered.

Wife to husband frowning over household bills: "Do what the government does—raise the debt ceiling."

Husband, looking up from newspaper, to wife: "What's happened between you and the retail merchants, dear? I see they say business is off."

Suburban Sanctuary

Late in the fall a suburban couple received 100 tulip bulbs from a friend in Holland. The wife kept asking her husband to plant them, but he delayed until in desperation she did the job herself. Naturally he was delighted—until the flowers came up in the spring and he saw that his wife had planted them so that in glowing colors they proclaimed: "John Is Lazy."

THE UNSUNG HAZARDS OF SUBURBIA

WILL STANTON

I THINK it's time we took some of our attention from outer space and did some research on the hazards of suburban living. I offer this report as a sort of steppingstone.

The time I hurt my arm was a stormy Saturday night. I drove to the doctor's house. "It doesn't really amount to much," I said, "but Fran thought you should take a look. A hot wheelbarrow fell on it."

"I see," said the doctor. "There's nothing wrong with a little skylarking—at least for a younger person. But a man with responsibilities—"

"Listen," I said. "We were just having a little family cookout."

"I know. Sometimes these things start out very innocently."

"If you'd let me finish telling you," I said. "I had just got a good fire going when the rain started, so I propped the wheelbarrow over it upside down. Then a little later I was reaching under to turn the hamburgers—"

"Well," the doctor said, "we'd better have a look."

As I had expected, it wasn't serious—my accidents never are. Sometimes I think the worst thing about them is the absurd explanations they always seem to involve me in. Like the spaghetti sauce.

We were having a big crowd in for dinner, and Fran was going to serve spaghetti. The tomatoes and peppers were ripe, so she made a lot of sauce. She left the kettle on the counter by the kitchen door while she cleaned the dining room. Jeannie had been watching her mother vacuum, and when Fran stopped to answer the phone I guess there was something about the cleaner hose and the kettle of sauce that was just too much for the child. Anyhow, when I came home I found everybody in tears and the household disorganized. I called the repair service.

"What seems to be the trouble?" the fellow asked.

"The vacuum cleaner doesn't work," I said. "Something's in it."

"What do you think it is?" he asked me.

"Spaghetti sauce," I said.

"I see," he said. "How much?"

I said about eight quarts. "We had a lot of extra tomatoes," I explained.

"I understand," he said. "Well, we try to put out a good sturdy machine, but it isn't built . . ."

I tried to explain to him that it was an accident—that my little girl didn't know any better.

"That's the story I get all the time," he said. "In the old days parents knew how to make their kids mind."

"Jeannie minds," I said, "but nobody ever told her not to do it."

"No," he said, "of course not. Too busy going to parties, and letting some baby sitter raise your kids. And what's the result?"

"You look after the vacuum cleaner," I said, "and let me worry about the kids."

"That's up to you," he said. "Mind if I ask you a personal question?"

I said I didn't mind.

"What did it sound like?"

That has bothered me ever since.

I hate to talk to repairmen anyhow. They treat you like a child just because you don't have a lot of technical information at your finger tips. I suppose if I devoted time to it I could learn the difference between 6-volt and 12-volt, AM and FM, and so on. But I'm old-fashioned enough to want to spend these precious moments with my family and flowers.

Just try to explain this philosophy to some lawn-mower mechanic. I did.

"That's fine," he said. "Is your mower two-cycle or four-cycle?"

"I'm not sure," I said. "I've had it only a short time."

"Let's look at it this way," he said. "Do you put oil in the gas or not?"

I decided to compromise. "Yes," I said. "I put some oil in sometimes."

"If it's a four-cycle, you're not supposed to put any in," he said.

All I was trying to do was give him answers that would make him happy. "I never put much in," I said. "You know—just a little from time to time."

"If it's two-cycle, you should use half a pint of oil to a gallon of gas."

"That's what I meant by a little," I told him. "About half a pint."

He made some remark I couldn't quite catch. Then,

"Bring it over," he said. "We'll see what we can do."

There was something in his tone that was a little condescending. This always annoys me. I wouldn't mind their overcharging me so much if they'd show me a little more respect.

I suppose that living on the threshold of catastrophe has made me extra cautious. Whenever an emergency arises, I try to consider every contingency—but so far there has always been something I've overlooked. I'm thinking now about the incident of the tarpaulin.

I had it rigged up as a sort of awning at the end of the porch—making a place for the kids to play, to put the lawn mower and so on. I fastened the outside corners to a couple of trees, one inside corner to the bracket that holds the TV cable, the other to a downspout. The possibilities for a mishap didn't occur to me until we were on vacation at the cabin.

We were having a heavy rainstorm, and I suddenly realized that the tarp, suspended like a hammock, would hold a great deal of water, and something would have to give. It would cost about $20 to replace one of the trees; the downspout and gutter would probably run a little higher. The bracket for the TV cable was pretty flimsy, but the cable itself was strong—possibly strong enough to pull over the antenna.

Our neighbors, the Baxters, would be aware of the problem, since the tarp was right in line with their living-room window. However, it was doubtful that Baxter would do anything about it voluntarily—he had got too much pleasure from my mishaps in the past. Still, he could hardly refuse a direct request. I didn't want to alarm Fran, so I went into town to send him a wire. I thought hard about how to word it.

Although Baxter is free with his advice and criticism, he is about as clumsy as they come. In the event that no damage had yet been done, I didn't want him adding his weight to any of the ropes and possibly falling into the tarp and pulling everything down. The simplest solution, I decided, would be to poke a hole in the tarp and let the water out. So I wired him: PLEASE CUT HOLE IN BOTTOM OF TARP—WILL EXPLAIN LATER.

A couple of days afterward we were getting ready for a picnic. "Do you think we should take the tarp along?" Fran asked me.

"What tarp is that?"

"The one you had rigged up by the porch," she said. "I thought we should bring it, so I had Junior take it down."

"I see." By this time Baxter would probably have my wire framed. "Whatever you want," I said.

"It's so lovely today," Fran said. "I just hate the thought of going home."

I nodded. "I know just how you feel."

———————— • ————————

Gardener feeding scrawny sapling: "Don't you want to grow up like other trees? Don't you *want* a nest of robins in your hair?"

Friend to neighbor after house-hunting trip: "The trouble with the American suburb is that everybody who dreamed of getting away from it all arrived at the same time."

On the first day of springtime my true love gives to me: five packs of seed, four sacks of fertilizer, three cans of weed killer, two bottles of insect spray, and a pruning knife for the pear tree.

Husband, lounging on sofa, to wife: "I'll think about spading the garden in a little while. Right now I'm thinking about painting the screens."

Wife to husband relaxing on terrace: "The trouble with suburban living is no matter where you sit you're always looking at something you should be doing."

Sweet peace attend as night's shades lower—and darkness stills each power mower!

Nothing ruins a neighborhood for the average husband like having an enthusiastic gardener move in.

Husband to wife, after paying off mortgage: "Well, dear, we've survived the lien years!"

———————— • ————————

---•---

Home-owner, fishing in flooded basement, to friend: "We gave up trying to keep it dry and had it stocked."

Man with flourishing garden to envious neighbor: "There's really nothing to it. I planted the seeds indoors, then transplanted them to a cold frame, then after careful nurturing I threw them out and bought these plants at a nursery."

What people miss most when they move to the suburbs is the train.

Suburbia is where the developer bulldozes out the trees, then names the streets after them.

Man to neighbor: "Let's make a deal. I'll stop keeping up with you, if you'll stop keeping up with me."

After heavy snowfall, wife to shoveling husband: "Try to think of each flake as a fluffy little friend."

Generations Apart

A father was discussing life with his nine-year-old son and the talk turned to the olden days, in the late 1930s, when Dad was young. The son was incredulous that his father could have enjoyed life way back there during the Dark Ages when there were no TV dinners, pizza pies, transistor radios, space shots or color television.

"You know, Dad," he mused, "when I think of you as a little boy, I always think of you in black and white."

Young voice on the bus: "I'll say this for my old man—he tells it like it used to be."

---•---

RUMPELSTILTSKIN,
HE SAID HIS NAME WAS
WILL STANTON

THE other evening the kids were watching a TV show about this widow whose two small children pick up a stray dog they want to keep. The kids plead, the dog walks on its front legs and counts to ten, but the mother says there's no money for a license and brushes away a tear. In the end, of course, the kids get to keep the dog and everything works out fine. It was so phony I couldn't stand it.

"That's the stupidest waste of time I've ever seen!" I said to my wife. "What drivel! What mush!"

"But the kids liked it," she said.

"That's the tragedy," I replied, flinging *TV Guide* across the room. "The kids don't know the difference." I withdrew a tattered volume from the bookcase. "Everyone sit down," I said. "Listen to a *real* story, the way they used to tell them."

A word of advice to all parents: don't criticize an idiotic TV show until you've reread a few of the old classics—like Rumpelstiltskin. In case you've forgotten how it goes. . . .

There's this poor miller who has a beautiful daughter and one day he tells the king she can spin gold out of straw. (To make himself seem important, the book says, but it seems sort of dumb to me. One chance in a lifetime to speak to a king and you throw him a curve like that.)

Usually you picture a king as a man of the world. When he hears a story like this he's going to be a little skeptical. He's going to say, "If your daughter can spin gold, how come you're so poor?" But the king is even stupider than the miller. He believes him.

The king takes the girl to a room full of straw and tells her to spin it into gold by morning or she'll die. Then he walks out. Now if I thought some girl could spin gold out of straw, I'd stick around to see how she did it. Not the king. He doesn't seem to have much of an attention span. Ten seconds maybe.

Naturally the girl doesn't know what to do, so she starts to cry. Just then a little man comes in and asks why she's bawling. She tells him her problem and he asks what she'll give him to spin the gold. She says her necklace, and it's a deal—one necklace for a room full of gold. Chances are she's the only person in the world whose life depends on spinning straw into gold and in walks the one person who knows how. Talk about luck!

The next day the king is very pleased and takes her to a bigger room full of straw. Same setup as last time—she cries, in comes the little man, she gives him a ring, he spins the gold, the king is happy. He tells her if she spins one more room full he'll make her his wife.

This time when the little man asks what she'll give him, she says she doesn't have anything. Well, what would you expect a poor miller's daughter to have? In fact I'm beginning to wonder where she got the necklace and the ring. So the little man says she must give him her first child and she says okay. (She's inclined to say the first thing that comes to her—a lot like her father that way.)

The next day she becomes queen and in a year she has a child. Now you'd expect the average woman in this situation to be a little tense, a little edgy. No, the queen "thought no more of the little man." All he's done is spin three rooms full of gold, save her life, jump her from miller's daughter to queen, and make her promise him her first child, but all this slips her mind. Somehow you get the feeling she's not a very deep thinker. Remember back when the king offers to marry her? She's only known him two days and he's threatened to kill her three times. She marries him anyhow.

At any rate the little man shows up one day and asks for the baby he was promised. The queen is terrified and offers him all the riches of the kingdom. This is typical thinking on her part. Here's a man who can make gold out of straw and she offers him money.

But the little man turns her down. "No," he says, "I would rather have something living than all the treasures of the world." To me, this is pretty touching—the little fellow has a heart. In fact he's the only character in the story who shows any good qualities whatsoever.

The queen falls back on her specialty. She cries. The little man takes pity on her and says if she can guess his name in three days he won't take the child. He doesn't have to do this, you understand. He's just trying to give her a break.

So the queen sends out a messenger to ask for all the names he can find, but she can't get the right one. What the king is doing all this time I don't know. If my wife suddenly started sending messengers all over the country collecting names I'd want to know what was going on.

On the third day the messenger sees the little man and discovers his name is Rumpelstiltskin. Of course the queen is delighted. Pretty soon the little man shows up and asks if she knows his name. Now the custody of a child is at stake and this is no time to clown around. But the queen has to be cute. She asks if his name is Jack. No. Harry? No. "Then," she says, "perhaps your name is Rumpelstiltskin!" I can just hear her—that smug, infuriating tone women use when they happen to be right about something. The little man goes into a rage, stamps his foot into the ground, splits in two and that's the end of him.

That's as far as the story goes, but I can't see it ending there. It's been over a year since the last batch of gold. "Queen, how come you never spin me gold anymore?" the king says. "Before we were married you used to spin it all the time."

"It wasn't me, it was a little man by the name of Rumpelstiltskin," she says, and tells him the whole story.

The king is pretty upset. "You mean to say you spent three nights alone with some troll?"

"Just spinning was all," she says.

"And a year later he comes around and wants the child," the king says. "Is that your story?"

"It's the truth," she says.

"And you expect me to believe you were just spinning?" The king takes off his crown and slams it on the floor. "You think I'm stupid or something?"

"Well . . . ," she says, and so on and so forth.

No, I've decided I'm not going to push the old classics on the kids. It won't be long before they'll be complaining about what *their* children are watching. "How can they stand this idiotic stuff? Remember that show we used to watch—about the fellow whose mother was an automobile?" And they'll nod and smile with that faraway look. I wouldn't take that away from them—not for all the spun gold in the world.

I think I just lost contact with my little girl. While reading the advertisements in a popular New England magazine, I noticed an appealing vacation spot. "Wouldn't you love to go to the Holly Farm Inn?" I asked my 13-year-old daughter.

Peering up at me from a comfortable sprawl on the living-room rug, she replied, "Maybe. Just what do people do at a farm-in?"

Frowning father to small son: "When I was your age I walked two blocks to the school bus every morning!"

Want ad placed by a ten-year-old boy in a Lancashire, England, paper: "I wish to contact men who were in the fifth grade in 1923 and who knew my father at that time. Object: to find out if he was as good a student as he tells me he was."

Small boy to dad reading bedtime story: "Fiddlers three? Don't you mean a three-piece string combo?"

Father to teen-age son: "When I was your age, I would have felt lucky to use the family car whether I agreed with the bumper sticker or not."

Three generations were represented at the dinner table. When the father mentioned Will Rogers, the son said, "Daddy, you mean Roy Rogers." Then the grandfather looked up and asked, "Who's Roy Rogers?"

Junior, who now has a job in a big establishment downtown, asked Grandpa if he ever had to be careful lest he "bend, fold or mutilate" his IBM card, and Grandpa wanted to know what that was. When Junior told him, Grandpa said he probably would have sweat the card through—and Junior wanted to know what *that* was.

Head of the House

BATTLE-TESTED HINTS FOR THE HOUSEBOUND HUSBAND

MARC DROGIN

WELL, now I know what it's like to run the house. Perhaps some of the fascinating little things I learned over the past 56 hours and 35 minutes, while my wife was lying leisurely in a hospital, can be of value to my fellow man. They are details learned and tested under battle conditions. They were bought with blood.

First, some mealtime hints. A balanced meal is whatever gets hot all at the same time. A snack is what doesn't.

Do not feed a one-year-old anything that looks as though it could be squeezed through the playpen mesh. It will be.

Anything tastes better to a three-year-old if you say he can't have it. Anything tastes better to a one-year-old if the dog has it. Anything tastes better to the dog if you get nasty when he takes it off the table a second time.

Strained vegetables and liver with cookies on it will not fool anybody.

Keep in mind that ashtrays will always land bottoms up, that feathers are hard to sweep up and that a little debris makes a house a home. Dishes will always dry by evaporation if left alone. Babies, only occasionally.

It is an incontestable fact of nature that the diaper-rash ointment will always be in the other room.

The attention span of a three-year-old is 7.3 seconds. A one-year-old has never heard about attention spans. The attention span of a dog is approximately twice the length of whatever you hit him with.

There is a game called Let Daddy Sleep, Dammit, but nobody will ever play.

As to your wife, remember that the dear thing is in the hospital and should be telephoned every day or so. Make it a practice never to mention anything that is happening. Let the baby tooth embedded in the end table come as a surprise. Later.

Do not ask on the third day where she put the diapers. Women don't have that kind of sense of humor.

Ask rather offhandedly if she'll be home tomorrow. Ask casually, "*When* next week?" Never weep over the telephone.

With masculine strength and iron will, and with a little common sense, 56 hours and 35 minutes can be made to flit by as if they were only a month or two. And to complete the overall picture of confidence, for your wife's return here's a nice little touch: have the children prop you up in a casual position in your easy chair as she's about to arrive.

Just try not to twitch. It's a dead giveaway.

———— • ————

I thought you were going to your lodge meeting?"

"It was postponed. The wife of the Grand Exalted Invincible Supreme Potentate wouldn't let him out tonight."

Tell me, Tom, who is the boss in your house?"

"Well," Tom answered thoughtfully, "Margie assumes command of the children, the servants, the dog and the parakeet. But I say pretty much what I please to the goldfish."

A man returning home unusually late was tiptoeing into his bedroom when his wife woke up. "Is that you, John?" she asked sleepily.

"Well," he answered, "it better be."

Father grumbling to his two youngsters, as he reluctantly gets ready for an evening out: "Other kids make their mothers too tired to want to go out, but not *you*."

Heard in a New York bar: "My boss won't let me make personal calls at the office, and my wife and daughter won't let me make them at home."

Saleswoman at lingerie counter to male shopper: "Could you be a little more explicit than 'big and fat'?"

———— • ————

Husband to jeweler: "What's good for the fourth day after a wife's birthday?"

Psychiatrist to male patient: "And did this feeling of insignificance come on suddenly or develop normally with marriage and parenthood?"

According to one father, his family consists of three members: nobody, everybody, and anybody who's anybody. When a difference of opinion arises, says the father, his teen-age daughter invariably prefaces her remarks with, "Anybody who's anybody knows that. . . ." His wife usually claims that, "Everybody knows that. . . ." His own opinions, he reports, are usually met with a chorused, "Nobody believes that these days."

The last word in an argument is what a wife has. Anything a husband says after that is the beginning of another argument.

Mother's authority in our home became clear when my father, after assigning new duties to my sister and me, said, "We think it's a very good idea, and so do I."

The Better Half

Frazzled wife in kitchen to home-coming husband ardently embracing her: "Why can't you come home exhausted like other men?"

A wife, complaining that her husband hadn't taken a good look at her in five years: "If anything happened to me I don't think he'd be able to identify the body."

CONFESSIONS OF A FRUSTRATED HOUSEWIFE OR MY LOVE AFFAIR WITH THE WASHING-MACHINE MAN

JOYCE KISSOCK LUBOLD

THE all-American housewife is, let us agree at the very beginning, faithful—both to her husband and to her wedding vows. Although she may enjoy reading those novels of suburbia that turn every residential street into a beehive of amorous intrigue, she knows very clearly the difference between that kind of fiction and her own kind of reality. In real life, her job consists of a frenzied round of washing, cleaning, cooking and circular running. Quite aside from love, we housewives are too busy, too harried, to prance lightfootedly along any primrose path. Infidelity is simply not for us.

However, at this very moment, I'm carrying on what certainly amounts to a full-blown romance. I am going through all the sweet, stylized motions of a great love affair: the first timid overtures, the long-awaited meetings, the baffling, turning tides of love and hatred intermingled. I'm doing these things; so is my neighbor, and so, very probably, are most other housewives.

My men change from time to time. Some weeks, I fling myself at only one man; other weeks, I find with dismay that I am fluttering with mad, false gaiety among four or five, for whom I must transform myself into the most flirtatious of plantation belles every time some major appliance breaks down.

Now, you take Charlie Gant. Charlie, bless his sullen soul, is the only man in town who is qualified to diagnose the strange tremors and fevers to which my washing machine is prone. Drawn to his charm or no, I *must* get along with Charlie, since I cannot get along without him. Charlie is a proud man, and he walks the streets of our town with the serious, heavy tread of any despot. For it is he alone who decides between the thrilling promise: "Be over this morning," and the chilling: "Maybe next week."

And so begins the affair.

At 9:37 of a Tuesday morning, my washing machine gives a single great *yawp!*, swirls its load of wash around at breakneck

41

speed for a moment, and then, grinning hugely, disgorges an enormous quantity of gray, soapy water onto the kitchen floor. With shaking hands, I dial Charlie's phone number, desperate for the sound of his reassuring voice.

His wife answers! She asks my name. I offer my phone number instead. I hang up, forcing myself to be calm, steeling myself to wait.

Now the water oozes sluggishly into the cellar, and mechanically I go about my chores, to the beat of an anxious little song: "When-will-he-call? Will-he—horrors!—call-at-all?" The water drips on.

The phone rings. It is Charlie! I am overwhelmed with joy. But careful. I must be gay and bright. Charlie hates to hear a woman whine.

"Mr. Gant! Thank you so much for calling back." (Be light! Never let him guess how much you need him.) "I ran into an odd bit of trouble with my washer this morning. It's a leak of some kind, and the water is *pouring right down*—" (Careful. You *mustn't* panic. Charlie wants his women brave.) "And so I wondered if you might like to drop by this morning or—" (Don't push him.) "—this afternoon."

And then his familiar voice, so gruff, so proud, so positive. "Got a lot of calls to make today, Mzz." (Charlie calls me "Mzz.")

"Oh, of course. I know how busy you always are." (Go softly with your flattery. This man knows all the tricks.) "But I did hope you could squeeze me in." (Little giggle.) "I just don't know what to do. I'm just so upset." (*Now*. Cling to him. Forget your pride. This is the moment.) "I really need you, Mr. Gant. Any time you can make it."

"Yeah. Well, I'll try to drop by. Sometime after lunch." And in his dear abrupt way, Charlie hangs up. (My, but he's gruff today. It's because he feels he's given in to me. I know his moods.)

All this pretty well shoots the morning for me. This kind of thing may have been all in a day's work for the ladies of the French court, but I have to sit down with my feet up for ten minutes or so, just to get my breath back. I dare not tarry for long, though, because there's a lot to be done to make ready. You can't do too much for Charlie. I mean, if he sees some tendency to grovel, it does not displease him.

First, the dishes. (Charlie Gant likes to spread his tools on the kitchen table.) Then I make a pot of coffee. (He likes it strong and bitter.) I put the baby down for a nap and the four-year-old in front of the television set. (Kids make Charlie nervous.) It is right about then that I hear his ring at the door.

"Hel-*lo*, Mr. Gant," I carol as I open the door.

He walks silently into the house. I walk behind him. We reach the kitchen and turn face to face. As he stands there, so long awaited, I find myself in the second stage of the affair. For love is akin to hate, and joy lies closest to sorrow. We are caught in the inexplicable surge of antipathy that lovers know when they try, too hurriedly, to reknit old ties.

"Machine's still full o' water," Charlie says with strong distaste.

"I know it is," I say shortly. "That's why I called." (He is a boor. I hate him. Hate him.)

"Can't do a thing with the water in her," he says, his toolbox still held tightly in his hand.

"Neither could I," I say, fighting this unreasoning hate. There is a terrible silence, a mute struggle between us.

And then *he* gives in. "Well. We can't do a thing until we get rid of it, can we?" he says as he finally puts down his toolbox.

Ah, the shrewdness of that "we." I melt again; the icy hatred vanishes. "I didn't like to fool with it until you were here," I say archly. He smiles at me and then disappears behind the washing machine. (I love this man. Love him.)

I turn the timer when he tells me to, and finally the machine lurches reluctantly into its drain cycle as Charlie and I, bound by our extraordinary camaraderie, watch the water slowly recede.

"Appears you've run right through that water-level switch again," Charlie says, and the sternness in his voice chills me.

"Do you think you might be able to do something special with it?" I ask falteringly.

"Dunno. Doesn't look good." (Charlie never really gives in to me. That's the thing about him.) "I'll give her a try, but I dunno," he says.

"I'll get some coffee for you," I say, acknowledging dismissal.

Now he works at his task and I at mine, as a warm, friendly atmosphere comes to fill the room. In time, the job is done. "I'll try not to phone again too soon," I say gaily, yet wistfully, as Charlie leaves.

The door shuts on his dear retreating form. I sink exhausted on a chair. There is a cry of dismay from my four-year-old. I reach the living room just in time to see our television picture glare and go black. It's all to do again. And with a different man!

C ity Hall," said the switchboard operator, answering a call. There was no sound on the other end of the line. "City hall," the operator repeated. Still no reply.

Finally, after the third time, a rather nervous female voice said, "Is this really city hall?"

"That's right, madam," said the operator. "With whom do you wish to speak?"

There was an embarrassed silence. Then the female voice said softly, "I guess nobody. I just found this number in my husband's pocket."

R ing Lardner was once requested by a girl reporter to contribute to a symposium about the virtues of wives. The idea was to show that without their sturdy helpmeets by their sides, most gents would now be in the gutter. Mr. Lardner surprised the lady by replying as follows:

"I was never one to keep a diary, and so must depend on an unsteady, Volsteady memory for the things my wife has done for me. In 1914 or 1915, I think it was July, she cleaned my white shoes.

"In 1918 she told the man at the draft board that she and three kiddies were dependent on me for support. In 1921 and again in 1923 she brought in some ice, White Rock and glasses.

"She dusted my typewriter in 1922. Late one night in 1924 we got home from somewhere and I said I was hungry and she gave me a verbal picture of the location of the pantry. Once a man named Morris called me up and she told him I was out of town.

"The time our car stalled she suggested it must be out of gas. Another time I quit cigarettes and she felt sorry for me.

"Once, on an overnight train trip, we had a section in a sleeping car, and just as I was nearly crazy trying to guess whether I should take the lower or upper berth she solved the problem by crawling into the lower. And once when a waiter was going to put two lumps of sugar in my coffee, my wife stopped him. She didn't touch him or call him a name; she just said, 'Only one lump!' And he did not put the other lump in."

Husband visiting wife in hospital: "Oh, sure, I clean and dust and wash the dishes and make the bed—though not as often as you did of course."

During a week when her husband and all three children were sick at home, the harassed young wife commented: "The toughest thing about being a housewife is that you have no place to stay home from."

A harassed housewife, describing a day that had been filled with frustrations, wound up with: "I even got a busy signal on Dial-a-Prayer."

Mop-in-hand wife answering phone while husband relaxes: "This is 'labor'—would you like to talk to 'management'?"

WHAT *NOT* TO SAY TO YOUR HUSBAND

CYNTHIA LINDSAY

GETTING along with a husband requires far more than the ability to look pretty and unharassed during domesticity's trying moments. It requires a basic instinct to know what *not* to say and when not to say it.

You never know what may have happened to the man a few minutes ago. He could have had a run-in with the boss—so he thinks you're extravagant when you tell him you want a hair ribbon from the dime store.

On the other hand, he may have put through a big deal, been complimented by the president of the company or had his secretary tell him he reminds her of Walter Pidgeon. In which event he may say, "It's high time you had a fur coat." You never know.

Try to case the situation before you commit yourself to any statement. But don't think too long without saying something, 45 because then he is going to ask, "What are you sulking about? You haven't said a word since I got home."

Here are ten rules, tested in every home and divorce court in the country, on what you must never bring up if you want a sublime marriage:

1. Never say, "How do I look?" You're wasting your time and his. If you don't look all right, he will notice. If you do, he won't. A straggling hair, slip showing or crooked lipstick will catch his eye immediately. A new hair-do, loss of four pounds or a smart dress—never. The best you can hope for as an answer to the question is, "Fine, dear"—while he reads the sports page.

2. When he says, "Sometimes I think my mother is crazy," do *not* say, "She certainly is." He will reply, "Well, I don't mean really crazy—" and you will say, "But *I* do." Then you're really into it. And presently it will come out that you attacked his sainted parent.

When he says his mother is crazy, just say, "Poor lady, she's old and lives alone—we really should see more of her." "Over my dead body," he will reply, and devote the rest of the evening to proving to you that his mother is off her rocker.

3. Never tell him you're tired. *He's* tired. *You* don't plan your day right. When he asks, "How was your day?" don't under any circumstances tell him. If you are lucky enough to get a "How are you?" it is permissible to say, "Fine—maybe a little beat." But if you see a glimmer of sympathy, do not press your luck, because if you go on, a glazed look will cloud his eyes and without looking up from the paper he will mumble, "That's nice, dear."

4. Never say, "I don't know how Helen can stand it. Charles is getting impossible."

You have now attacked a male. If friends are having marriage difficulties, the woman is wrong. Your statement will be countered with, "Poor Helen, indeed. If she would stay away from that idiotic women's club, and see that dinner was on the table, there wouldn't be any trouble."

The danger of this kind of discussion is that it may remind your husband of something *you* haven't done. It's best to say, "It does seem a shame about the Stewarts—I'm afraid they aren't getting on." Then you haven't taken sides. No point in trying to understand. Just accept it.

5. Never tell him about a past love or a gentleman who got fresh with you at the dance the other night. In the first case his answer might be, "Well, if he was so all-fired great, why

didn't you marry him?" This can end in tears.

In the second case he won't be jealous, which is what you hoped for. He will think you are making it up to make him jealous, which you probably are.

6. Don't start any sentence with, "Never mind, I'll do it," or "Aren't you ever going to—?"

First, you'll have to. Second, he isn't. These are the two most bullhead-making approaches in marriage.

7. Don't discuss the price or quality of his apparel. His clothes are a basic necessity. Yours are sheer frivolity. Everybody at the office has more suits than he has. "Did you *have* to buy that dress? Why didn't you get a really smart black one?"

8. Never say, "You're always talking sports. Don't you think it's time you let me in on what you're talking about?"

When you consider the possible outcome of this statement, it is blood-chilling. He may decide, all right, he will. So he takes you to a baseball game and is prepared to be kind and instructive. He is not, however, prepared for you to ask where the goal posts are.

9. Never ask if he enjoyed his nap after he has snored his way through an evening of television. He was *not* asleep; he was resting his eyes. He heard every word of it.

10. Never tell him your dreams. I woke my husband one night and said, "I just had the most horrible dream. I was having an operation in a hospital in a strange city. It was awful. I was crying for you, and they couldn't find you anywhere."

He just rolled over and said, "Did you try the club?"

Out of Control

After the birth of his eighth child, a friend of mine received a letter of congratulations from the local Planned Parenthood association—along with a card he was to return if he desired professional help in the future. My friend sent back the card with this notation: "Where were you when I needed you?"

Snatch of overheard dialogue: "You know what they call people who use the rhythm system of birth control?"

"No. What?"

"Parents."

There's a story going the rounds about a new baby who was born grinning from ear to ear and wouldn't stop smiling. Finally, the doctor, who had never seen anything like this before, called in some of his colleagues to have a look. One of them noticed that the baby had his right hand clutched into a fist, so he reached down and opened it. Inside the hand was—The Pill.

Wife, knitting tiny garment, to husband: "Oh, I meant to tell you—it wasn't psychosomatic after all."

En route to the supermarket one Saturday morning, I became interested in a family walking in front of me. The young father pushed a wide baby carriage with a pair of chubby twins inside. On one side of him, a small girl, carrying a big brush, held on to him. On the other side walked an older boy with a stack of leaflets in his hand. At the first lamppost, they all stopped. While the father lifted a pot of glue from the carriage, the boy handed him one of the leaflets and the girl extended the brush. The father brushed glue onto the paper, stuck the handbill on the lamppost, put the pot away, and they all moved on.

Amused by the teamwork, I stopped to read the large, bold letters on the handbill: SUPPORT BIRTH CONTROL.

A young housewife in our town was asked by her neighbor, who had just dropped in. "What is that you're taking, my dear, the Pill?"

"No," was the worried reply. "This is a tranquilizer. I forgot to take the Pill!"

If nature had arranged for wives and husbands to have children alternately, there would only be three in a family.

Man on park bench to small boy: "And whose little population explosion are you?"

Young matron resigning from job, "My reason will soon be apparent—and so will I."

Help!

ALL UP IN A HEAVAL

JOSEPH HENRY JACKSON

For quite a while now we have been wondering about the Trotts. We have never seen them but we feel they are almost friends. Marta, who told us so much about them, seemed to us at first the ideal helper we had sought so long. The Trotts had written sincerely and warmly To Whom It Might Concern.

For the three months Marta stayed with us she was all we hoped. But we began to see that Marta still lived with the Trotts in spirit if with us in the flesh.

We understood this when we realized that we were coming to know a surprising lot about the Trotts' family life. Mrs. Trott, we learned, wore a transformer. Mr. Trott was a pharmist. He played a flute after dinner; the music was lovely, Marta said—clear as a hound's tooth. Perhaps it was his training at the prescription slab that taught him to make a better Old Fashioned than I did. Marta said Mr. Trott always put a dash of angora bitters in his.

As the weeks passed, we began to see the Trotts more and more plainly. Order ruled in the Trott household; times, dates and schedules were scrupulously observed. When we assumed she would change her night off because we had unexpected guests, Marta said Mrs. Trott would not have taken such a thing for granite. "She would never put me in a lurch!"

Mrs. Trott, we learned, often had ladies in for tea, and sometimes for a game of option bridge. Marta had never minded doing up the cups and plates. But there was no doubt about her feeling

49

that we might better have done such things with more style. Mrs. Trott made her tea in a semaphore, a handsome brass one.

It was not long before we came to have in our minds' eye a partial picture of the Trott living room with books that come by mail from the Literary Glide, and the derogatypes of Trott relatives on the walls.

Mrs. Trott was one for sayings, it appeared. She often said she didn't believe in stirring up a harness nest. Now and then, we thought, Marta felt she spoke too much of the Trotts. At such times she would close the subject. "Excuse me!" she would say. "I was just talking out loud!"

Inevitably Marta went back to the Trotts. It was, we believe, our lack of neatness that was too much for her. What with our child and a cat and the fact that we were too busy most of the time to be as tidy as we should—as tidy as the Trotts—Marta felt that our house always looked like the raft of God, and she never felt wholly at home in it. She did not like it, she said, when things were all up in a heaval.

A friend gave Dorothy Parker a young alligator, some three feet long. Not knowing what else to do with it, the author put it in her bathtub. She went out shopping, and when she returned she found this note from her maid, who had come in during her absence: "I have resigned. I refuse to work in a house where there is an alligator in the bathtub. I would have told you this before, but I did not think the matter would ever come up."

A wealthy Canadian advertised for a cook, offering top wages, minimum working hours and luxurious living quarters. Deluged with answers, she chose a woman from out of town and scribbled off a note offering her the job.

A few days later came the reply. "Dear Madam: Sorry to have to turn down your offer, but handwriting analysis is my hobby and after examining yours, my book tells me that you would be too hard a person to work for. Thanks anyway."

An ad in the Newark, Ohio, *Advocate:* "Wanted — experienced housekeeper; good wages. Two in family; good referee essential."

In a trim bungalow near Manhattan lived a rising young novelist and his wife, presided over by a beautiful Scandinavian servant whom everybody described as a perfect gem. This paragon one day approached her mistress in tears and announced: "I must leave on the first of the month."

"But why?" demanded the housewife. "I thought you were perfectly happy here." It wasn't that, sobbed the maid; she had met a handsome soldier a few months before, and now — and now — "Don't do anything until I've consulted my husband," said the wife. She was back from his study in a trice. "We have decided that you must stay," she announced. "We will adopt your baby."

In due course, a son appeared upon the scene, the author adopted him legally, and all was serene for another year, when the maid again announced that she was leaving. This time she had met a sailor. The author and his wife went into another huddle, and the maid was told, "It is unfair to bring up a child alone. We will adopt your second baby."

The second baby was a darling little girl, and the bungalow resounded with happy laughter. Then the blow fell. The maid resigned again. "Don't tell me," gasped the wife, "that this time you met a Marine."

"It's not that at all, ma'am," said the servant with dignity. "I'm resigning because I simply cannot work for such a big family."

One housewife to another: "With a completely automatic kitchen and laundry, I let the maid go and hired a mechanic!"

A Mrs. Gallagher of Tyrone, Ireland, in the course of hiring a new maid, interviewed several local girls. Finally one was selected and told to report for work the next morning. The following day when the doorbell rang, Mrs. Gallagher was surprised to see a total stranger standing on the doorstep. "You hired me yesterday, ma'am," said the girl.

"But you're not the maid I interviewed," gasped the matron.

"Ah, no, ma'am, I'm not meself," explained the girl. "She's sick. I'm me sister."

When I made a house call on some sick youngsters, their mother told me that she was expecting her fourth. She had announced the same news to her maid that morning, and the maid had promptly baked and beautifully decorated a cake. On the top, lettered in icing, was the message: "FAREWELL."

A young physician and his wife had considerable difficulty teaching a new maid to answer the telephone properly. In spite of repeated instructions she persisted in answering "Hello," instead of "Dr. Jones' residence." After many practice sessions, everything seemed to be all right. Then one morning the extension in the bedroom rang, and the maid, busy making the bed, grabbed the phone and blurted: "Dr. Jones' bedroom."

Two nursemaids were wheeling their infant charges in the park when one asked the other: "Are you going to the dance tonight?"

"I'd love to," the other replied, "but to tell the truth I'm afraid to leave the baby with its mother."

It was an important dinner, and the host, giving last-minute instructions, reminded the cook not to serve the salad dressed, but to serve it undressed, since he wanted to take care of that detail himself. But at the salad course he was horrified to see the cook, clad only in her slip, come through the door carrying the salad bowl.

"What's the meaning of this?" he asked.

"You said undressed," she retorted, "but this is as far as I go!"

One day the Mexican girl who worked for us told me she was quitting. When I asked why, she said, "I'm in the family way."

"You can't be! Who is it, Maria?"

"Your husband and your son," she replied.

Horrified, I demanded an explanation.

"Well," she replied, "I go to the patio to clean and your husband say, 'You're in my way.' I go to the living room to clean and your son say, 'You're in my way.' So I'm in the family way and I quit."

The housewife was looking over the new maid's references. "Do you think you will settle down here?" she asked, after a while. "You seem to have left a good many places."

The girl smiled confidently. "Yes, ma'am," she replied. "But I didn't leave any of them voluntarily."

Pardon My Language:

LINGUISTIC LAPSES

THE LOWER ORDERS of creation are good linguists. Though they don't seem to get much fun out of it, ants communicate perfectly, as do bees. They're not confused by language. But we are. Language has been described as a device for concealing thought. It's also a device for impeding communication. Bernard Shaw remarked that England and the United States were two countries divided by a common language. That vast network of booby traps called words is at work all the time. Of all these traps the most baffling is described on page 67, in Corey Ford's "Do You Talk Double-Take?" I would gladly have made him a present of a sample I once made up myself. It was an imaginary deathbed utterance by Samuel Goldwyn: "I never thought I'd live to see this day!" Apropos of the booby traps foreigners fall into when they use our noble tongue, it may be remarked that we, perhaps the world's worst linguists, don't have much right to laugh. I can still remember an incident when I was traveling by train in Germany. A middle-aged American, his face drawn in moderate anguish, came charging down the corridor, and seeing another obvious American, took me by the shoulder and gasped out: "For God's sake, tell me quick, am I a Damen or a Herren?"

Language Barriers

A Filipino schoolteacher wrote the following letter of resignation to the American superintendent in her best English: "I wish to resignate. My works are too many and my salaries are too few. Moreover, my principal makes many lovings to which I say 'Oh, not.'"

Two American women stopping at the Hotel Tivoli in Lisbon wanted another chair in their room. The steward who answered their ring could not understand English. One of the women pointed to the only chair in the room, then tried pantomime, seating herself in an imaginary chair. With a knowing smile, the steward bowed and motioned for her to follow him.

At the end of the corridor, he stopped, smiled and bowed again, and pointed triumphantly to the door of the Ladies' Room.

Mr. Goldberg, returning from Europe, was assigned by the head steward to a table for two. Here he was presently joined by a polite Frenchman who, before sitting down, bowed, smiled, and said, *"Bon appetit."* Not to be outdone, Mr. Goldberg rose, bowed, and said, "Goldberg."

This little ceremony was repeated at each meal for three days. On the fourth day, Mr. Goldberg confided his perplexity to a man in the smoking lounge: "It was like this, you see. This Frenchman tells me his name—Bon Appetit—and I tell him my name—Goldberg. So we are introduced. That is good. But why keep it up day after day?"

"Oh—but you don't understand, Mr. Goldberg," replied the other. *"Bon appetit* isn't his name. It means 'I hope you have a pleasant meal.'"

"Ah!" exclaimed Goldberg. "Thanks."

That evening it was Mr. Goldberg who arrived late for dinner. Before sitting down he bowed ceremoniously, and said, *"Bon appetit."*

And the Frenchman rose, smiled, and murmured, "Goldberg."

When Captain Cook discovered Australia, his sailors brought aboard ship a strange animal whose name they did not know. Sent ashore to inquire of the natives, they came back and said, "It is a kangaroo." Many years passed before it was known that when the natives were asked to name the animal and said, "Kangaroo," they meant, "What did you say?"

A Pasadena girl took a job as a forelady in a shop employing several Mexican women. The first morning she addressed each of them cordially in her high school Spanish. The women shrank from her. When the same thing happened next day, the mystified girl told the boss. He asked her what she had said to them. "Just good morning," she replied.

"But how did you say it?"

"I said *'Buenos Dios, Buenos Dios!'*"

The boss howled. "If you wanted to say good morning you should have said *'Buenas dias.'* You've looked at each of these women the first thing in the morning and said 'Good God, Good God!'"

A Pan American World Airways employe in Accra advertised that he wanted a kerosene refrigerator and received this reply: "I have the honour most respectfully to submit this my humble application soliciting for employment as a kerosene refrigerator. I successfully passed the seventh standard at Oboden Methodist Middle School and hold documents testifying my character and ability."

At a dinner party in New York, a South American visitor was telling about his country and himself. He concluded, "And I have a most charming and sympathetic wife, but, alas, no children." Then, as his companions seemed to expect further enlightenment, he continued haltingly, "You see, my wife is unbearable."

This was greeted with puzzled glances, so he sought to clear the matter up: "I mean, my wife is inconceivable." Seeing that this, too, was not understood, and floundering deeper and deeper in the intricacies of English, he finally explained triumphantly: "That is, my wife, she is impregnable!"

A firm experimenting with an electronic brain designed to translate English into Russian fed it the words: "The spirit is willing but the flesh is weak." The machine responded with a sentence in Russian which meant, a linguist reported, "The whisky is agreeable but the meat has gone bad."

A Londoner wound up a business trip to the Orient with a visit to Taipei. At a luncheon he was asked to say a few words. Since he spoke not a word of Chinese, his address was to be translated by an interpreter sentence by sentence.

"Well," he began, "I just want you to know that I'm tickled to death to be here."

A look of agony appeared on the interpreter's face. "This poor man," he said in halting Chinese, "scratches himself until he dies, only to be with you."

A firm in Singapore was surprised to receive an inquiry from Saigon for 12 million trombones. Even though orders are pouring into Singapore from the American services in Vietnam, this did seem rather excessive.

Then the French commercial attaché solved the problem—*trombone* is the French word for paper clip.

During a United Nations discussion on aid for under-developed countries, an American delegate drew attention to the connection between health problems and the provision of privies. An interpreter, not knowing what a privy was, translated it into French as "private law." His colleague immediately spotted his mistake and passed him a note with just two letters on it: W.C.

The first interpreter glanced at the note, smiled indulgently, scribbled a reply and passed it back. "You run along," his astonished colleague read. "I'll be all right."

Red Smith, the sports columnist, was an honored guest one evening at a banquet tendered by the Don Q Rum Company in Puerto Rico. Smith delivered his speech nobly, but for one detail—he persisted in referring to his hosts as the "makers of that wonderful Bacardi rum."

Every time he mentioned the competing name "Bacardi," a mortified Don Q official would jump up and correct him with, "Don Q, *señor,* Don Q."

And every time Red Smith answered graciously, "You're welcome."

---●---

A Chinese student at the University of Michigan who memorized phrases from an etiquette book had his first opportunity to try them out at a reception given by President Ruthven. When a cup of tea was handed to him, he solemnly responded: "Thank you, sir or madam, as the case may be."

An American visitor in a Montreal restaurant went to the washroom, turned on what he thought was the cold water and was scalded with hot water. "This is an outrage!" he screamed at the manager. "Why aren't your taps properly marked?"

The manager patiently explained. "Look," he said. "This tap is marked C. That stands for *Chaud*, which is French for 'hot.' You should know that when traveling in Quebec."

The customer stood abashed. Then he made a discovery. "Wait a minute, the other tap is marked C, too. What about that?"

"But, of course," said the proprietor. "That stands for 'Cold.' This is a bilingual restaurant in a bilingual city, my friend."

---●---

MISHAPS WITH ANOTHER LANGUAGE

FRANK MOORE COLBY

I READ French off and on for years, but when I tried to speak it I realized the chasm that cut me off from the real French language. So I tried a phonograph, and after many bouts acquired part of a sermon by Bossuet and real fluency in discussing a quinsy sore throat with a Paris physician, in case I ever went there and had one. I then took 14 conversation lessons and should, if I had kept on diligently, have been able at the age of 85 to inquire faultlessly my way to the post office. I could already ask for butter and sing a song written by Henry IV. But these methods were too slow or led in directions I did not wish to go.

So I scraped acquaintance with every Frenchman whom I heard talking English badly, and became immensely interested in his welfare. I introduced visiting Frenchmen to French-speaking Americans, and sat, with open mouth, in the flow of their conversation. I fastened upon an unfrocked priest who wanted to become completely American and forget France, and as I was trying to reverse the process, I rather got in his way. I took to the streets at lunch time and tried newdealers, bookshops, restaurants, invented imaginary errands, bought things I did not want, and exchanged them for objects even less desirable. That kept a little conversation going from day to day, but on the whole it was a dry season. I had always heard that the French are clannish and hate to learn another language, but most of my overtures in French brought only English upon me. I was always diving in French and they were always pulling me out again. They thought they were humane.

Then I fell in with M. Bernou, whose English and my French were so alike that we agreed to interchange them. We met daily for two weeks and walked in the park, each tearing at the other's language.

Our conversations, as I look back on them, must have run about like this:

"It calls to walk," said he, smiling brilliantly.

"It is good morning," said I, "better than I had extended."

"I was at you yestairday ze morning, but I deed not find."

"I was obliged to leap early," said I, "and I was busy standing up straight all around the forenoon."

"The book I prayed you send, he came, and I thank, but positively are you not deranged?"

"Don't talk," said I. "Never talk again. It was really nothing anywhere. I had been very happy, I reassure."

"Pardon, I glide, I glode. There was the hide of a banane. Did I crash you?"

"I noticed no insults," I replied. "You merely gnawed my arm."

Gestures and smiles of perfect understanding.

I do not know whether Bernou felt as I did on these occasions — like a child. For they said I ought to think in French, but when there is so little French to think with it divests the mind of its acquisitions of 40 years. Knowledge of good and evil does not exist, the sins have no names and the mind is like a rather defective toy Noah's ark. From the point of view of Bernou's and my vocabulary, Central Park was as the Garden of Eden, with new and unnamed things everywhere. A dog, a tree, a statue taxed our powers of description, and on a complex matter like a policeman our minds could not meet at all. We could only totter together a few steps in any mental direction. For my part I shall always feel toward Bernou as my childhood's friend. I wonder if he noticed that I was an old, battered man.

Deft Definitions

Minor operation: one performed on somebody else.

Spare tire: The one you check the day after you have a flat.

Short cut: A route on which you can't find anybody to ask where you are.

An opportunist: Any man who goes ahead and does what you always intended to do.

Nagging: The constant reiteration of the unhappy truth.

Secret: Something you tell one person at a time.

Nonchalance: The ability to look like an owl when you have acted like a jackass.

Punctuality: The art of arriving for an appointment just in time to be indignant at the tardiness of the other party.

Rare volume: A borrowed book that comes back.

Diet: A short period of starvation preceding a gain of five pounds.

Compromise: A deal in which two people get what neither of them wanted.

Bargain: Something you cannot use at a price you cannot resist.

Sense of humor: What makes you laugh at something which would make you mad if it happened to you.

Neurotic: A person who, when you ask how she is, tells you.

Intelligence: A sterling quality possessed by anybody who will listen attentively to what you have to say and nod in agreement.

Efficiency: The knack of getting someone to do a job you dislike.

Perfect guest: One who makes his host feel at home.

Apology: Politeness too late.

Junk: Something you keep ten years and then throw away two weeks before you need it.

Woman Driver: A person who, when obeying every rule, is blamed for slowing down some man who isn't.

Cookbook definition of eternity: Two people and a ham.

Traffic Light: A trick to get pedestrians halfway across the street safely.

Pedestrian: Man who thought there were still a couple of gallons of gas left in the tank.

Family swimming pool: A small body of water completely surrounded by other people's children.

Bachelor: A man who leans toward women, but not far enough to altar his stance.

Overweight: Just desserts.

Ostentation: That showy quality deplored in anything we can't afford.

Wood: That remarkable material which burns so easily in a forest and with such difficulty in the fireplace.

Will power: The ability, after you have used three fourths of a can of paint and finished the job, to close the can and clean the brush, instead of painting something else that doesn't really need it.

Perfect timing: Being able to turn off the "hot" and "cold" shower faucets at the same time.

A distinguished commentator is one whose predictions are forgotten by the time circumstances prove them wrong.

When the other guy is laid off it's a reccession. When it happens to you it's a depression.

Exhilaration is that feeling you get just after a great idea hits you, and just before you realize what's wrong with it.

An American professor met three staid members of the Académie Française in Paris and asked for their definition of *savoir-faire,* which he wanted to include in his modern dictionary. "Eet is not deefeecult," one said. "Eef I go home and find my wife kissing another man and I teep my hat to them and say: 'Excuse me,' that is *savoir-faire."*

"Not quite," said the second. "Eef I go home and find my wife kissing another man and I teep my hat and say: 'Excuse me. Continue,' that is *savoir-faire."*

"No—not quite," rumbled the third, fingering his beard. "Eef I go home and find my wife kissing another man and teep my hat and say: 'Excuse me. Continue,' and he *can* continue—*he* has *savoir-faire."*

Among the English language's many puzzling words is "economy," which means the large size in soap flakes and the small size in motorcars.

Since we say a herd of cattle, a pack of wolves, a pride of lions, etc., why not a piddle of puppies . . . a trip of hippies . . . a wince of dentists . . . a lurch of buses . . . a wrangle of philosophers . . . a shrivel of critics . . . a descent of relatives.

Mummies are Egyptians that were pressed for time.

———————•———————

EPIGRAMMATICALLY SPEAKING
AMBROSE BIERCE

Absurdity. A statement or belief manifestly inconsistent with one's own opinion.

Acquaintance. A person whom we know well enough to borrow from, but not well enough to lend to. A degree of friendship called slight when its object is poor or obscure, and intimate when he is rich or famous.

Advice. The smallest current coin.

Bore. A person who talks when you wish him to listen.

Calamity. A plain reminder that the affairs of this life are not of our own ordering. Calamities are of two kinds: misfortune to ourselves, and good fortune to others.

Consult. To seek another's approval of a course already decided on.

Coward. One who in a perilous emergency thinks with his legs.

Duty. That which sternly impels us in the direction of profit, along the line of desire.

Edible. Good to eat, and wholesome to digest, as a worm to a toad, a toad to a snake, a snake to a pig, a pig to a man, and a man to a worm.

Education. That which discloses to the wise and disguises from the foolish their lack of understanding.

Egotist. A person of low taste, more interested in himself than in me.

Fashion. A despot whom the wise ridicule and obey.

Hospitality. The virtue which induces us to feed and lodge certain persons who are not in need of food and lodging.

Litigation. A machine which you go into as a pig and come out of as a sausage.

Noise. A stench in the ear. Undomesticated music. The chief product and authenticating sign of civilization.

Patience. A minor form of despair disguised as a virtue.

Peace. In international affairs, a period of cheating between two periods of fighting.

Politeness. The most acceptable hypocrisy.

Revolution. In politics, an abrupt change in the form of misgovernment.

Stating the Oblivious

DO YOU TALK DOUBLE-TAKE?
COREY FORD

YOU CAN'T blame me for making a mistake," my friend Bunny said the other day. "After all, none of us are human." I was trying to figure that one out when she added thoughtfully, "I may be wrong, but I'm not far from it."

Bunny is a skid-talker. Skid-talk is more than a slip of the tongue. It's a slip of the whole mind. In effect, it puts one idea on top of another, producing a sort of mental double exposure—and my friend Bunny is a master of the art. When her husband, a prominent Hollywood director, completed a screen epic recently she told him loyally, "I hope it goes over with a crash." She was very enthusiastic after the preview. "It's a great picture," she assured everyone. "Don't miss it if you can."

That's the insidious thing about skid-talk—you're never quite sure you've heard it. Skid-language is like a time bomb; it ticks away quietly in your subconscious; and suddenly, a few minutes later, your mind explodes with the abrupt realization that something about the remark you just heard was a trifle askew.

"If George Washington were alive today," Bunny told me once, "he'd turn over in his grave." On another occasion she opened a debate with the challenging sentence, "For your information, let me ask you a question."

The simplest kind of skid-talk consists of mixing words. For example:

"Too many cooks in the soup."

"From time immoral."

"There I was, left holding the jackpot."

"It was so dark you couldn't see your face in front of you."

"I want some hot-water juice and a lemon."

A devoted mother added another gem to my collection: "I'm going to have a bust made of my daughter's head." And a stranger whom I discovered feeding pigeons in Central Park explained to me with quiet dignity: "I believe in being dumb to kind animals."

Sometimes a skid-talker will turn an entire sentence inside out so effectively that the listener can't possibly set it straight again. I keep wondering about a statement I overheard the other day at the station: "He tells me something one morning and out the other." And I have yet to discover what's wrong with Bunny's advice to a young married couple: "Two can live as cheaply as one, but it costs them twice as much."

Bunny is a natural skid-zophrenic. "I'm a split personality all in one," she describes herself happily. She lives in a handsome country place of which she says dreamily, "Isn't it pretty? The lake comes right up to the shore." "I went to a wonderful party," she said of a recent celebrity-studded banquet. "Everybody in the room was there." She made sure to thank the hostess as she departed. "Darling, that was the best dinner I ever put in my whole mouth."

Bunny's insults are equally bewildering. "I never liked you, and I always will," she told a screen star frankly. And a perennially young starlet is still trying to decipher Bunny's candid appraisal: "You're old enough to be my daughter."

The best skid-talk fuses two thoughts together, creating a new shortcut which speeds up the language. I remember a New Year's Eve party when Bunny became fearful that the sounds of midnight revelry might disturb the neighbors. "Don't make so much noise," she told the celebrants. "Remember, this isn't the only house we're in."

I had an affectionate note from Bunny recently. "Come see us again soon," she wrote. "We miss you almost as much as if you were here."

———— • ————

Widow, asked whether she would ever marry again: "I'd certainly have to think twice about giving *that* a second thought."

A young prep-school lad we know is still trying to decipher the following letter from his current girl friend:

"Dear John, I hope you are not still angry. I want to explain that I was really joking when I told you I didn't mean what I said about reconsidering my decision not to change my mind. Please believe I really mean this. Love, Grace."

A local radio announcer commenting on hazardous driving conditions: "Please don't do any unnecessary driving unless it's absolutely necessary."

From an auto-accident report to an insurance company: "My car sustained no damage whatsoever and the other car somewhat less."

Sign just outside a bridge-construction job: "No Unauthorized Trespassing."

———— • ————

As they watched a TV newscast, a woman said to her husband: "It seems to me that the majority of people in this country belong to some minority group."

Mayor Richard J. Daley of Chicago, asked by reporters to comment on a trucking strike, offered this comment: "What keeps people apart is their inability to get together."

After the warning bell announced the Louvre's closing, one old museum guard grumbled to another as they shepherded the crowds out, "Every day for 20 years it's been the same. There's always somebody who's the last to leave."

Insurance Claimants Tell How Auto Accidents Happen:

I misjudged a lady crossing the street.

I collided with a stationary streetcar coming in the opposite direction.

I heard a horn blown and was struck in the back—a lady was evidently trying to pass me.

A pedestrian hit me and went underneath my car.

My car was stolen, and I set up a human cry but it has not been recovered.

If the other driver had stopped a few yards behind himself, the accident would not have happened.

Troubles at North Dakota State Relief Headquarters:

Please send my money at once as I need it badly. I have fallen into errors with my landlady.

I am very annoyed that you have branded my oldest boy illiterate. Oh, it is a dirty lie, as I married his father a week before he was born.

Sir, I am forwarding my marriage certificate and my two children, one of which is a mistake as you will see.

Mrs.—has had no clothes for a year and has been regularly visited by the clergy.

I have no children as yet, my husband is a bus driver and works day and night.

In accordance with your instructions, I have given birth to twins in the enclosed envelope.

Emergency Investigators Report City Problems:

The man has had two operations and is now rid of his money entirely.

This man was hit by an automobile and speaks broken English.

The children need thorough cooking.

Milk is needed for baby and father is unable to supply it.

Although applicant's wife looked worried and despondent, her canary was singing cheerfully.

This is a cheerful colored family. There is no food in the house and the children are fading.

Overheard on a bus: "Oh, I feel some better this morning, but I always feel bad when I feel better because I know I'm going to feel worse."

A nervous little immigrant woman upon arrival in America was asked, "Do you advocate the overthrow of the government of the United States of America by subversion or violence?"

She thought a moment, then made her choice. "Violence," she said.

The Federal Aviation Agency's rules for takeoffs and landings of jet-powered transports include this sentence: "The takeoff distance shall not be greater than the length of the runway."

On a Chicago billboard: "Now you can borrow enough to get completely out of debt."

Unmarried?" asked the census taker.

"Oh, dear, no," replied the prim little lady, blushing. "I've never even been married."

There are persons who have a gift for what may be called the wolf sentence in sheep's clothing. It is not double talk, exactly. It sounds innocent enough until you begin to think it over to find out what it means. Then it is apt to drive you loony. Our favorite master of the wolf sentence is a lady in Hollywood. She's gotten off such mots as these:

"There are lots of nice people in Hollywood, but not many."

"Isn't he handsome — that other-looking fellow?"

"She had more money than she could afford."

Gertrude Stein once got off this wolf sentence: "She was the kind you liked better the more you saw her less."

A classic of its kind was this sign in an army mess hall in Britain during the war. Printed in big black letters across the exit, it read: "Kindly Let Those Who Are Going Out First." That sentence drove us crazy, and I thought it would never be topped. But it was, in a San Francisco bar. I was standing next to a guy who was being pestered to death by a frightful bore. At last he snapped: "Look, if you don't get out of here and leave me alone, I'll find somebody who can!"

Malapropriety

Our maid asked for an advance on her week's salary. "Our preacher is leaving the church this Sunday," she told us, "and the congregation wants to give him a little momentum."

When I offered my neighbor a lift into town, the combination of my old jalopy and the back roads gave us a real jouncing. At his destination he said, "I can't tell you how much I appreciate this. I hope someday I'll be able to recuperate."

Describing the school concert, a proud parent said: "The glee club sang several selections Acapulco."

She may be a good mother," said one woman to another, "but her housekeeping certainly is halfhazard."

Our young nephew, who lives on a ranch, was staying with us so that he could attend school in Denver. As he dressed for his first dance, I asked him if he was taking a date. "No," he said. "I'm just going stud."

Just before the 1956 convention, the Democratic platform committee held public hearings to give interested groups and individuals an opportunity to present their views. A man who had expressed great concern about the magnitude of federal spending got confused under the questioning of a committee member. Finally he shouted in desperation, "Senator, if we don't stop shearing the wool off the goose that lays the golden egg, we are going to pump the well dry!"

Alice Roosevelt Longworth tells about a merchant seaman who was being investigated under the McCarran Act. "Do you," asked the interrogator, "have any pornographic literature?"
"Pornographic literature!" the sailor burst out indignantly. "I don't even have a pornograph!"

A clerk in a store announced to another clerk: "I treat all my customers alike. I don't use discretion with anyone."

At a ceremony in the Princeton University chapel, an old lady buttonholed an usher and commanded, "Be sure you get me a seat up front, young man. I understand they've always had trouble with the agnostics in this chapel!"

Telling of a member expelled from her club, a woman said: "They dismembered her."

After a bad fall, a man reported: "I thought I had broken a shoulder but I found I had only pulled a liniment."

At a Washington dinner party someone teased Senator Margaret Chase Smith about her chances for a presidential nomination: "Tell us, Margaret, what would your platform be?"

Without thinking, she blurted: "I'm for two mails a day."

To the other guests—only half-hearing what had gone before—that sounded like an off-color remark. "Margaret!" gasped one woman.

The lady senator hastily corrected: "I meant to say I would favor two deliveries a day"—and everyone howled.

At the peak of the Saturday-afternoon traffic in a New York town, when parking places were nonexistent, a distraught-looking matron hurried into a shop. Pushing past several customers, she said excitedly, as she waved toward the street, "Can you wait on me, please! I'm double-breasted!"

A young woman telephoned my brokerage office and placed an order for a few shares of stock—the first she had ever bought. The next day she called again, and after asking me to buy five additional shares for her, she said excitedly, "Oh, boy! I'm becoming a regular raccoon!"

A plump, good-natured shipmate of mine on the U.S.S. *Maryland* was teaching himself to play the saxophone. One evening he played a number of current tunes well enough for me to recognize them. "My goodness," I said, "you're getting quite a repertoire."

His pudgy face fell. "I guess you're right sir," he replied. "I've been sitting around on it too much lately."

The minister was delivering a rousing sermon on the evils of gossip. "If there is anything I hate," he said vehemently, "it is a tongue-bearing, tale-wagging woman!"

———————— • ————————

At a dog show in Los Angeles, a spectator asked an attendant to direct him to the Labradors. "All the way down the aisle," said the attendant, "and the first door to the right."

Although my mother is a strict teetotaler, she is fond of a relative who is somewhat of a tippler. Mother telephoned her one morning and was told by the maid that her mistress probably would not be up before noon. Hanging up the receiver, Mother turned to me and remarked, "I guess Helen must be in bed with a leftover."

Hammered Grammar

WHICHCRAFT
JAMES THURBER

THE relative pronoun "which" can cause more trouble than any other word. Foolhardy persons sometimes get lost in which-clauses and are never heard of again. My distinguished contemporary, H. W. Fowler, in his *Dictionary of Modern English Usage,* cites a tragic case of an adventurer who became involved in a remarkable which-mire. Fowler has followed his devious course as far as he safely could on foot: "Surely what applies to games should also apply to racing, the leaders of which being the very people from whom an example might well be looked for. . . ." Not even Henry James could have successfully emerged from a sentence with "which," "whom," and "being" in it. The safest way to avoid such things is to follow Ernest Hemingway. In his youth he barely escaped with his mind when trapped in the following which-clause: "It was the one thing of which, being very much afraid—for whom has not been warned to fear such things— he. . . ." Being young and powerfully built, Hemingway was able to fight his way back and begin again. This time he skirted the morass this way: "He was afraid of one thing. This was the one thing. He had been warned to fear such things." Today many happy writers are following in the trail Hemingway blazed.

75

Trying to cross a paragraph by leaping from "which" to "which" is like Eliza crossing the ice. The danger is missing a "which" and falling in. A case in point is: "He went up to a pew which was in the gallery, which brought him under a colored window which he loved and always quieted his spirit." The writer, worn out, missed the last "which"—the one that should have come before "always." But supposing he had got it in! We would have: "He went up to a pew which was in the gallery, which brought him under a colored window which he loved and which always quieted his spirit." Your inveterate whicher in this way gives the effect of tweeting like a bird or walking with a crutch, and is not welcome in the best company.

It is well to remember that "whiches" multiply like rabbits. Take a sentence like: "It imposes a problem which we either solve, or perish." The writer of a monstrosity like that tries to reconstruct the sentence, and gets: "It imposes a problem which we either solve, or which, failing to solve, we must perish on account of." He gets a drink, sharpens his pencil, and grimly tries again: "It imposes a problem which we either solve, or which we do not solve, and from which. . . ." The more times he does it, the more "whiches" he gets. The way out is simple: "We must either solve this problem, or perish." Never monkey with "which."

———— • ————

While examining an inductee, an Army medic noticed a scar on the boy's scalp and asked about it. "I got it from being drugged," said the inductee. The doctor, failing to see the connection, asked him to elaborate. "Well," the inductee said, "I was working on a ranch. My horse bolted, my foot got caught in the stirrup and I was drugged."

———— • ————

Newsweek quotes the Savannah, Georgia, *Morning News* in the throes of grammar trouble: "The investigators theorized that the two must have lain down on the two must have laid down on the two must have layed down on the tracks and fell asleep."

We just heard about a little boy who said to his teacher, "I ain't got no pencil."

She corrected him at once: "It's 'I don't have a pencil.' 'You don't have a pencil.' 'We don't have any pencils.' 'They don't have any pencils.' Is that clear?"

"No," said the bewildered child. "What happened to all them pencils?"

Winston Churchill had submitted a draft of an important wartime speech to the British Foreign Office for comment. The draft was returned with no comment whatever on content; but where he had ended a sentence with a preposition a Foreign Office purist had careted the preposition into its stiffly grammatical position.

At this, the Prime Minister flew into a lather. To the offending purist he dispatched a note. "This is the type of arrant pedantry," read the note, "up with which I will not put!"

If lawyers are disbarred and ministers unfrocked, perhaps electricians get delighted . . . Far Eastern diplomats disoriented . . . cashiers distilled . . . alpine climbers dismounted . . . piano tuners unstrung . . . orchestra leaders disbanded . . . artists' models deposed . . . cooks deranged . . . nudists redressed . . . office clerks defiled . . . mediums dispirited . . . dressmakers unbiased.

In Grosse Pointe, Michigan, a teacher appealed to parents through an ad in the *News:* "If you are not satisfied with your child's progress in school, why not have he or she tutored by an experienced teacher recommended by the Detroit Board of Education?"

London's *New Statesman and Nation* conducts weekly "competitions" in epigrams, limericks, etc. Recently readers were asked to play a game originated by Philosopher Bertrand Russell. On BBC's *Brains Trust* program he had humorously conjugated an "irregular verb" as "I am firm; you are obstinate; he is a pig-headed fool."

Among the winners picked by the *New Statesman* were the following:

I am sparkling; you are unusually talkative; he is drunk.

I am righteously indignant; you are annoyed; he is making a fuss about nothing.

I am beautiful; you have quite good features; she isn't bad-looking, if you like that type.

I have reconsidered it; you have changed your mind; he has gone back on his word.

I am an epicure; you are a gourmand; he has both feet in the trough.

I am fastidious; you are fussy; he is an old woman.

I have about me something of the subtle, haunting, mysterious fragrance of the Orient; you rather overdo it, dear; she stinks.

The plural of "whim" is "women."

In Other Words . . .

ENGLISH INTO ENGLISH
ROBERT PAUL SMITH

IN HIS book *Translations from the English,* Robert Paul Smith bridges the gap between the spoken word and its unspoken meaning. Here are a few handy translations:

Translation from the Repairman

"First thing in the morning."

By the end of next week.

"Soon as I get a man free."

End of the month.

"Next week."

Next month. For house painters (outside), within six months; house painters (inside), as soon as it's cold enough so that all the windows have to be closed.

"It's a characteristic of that particular year."

That always was a bad model.

"If it was mine . . ."

If it was his, he wouldn't have it. He'd sell it to you.

"Trust me. If it's not what you want when I'm done, you don't owe me a dime."

When it's done, you don't owe him a dime. You owe him $340 for labor and $37.50 for materials.

Translation from the Teacher

"Oh, I wouldn't worry about that. At this stage, it's the social adjustment that counts."

The child cannot read, write or count beyond nine, but has stopped throwing modeling clay into the sand box.

"He has a considerable grasp of spatial values."

He can get a glob of finger paint *all over* a sheet of paper. And, without half trying, he can spatially extend it over his body, his T-shirt, his shoes, dungarees and, unless restrained, you.

"It's been a real pleasure having him in the class this year. He's developed so."

It's the end of the term, the teacher is getting married and quitting—why hold grudges?

Translation from the Saleslady

"All the newest models cling that way."

You wear size 14 but all they have is a 12.

"The most amusing hat."

Over $40.

"But, Madam, it helps give you height."

You're dumpy and the hat has a feather sticking up.

"But Madam has the height for it."

You're six feet two and the hat is flat.

"Well, perhaps just a tiny tuck here and let it out just the least bit here and possibly . . ."

The alterations will cost more than the dress.

Translation from the Wife

"It isn't what you said, it's the way you said it."

You said she didn't darn your socks, and she didn't, but she has no reason handy at the moment.

"Me? Angry?"

She. Angry.

———————— • ————————

I've always had an admiration for people who can say minor things in a major way. One of my acquaintances once told me that his "balance sheet shows a reshuffling of proprietary interests," which impressed me considerably. I subsequently found out what he meant was that his car had been repossessed, but my admiration dimmed not a whit. He was the kind of a guy who would give someone four quarters for a buck and describe it as "taking part in a currency-exchange program." I like that. It has class. Furthermore, I think I am catching on. I recently sold a busted Japanese camera and described it as "disposing of a segment of my foreign holdings."

I'm a plain, blunt man, Mr. Williams," says my friend with unnatural heartiness; and he means by that that he is a cunning, subtle, diplomatic sort of fellow who is about to tell some lies. Whenever anyone, either avoiding your gaze or uneasily challenging it, says aloud the pronoun "I" followed by a claim to some definite virtue, you may safely expect a lie, or a lecture, or both:

"I'm only thinking of you, dear" means *I am now about to get a bit of my own back.*

"I don't want to make you unhappy" means *I will now repeat to you certain malicious gossip which will reduce you to sleepless misery.*

"I'm bound to admit" means *I will now confuse the main issue.*

"I'm not one to criticize" means *I shall now proceed to find fault with all you have done.*

"I'm as broad-minded as anyone" means *All my ideas on this subject are hopelessly out of date.*

"I hope I know my place" means *I am about to step right out of it and tell you a few home truths.*

"I'm a tolerant sort of fellow" means *I can't endure you another moment and am now preparing to throw you out of the house.*

Once again child psychiatrists are favoring as a form of treatment "practical negative reinforcement." That's the scientific term for spanking.

Fred M. Hechinger, education editor of the New York *Times,* criticized jargon in the field of education. He said that if an educational publishing house had printed Budd Schulberg's famous book *What Makes Sammy Run?* they would have called it *Motivational Research of Sammy's Potential.*

Woman, in kitchen preparing supper, to visitor: "It's a clever new way of getting rid of leftovers. You make it exactly like hash, but you call it recycled roast."

Communications Gaps

THE MOST
NERVE-SHATTERING WORD
IN THE LANGUAGE

H. ALLEN SMITH

L ULLABY." "Golden." "Damask." "Moonlight." Do these words seem esthetically attractive to you? They have appeared with some regularity on lists of "the ten most beautiful words in our language." Along with "luminous," and "hush," "anemone," "mother" and various others. These lists appear from time to time in the public prints. But I can't recall ever seeing a list of the ten ugliest words in the language.

Almost every literate person has in his head an agglomeration of words that can cause him to wince, and even shudder, such as "agglomeration." I lay claim to several hundred of the uglies. "Mulcted" almost nauseates me. I cringe in the face of "albeit," and/or, "yclept," "obsequies," "whilom," and "tinsmith." Want to hear a *real* ugly word? "Ugly."

But my own nomination for the meanest and low-downest and ugliest word of all is "Oh." Said twice, with maybe a hyphen, this way: "Oh-oh." In its maximal ugliness, it is customarily spoken softly with inflections that would curl the toes of a sandy-land mule.

Something is wrong, let us say, with the engine of your car. You take it to the garage. The mechanic lifts the hood and pokes around a bit and then you hear him murmur, "Oh-oh." The wretched creature says it in such a quietly dramatic manner that you know instantly that your whole motor has to be derricked out and thrown away and a new one put in.

Consider our friends, the dentists. Most of them have enough gumption (beautiful word!) to conceal their opinions and judgments, but sometimes you'll run across one who forgets his chairside manner. He'll be inspecting a big molar in the back, and suddenly he'll say, "Oh-oh." Or he'll come out of his darkroom carrying an X ray taken a few minutes earlier, and he'll put it up against the light, and he'll look at it briefly, and then his head will give a jerk and he'll say, "Oh-oh." You know at once, without ESP, precisely what is meant. Out. All of them. From now on, plates. No apples. No corn on the cob. No a lot of things.

Physicians as a general thing have schooled themselves carefully to conceal any sinister condition they may find during an examination. Yet I have run across one offender in my checkered medical career. He was giving me the annual checkup. He took my blood pressure and tapped me for knee jerks and scratched me on the bottoms of my feet for God knows what and stethoscoped me front and back and had me blow into a machine to test my "vital capacity" and then he turned the electrocardiograph loose on me. As he studied the saw-toothed dossier on my heart, his brow crinkled and I heard him say, quite softly, "Oh-oh." Everything inside of me suddenly bunched together in one large knot.

"What is it?" I demanded. "Whad you find there?"

"It's nothing, really," he said.

Nothing! Cancer of the heart is *nothing?* It had to be at least that.

"I heard you say 'Oh-oh,'" I told him. "Come on. Tell me. I'm a man. I can take it. Let me have it straight."

"Okay," he said, and I steeled myself and began to turn chicken. "I said 'Oh-oh' because," he went on, "I just happened to think that I haven't made out my tax return yet, and the deadline is tomorrow."

I quit him the next day. I can't use a doctor who is mooning over his income-tax return while he is looking at the record of my frightful heart disorders. I don't want a doctor *ever* to say "Oh-oh" in my presence, unless perhaps he has dropped his sphygmomanometer on the floor and busted it. Even in that contingency I think he should employ a more masculine expression. I would.

"Oh-oh" is the most frightening, nerve-shattering locution to come into general usage since Noah Webster's day. It should surely be forbidden by federal statute.

———— • ————

A subscriber who called the Cleveland *Plain Dealer* to ask the capital of Alaska was told, "Juneau."

"If I knew," she retorted, "I wouldn't be asking you!"

In the midst of a busy morning, the county agricultural agent got a call from a woman who said she was starting a chicken farm and wanted to know how long she should leave the rooster with the hens.

"Just a minute," said the agent, who was busy talking on another phone.

"Thank you very much," said the woman, and hung up.

An English university professor was waiting in the bitter cold for a train to London when the non-stop Cornish express astonishingly stopped at the station. The professor promptly got on board. He had one foot in the carriage when a railway official called out: "You can't get on here, sir. The train does not stop."

"That's all right," said the professor. "If it doesn't stop, then I'm not on it."

A Midwestern university held entrance exams for a group of ex-GIs. One of the questions was, "Name two ancient sports."

An ex-sergeant racked his brain and finally came up with an answer that passed him. He wrote, "Anthony and Cleopatra."

In a delivery of books from a department store, I was charged for one I did not receive. I telephoned the store and was promised that my account would be credited with the amount of the missing book. But the next day a delivery-man came to pick up the book. Again I called the store. I explained in detail that I had been charged for a book I did not receive and that now a driver had come to pick up the book.

"Did you give it to him?" asked the clerk.

———— • ————

My friend called a Venetian-blind repairman to come pick up a faulty blind. The next morning, while the family was at breakfast, the doorbell rang. My friend's wife went to the door, and the man outside said, "I'm here for the Venetian blind." Excusing herself in a preoccupied way, the wife went to the kitchen, fished a dollar from the food money, pressed it into the repairman's hand, then gently closed the door and returned to the table. "Somebody collecting," she explained, pouring the coffee.

An insurance agent made an appointment with a woman to go to her home and talk policies. "You may find me in a dilemma," she warned him.

"Oh, that's all right," he assured her. "My last prospect was in a kimono."

QUESTIONS I NEVER FIGURED OUT ANY DECENT ANSWERS TO
ROBERT PAUL SMITH

Very Early

Kitchy koo? Ooz issums, issums?

What's your name?

Where's his nose [tongue, big toe]?

What do you think you're doing with the egg beater and the cat?

How can you lose a mitten [Teddy bear, handkerchief, pants]?

Early

What makes you think you're so smart?

Who told you you could pitch?

Would you rather have a million trillion dollars or be Tom Mix?

Whatever gave you the bright idea you could parachute off the garage roof with an umbrella?

You call those hands clean?
How can you lose a glove [library book, pencil, sweater]?

Later
What do you mean, you *can't* understand algebra [ancient history, geometry, quadratic equations]?
What gives you the idea that you're the only one who knows anything?
You call that cleaning your room?
How'd you like a punch in the nose?
Who told you you could play center?
How can you lose a bicycle [50-cent piece, pair of eyeglasses]?

Even Later
Where's the fire, Mac?
Whatever made you think I cared the first thing about you, just because I let you kiss me good-night?
Is any girl worth all that moping around—a boy your age?
Don't you think I was ever young myself, Son?
When will you learn that you can't go around saying whatever you think?
For this we sent you to college?
Would you rather be happy and dumb or miserable and smart?
Are you seriously trying to tell me that you *lost* your eyeglasses [sneakers, hat, wallet]?

Much Later
How can you speak that way to me?
How can you speak that way to your very own child?
Who ever told you you knew how to balance a checkbook [invest in stocks, make hotel reservations, speak to a headwaiter]?
Listen, Jack, when you gonna get wise to yourself?
Don't you have any opinions about anything?
Don't you care?
Do you think I'm putting on weight?
Do you really, but really, like this hat? You're sure it isn't silly?
Gee, Dad, weren't *you* ever young?

Right Now
Neighbor, have you given any thought to the future?
Waddia know good?
Waddia know for sure?
Will you never learn?

Typographical Terrors:
THE PRINTED WORD

W HEN Gutenberg developed movable type, the last thing he suspected was that it would prove to be the cradle of humor. Take newsbreaks—you'll find a good selection under "Slips That Pass," on page 100. Newsbreaks put the lie to the notion that there are no new jokes. These couldn't have existed until the printing press came along. Just as, I suppose, the humor that springs from misspelling (see "Spellbound," page 96) could not arise until spelling had been standardized. Bernard Shaw, arguing for simplified spelling, once made neat use of the old "fish" wheeze. "Fish" should, of course, be spelled G-H-O-T-I: "gh" as in "tough," "o" as in "women," "ti" as in "emotion." The hilarious story about Nunnally Johnson (page 95) reminded me (I learned this from Martin Gardner's fine edition of Bombaugh's *Oddities and Curiosities of Words and Literature*) that the British army once boasted a major named Teyoninhokarawen.

Sign Language

On a British Columbia automobile association vehicle: "Call us at any hour. We're always on our tows."

On electric-company truck: "Let us remove your shorts."

A sign on a construction project at a hospital in Richmond, Virginia, says: "All men on the job must wear safety hats." Under this, someone has carefully added: "Regardless of their political opinions."

Near the busy terminal of a trucking firm in Paterson, New Jersey, a large billboard proclaimed: "This Is a Trucking Company That Never Sleeps." Crayoned neatly beneath was: "And neither do its neighbors!"

A piece of graffiti on the wall of a New York office building says: "Legalize Mental Telepathy." Under it, someone has added: "I knew you were going to say that."

A Fire Island, New York, beach house named "Psychottage" has a small roadway behind it called "Psycho-Path."

A Chicago beauty salon calls itself "Curl Harbor."

A sign at the entrance of the women's clothing section of a Detroit department store reads: "Ladies Ready to Wear Clothes." Underneath in bold masculine handwriting, someone has added: "It's about time!"

The owner of a meat market rigged up a device. Instead of the digits showing the amount of the sale on his cash register, this sign pops up: "Tell It to Your Congressman!"

Ecological bumper sticker: "Support Your Local Planet!"

On the wall of a building near his residence, director Mike Nichols noticed a chalk inscription one morning that read: "I LOVE GRILS." The next morning a line had been drawn through this and a new line printed below: "I LOVE GIRLS." The third day that line had been crossed out, too, and a third line substituted—in letters twice as large. It read: "WHAT ABOUT US GRILS?"

Large sign at the entrance to the Million Dollar Museum in White's City, New Mexico: "We do not have the gun that killed Billy the Kid. Two other museums have it."

Sign posted at a power station in Ligonier, Pennsylvania: "Nine Out of Ten Turkeys Prefer Electric Roasting."

In obstetrician's office: "Pay-as-you-grow."

A sign in front of a shoe repair shop pictured several styles of rubber heels and a beautiful girl who was saying, "I'm in love with America's Number 1 heel." Underneath in small feminine handwriting, someone had added, "Too bad, sister! I married him."

Posted on the front of a bookstore in Minneapolis: "I open Monday through Saturday at about 11:00 or noon, but occasionally as early as 9:00 or 10:00. But some days as late as 1:00. I close about 5:30 or 6:00. Occasionally on Saturday, I close at 4:30 or 5:00, especially when the world seems dreary."

A table labled "Desirable Weights for Women" was posted on the bulletin board of a Washington, D.C., hospital, provoking groans from the well-nourished secretaries on the staff. But scowls changed to grins a few days later when a new list was posted next to the old one. Adding 10 to 15 pounds in each height category, it was labeled: "Weights for Desirable Women."

Soon after a London baker hung up a sign outside his shop advertising "Vienna Rolls," someone added, "London Swings."

Above the washbasin in my husband's office, the boss had put a large "Think!" sign. Directly below, someone hung a small hand-lettered sign saying: "Thoap!"

Toward the end of the deer season last year, a "Deer Crossing" sign on a California highway had another sign fastened to it, evidently by a disappointed hunter. It read: "Promises! Promises!"

Note on a Greenwich Village bulletin board: "Dear John, Come home, forgive and forget. I have destroyed that cherry-pie recipe. Helen."

Bona-fide double billings on movie marquees:
In Edinburgh: THE GENTLE SERGEANT – THE UNKNOWN MAN.
In Fayetteville, Tennessee: I AM A CAMERA – OVEREXPOSED.
In Houston: LADY GODIVA – RUN FOR COVER.
In Detroit: LOAN SHARK – EVERYTHING I HAVE IS YOURS.
In Fort Worth: AN AMERICAN IN PARIS – THE BIG HANGOVER.
In Los Angeles: TRAPEZE – EMERGENCY HOSPITAL.
In Hollywood: THE SEVENTH VEIL – GREAT EXPECTATIONS.
In Los Angeles: GO FOR BROKE – LAS VEGAS STORY.
In Toronto: HOLIDAY AFFAIR – LET' S MAKE IT LEGAL.

Written on a rock in southern West Virginia is a highway sign which reads: "You Must Pay for Your Sins." Underneath in smaller but still legible print, someone has added: "If you have already paid, please disregard this notice."

Inscription for a Fly Swatter: "The hand is quicker than the eye is, But somewhat slower than the fly is."

Posted in an office of a U.S. air base: "Do Not Undertake Vast Projects with Half Vast Ideas."

What's in a Name?

In San Francisco, attorney Bert Hirschberg asked Nick Versus, "Are you married?"
Nick: "No. Why?"
Bert: "Well, if you were and you wanted to dissolve the marriage, I'd handle the case free just for the thrill of filing Versus vs. Versus."

After several unsuccessful attempts to get our electric bill corrected, my husband wrote a detailed complaint, closing his letter with these words: "I suggest you remedy this situation at once, because I am, Thoroughly, T. Dolph."

My friend R. B. Jones doesn't have a first or middle name — only the initials R. B. This unusual arrangement was never a problem until he went to work for a government agency. The government is not accustomed to initialed employes; so R. B. had a lot of explaining to do. On the official forms for the payroll and personnel departments, his name was carefully entered as R (Only) B (Only) Jones. Sure enough, when R. B. got his pay check, it was made out to Ronly Bonly Jones.

Inmates of the Iowa State Penitentiary refer to it as "The Walled-Off Astoria."

A group of women searching for a name for a new club decided on "The Vicious Circle."

Writer Thyra Samter Winslow named her tiny house in Manhattan "Writer's Cramp," Ann Sothern called her Beverly Hills place "Sothern Exposure," and Bill Boyd called his house in the hills high above Malibu "The Boyd's Nest."

Sign on a house trailer: "Reluctant Draggin."

Nunnally Johnson, Hollywood screenwriter-producer, is fascinated with unusual names. Some time ago when someone referred to an actress named Giselle Werbischek Pfiffle, he insisted on looking up her name in the telephone book and calling her himself. The ensuing dialogue went like this:

"Is this Miss Giselle Werbischek Pfiffle?"

"Yes . . . ?"

"This is Nunnally Johnson."

"Who?"

"Nunnally Johnson. You don't remember me?"

"No, I don't believe I do."

"I'm sorry. I must have the wrong Giselle Werbischek Pfiffle."

A friend received a letter from a large oil company stating that his impeccable credit rating entitled him to a credit card by return mail. He bit. In answering the questions, he wrote across the top of the application, "Flattery works." The credit card arrived promptly. It was made out to:

> *Mr. Curry Joyce*
> *Flattery Works*
> *Euclid Ave.*
> *Chicago, Ill.*

William Fox Harkins weighs only 160 pounds, so he and his office staff were puzzled when a letter came addressed to him as William Fatty Harkins. Only when his secretary pored over the new telephone directory did the answer suddenly become obvious. Lawyer Harkins is listed, quite naturally, as "Harkins, Wm F atty."

Upon completing our mission at an air base near Samsun, Turkey, our crew made reservations with a local airline for the trip back to our base in West Germany. The reservation-request form had space for only three names of the four in our party, so we noted that there was another name on the reverse side. When the tickets arrived, we found one each for Lt. Joe Turner, Mr. Cummings, Mr. Kieper and a Mr. See Backside!

Spellbound

A European student, confused by English spelling, submitted this poem to his professor of literature:

The wind was rough
And cold and blough;
She kept her hands inside her mough.

It chilled her through,
Her nose turned blough,
And still the squall the faster flough.

And yet although
There was no snough,
The weather was a cruel fough.

It made her cough,
(Please do not scough);
She coughed until her hat blew ough.

The mail-order catalogue played an important part in my primary education. When I asked my dad what a shoe tree was, or an awl, or a casting rod, he would show me pictures in the catalogue. It was a spelling aid, too. "How do you spell 'genuine'?" I once asked him.

"Look it up in the catalogue," he replied.

"But how can I find it?"

"Turn to the saddles," he told me, his voice betraying his disappointment that his child was so dull. "See, it's right here. 'First Quality Saddles. Genuine Leather.'"

Three successive notices from the classified column of a small Connecticut weekly paper tell their own story:

March 22nd: "For sale. Slightly used farm wench in good condition. Very handy. Phone 366-R-2. A. Cartright."

March 29th: "Correction. Due to an unfortunate error, Mr. Cartright's ad last week was not clear. He has an excellent winch for sale. We trust this will put an end to jokesters who have called Mr. Cartright and greatly bothered his housekeeper, Mrs. Hargreaves, who loves with him."

April 5th: "Notice! My W-I-N-C-H is not for sale. I put a sledgehammer to it. Don't bother calling 366-R-2. I had the phone taken out. I am NOT carrying on with Mrs. Hargreaves. She merely L-I-V-E-S here. A. Cartright."

An American impresario, preparing a concert program, instructed his new secretary to expand all abbreviations—Op. into Opus, for example—before sending the program to the printer. Later, in the printer's proof, he found: "Bach: Massachusetts in B Minor."

George Ade was sitting with an eight-year-old friend one afternoon when she looked up from her Hans Christian Andersen and asked, "Does m-i-r-a-g-e spell marriage, Mr. Ade?"
"Yes, my child," he replied.

Joel Chandler Harris was in his office when one of his reporters called out, "Do you spell 'graphic' with one 'f' or two?"
"Well," Harris answered, "if you're going to use any at all, Bill, I guess you might as well go all the way."

A few years ago, the telephone company in a midwestern state, after publishing a directory with certain abbreviations, received this letter from a subscriber: "Gntmn: Yr abbr of our town of Commerce as Comre in ur br new tel drctry is unfr, unclr, unplsnt, unecsry."

Extract from a schoolgirl's letter home: "We all have to have a dictionary here, so I have asked for one to be ordered for me. I hope you don't mind. Apparantly Miss Foster thinks they are essensual."

To encourage better spelling, somebody on the Chicago *Daily News* put up this notice on the bulletin board: "Let's set our sights high. Let's learn to spell JUDGMENT correctly. Let's repeat to ourselves each day, 'Today I will spell JUDG-MENT without an E.' Who shall be the first to announce this accomplishment? Praise be unto him. Deranged."

Right next to this a reporter pinned up: "Dear Deranged, I tried to spell judgment without an 'e' and it came out judgmnt. Now I'm in a predicamnt. Confusd."

Crossed Wires

An Atlanta man, who found there was no reservation for him at the Cloister Hotel in Sea Island, was telephoning Western Union to advise his wife of the change in plans. The taking of name and address was handled by the operator in the best impersonal—almost mechanical—tradition. But when he gave the message: "No soap at Cloister. Staying at King and Prince," there was a long pause. Then, throwing aside all company policy, the horrified operated blurted out, "Oh, sir, I'm sure if you'd asked the Cloister they would have given you some soap!"

A telegram given over the phone to a Western Union operator was to go to Mary Anne Wolfe. It arrived addressed to: "Mary Ann Withany and Wolf Withany."

A member of the National Board of the YWCA, traveling in the West and finding some of her plans suddenly altered, decided to return at once to her home in Chicago. Accordingly she left the train at Reno and sent from there a telegram to her husband: "HAVE SUDDENLY CHANGED PLANS. RETURNING HOME AT ONCE. LOVE." She handed this to the young woman operator who read it thoughtfully and then said, "I hope you won't mind my saying it, madam, but it does do me a lot of good to send a message like this *once in a while.*"

When the Lunt-Fontanne comedy *O Mistress Mine* was playing on Broadway, a man in Washington, D.C., wired a New York friend to get him a pair of tickets for the following Saturday night. This the friend was able to do, and he promptly wired: "MISTRESS OKAY FOR SATURDAY."

The Washington man read the wire and chuckled. Penciled below the message were the words: "Western Union prefers not to transmit this type of message."

When I had to make an unexpected trip to a city with which I was unfamiliar, I selected a hotel at random from a hotel guide and asked my secretary to wire for a room to be held for me. The title "The Reverend," which she used in the message, must have given the receiving operator some concern. For this telegram came back to me: "DO NOT FEEL HOTEL BLANK DESIRABLE FOR YOU HAVE RESERVED ROOM HOTEL WHITE (SIGNED) WESTERN UNION."

On my birthday I received a telegram relayed over the telephone by a Western Union operator with the happiest voice imaginable. It did indeed brighten my day. A week later, I received a telegram from my father bawling me out for not writing home. I was sure the same woman was reading the wire, but the voice was harsh and cold.

Afterward I said, "What's the matter with your voice?"

"Nothing," she replied in normal tones. "I always try to convey not only the words of the message, but also the intent."

A director on location couldn't understand why his wife blew her top when she received the following wire from him: "HAVING WONDERFUL TIME, WISH YOU WERE HER."

When his son was born humorist Bugs Baer sent this telegram to his wife: "I HEAR YOU HAD A BOY IN YOUR ROOM LAST NIGHT."

Slips That Pass

Ad in the Batavia, New York, *Daily News:* "Odd jobs wanted by handy man, trimming hedges, shrubs and others."

From a church bulletin: "Ushers will swat late-comers at these points in the service."

Sign on New York City employment-office door: "Good girl wanted bad."

A notice in the Bridgeton, New Jersey, *Evening News:* "Elder Valese, pastor of the Soul Stirring Church, Brooklyn, will speak here at eight o'clock. She will bring a quart with her and they will sing appropriate selections during the service."

In an Ohio paper: "The operator of the other car, charged with drunken driving, crashed into Miss Miller's rear end which was sticking out into the road."

From the social column of the Asheville, North Carolina, *Citizen:* "A musical program was presented during the afternoon. Mrs. Melvin Tilson, accompanied by Mrs. C. Fred Brown, sank two numbers."

Notice in the Prescott, Arizona, *Courier:* "To whom it may concern: C. H. Elliot doing business as Pat's Mobile Home Movers and Mobile Home Service, is no longer connected, in any way what so ever."

Church note in *The New Forest Magazine,* England: "In future the preacher for next Sunday will be found hanging on the notice board."

The wrapper on prepacked puff pastry on sale in England advises: "Enough in the packet for four persons or 12 little tarts."

From a *Business Week* article on the marriage rate and its effect on retail sales: "It should be at least a year or two before the bulge appears in the marriage figures."

Heading on column of figures published by Census Bureau: "Population of U.S. Broken Down by Age and Sex."

From the Personals in the Tacoma *News-Tribune:* "Due to illness of the owner, Milton's Barbershop will be operated by a competent barber until owner's return."

A lawyer's secretary, billing a client with whom her boss had had many long conferences, issued this statement: "Bull rendered—$50."

Ad submitted to travel guide: "Cocktail lounge. Continental cuisine. Mid-Evil atmosphere."

Classified ad in the Harrisburg, Pennsylvania, *Patriot:* "51 acres of timberland, traversed by mountain streams, with the stone ruins of an old mill. An ideal retreat for the mature lover."

From the Tulsa, Oklahoma, *World:* "It is permissible to spank a child if one has a definite end in view."

In the Monterey, California, *Peninsula Herald:* "The area in which Miss Garson was injured is spectacularly scenic."

A Chicago restaurant menu offered: "Today's Special—Dreaded Veal Cutlets."

The Tonopah, Nevada, *Times-Bonanza* reports: "The writer and his bitter half were overnight guests of Mr. and Mrs. Vern Smith."

From the Allentown, Pennsylvania, *Lentz Post News:* "Mrs. Jones, a strained elocutionist, will give readings."

The following correction appeared in a small-town paper: "Our paper carried the notice last week that Mr. John Jones is a defective in the police force. This was a typographical error. Mr. Jones is really a detective in the police farce."

Ad from Fremont, Nebraska, *Tribune:* "For Sale—Young dressed hens. Absolutely clean and ready for the rooster."

In Colorado Springs *Gazette Telegraph:* "The incumbent mayor exhumed confidence before the polls closed."

From the San Diego *Tribune:* "A party of young people followed the bride and groom to San Diego, hoping to surprise them in the hotel lobby. When they arrived the newlyweds had already gone up to their doom."

In an English paper: "A committee of ladies, with Mrs. Roberts as leader, threw themselves into the tea, which proved a masterpiece."

From a bulletin of the Tuscon Art Center: "Figure Class I. A studio course working directly from the human figure. Anyone wishing to take advantage of the model without instruction may do so."

From the Pittsfield, Massachusetts, *Berkshire Eagle:* "The accident occurred shortly after 1 p.m. Pickett took his eyes from the road momentarily to look at a trick going in the opposite direction."

From the Andrews County, Texas, *News:* "Refreshments of cake squares, iced in pink and glue, were served."

An ad in the Hartford, Connecticut, *Times:* "LOVALON BRA is the bra for you. For mother, daughter and sister, too, its so lovely and so mashable."

From a report of a council meeting in Ottawa, Illinois, *Republican-Times:* "Moved by Commissioner Doherty that the report of E. T. Burke, Fire Chief, be approved and placed on fire."

From the Lynchburg, Virginia, *Daily Advance:* "'I's very happy,' said Olga, a medical student, in perfect English. . . ."

From the Yeovil, England, *Western Gazette:* "The first swallow has arrived at Devizes. It was spotted by Police Constable John Cooke, of Seend, whose hobby is birdwatching, sitting wet and bedraggled on telephone wires."

From the New Bethlehem, Pennsylvania, *Leader-Vindicator:* "Obviously a man of sound judgment and intelligence, Mr. Rau is not married."

Society note in the Denver, Colorado, *Rocky Mountain News:* "She looked like the belle of a court ball with the gown and her hair piled high on her head."

From a society note in the Salt Lake City *Deseret News:* "The young bride-elect is a has been residing at 250 Fifth East Street."

From a motorcycle handbook: "To Retime Engine—This operation should be entrusted to our service stations, as it requires special fools."

From Newark, Delaware, *Weekly:* "He is a graduate student in the Episcopal seminary at Cambridge, which is afflicted with Harvard University."

Want ad in *The Wall Street Journal:* "Executive secretary, now employed, desires more active or pressure position with man of affairs."

From *True Romance:* "I stared soberly into my mirror that night as I combed my lone straight hair. I knew I was not very pretty."

Help-wanted ad in Washington *Post:* "Widower with school-age children requires person to assume general housekeeping duties. Must be capable of contributing to growth of family."

From the Jacksonville, Florida, *Times-Union:* "The sewer-expansion project is nearing completion, but city officials are holding their breath until it is officially finished."

Ad-Libs

Ad in *Billboard:* "Lion tamer wants tamer lion."

From the Hastings & St. Leonards, England, *Observer:* "House to let. Furnished with period pieces from an unfortunate period."

Real-estate ad in program of The Barn Playhouse, New London, New Hampshire: "For Sale. Business site in large city. Busy intersection with traffic light out of order. Just the right spot for doctor or lawyer."

Headline of an ad in a New York bus: "FOR A SUCCESSFUL AFFAIR, IT'S THE EMPIRE HOTEL."

Our award for the most-mentally-jumbled-copywriter-of-the-year goes to the creator of this Philadelphia department-store copy: "For you alone! The bridal bed set. . . ."

The slogan "Send me a man who reads," which heads the International Paper Company ads, elicited this revised version from a high-school girl: "Send me a man. Who reads?"

Advertising men, in their search for new ideas, turn to many sources—even to the public. In a series of ads, Eagle Shirtmakers asked readers to aid in conjuring up new creative names that could be applied to the color of men's shirts. Among entries received were: gang green, unforeseeable fuchsia, Freudian gilt, navel orange, dorian gray, statutory grape, willie maize, unshrinkable violet and whizzer white.

A San Diego store attaches this label to every package of seeds: "Warning—after planting, step back quickly!"

A hotel in the Rocky Mountains advertised: "If you can't sleep here, it's your conscience."

Advertisement for Webster's carbon papers: "The greatest thing in carriages since babies."

One life-insurance company distributes match books with these words of caution: "Before you scratch, please close folder (especially if a policyholder)."

Ad in the Green Bay, Wisconsin, *Press-Gazette:* "'Twas the night before Christmas, and all through the house, not a creature was stirring, not even a mouse—Canadeo Exterminating Co."

From an ad for Bennett's, Inc., a Toledo, Ohio, furniture store: "This is a truly nice chair. It has everything in it that 20-odd generations of custom upholsterers have learned to build in. But it doesn't 'do' a thing. It doesn't recline, nothing pulls out. There are no buttons or levers, and you can't revolve it for television—or anything else—it just doesn't revolve. It's on legs.

"So far as the table is concerned, we're almost embarrassed. There are no leaves to lift up, nothing pulls out or up. It doesn't extend nor does it pop up. You can't, in fact, do one thing with it except put it under a lamp. It doesn't even have a drawer.

"The lamp is in the same league—all it does is light. Pull the chain on a couple of brass sockets and you've had it. No swivels, no reflectors, nothing on the ceiling, and no music.

"We submit all three as our contribution to sanity in a world of design that becomes more confusing by the hour—and in the firm conviction that somewhere in these parts there's a gent who would just like to sit down comfortably and read his paper."

From an ad for The Springs Cotton Mills in *Newsweek:* "Springmaid sheets are known as America's Favorite Playground."

From a West Roxbury, Massachusetts, monument firm's ad in the Boston *Globe:* "There's still time to get under the deadline."

Help-wanted ad in the Camden, Maine, *Herald:* "Man with flair for public relations needed to superintend Camden dump. Ability to visualize total job perspective beyond immediate appearance could be an asset. Chance to meet and work closely with all types of people. First choice on antiques, bric-a-brac and leftovers. Selection of all leading newspapers and periodicals for coffee breaks. Unequaled opportunity for bird-watching enthusiast specializing in gulls."

A classified advertisement in the *Brown Daily Herald* read: "Will the person who borrowed my metronome please return it? I rely on the rhythm method."

Ad in Ann Arbor, Michigan, *News:* "Four-poster bed 101 years old with springs. Perfect for antique lover!"

A San Francisco art dealer, who dreams of living weekends in a log cabin deep in the woods, placed a classified ad to that effect in the papers. His wife, who has other ideas, placed an ad to run directly beneath it, reading: "Disregard previous ad."

From the Lubbock, Texas, *Avalanche-Journal:* "Need a sympathetic companion? Basset puppies are all ears."

Help-wanted ad in *The Wall Street Journal:* "Mediocre accountant. Disreputable company has recently acquired obscure widget firm as a tax loss and wishes to continue its unprofitable operation by hiring an inept apathetic accountant. A disinterested attitude while working for this bewildered management is the key to securing this job. Position offers little and gives less with probable reduction in your current earnings."

Advertisement in the Three Rivers, Michigan, *Commercial:* "GE Automatic Blanket—Insure sound sleep with an Authorized GE Dealer."

Advertisement slogan for perfume-mist in plastic containers: "No bottles to break—just hearts.

A young ad executive was called down by his boss for overwriting some copy. His mentor's memo read simply: "I've told you 40,000 times—stop exaggerating!"

Ad for a snow blower: "Does your heart good to watch it work!"

Ad for drip-dry jersey dress: "Freedom from the Press."

The great advertising men don't all hang out on Madison Avenue. One of them must peddle space for the Scarborough, Ontario, *Mirror,* helping his clients concoct ads like these two, which are for entirely separate, if similar, enterprises:

"Jack, please come home," ran the first one. "I have rented reducing equipment from Stephenson's Rent-All."

"Jack, don't go home," warned the second ad. "She's also rented a floor sander, wallpaper steamer, paint sprayer, power saw and rug shampooer from Morningside Rent-Alls."

Announcement in the Pullman, Washington, *Herald:* "Wanted: State trooper applicants. Applicants must be six feet tall with a high-school education, or 5' 11" with two years of college."

Classified ad: "Man wanted to work in dynamite factory; must be willing to travel."

Help-wanted ad in the Kirkwood, Missouri, *Advertiser:* "Permanent part-time angel for pediatrician's office; receptionist, bookkeeper and diplomat; previous experience in boiler factory desirable."

Ad in the Salt Lake City *Tribune:* "Get a lot for a box top! Hillside, 2 level, with a stream. Just send cap from unopened fifth of Old Crow together with $2500."

In Good Form

A bus repairman was filling out a report on a highway accident. When he came to the question, "Disposition of passengers?" he wrote: "Mad as Hell."

A village character of my acquaintance was filling out an income-tax blank and came to the part marked "Do Not Write in This Space." Incensed at this limitation on his personal liberty, he penciled in the forbidden space: "I will write where I damn please."

A New York hotel whose clientele includes many salesmen and buyers keeps a record of the companies represented by the guests. A breezy woman buyer from the West, after putting her name and address on the registration card, seemed to be brought up short by the query: "Firm?" She nibbled the end of her pen for a moment, then wrote: "Not very!"

The business manager of a Philadelphia newspaper, checking office life-insurance applications, came across one in which an employe named his wife beneficiary and then filled out the space headed, "Relationship to you," with the word: "Nice."

When a customer closes an account at the Chemical Bank & Trust Co. in Houston, the president sends a letter of regret and asks the former customer to return an attached card listing possible reasons for closing the account. One card was returned by a young woman with this note: "I married Account Number 510-173."

After the woman across the street backed out of her driveway into the side of our car, my husband sat down in disgust to fill out the accident report. Where the form read "Condition of driver," he indignantly penciled: "Woman."

The personnel man received a questionnaire which asked, among other things: "How many people do you have, broken down by sex?

His answer: "Liquor is more of a problem with us.

In filling out a form for the records of the Brooklyn Dodgers, one outfielder, on the line asking "Length of residence in home town," wrote: "About 40 feet."

The employment clerk, checking over the applicant's papers, was amazed to note the figures 107 and 111 in the spaces reserved for "Age of Father, if living" and "Age of Mother, if living."

"Are your parents that old?" asked the surprised clerk.

"Nope," was the answer, "but they would be if living."

A laborer applying for a factory job struggled through an application form and came to the query: "Person to Notify in Case of Accident." He wrote: "Anybody in sight."

A young Texas grade-school teacher was filling out a health questionnaire for the coming term. Weary after a difficult first semester, she was ready for the query, "Have you ever had a nervous breakdown?"

In big letters she wrote: "NOT YET, BUT WATCH THIS SPACE FOR DEVELOPMENTS."

When a medical student, applying for a scholarship at his university, was asked why he needed assistance, he wrote: "My wife and I are now separated, and this has left me as my sole means of support."

One of the queries on the questionnaire sent by the summer-camp director was "Is your daughter a leader or a follower?" My husband described our energetic seven-year-old thus: "She is a leader without any followers."

A young man applying for a teaching position, in response to a query about marital status, wrote: "Eligible."

The application blank sent in by a woman trying for a teaching job in a Texas school system had a very flattering picture attached with this note: "I don't have a recent photograph of myself, but am enclosing one of my high-school daughter. We look very much alike."

A teacher, asked in a survey for three reasons for entering her profession, responded: "June, July and August."

A starlet filled in a studio publicity questionnaire concerning her pet aversions with: "I haven't any—I adore all pets."

The Victoria, B. C., *Times* instructs the carrier boy to interview people who quit the paper and send in the reason for their canceling. One boy submitted this message: "The news upsets Mrs. Smardon."

Insurance salesman to customer: "You've filled in this application all right except for one thing, Mr. Perkins— where it asks the relationship of Mrs. Perkins to yourself, you should have put down 'wife,' not 'strained.'"

A Topeka, Kansas, assessor recently ran across the best answer yet to the question on the tax assessment blank: "Nature of taxpayer." The answer: "Very mean."

In Northampton, Massachusetts, a Smith College freshman scrawled as her denominational preference: "I like to be called Betty."

———— • ————

The
Money Game:
BUSINESS AND FINANCE

S AMUEL JOHNSON, not usually given to mellow moods, once remarked, "There are few ways in which a man can be more innocently employed than in getting money." This innocent business (which Calvin Coolidge suggested was America's *only* real business) has nonetheless generated a type of humor notably cynical. Analyze the wry jokes that follow and what do you discover? That taxes are a vast governmental con game; that to beat the game you have to become a con artist yourself; that the stock market is a sucker trap; that all women are financial mental defectives; that ruinous inflation is as inevitable as day and night; that bankers, labor leaders, and salesmen are the ordained enemies of the human race; that businessmen have the natural charm of an anaconda (Kin Hubbard may have been thinking of businessmen when he said of bees: "A bee is never as busy as it seems; it's just that it can't buzz any slower"); and that it's all as funny as can be, isn't it? It's as if John Q. Citizen had nothing left but his sense of humor to save him from being battered to a financial pulp. This situation will persist until it is discovered by the Internal Revenue Service, at which time Congress will clamp a tax on jokes, with a depletion allowance for humor originating in Texas.

(The above remarks were written on April 15.)

Taxing Situations

An auditor in the Manhattan district office of the Internal Revenue Service received a return from a woman over 65 claiming seven children as dependents. The auditor noted that the previous year she had claimed only two children. The woman was duly summoned and asked to explain.

"The cat had kittens," she said. The auditor replied that kittens might cost money but they can't be claimed as dependents.

"Young man, you must be mistaken," she said. "I've been claiming the parents for years."

An income-tax consultant, uncertain as to whether a client's wife was entitled to double exemption for being 65 years old or over, wrote the husband asking for information. After some delay he received this answer: "My wife says she is not 65 and never will be."

Letter to Collector of Internal Revenue, Boston: "From the letterhead you can easily see that I am in prison. I'd like to know if the $800 which I stole has to be reported by me."

A woman appeared in a Minnesota tax office with a return on which there was a deduction of $500 for bad debts. When that item was questioned, she replied haughtily that they were her own bills she owed to people about town, and that she knew they were worthless because she had not paid any of them in the last two years and did not intend to pay any of them.

Matron to Internal Revenue agent: "If the Government isn't a dependent, what is it?"

Internal Revenue agent to taxpayer under fire: "Your return blew three tubes in the computer."

Woman in Internal Revenue office: "But surely you're not going to tax me on money I've *spent!*"

Over the incoming door at the Los Angeles tax bureau is a sign: "Watch Your Step." Over the outgoing door is: "Watch Your Language."

The Internal Revenue Service suggests double-checking of income-tax arithmetic. This will give you two answers, instead of the three you get by triple-checking.

An Internal Revenue Service man, asked if birth-control pills were deductible, replied, "Only if they don't work."

The only time the average child is as good as gold is on April 15.

Tax loopholes are like parking spaces—they all seem to have disappeared by the time you get there.

Puzzled by a term on my income-tax form, I telephoned the nearest Internal Revenue office for interpretation.

"Capital gains?" echoed the young woman who said she would help me. "Capital gains? If you don't know what they are, you don't have any."

Albert Einstein once admitted that figuring out his U.S. income tax was beyond him—he had to go to a tax consultant. "This is too difficult for a mathematician," said Einstein. "It takes a philosopher."

Matronly type to Internal Revenue inspector: "I wish you people were half as fussy about how *you* spend it as you are about how *I* spend it!"

Income-tax expert: Someone whose fee is the amount he saves you in making out your tax.

An anonymous New York taxpayer sent a letter to the State Comptroller's office in Albany saying that he had cheated on his income tax ten years ago and had not been able to get a good night's sleep since. He enclosed $25 and added: "If I still can't sleep, I will send the balance."

Clerks in the Indianapolis tax office were taken aback by a blank tax return which was accompanied by this note: "You were notified several times that I have been dead for four years. Please send no more of these blanks."

Doleful complaint in a letter received by the Atlanta Internal Revenue Service office: "From what I can understand that you want me to send to you I don't have it at all."

Boston police reported that a woman ran back into a burning house after dashing to safety. She returned shortly, however, unharmed—and clutching a carefully filled-out income-tax return.

One man to another: "I wanted my son to share in the business but the government beat him to it."

Internal Revenue agent to worried taxpayer: "Yes, Mr. Chilton, I'm afraid we *do* want to make a federal case out of it."

Wife reading completed income-tax form: "What's the idea—charging my beauty treatments off as a loss?"

Inflationary Tendencies

When government spends more than it gets, and when labor gets more than it gives, that empty feeling in your pocket is inflation.

Overheard: "I hope they don't raise the standard of living any higher. I can't afford it now."

One day at the office we were discussing the rugged effects of inflation. One man remarked that his wife had found a way to beat it. "She spends my salary during the first week of the month," he explained, "before its purchasing power diminishes."

Inflation marches on, making it possible for people in all walks of life to live in more expensive neighborhoods without even moving.

Announcement in *Sunset By-Lines,* publication of American Legion Post 165: "Because of the increased cost of printing and mailing, taxes and inflation, this publication comes to you twice as free as it used to."

National debt: Something that is always located just beyond comprehension.

Mass Observation, a British poll organization that feels the public pulse on timely topics, recently asked members of the middle class: "Given a one-tenth reduction in income, where would you make your cuts?"

Replied one dismal country parson, "Across my throat."

On the office wall of the New York *Daily News* controller: "There is no such thing as petty cash!"

One of the richest men in the world, oil tycoon Paul Getty, was being interviewed in London. "If you retired now," asked a reporter, "would you say your holdings would be worth a billion dollars?"

Getty paced up and down the room, mentally adding. "I suppose so," he said. "But remember, a billion doesn't go as far as it used to."

A banker went to the doctor for a checkup. Finally came the doctor's verdict, "You're as sound as a dollar!"

"As bad as that!" exclaimed the banker. And he fainted dead away!

Man, returning home from work, to wife: "The good news is I'm in the vanguard of the fight against inflation. The bad news is—I'm fired."

---•---

Farmer, paying lunch check, to a friend: "According to what they charged for that ham sandwich, I've got a hog that's worth $3060."

Clerk to tycoon boss: "I'd like a raise so I can have some savings that can be nibbled away by inflation, like everybody else."

Stock Exchanges

HOW I ALMOST MADE A KILLING IN THE STOCK MARKET
FRED SPARKS

I SHOULD HAVE known better. My family's financial history has been a succession of Black and Blue Days. We haven't missed a financial panic since Black Friday, 1869, when Jay Gould tried to corner the gold market and wiped out Great-Grandfather.

Our tradition has been "Buy High, Sell Low." Grandfather adhered religiously to it in the bubbles of 1893, 1900 and 1907. My father carried on nobly. In 1926 he bought, by mail, "beachside" lots, a week before the Blue Thursday when Florida's land boom collapsed. Undaunted, he saved industriously for the next three years and accumulated a nice pile—just in time to get in on Black Tuesday, 1929.

After that, at least once a week, Father gave a dinnertime lecture on the Fallacy of Gambling in Securities. It went this way: Don't buy on margin. Don't take tips. Buy only blue chips. Keep at least two thirds in cash and bonds. And don't let your investments interfere with your profession. He would end up by slamming the table with his fist and bellowing his battle cry: "Remember Black Tuesday!"

His advice stayed with me. When, in 1949, I began earning more than I spent, I put my savings in bank accounts and high-grade bonds. But because I lived abroad during the booming 1950s, my determination to avoid speculation was never really tested. I resided in places like Thailand and Iran, where, when you talk about "the Exchange," they assume you're referring to students.

The moment I returned to the United States in late 1960, however, I began hearing that "Jim made a fortune in the market," that "Jack cleaned up in oils and retired on his 40th birthday." My old friends' conversation was spiced with remarks about "growth stocks," "mergers," "splits." Even at literary gatherings the most discussed author was Dow-Jones. Without a single stock, I was, securities-wise, a "square." But slowly I caught the fever.

One night in mid-1961 a man whose judgment I have always respected said, "Fred, are you in United Necktie?"

"No, just a few bonds and a savings account," I replied.

"You keep money in the *bank?*" he said. "That's like locking a racehorse in a closet. Take it out and get into a rocketing stock like United Necktie."

"How do I know it will go up?"

"Man, oh, man! Have you lost faith in this country?"

The next day my friend, always helpful, took me to meet his broker. The moment I heard the exciting tap-tap of the ticker and saw the magic numbers being changed on the board, the ten generations of gambling blood within me began to boil. I told the broker I would withdraw $10,000 from the bank and buy 400 Necktie at 25.

"Outright?" asked the broker.

"Of course not!" my friend butted in. "On margin."

"Margin!" I gasped. "My father——"

"Your father," he interrupted, "lived in the horse-and-buggy days. For $10,000 at the current 70-percent margin you can buy 571 shares of United Necktie. Every time it goes up $1 you'll make $171 more than if you bought outright."

He had something there. Mentally, I unfastened my safety belt. I turned to the broker and commanded: "Margin!"

Three days later my friend cheered over the phone: "Necktie has hit 35. It's bound to break 100!"

Converting my bonds, I acquired another bundle of Necktie. Father's picture on the mantle seemed to be staring at me. I put it in a drawer.

I started carrying around a copy of *The Wall Street Journal* and dreaming of owning that Riviera villa. As the market rose I nightly doodled my paper profits. Suddenly I found it impossible to live within my usual budget. When Necktie hit 50 I was roughly $20,000 ahead—two years' hard work. Why scrimp? I ordered a custom-tailored suit, shifted from house gin to brand Scotch, had two teeth capped and presented my tipster-friend's wife with a fine brooch.

I had to borrow money to live on. For, while my expenses mounted, my income had been reduced by the interest formerly received from the bonds and the bank account. And I owed the broker margin interest.

By April 1962, Necktie, which had reached a high of 83, began slipping . . . 78 . . . 74 . . . 73 . . . 69. . . . Like everybody else, I asked an expert the reason. "A technical readjustment," he said.

The commonly held idea is it is *easy* to make money, or even to lose money, in the market. I soon found that this is an utter fallacy. Though I neglected my profession, I don't know when I have worked so hard. Daily I read three market letters. They confused me. One, trying to explain the slide in the market, said, "The first thing we've got to remember is that the '60s are not the '50s." Every time I turned on the TV to get latest developments there was a government official, grinning like a Halloween pumpkin, telling a reporter he was simply overjoyed with business prospects.

As Necktie went to 60 I covered scratch pads and tablecloths with: "60 × 1000 = 60,000 − 20,000 = 40,000 PROFIT!"

Not for long, Necktie went to *25!* I stayed up all night. Should I get out, even? Then I thought of the U.S. Marines, of John

Paul Jones. "I shall never surrender or retreat," I cried.

One noon I went into a restaurant and ordered shrimp, steak, ice cream, coffee. Then I walked over to a ticker kept there for the convenience of the customers. The market was down six points . . . then another five! I canceled the shrimp. Dow-Jones industrials down another half point, down another full point! I canceled the steak. Dow-Jones down *so far* $14! I canceled the ice cream and lunched on black coffee and an aspirin.

To meet margin calls I sold the blue chips that I had been holding onto.

For weeks I didn't know what was going on in the world. I'd turn quickly to the stock tables, ignoring page one. When I bought some shirts the clerk asked, "How will you pay, sir? Check or cash?" I replied, "Margin."

On the morning of May 28 (Blue Monday) I was driving to the country when I heard a radio report: "Extremely sharp break in the market."

I did a U-turn and sped downtown. My broker's board room was jammed. Those of us who owned cats and dogs talked to one another without introductions, the way people always do in times of stress. One woman, sold out for failing to put up more margin, made a remark widely used that day: "There's nothing wrong with the economy of this country," she said. "It's just that *I* haven't got any money left."

Necktie at 12! I asked my broker, "Should I sell?"

"Listen," he said, "you've still got a few points before another margin call. Don't panic! Don't be one of those who buy high and sell low."

But, as the afternoon wore on, the market galloped wilder than Paul Revere. I was caught in the tide with all the other sucker fish. I *did* panic. I told my broker, "Sell my Necktie at market!"

I went home, took a sleeping pill and slept for 14 hours. The next day, the evening paper read: "MARKET IN REMARKABLE RALLY." United Necktie was at 25 again.

The other night my nephew came to dinner. I told him about the dangers of speculation, repeated my father's five points and ended my lecture by bellowing, "REMEMBER BLUE MONDAY!"

An account executive of a Cincinnati stock-and-bond firm telephoned an elderly woman client who had purchased her first stock, ten shares of Proctor & Gamble, and excitedly told her that Proctor & Gamble just announced they were going to split.

"Oh! What a shame," replied the woman. "They've been together so long!"

George Olmsted, Jr., chairman of a Boston paper firm, comments on the stock market: "It would seem that if you want to be one of the glamour issues and have the price of your stock go through the roof, you need to be selling either a copier or a contraceptive. Reproduction or no reproduction—nothing in between."

The young woman had just married a stockbroker. When asked by a friend how they met, she replied, "Oh, we were introduced by a mutual fund."

A Minneapolis stockbroker's secretary was introduced to the president of one of the more successful local firms. "I'm so glad to meet you," she bubbled. "You went up today!"

Two Fort Worth stockbrokers: "Let's talk about something else besides business."

"Okay, let's talk about women."

"Good idea. Common or preferred?"

Financier's wife to guests: "Speak softly, Edward always says, but carry a big portfolio."

Will Rogers: Don't gamble. Take all your savings and buy some good stock and hold it till it goes up, then sell it. If it don't go up, don't buy it.

Don't Bank on It

DEAR BANK, I'M UNBALANCED

DERECK WILLIAMSON

ANOTHER defeat in my long and unsuccessful war with banks was recorded recently when I became involved in a "your number, our number" skirmish. Just before lunchtime, I realized that I had no money. I didn't have my personalized checkbook (available in 18 decorator colors) with me, so I phoned my wife and asked her to read the number on our checks.

She said the checks were covered with numbers, and asked me which one I wanted. I told her I didn't want the number at the upper right, which is the consecutive check number. Nor the improper fraction near the dateline, which tells the bank where it is located.

My wife said that left two long numbers at the bottom of the check: "In the beginning is a vertical line shorter than a one, but sort of thicker. Then there is a colon, but the dots are square. Then come zero, two, one, two; then two cute little square dots in a row; and then a skinny little line the same height as the dots. Then zero, three, four, nine; then one of those stunted ones again; and then another square colon.

"The second number is shorter: five, seven, question mark, space, two, zero, a deformed six, space, then five with two little lines, and a square colon but with the bottom dot missing this time."

My wife said she felt a headache coming on, so I thanked her, hung up, and plunged into a study of the two numbers I had written down. The bank probably would want the longer number. I decided to eliminate the little lines and square dots, evidently put there as light reading for the computer. That left 02120349.

I went to the bank and asked for a blank check, explaining that I had an account there and that I had left my purple plaid checkbook at home. The teller was dismayed. "Don't you have one of your checks with you?"

"No, but I have the number," I announced proudly. "It's 02120349!"

"That's *our* number," she snapped. "We must have *your* number."

I consulted my scrap of paper. "You mean 572065?"

"That sounds more like it," said the teller. She handed me a blank check, and I cashed it—after putting *my* number on it.

Deciding to make the best of a bad thing, I carefully memorized my own bank number. Thus it was with confidence that I marched into the bank the other day, wrote my number with a flourish on a deposit slip, and promptly lost the battle of the *yellow* deposit slip vs. the *white* deposit slip.

I have a "regular" checking account, which means that I must maintain a certain minimum balance or else I will be charged for cashing checks. (I am *always* charged for cashing checks.) In a "special" checking account, you are routinely charged for cashing checks. I don't know why I got a regular checking account, except that it sounded better. A special account could mean "special attention" from the bank, and I wanted to avoid that at all costs.

You must fill out a white deposit slip for a regular account, and a yellow slip for a special account. There weren't any white slips at the counter, so I made out a yellow slip. I crossed out the word "special" and wrote in "regular."

"No, no!" shouted the teller. "You want a white slip!"

I tried to explain that both slips were exactly the same except for the color, plus one word which I had changed. It was no use; nobody listens to a bank customer with a record of previous offenses, including not knowing his own number. She pushed through a white slip and instructed me to make it out properly.

I filled it out, passed it back and completed the transaction. As I crept out the door, I felt folded, spindled and mutilated.

———— • ————

After living for some weeks on an unofficial overdraft, my friend received the following letter from his bank: "Dear Sir, We would be most grateful if we could revert to the old system of *you* banking with *us.*"

———— • ————

A senior loan officer was standing by the desk of a junior loan officer when the telephone rang. The junior officer answered, saying, "No . . . no . . . no . . . yes . . . no," and hung up. The senior officer questioned him immediately. What had he said "yes" to?

"Don't worry," said the junior officer reassuringly. "I said 'yes' only when he asked me if I was still listening."

Matron, leaving withdrawal window at bank, to friend: "That's what I like about banks—they never ask you what in the world you're doing with the money."

Prospective borrower at loan company: "Just enough to tide me over until I can get a credit card."

On a bank official's desk: "In this office, the word 'no' is a complete sentence."

A San Francisco bank cashier cashed six phony checks for the same forger within a two-week period. When police and the bank's manager asked the girl why she suspected nothing and kept cashing the checks, she explained, "Because he looked familiar."

Loan officer to customer: "And one of life's disappointments, sir, is discovering that the man who writes the bank's advertising is *not* the one who makes the loans."

Woman to banker: "I'd like to open a joint account with someone who has money."

Business as Usual

A New Yorker passing Fulton Fish Market spotted two tubs of live softshell crabs, side by side. One tub had a sign reading, "$2.50 a dozen"; the other a sign reading, $1.50 a dozen." While he watched, a crab pulled himself up laboriously from among his fellows, attained the rim of the tub and climbed into the $2.50-a-dozen receptacle. "That's the sort of thing," the gentleman observed, "that can happen only in the U.S.A."

At a Washington party some years ago two well-known reformed lobbyists were comparing notes on how the five-percent business had fallen off. One asked the other, "How's business?"

"Well, you know how it is," said the other. "This business is like sex. When it's good, it's wonderful. When it's bad— it's still pretty good."

Overheard on the bus: "The sad story of my business career is that I started out on a shoestring the year everybody started wearing loafers."

The young son of a dress manufacturer in New York's garment district was asked by his teacher to tell how many seasons there were and to name them. "Two," the boy said. "Busy and slack."

American wife to husband at Rome's Trevi Fountain: "You're probably the first person to toss a coin in the fountain and wish for the stabilization of the international wool market."

Executive to employe: "I can't approve your expense account, Argyle, but we'd like to buy the fiction rights to it."

One man to another: "We're a nonprofit organization. We didn't mean to be—but we are."

I know of one who became a person of large doings because on a day he wore, by accident, the wrong pair of trousers. They sorted very ill with his upper gear; consequently, that day, instead of trotting all about the office as usual, he remained assiduous at his desk with the incongruent pantaloons well hidden. He summoned to him all those from whom he required information, even asking the head of the firm, by telephone, to step in when he next went by. He discovered, by the end of the day, that he had dispatched more business than he usually did in a week; he wasted no time in genial to-and-fro; he strongly impressed valuable customers by not rising from his chair. He remained bashfully until all his colleagues had gone home, and so happened to catch an important long-distance call. He specialized in staying at his desk thereafter. By sitting still he rose to the top of the tree. It was the sheer hazard of a wrong pair of trousers.

Company executive to junior executives: ". . . and when Mr. Biglee's son starts working here tomorrow he'll have no special privileges or authority. Treat him just as you would anyone else who was due to take over the whole business in a year or two."

Chairman of the board to other members: "Of course, it's only a suggestion, gentlemen, but let's not forget who's making it."

A good many concerns have learned the value of using a specific chair for unwelcome guests. An ordinary office chair can be made most uncomfortable—for prolonged visits—by cutting an inch or so off the front legs. The caller slips forward. A set of muscles gets tired—though the visitor does not know why he is uncomfortable. The manager of a Chicago office kept track of the time wasted by visitors who called on him during the week. Then he installed a specially prepared chair. The wasted time decreased 80 percent.

A friend lamented to John D. Rockefeller that he had not been able to collect a $50,000 loan made to a business acquaintance.

"Why don't you sue him?" asked Rockefeller.

"I neglected to have him acknowledge the loan in writing."

"Well," said the oil tycoon, "just drop him a letter demanding the $100,000 he owes you."

"But he owes me only $50,000."

"Precisely," said Rockefeller. "He will let you know that by return mail—and you will have your acknowledgment."

Tired businessman's observation: "It's simply fantastic the amount of work you can get done, if you don't do anything else."

At a businessmen's convention, four old cronies, all pillars of the same community, got together in a hotel room and before long they were discussing their shortcomings. "Well, said one, a leading businessman known as a teetotaler, "I confess I have a little weakness. I like to drink. But I never let it interfere with my work. Every now and then I go off to another town, take a room in a hotel, have a little binge and come back home again, none the worse for wear."

"I have to confess my weakness is women," said another. "Now and then—a lonesome widow—very discreet, you know, and nobody's the wiser. . . ."

"Mine is betting," said the leading banker. "When I get a chance, I put a little on the horses. Not much—but I just have to give in to my weakness now and then."

They all looked expectantly at the fourth member of the group, but he didn't seem inclined to volunteer anything. "Come on, now," they said, "how about you?"

"I—I—just don't want to tell . . ." he stalled.

They all looked askance. What sinister vice was he covering up? They coaxed and coaxed and finally told him he was damned unfair, since they had all been so frank.

"All right," he said reluctantly. "If you must know—it's gossip. And I just *can't* wait to get out of this room!"

In the business world an executive knows something about everything, a technician knows everything about something —and the switchboard operator knows everything.

Disconsolate husband to wife: "That new blood I infused into the corporation just asked for my resignation as chairman of the board!"

Beggar to businessman: "You see, sir, my federal anti-poverty grant is now contingent on my ability to raise matching funds in the private sector."

The big business executive was in the waiting room on the maternity floor of the hospital. While other expectant fathers paced the floor and thumbed nervously through magazines, he sat at a table working furiously at a sheaf of papers he had taken from his bulging brief case.

After some hours a nurse came into the room and spoke to him. "It's a boy, sir," she said.

"Well," snapped the executive without looking up from his work, "ask him what he wants."

A girl approached a businessman in a San Francisco office-building lobby, asking, "Would you donate to the Sexual Freedom League?"

The businessman answered gruffly, "I give at home."

A New York merchant came into his office looking haggard and wan from persistent insomnia. "Count sheep," advised his partner. "It's the best known cure."

The next morning the merchant looked more bleary-eyed than ever. "I counted up to 50,000," he told his partner. "Then I sheared the sheep and made up 50,000 overcoats. Then came the problem that kept me awake all the rest of the night: *Where could I get 50,000 linings?*"

Hitting the Pitch

The manager and one of his salesmen stood before a map on which colored pins indicated the representative in each area. "I'm not going to fire you, Cartwright," the manager said, "but just to emphasize the insecurity of your position I'm loosening your pin a little."

How you getting along?" the veteran salesman asked the fledgling.

"Rotten. I got nothing but insults every place I called."

"That's funny," the old man mused. "I been on the road 40 years. I've had doors slammed in my face, my samples dumped in the street. I been tossed down stairs, been man-handled by janitors—but insulted? Never!"

Insurance agent to would-be client: "Don't let me frighten you into a hasty decision. Sleep on it tonight. If you wake up tomorrow, let me know then."

The proprietor of a highly successful optical shop was instructing his son as to how to charge a customer.

"Son," he said, "after you have fitted the glasses, and he asks what the charge will be, you say: 'The charge is $10.' Then pause and wait to see if he flinches.

"If the customer doesn't flinch, you then say, 'For the frames. The lenses will be another $10.'

"Then you pause again, this time only slightly, and watch for the flinch. If the customer doesn't flinch this time, you say, firmly, 'Each.'"

Man to auto salesman: "My trade-in is one of those marvelous '67s you went into ecstasies about when you were selling it to me."

A salesman of superability was nevertheless dissatisfied with life and decided to end it all. He had climbed a bridge railing and was about to jump when a policeman appeared. "Hey!" shouted the officer. "You can't do that!"

"Why not?" challenged the salesman, and went on to argue the point with the policeman. After several minutes they both jumped.

An insurance salesman was getting nowhere in his efforts to sell a policy to a farmer. "Look at it this way," he said finally. "How would your wife carry on if you should die?"

"Well," answered the farmer reasonably, "I don't reckon that's any concern o' mine—so long as she behaves herself while I'm alive."

A traveling salesman, held up in the Orkney Islands by a bad storm, telegraphed to his firm in Aberdeen: "Marooned by storm. Wire instructions."

The reply came: "Start summer vacation as of yesterday."

A shy young man came into the office of a go-getter sales manager, timidly approached the desk and mumbled, "You don't want to buy any insurance, do you?"

"No," was the brusque reply.

"I was afraid not," said the embarrassed chap, starting to back toward the door.

"Wait a minute!" exclaimed the sales manager. "I've dealt with salesmen all my life, and you're the worst I've ever seen. You have to inspire confidence, and to do that you've got to have it yourself. Just to give you confidence that you *can* make a sale, I'll sign for a $10,000 policy."

Signing the application, the sales manager said, "What you have to do is learn some good techniques and *use* them."

"Oh, but I have," returned the salesman. "I have an approach for almost every type of businessman. The one I just used was my standard approach for sales managers."

Businessman to salesman: "I like your approach—now let's see your departure!"

Car salesman: "And it's priced just over the car which is priced a few dollars above the car which costs no more than some models of the lowest price cars."

As district manager for a vacuum-cleaner company, my main job was hiring men and training them. To help a new man become familiar with the product, I suggested that he demonstrate it to his wife. The next morning I asked him how he got along.

"I did what you told me," he said. "And when I finished, I asked my wife, 'Would you buy it?' She said, 'Yes.' Then I asked her, 'Why?' She replied, 'Because I love you!' "

Labor's Love Lost

THE FUTURE OF
THE FIVE-HOUR DAY?
JACK ALTSHUL

T**HE FIVE-HOUR** day won recently by a New York electricians' union *could* turn out to be a Pyrrhic victory. Other trades in the construction industry have high-voltage ideas about leisure time, too, and the way their union leaders have been getting workers less-work-and-more-pay contracts every year, it may not be long before the men begin to wonder what to do with all their idle hours.

Of course, they won't have much of a problem if they have working wives. Let us consider, for instance, a typical day in the life of Virgil Trauma, a plumber, and his wife, Ophelia, a secretary, about eight years hence.

Virgil starts work at seven in the morning, so he has long since departed from the house by the time his sons, James Hoffa Trauma, 8, and Van Arsdale Trauma, 6, start preparing their jet-cereal breakfast. The boys rush off to school after dutifully awakening their mother, and Ophelia settles down to the coffee Virgil left for her. At 9:30 she is picked up by the car pool, and the four gals have all the way to work to discuss what Hubby cooked for dinner the night before.

Virgil returns home at 12:30 and stretches out in the easy chair with a copy of the nation's best-selling magazine, *Hubby's Home Companion.* He gets through such articles as "The Office Boy—A Threat to Your Marriage?" and "Busy-Day Meals for Busy Boys" before he is interrupted by a knock on the door. Hector Complex, a strapping pipe fitter and next-door neighbor whose union won him a four-hour day, wants to borrow a cupful of sugar to finish an upside-down cake. They make a date to go supermarketing later in the day, and Virgil busies himself with cleaning the house. At three o'clock, Van Arsdale and James H. come bouncing in from school, and Virgil is horrified to see that their shoes are soaking wet. "You just wait till your mother gets home!" Virgil barks.

At 3:30 Virgil and Hector keep their shopping date. In the store they stop to say hello to Hal Neurosis. Hal serves on more committees than anybody else in town. His current interest is in forming a local chapter of the national "Equal Rights for Men" association, which is plunking for an eight-hour day for the working man, so he can catch up with the working woman. Both Hector and Virgil agree that they'd like to join, and Hector volunteers to hold the first meeting at his house. "I hope the boys like my upside-down cake," he ventures shyly.

Back home, Virgil gets busy preparing dinner, and is interrupted only six times to break up fights between his warring children. The shrimp-and-cream-cheese casserole is in the oven when the phone rings. It is Ophelia. "I won't be home for dinner," she says. "The girls have decided to have a couple of beers and go bowling. We've got to have some relaxation, you know. After all, we do work a *full* day."

Virgil removes the casserole from the oven. The boys refuse to eat it, and rustle themselves up another package of jet cereal. Wearily, Virgil gets them to bed. At midnight, Ophelia hasn't come home yet, so Virgil turns in, too. He falls asleep to the wonderful vision of the "Equal Rights for Men" boys marching on Washington and winning an eight-hour day.

———————— • ————————

Union leader reading bedtime story to his child: "Once upon a time-and-a-half. . . ."

Samuel Gompers, the great labor leader, was once asked what American Labor wanted, and his response may well be the most eloquent speech he ever made.

"More," he said.

A movie house showing a popular thriller was being picketed, but crowds continued to throng into the movie. Union officials decided a drastic step was necessary.

The next day a lone picket stood silently by the box office. His sign read: "The hero's uncle did it."

———————— • ————————

A Broadway play, *Mid-Summer,* which featured a slatternly maid who flipped a duster casually around a hotel room and went out, was picketed until the management agreed to run the following program note: "The character Rosie is intended to bear no resemblance to actual hotel maids of the present day. The producers recognize the fact that the 7000 maids who are members of the Hotel and Club Employes Union, Local 6, New York, are industrious and able."

One chorus girl to another: "He's only a tycoon, but he spends money like it was out of a union welfare fund!"

In St. Louis, Missouri, a contractor who held up a $500,000 building job until a robin that had built a nest on the site could hatch her eggs explained: "I'm no bird lover. I just respect a fellow contractor."

Assistant reporting to corporation president: "A guaranteed annual wage, a guaranteed annual bonus, a guaranteed pension plan is fine with the employes, Chief. Except they would like a guarantee you won't go broke."

It was a heated discussion of election procedures in the labor unions, and the group was evenly divided as to their honesty until one young man said, "I know the elections are crooked. In our last election I ran for shop steward of our local and voted for myself three times, but when the returns were completed, I never got a vote!"

In Philadelphia an official of the AFL-CIO Transport Workers Union received this letter: "My sister, who lives in New York City, wrote me that you had a strike against the bus lines there. For five days she had to walk to work and because of that she lost seven pounds, which makes her look a lot better. Not only that, but she met a guy walking to work one day, and he was a bus driver on strike. Now they are going to get married. Why can't you have a strike here in Philadelphia?"

A labor leader went to a matrimonial agency. "Is this a union shop?" he inquired. Assured that it was, he picked out a picture of a luscious 25-year-old and said, "I'll take her."

"No, you have to take this lady," said the manager, showing a picture of a gray-haired woman of 60.

"Why do I have to take her?" thundered the labor leader.

"She," said the manager, "has seniority."

A worker who was one dollar short in his pay envelope complained to the cashier. She looked at the records and said, "Last week, we overpaid you a dollar. You didn't complain about the mistake then, did you?"

"An occasional mistake I can overlook," replied the worker. "But not two in a row."

The entire personnel had been summoned to listen to a most important announcement by the chairman. "Ladies and gentlemen," he said, "for some time now the board has been aware that a rumor has been circulating. It is true: on the first of next month the whole plant will change over to full automation."

Rumble, rumble, rumble, went the multitude. The chairman raised his hand for silence, then went on. "Not a single person will be laid off. Wages will continue as before. Bonuses will be as usual. Holidays with pay, sick benefits and pension schemes will go on. Every member of the firm will be expected to appear for work on Wednesday of each week. Wednesday only."

There was a choked hush. Then, breaking the silence, came a plaintive voice from the back of the crowd: "What? *Every* Wednesday?"

A person who breaks his leg while dancing in the company elevator during his lunch hour because he likes his job may collect workmen's compensation, the Court of Appeals in Albany, N.Y., has ruled.

The court upheld an Appellate Division ruling which said that Robert Bletter should receive workmen's compensation for time lost after he broke his leg because he had been inspired to dance as an outlet for his good feeling about his job, his fellow employes and his supervisor.

A labor-union member was asked on a TV news program about his views on the Senate's investigation of labor racketeering. He stated that he thought his union was operated better today than in the past. "For instance," he said, "years ago you didn't know who was taking your money when you paid your dues—today you do."

When a young stenographer falls backward while applying lipstick in the company lounge during her lunch hour, can she claim that the resultant injury occurred in the course of her employment?

Yes, said the St. Louis Court of Appeals. It is a business axiom that comfortable employes perform their duties more efficiently, and since cosmetics are a source of considerable comfort to the feminine worker, the applying of lipstick is an on-the-job benefit to the employer.

From Nine to Five:
THE OFFICE ROUTINE

THE OFFICE" is one of the strangest inventions of modern man. (It's also, as Don Herold remarks on page 153, one of the least efficient: outside of watching a John Wayne movie, the coffee break is the most successful time-waster in existence.) The office routine would baffle any of our ancestors living 250 years ago. They'd find it hard to figure out why we are willing to spend a third of our day shut up in noisy rooms, doing things with bits of paper covered with words—creating them, filing them, shoving them around, multiplying them and, finally, forgetting them. Out of this baffling institution we extract considerable comedy. Maybe it's the officially accepted comedy of office life that helps make it tolerable: the stenogs who are always dumb, beautiful, or both; the juxtaposition of the contrasting atmospheres of sex and computers; the executive carefully trained to nonexecute; our genius for devising foolproof methods of soldiering on the job; the whole comedy of office class-distinctions, which makes the court of Louis XIV look like a hippie commune. What will happen to this curious little world of comedy when office work is fully automated and adventurous pilgrimages to the water cooler are no more? Perhaps, just to keep that world alive as a museum piece, the computers will be programmed for jokes.

Previous Experience?

Employer to beautiful blonde who has filled in job application: "Miss Jones, under 'Experience' could you be a little more specific than just 'Oh Boy!'?"

An employment office, checking references of a job applicant, asked one ex-employer: "Was he a steady worker?"
"Steady?" came the indignant reply. "He was motionless."

Home-coming husband to wife: "Whew! I took an aptitude test this afternoon. Thank goodness I own the company!"

Young girl to prospective employer: "Before I accept this job, Mr. Slawson, I think it only fair to tell you there won't be any opportunities for advances."

An employment office was checking on an applicant's list of references. "How long did this man work for you?" a former employer was asked.

"About four hours," was the quick reply.

"Why, he told us he'd been there a long time," said the astonished caller.

"Oh, yes," answered the ex-employer, "he's been here two years."

It is customary when being interviewed for the job of salesgirl to be asked, "Who is the most important person in this store?" To which most applicants dutifully reply, "The customer." Recently an applicant was being interviewed by our store manager, and when he came to the big question she shyly half-asked, half-answered, "The manager?" She was hired.

From the Los Angeles *Times:* "Large defense products plant has excellent opportunity for assistant office manager. This is not an executive position; job entails considerable work."

Want ad in San Antonio *Evening News:* "Executive Director, from 24 to 40. To sit at desk from 9 to 5 and watch other people work. Must be willing to play golf every other afternoon. Salary, over $350 to start. WE DON'T HAVE THIS JOB! WE JUST THOUGHT WE'D LIKE TO SEE IN PRINT WHAT EVERYONE IS APPLYING FOR."

Applicants for jobs on Kentucky Dam, when the project was starting, had to take a written examination. One chap read the first question: "What does 'hydrodynamics' mean?" hesitated, then wrote: "It means I don't get the job!"

A young woman filling out an application blank in a West Coast airplane factory pondered over the last question, "What are your aims and ambitions?" then wrote, "I want to go as far as my education and sex will allow."

The personnel manager looked up at the young man seeking a job. "Tell me," he said, "what have you done?"

"Me?" answered the startled applicant. "About what?"

A matronly woman filling out an employment application came to the line marked "age." Here she hesitated a long time. Finally the personnel manager leaned over and whispered, "The longer you wait, the worse it gets."

When a woman filling out an application came to the square marked "age," she didn't hesitate. She simply wrote: "Atomic."

Pooled Resources

Office girl to good-looking new girl: "Mr. Hartnig? Keep going until a red-haired man winks at you, then turn right and go all the way back to a hoarse voice that says 'WOW'—turn left until you run into a low whistle, and you're there."

One office worker to another, as shapely secretary walks by: "Who said she was all thumbs?"

The green-eye-shadow fad swept through our office-girl staff like a plague one summer. One particularly hot, humid day, a group of visiting engineers came to tour our building, and one of them asked the guide if he could check the humidity controls.

After studying the dials a long time, he turned to our office manager and said, "Just as I thought. It really should be much lower. Your girls are beginning to mildew."

Office girl, leaving on vacation, to substitute: "While I'm gone, you'll continue what I was working on—but that doesn't include Mr. Haynes!"

Employer to stunning secretary: "You understand that the job is temporary? As soon as my wife sees you, you're through."

One secretary to another: "The efficiency expert has had his eye on me a lot, lately. I don't know whether to act busy or interested."

Office men, discussing new girl in accounting department: "She may not know a debit from a credit—but she certainly adds up."

Glamour girl to male fellow worker: "Yes, I can tell you how I got *my* raise, but I don't think it will help *you* much."

Personnel director introducing mini-mini-skirted file clerk to new employe: "This is Miss Taylor—Miss Taylor sorts out the men from the boys."

Ad in Thompsonville, Connecticut, *Press:* "WANTED—Man to manage Accounting Department in charge of 20 girls. Must like figures."

Secretary to office wolf: "I'm sorry, William. I ran you through the computer last night, and you just didn't make it."

Take a Letter

Asked how she liked her new boss, a young secretary remarked, "Oh, he isn't so bad, only he's kind of bigoted."

"How do you mean?"

"Well," explained the girl, "he thinks words can only be spelled one way."

Miss Wilcox," a chap told his new secretary firmly, "always add a column of figures at least three times before you show me the result."

The next day she came in with a broad smile. "Mr. Johnson," she said, "I added these figures ten times."

"Good. I like a girl to be thorough."

"And here," she said, "are my ten answers."

Employer to new secretary: "Briefly, Miss Finch, your duties will be to take dictation, answer the phone, do some filing and stay single!"

Before my husband and I went on a cruise to celebrate our 50th wedding anniversary, I told his secretary that I wanted this trip to be a complete rest for him. No matter what happened, she was not to write him about it. At our first port my husband received this letter from his secretary: "Our first catastrophe happened this morning, but I won't write you about it. . . ."

A publisher's secretary incurred his ire by presuming to make some necessary grammatical changes in a letter he had dictated. "I want my letters typed exactly as I dictate them!" he stormed. "Is that *quite* clear? Now take this."

That afternoon, the secretary planked this letter on his desk:

"Dear Smythe: The idiot spells it with an 'e.' Thinks it's aristocratic. His old man was a janitor. With regard to your letter of—look it up. Anybody who can read that handwriting deserves a medal. You ask the best discount we can allow on 5000 juveniles, assorted titles. In order to make any profit at all we cannot go above—hey, Lew, what do you think Smythe will stand for on that juvenile deal? Forty-five percent? Hm-m-m—our accountants figure that forty-three percent is the furthest we dare go. The extra two percent is for that damn 'e' he sticks on his name. Trusting to receive your esteemed order, etc., etc., etc."

A businessman hired a new secretary, and the first morning she worked for him he dictated a letter to his wife, who was away on a trip. When she brought the letter back to him for his signature it was perfect, with one exception. She had omitted his final words, which were, "I love you."

"Did you forget my last sentence?" he asked.

"Why, no, I didn't forget," she said. "I just didn't realize that you were dictating."

Returning to his office after lunch, the executive found this memorandum on his desk: "Your wife called. She wanted to remind you of something which she couldn't remember but thought you would."

Secretary on bus: "And furthermore, comma——"

When a Cleveland tycoon handed his secretary the papers for a big deal, he told her gravely, "This is hot stuff, so file it away carefully." She did, too—in a large manila envelope marked "HOT STUFF."

Suddenly called out of town, a Chicago news commentator told his new secretary: "Write Allis-Chalmers in Milwaukee. Say that I can't keep that appointment Friday. I'm off for Texas. I'll telephone when I get back. Sign my name." Upon his return, he found this carbon waiting:

Alice Chalmers
Milwaukee, Wisconsin
Dear Alice:
   I'm off for Texas and can't keep that date . . .

The man promptly phoned the tractor company and said, "I hope you haven't received a certain letter."

"Received it!" came the reply. "It's been on the bulletin board for three days!"

As secretary to a busy executive, I screen his incoming phone calls. When I answered recently, a youthful male voice inquired, "May I speak to Mr. Baird?" Automatically I said, "May I ask who is calling?"

"Sure," replied the cheerful voice. "I'm the fellow who wants to speak to Mr. Baird!" I put the call through.

Executive secretary to boss: "'A voice crying in the wilderness' would like to speak to you. I believe it's your son."

It had been one of the boss's bad days, and in the last few minutes his secretary brought him a letter for his signature. He signed the letter, but not until he had the stenographer put it back in the typewriter and add: "P.S. Please excuse errors. Dictated to a poor stenographer."

After he had left the office, the girl took the letter from the envelope, and added: "P.S. #2. The reason I am so poor is because he pays me only $25 a week."

The new secretary was a stunningly beautiful blonde, and her boss was the envy of his co-workers. He was disillusioned about her, however, after he dictated a letter to a publisher, told her to sign his name and mail it. For the address, he handed her the publisher's letterhead.

Next morning the mail room returned the letter for lack of sufficient address. The envelope read: "Macmillan Company, New York, London, Tokyo,"

Personnel Relations

ME
GO
NOW

BILL CONKLIN

I N THE advertising agency where I work as a copywriter, the word has long since gone around that I am vaguely daffy. It's true. I rarely say what I mean. I'm a lad who becomes involved in impossible situations. I quite literally get into things. (For example, a lamp shade once got stuck on my head in the middle of a rather exciting meeting.) And things have worsened steadily since Glenn Gordon came in as creative head of our agency.

The first time Glenn ever saw me was the day Gregory Peck toured our offices, gathering background for a movie role. At the moment I was in the art department, waiting for an artist friend to return from lunch. Sitting at a drawing board, idly drawing rectangles, I suddenly looked up to see Glenn Gordon, Gregory Peck and other important folk filing into the room. Sizing up the situation quickly, I did what I maintain was the right thing. Glenn Gordon was there to show Mr. Peck artists. I became one. I drew rectangles furiously.

"This is what we call the bull pen," Glenn said. "Here our rough ideas are rendered into finished layouts to show clients." He smiled at the artists in the bull pen. He smiled at me. Gregory Peck smiled at me. I smiled back.

As soon as they left, I decided not to wait around for the artist any longer. I scribbled a note for him to call me, took a short cut to my office and spun a piece of copy paper into my typewriter. Shadows fell across my opaque-glass cubicle. Voices murmured. I looked up, appalled. There were Glenn Gordon, Gregory Peck, the others.

"This is a typical copywriter's office," Glenn began. "Here,   *147* basic copy is pre——" He stared at me and his mouth hung open, caught on a syllable.

I smiled at him. I smiled at Gregory Peck. The group moved on and I returned to my work, but my heart wasn't in it. The battle was joined. I knew with a dread certainty that Glenn and I would meet in the lists again.

Sure enough. A week later a secretary had her purse stolen. Presuming it taken by a transient messenger and hoping at least to recover the bag, she asked me to search the wastebasket in the men's room. I went in and began looking through the big basket. Glenn Gordon entered. It didn't occur to me that he had no idea why I was examining crumpled paper towels in the lavatory of a hundred-million-dollar advertising agency. I saw it only as a good time to explain the Peck incident.

I rose up from the basket and said, "About Gregory Peck, sir. I wasn't twins the other day. I was in the art department to see about cutting up some horses." (It didn't come out right, as usual, but I *had* been there that day to get some horse photos trimmed and mounted.) Glenn backed away slowly, nodding and smiling pacifically, and bolted out the door.

After that, things went smoothly until the day we came face to face in the production department. Glenn motioned me to a chair. Obviously he needed to know more about me and, wonderfully enough, I was more than equal to the occasion. We sat calmly together and chatted easily about a variety of things. As we talked, Glenn became visibly relieved.

I decided to quit while I was ahead. I stood up quickly and leaned toward Glenn to say good-by. A simple "So long" or "Nice talking with you" would have sufficed. But as I searched for the appropriate farewell, my mind (never very stable) gave way completely. No words came. Glenn, having no inkling that I meant to leave, unable to understand why I was suddenly towering over him silently, froze like a frightened rabbit.

My mouth began to move wordlessly. Finally I managed to speak. "Me go now," I said hoarsely, and walked away.

Why I said that—like most of the things I do—had an explanation, but it's the kind that never can be given without adding to the confusion. I had been reading about Robert Benchley. Once, during a bad play involving a character who spoke pidgin English, he had said "Me go" and had left the theater. I suppose that the phrase stuck in my subconscious until that terrible moment. Then it tumbled out to help do me in.

Soon there was another incident. The time, 4:20 p.m. of a hectic day. I had just escaped from a meeting where I had warmly shaken hands with a colleague at the agency instead of the client. I was headed for the 11th floor and the sanctuary of my own office, where I often have things in control. The elevator door opened and there, naturally, was Glenn Gordon. He smiled resolutely and said, "Hi, there, how are you?"

I stepped aboard and answered, "Hi! Just getting back from lunch?"

Convene all the authors of all the articles on how to succeed in business. Ask them to select the one phrase *not* to be uttered to the boss at twenty past four in the afternoon. "Just getting back from lunch?" would score an enthusiastic victory by acclamation. Do believe me, that isn't what I meant to say. I meant to say something else. Exactly *what,* I really do not know.

That was Tuesday. Wednesday was worse. I took a late lunch and celebrated a crisp January day in Manhattan by buying my fiancée a huge stuffed poodle. On my way back I saw a pair of earrings I thought she would like, and bought those, too.

It was midafternoon when I returned to my desk. Sitting there, my quixotic mind far from advertising, I had a clever idea. I decided to put the earrings on the dog's ears and thus give both presents an original touch. I unwrapped the big poodle and hoisted it up onto my desk. Carefully I took a floppy ear in my hand and began fastening a gold, bell-shaped earring to it.

Fate was tempted. Fate replied. As I bent earnestly to my task, Glenn Gordon came down the aisle .and glanced in my office. Everywhere about me dedicated copywriters were hard at work. Typewriters were singing the praises of myriad products—*I* was putting earrings on a stuffed poodle. I realize now it must have been, on top of everything else, almost a traumatic experience for Glenn. I grinned a foolish grin and said noncommittally, "Dog."

In movies and plays I have often seen and admired a well-executed double take. Glenn performed not one, not two, but three takes. He stared, opened his mouth to speak, then rushed away. I have not seen him since.

I go about my business these days with firm purpose, but I open each pay envelope with trepidation. One of these times a pink slip of paper will flutter to the floor. Then, sadly enough, it really will be time to say, "Me go now."

Boss to feet-on-desk clerk: "I'm going to mix business with pleasure, Gardner. You're fired."

Charles Lamb disliked office life and was inclined to be uncertain about his office hours at the India House. One day his chief said to him, "Mr. Lamb, I notice you come very late to the office."

"Yes, sir," replied Lamb, "but you will also notice that I leave early."

By the time his superior had worked that one out, Lamb was gone.

Employer to departing executive: "In a way, though, I'll be sorry to lose you. You've been like a son to me: insolent, surly, unappreciative."

One executive to another leaving president's office: "He calls it delegating authority—I call it passing the buck!"

Boss to executive assistant: "Benson, must you concentrate all your imagination, initiative and daring into your expense account?"

Boss to tardy office boy: "Instead of a gold watch in 45 years when you retire, we've decided to give you an alarm clock *now.*"

Girl, who works for a top radio-TV executive, exploding to a friend: "My boss has a split personality—and I loathe them both."

Personnel manager to prospective employe: "Oh, we have our own special type of incentive plan, Mr. Fenton—we fire at the drop of a hat!"

The head of an advertising agency was emphasizing to an employe the necessity of high-pressure advertising. "Repetition, repetition is the keynote," he said, pounding the desk. "Harp on your product in every way possible, cram it down people's throats, make yourself sickening if you have to, but don't ever forget to repeat and repeat! It's the only way to get results. Now what was it you wanted to see me about?"

"Well, sir," answered his employe, "I'd like a raise. A raise! *A raise!* A RAISE!"

Boss to computer salesman: "Something small—I just want to replace one smart aleck."

On Company Time

EARLY TO BED
AND LATE TO RISE . . .
DON HEROLD

I'VE DECIDED that getting up and going to work is just a form of nervousness, so I keep calm and stay in bed. It takes arrogance and courage, but I stay right there until I get some work done. Then I may go down to my office and play.

When I say play, I mean dictating letters, answering the telephone, holding "conferences" and doing those other office chores that most people call work.

One of the reasons I stay adamantly in bed in the a.m. is that I am an unusually energetic person, without a lazy bone in my body, and my natural impulses are to leap up, shave and dress in a jiffy, rush to the office, and start the day busily, achieving practically nothing. Instead I force myself to start what I consider real work at seven o'clock or eight, or whenever I wake up, and to stay at it and finish it before I waste any pep on the useless, unimportant, conventional movements of rising and getting to an office, or distracting myself with the morning paper and the morning mail.

I never look at my mail until afternoon. Looking at the mail first thing in the morning is nothing but sheer boyish curiosity, mixed with a certain amount of laziness. A man who attends to his morning mail in the morning is letting other people decide how he is to spend his day. (I've observed over the years that most people accomplish little more every day than getting up and going to work.)

I tell myself that my work is somewhat mental, and that a person can come nearer to being 100 percent mental in bed than anywhere else. His galluses don't chafe, his shoes don't hurt, the angle of the chair does not annoy him, he does not have to figure what to do with his arms or legs. If he has a brain, he's practically nothing but brain . . . in bed.

Another advantage is that bed is the one place in the world where other people leave a man alone. People somehow regard bedrooms as sacred territory and do not, as a rule, crash in uninvited. Furthermore, people feel that a normal man in bed fairly late in the morning must be sick, perhaps with something infectious. Let 'em think so!

Ruskin was grasping for a seclusion similar to that which bed gives when, upon entering on a serious spell of work, he sent out cards reading: "Mr. J. Ruskin is about to begin a work of great importance and therefore begs that in reference to calls and correspondence you will consider him dead for the next two months."

Mark Twain was, of course, the patron saint of all bed workers. He was a sensationally sensible man, and he saw no point in getting up to write.

A more recent advocate of bed work was Winston Churchill, who remained in bed until late in the a.m., and went to bed again after lunch and, I believe, again later in the day. Thanks to this conservation of energy, he lived into his hearty nineties.

Another famous bed worker was Rossini, the composer. There is a story that once, while composing an opera in bed, he dropped one of the arias on the floor and it slid some distance away. Instead of getting up to retrieve it he merely wrote a new aria.

It is said Voltaire did most of his scribbling in bed, and that Disraeli wrote some of his greatest speeches while stretched out on the floor. And lawyer Louis Nizer says, "I prefer to work from a reclining position. Even my office chair tilts, and a hidden footrest permits me to recline sufficiently, without offending my client's notion of dignity. I have found justification for my lazy posture in medical journals which suggest that it takes strain off the heart and increases stamina as well as thinking powers."

My own theory is that an office is one of the least efficient inventions of modern man, and that it should be stayed out of as much as possible. If housewives only knew how most executive husbands fritter away their days, their awe of "Father at the office" would become one more shattered schoolgirl illusion. Most men get more real work done on their trips and vacations than they do all the rest of the year.

My regimen of relaxation brings all sorts of shame on my head. I am called a laggard, a bum, an escapist; I've also been accused of suffering from habitual hangovers. Perhaps I may even be accused of working for the Associated Mattress Manufacturers of America: if they can get everybody to spend 25 percent more time in bed, it will eventually boost mattress sales 25 percent. That's all right with me. What's good for the Associated Mattress Manufacturers is good for the country.

———— • ————

Man who received by mistake a pay envelope without a check, to accounting department: "What happened? Did my deductions finally catch up with my salary?"

Personnel man to trainee: "Or if you prefer, you may elect to skip coffee breaks entirely and retire three years early."

Whispered at the water cooler: "His pride's a bit hurt. He had to ride tourist in the company plane."

———— • ————

The only man who ever got all his work done by Friday was Robinson Crusoe.

One stenographer to another: "They not only give you a pension in this office, but you age here more quickly."

Overheard: "You are looking unusually cheerful today. Did you win the rat race?"

Receptionist to co-worker: "He waited for over an hour, then he said to me, 'Isn't it beautiful, our growing old together?'"

Computer repairman to company executive: "I've found the cause of your slowdown. The big computer is shoving all the work off on the little computer."

An Answer for Everything:
THE ART OF RIPOSTE

I'M NOT SURE I agree with J. A. G. Rice that "anyone
... can develop the art to a certain degree of perfection. ..." There *are* people who humorlessly persist
in trying to top every amusing remark made. They succeed
only in being reparteedious. Others seemingly never have
to pause for the right riposte. The philosopher Dr. Robert
Maynard Hutchins, after being inordinately praised in the
introductory remarks by the chairman, stepped to the

podium and said, "If I'm such a great man, why can't I stop smoking?" (If he had then looked down at the palm of his hand he would have noticed the audience.) Once when I was emceeing a quiz show called "Information Please" I warned the experts not to listen to whispered hints from the audience. "No eavesdropping," I said sternly. One of the experts, the late Franklin P. Adams, at once raised his hand. "Adams-dropping O.K.?" he inquired. Any man who can beat that can also beat a royal flush. They tell me this is a permissive era, so I'll try one more example. Once when Mayor James J. Walker was a guest at a Fourth of July celebration in London, he had to follow a toast to the reigning British sovereign. Said Mayor Walker: "Ladies and Gentlemen, I give you George Washington—first in war, first in peace, first in the hearts of his countrymen!" Slight pause. Then, "In fact, I've never understood how he happened to marry a widow."

The Apt Response

A new barber nicked a customer badly in giving him a shave. Hoping to restore the man's feeling of well-being, he asked solicitously, "Do you want your head wrapped in a hot towel?"

"No, thanks," said the customer. "I'll carry it home under my arm."

Dr. Abernathy, a famous London diagnostician, was once approached at a social function by a dowager who tried to wangle free medical advice. "Oh, Dr. Abernathy," she said, "if a patient came to you with such and such a symptom, what would you recommend?"

"Why, I would recommend Dr. Abernathy," he replied.

I WISH I'D SAID THAT

J. A. G. RICE

ABOUT two thousand years ago a man named Phocion waited wearily while his barber gave him a summary of the current Athenian political situation. At last the barber said: "And how would you like to have your hair trimmed?"

"In silence," Phocion replied. Phocion's is one of the first recorded examples of the verbal comeback, the crushing rejoinder which arouses in the bystander the envious reaction, "I wish I'd said that!"

Why, one often wonders, can't this art of repartee be learned? Thousands of us are masters of bedtime wit. When our verbal adversary is no longer on the scene, the perfect comeback flashes into our consciousness—brilliant, witty, superb. Why, then, can't we think on our feet and say it at the right time? It is purely a question of learning to speed up our brain turnover. Anyone, I believe, can develop the art to a certain degree of perfection with study and practice.

Few of us, of course, can ever achieve the high levels of the real masters. Voltaire was one. He was speaking highly of a contemporary. Said a friend: "It is good of you to say such pleasant things of Monsieur X, when he always says such unpleasant things of you." Whereupon Voltaire suggested mildly, "Perhaps we are both mistaken."

Joseph Choate, with his ability to think fast on his feet, was another master. Once, so the story goes, he was defending a case in Westchester County, suburban to New York City. The local lawyer for the plaintiff, desperate in his efforts to convince the jury, finally addressed them frantically: "Gentlemen! I hope that your decision will not be influenced by the Chesterfieldian urbanity of my opponent."

Mr. Choate arose.

"Gentlemen," he said, "I am sure you will not be influenced, either, by the Westchesterfieldian suburbanity of my opponent."

Good repartee is founded on several fundamental virtues. It must, certainly, be humorous. It must be unexpected, distinctly not the normal thing to say. It must be understandable: a comeback is useless if it is involved and poorly expressed.

The simplest form of comeback is the much-vilified pun. Puns are peculiarly irritating to many people. But a complete knowledge of punning technic leads to facility in the more complicated types. Don't be ashamed of a pun—if it is good. Practically every great writer that ever lived has tried his hand at them. But it takes a touch of genius to create a double pun in the manner of the playwright George S. Kaufman, who, after hour upon hour of terrible cards in an all-night session, announced sadly that he was being trey-deuced.

The mental procedure of the punster is something like this: His brain pounces on someone's luckless remark and selects from it a succulent word that seems to have possibilities. He rolls that word around hungrily on his tongue. Can he put it in a strange background which has nothing to do with its sense, but only with its sound? If he can't, can he locate a near neighbor to that word and put that neighbor to work? If he is able to do either, he will have created a pun, and probably an enemy.

For his family's peace of mind, the beginner will do a little practicing by himself. He will invent situations. Imagine, say, that a waiter has brought him some stale bread. What might he remark? Well, how about "Waiter, this is not well bread," or, possibly, "I'm sure this flour didn't bloom in the spring."

One simple trick is to take one word, marry it to another, and emerge with a creation hitherto unsuspected by the world. Examples: DeQuincey's characterizing an old lady as "in her anecdotage"; or the columnists' discovery that Repeal was an alcoholiday.

Another type of comeback is the deliberate misinterpretation of someone else's remark. It can be as poisonous as any potion ever conceived by a De' Medici. Consider, for instance, the member of the French Chamber of Deputies who had been a veterinary before he became a Radical politician. One day, during a bitter debate, an aristocratic Conservative sneeringly inquired: "Is it actually true that you are a veterinary, my good man?"

"It is, sir," said the Radical. "Are you ill?"

Deliberate misuse of a catch phrase, rather than a remark, is another effective comeback. Joe Williams, the sports writer, recorded one of this type in one of his columns. He was watching the murderous tenth round of the Baer-Carnera battle. As Carnera staggered to his feet, after the seventh or eighth knockdown of the fight, Williams turned to the man on his right, Heywood Broun, and said: "Gosh, but the big fellow certainly can take it!"

"Yes," said Broun doubtfully. "But he doesn't seem to know what to do with it."

Other examples: the remark, when attacking a grapefruit, "There's more in this than meets the eye," and Dorothy Parker's comment on a much-publicized actress: "She runs the gamut of emotions from A to B." There was also the reply of the critic who was asked his opinion of a certain play. "I wouldn't like to comment," he said. "I saw it under bad conditions. The curtain was up."

Subtle in form is the velvet-glove remark. It takes a simple, harmless sentence, and places it in a highly exotic situation, thereby making the sentence change character completely. A wicked old lady, seeing the tango danced for the first time, once demonstrated this for all posterity: "I suppose it's all right," she muttered, "if they really love each other."

The famous Whistler remark—don't stop me if you have heard it—is an excellent example. Whistler had made some particularly clever statement, and Oscar Wilde, notorious for his plagiarizing of other people's dinner conversation, burst out: "Heavens, I wish I'd said that!"

"You will, Oscar, you will," said Whistler comfortingly.

Another grouping of comebacks might be termed betterisms. The whole mental attitude of the betterist, who is generally a pretty unpopular human being because of it, must be "Well, now, that's very nice, but you might have said this. . . ." For instance, the after-dinner story in which the toastmaster introduced a speaker by saying:

"Here is an unusual specimen. You have only to put a dinner in his mouth and out comes a speech."

The gentlemen in question arose and said: "Before I go on, I would like to call attention to your toastmaster, who is also unusual. You have only to put a speech in his mouth, and out comes your dinner."

A mad expansion of the betterism can be recognized in the Marxist fancy—Groucho's discussion of the advisability of building a house near the railroad track. A worried look appears on Groucho's face. Suddenly he says: "I don't like Junior to cross the tracks on his way to the reform school!"

Which is obvious enough humor, and would remain unsung by this commentator, were it not for the fact that Groucho had not quite finished. "In fact," he continued thoughtfully, "I don't like Junior!"

In trying to develop one's wit, it is not necessary at all times to be original. It has been said that originality is generally undetected plagiarism. Don't be afraid to borrow or adapt other people's ideas—if those ideas aren't well known—but give credit. You'll get your credit because of the aptness of your choice.

To attain maximum facility, one must first of all keep trying. But remember that even the wildest sort of repartee must be relevant. Keep thinking of the things you might say, but don't say them unless you are moderately sure they are worthy of you.

The imagination must be developed, like a muscle, by constant use. This does not mean that the hopeful wag must develop a new vocabulary. Some of the funniest things that have ever been said have been couched in one and two syllabled words. Ring Lardner's description, for one, of the young baseball player in love: "He give her a look you could of poured on a waffle."

Finally, the manner of delivery is important. Nothing can kill a clever remark more quickly than uproarious laughter by its conceiver, or a smug expression on his face. The beginner must practice in front of his mirror—trying to seem completely oblivious of the fact that he is being humorous. The "deadpan" delivery is by all odds most effective.

Repartee can be deadlier than the rapier or the sword. Like all weapons of attack, it must be handled with care, lest it damage the user—who will find himself, if his choices are unwise, in something of the position of the young man being discussed by two young ladies.

"Oh, he is so tender!" said the one who was engaged to him.

"Perhaps that's because he's been in hot water so much," suggested the other.

How can I ever show my appreciation?" gushed a woman to Clarence Darrow, after he had solved her legal troubles.

"My dear woman," replied Darrow, "ever since the Phoenicians invented money there has been only one answer to that question."

The superintendent of an insane asylum noticed an inmate pushing a wheelbarrow upside down.

"Why do you have it upside down?" asked the superintendent.

"You don't think I'm crazy, do you?" was the reply. "I pushed it right side up yesterday and they kept filling it with gravel."

An old man had lived in an old house in a western town for 50 years. One day he surprised everybody by moving next door. When they asked him why he moved, he replied, "I guess it's just the gypsy in me."

Someone asked the French writer Jean Cocteau if he believed in luck. "Certainly," he said. "How else do you explain the success of those you don't like?"

Groucho Marx asked a lovely young tennis star appearing on his program about her training for future tournaments. "I need to improve my form and speed," she replied.

"If your form improves," said Groucho, "you are going to need all the speed you can muster."

George Washington had more ready wit than history seems inclined to credit to him and could very competently hold his own in repartee. One day, as he sat at table after dinner, he complained that the fire burning on the hearth behind him was too large and too hot. "But sir," rejoined a guest, "it behooves a general to stand fire."

"But," came the instant reply, "it does not become a general to receive it from the rear."

Asked how it felt to attend the dedication of his own statue, the honored man said, "Well, somehow, you begin to feel differently about pigeons."

Peter Donald tells about the time W. C. Fields was handed a highball and asked, "What would you like to drink to?"

"To about three in the morning," Fields replied.

Professor C. Northcote Parkinson's latest law is: "Delay is the deadliest form of denial." At a tea the other day, a man approached Parkinson and asked him to explain it. "I will," replied Parkinson, "in a few minutes."

Mr. and Mrs. Victor Borge met Sonja Henie, the skating queen, at a party. "My," Mrs. Borge said later, "she certainly looks young."

"Why not?" Victor commented. "She's been on ice all her life."

During the Depression, soon after President Hoover initiated a number of major recovery programs, he told former President Coolidge that he could not understand why the results were as yet so disappointing and his critics so vociferous.

"You can't expect to see calves running in the field," said Coolidge, "the day after you put the bull to the cows."

"No," replied Hoover. "But I *would* expect to see contented cows."

Pun in Cheek

After an arduous session of the Supreme Court, the Justices once decided on a three-day boat trip for relaxation. On the second day out the late Justice Cardozo, somewhat the worse for mal-de-mer, was leaning over the rail of the boat, which was rocking badly, when Chief Justice Hughes sauntered along. "Can I do anything for you?" said the Chief Justice.

"Yes," answered Judge Cardozo, "overrule the motion."

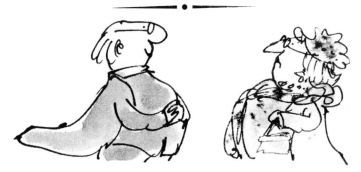

A bishop of the Methodist Church who was attending the annual meeting of the Women's Board of Foreign Missions had presented his views, when the president of the board took the floor.

"Bishop," she said firmly, "I cannot see this thing as you present it, and I will not be bullied!"

Bowing low before the lady, the bishop retorted, "Madam, neither will I be cowed."

Fannie Hurst, a fashionable author of her day, had acquired a beautiful figure by means of a rigorous diet, and fellow author Irvin Cobb followed her down Fifth Avenue for six blocks without recognizing her. Finally she said to him: "Aren't you going to talk to me?"

"Good Lord," said Cobb, "it's Fannie Hurst!"

"The same Fannie Hurst," she agreed laughingly.

"Not quite," said Cobb. "It may be the same Hurst—but it's not the same Fannie!"

A Main Line summer bachelor was dining with friends when a sweet young thing from next door came in. "Stay away from him!" warned the host. "He's a summer bachelor."

"Really?" murmured the modern generation. "How long have you been celibating?"

One of the contestants on Groucho Marx's quiz show was a young man named Lee. "One of the Virginia Lees?" asked Groucho.

"No, I'm from England," said the contestant.

"Oh," said Groucho, "one of the lend Lees."

When John D. Rockefeller, Jr., at the age of 77 married a woman in her 50s, the new Mrs. Rockefeller was jokingly called his child bride. "What did he give her for a wedding present?" a newspaperman asked. "Blocks?"

"Yes," replied a friend. "Forty-ninth and Fiftieth—on Fifth Avenue."

Touché

Two English schoolboys took a dislike to each other, and the hatred grew more intense as the years passed. One entered the Royal Navy and finally became an admiral; the other went into the church and eventually was made a bishop. Years later they met on a London railroad-station platform. They had changed, of course, and the bishop had grown very plump, but they recognized each other. The bishop swept up to the admiral, who was resplendent in his uniform with medals and gold braid glittering all over him, and said: "Stationmaster, from which platform does the 10:05 train leave for Oxford?"

The admiral promptly retaliated: "Platform 5, madam. But in your condition, should you be traveling?"

At a literary luncheon held shortly after the publication of her memoirs, Gypsy Rose Lee was preceded by author Walter Lord. At the conclusion of his talk, he remarked that just before the luncheon Gypsy had said to him: "Walter, your speech will be a hard act to follow, so to insure close attention to my speech, I've decided to take all my clothes off!"

Gypsy rose from her seat, smiled demurely at the audience and said: "Why, Mr. Lord, you know that isn't true. You know I'd never end a sentence with a preposition!"

As a visiting Englishman was driven up a Cincinnati street, he cast aspersions at the passing scene, particularly at what he termed the "hideous architecture."

"We call it Victorian," said his Cincinnati host.

When the late editor Harold Ross founded *The New Yorker* the original offices were modest and almost bare of equipment. One of the earlier members of the staff was writer Dorothy Parker. One day, during working hours, Ross met her in a restaurant downstairs. "What are you doing here?" he demanded. "Why aren't you upstairs working?"

"Someone was using the pencil," she explained.

The captain of a ship once wrote in his log, "Mate was drunk today." When the mate became normal, he was terribly chagrined and angry; he pleaded with the captain to strike out the record; he declared that he had never been drunk before, that he would never drink again. But the captain said, "In this log we write the exact truth."

The next week the mate kept the log, and in it he wrote, "Captain was sober today."

On her first visit to the South, a young niece heard the remark, "I was 16 before I knew damn Yankee was two words," once too often. The next time a southern belle uttered the much-repeated phrase the northern belle was ready.

"That's all right, honey," she said. "Until I came down here I always thought Robert E. Lee was a steamboat."

The late Uncle Joe Cannon was telling Chauncey M. Depew about a fish he had almost caught. "About the size of a whale, wasn't it?" asked Mr. Depew, softly.

"I was baitin' with whales," answered Uncle Joe.

The Duke of Wellington received a letter from a lady stating that she had put down his name for a subscription of £200 for a certain church. He replied, agreeing to her flattering assignment; but added that he, too, was interested in a needy church, and counting upon her liberality, he had put her down for £200; "and so," he concluded, "no money need pass between us."

A bumptious playwright who had a new show opening sent a couple of tickets for the first night to the mayor of the city with a note suggesting that the chief executive could bring a friend "if he had one."

The mayor returned the tickets with a courteous letter stating that previous engagements made it impossible for him to see the show the opening night, but he would purchase two tickets for the second performance—if there was one.

One day Mark Twain arrived in a Canadian hotel, and, glancing over the register, took note of the signature of the last arrival: "Baron——and valet." Twain signed, and when the clerk looked at the register, this met his eye: "Mark Twain and valise."

Men of Few Words

Shortly after Admiral Byrd's notable polar expedition returned from the land of ice, someone asked one of the men what one thing he missed most while away. "Temptation," was the answer.

Lord Beaverbrook's servants, it appears, never referred to him as "his Lordship" or "Lord Beaverbrook," but as "the Lord." When Randolph Churchill called at Arlington House, he was told by the butler, "I am sorry, sir, but the Lord is walking in the park."

"Oh," said Randolph. "On the lake, I presume?"

At a reception in Paris where there were many titled guests, the wife of an American general stepped up to the cocktail table. "Looking for something?" asked another guest.

"Yes, a bourbon."

With a courtly bow, he asked, "Would a Hapsburg do?"

W_{hy}," a man asked a friend, "do you always answer a question with a question?"

Replied the friend, "Why not?"

T_{wo} Amherst graduates attending the international radio-telegraphic conference in Madrid decided to give an Amherst dinner. Sixty-five delegates attended the affair at the Palace Hotel. To provide a grand climax for the party the hosts had sent a long cable to Calvin Coolidge, an Amherst graduate, explaining the situation and asking him to send a suitable message to be read at the dinner.

They also emphasized that the delegates had the privilege of free transmission of messages—a hint to the former President to expand his reply.

The dinner was marked by long speeches. Then came the big moment. One of the hosts arose and read the message from Coolidge.

It said: "Greetings."

T_{here} was a writer in England who not only appropriated a lot of Bertrand Russell's ideas for a book he was writing, but had the nerve to ask Russell to contribute an introduction when the work was completed. Lord Russell's reply consisted of two words: "Modesty forbids."

T_{he} late Senators Spooner, of Wisconsin, and Allison, of Iowa, were leaving the Capitol one evening when it started to rain heavily. "Do you think it will stop?" asked Spooner.

"Always has," answered Allison.

I_{nitiating} my young pupils into the mysteries of the French language, I explained that "Madame" was used in speaking of a married woman; "Mademoiselle," an unmarried woman; and "Monsieur," a gentleman. To see if the children understood, I turned to a boy who seemed rather bored and asked: "What is the difference between 'Madame' and 'Mademoiselle'?"

"Monsieur," came his prompt reply.

Recovering Their Wits

Opie Read, the humorist, was playing golf in a foursome when his ball landed in a sand trap. Hidden from view, he hacked away at the ball. When he finally drove it out and rejoined his friends, he was asked: "How many strokes, Opie?"

"Three."

"But we heard six!"

"Three," said Opie, "were echoes."

Once when Henry Clay failed to recognize a young lady, she said reproachfully, "Why, Mr. Clay, you don't remember my name!"

"No," answered the statesman in his most gallant manner, "for when we last met I was sure your beauty and accomplishments would soon compel you to change it."

Just as Al Jolson was about to go on the air in one of his radio programs, he got a long distance call from a pal in a distant city.

"The broadcast was great! You were marvelous, Al!" the friend gushed.

"But heavens, man!" shouted Jolson, "I haven't even started yet."

For a moment there was silence, then this comeback: "Yeah, but you forget the three hours difference in time. You're all through here."

An unusually understanding English wife, whose husband had been away on a business trip, received a call from the town's local gossip. "I feel I should tell you that I saw your husband at Blackpool last weekend," she reported, "walking along the beach with a very attractive blonde on his arm."

"Well, what would you expect him to have on his arm at his age?" the wife snapped. "A pail and shovel?"

Jimmy Walker, the former mayor of New York City, was gifted with a rare and spontaneous sense of humor. One night at a banquet Walker had been introduced and had just started to speak when the speakers' platform gave way. In the confusion and even as the platform was collapsing, Jimmy quipped: "Reminds me of some of the platforms I've run on."

At a reception in Washington, a young man was asked by a widow to guess her age. "You must have some idea," she said as he hesitated.

"I have several ideas," he admitted with a smile. "The only trouble is that I hesitate whether to make you ten years younger on account of your looks, or ten years older on account of your brains."

A lady approached her Congressman one day and held out her hand. "Now confess," she said, "that you've forgotten all about me."

He had. He knew her face, but his memory would serve him no further. But with a low bow he replied, "Madam, I've made it the business of my life to try to forget you."

Once when Eve Arden was appearing in summer stock, her co-star decided to spring a practical joke. In a scene where he and Eve spoke to each other across the stage, he had a phone in the actress's corner ring out in the middle of her recital. Eve retained enough stage presence to answer the phone. Thinking quickly, she turned to the prankster and said, "It's for you."

Pardon My Put-Down

When a woman was described as rude to her inferiors, Dorothy Parker is said to have asked, "Where does she find them?"

The Admiral heading a bureau in Washington refused to accept recommendations without numerous corrections, and the bureau's work lagged sadly. Prodded to speed up operations, the admiral summoned his staff. "Whatever bottlenecks exist," he concluded, "I demand that you get rid of them. Any comments?"

"Sir," said a reserve officer, "in my experience with bottles, I've observed that the necks are always at the top."

One night at a stuffy party, John Barrymore was trying to hide from the other guests. A notorious bore searched him out, however, and sat down beside him. "It's good to see you, Mr. Barrymore," he said. "You're the first person I've met tonight worth talking to."

"I must say," replied Barrymore, "that you're more fortunate than I."

At a party playwright George S. Kaufman was forced to listen to a bore relating a seemingly interminable story. Suddenly the man stopped and said, "Excuse me, I seem to be getting ahead of myself."

Kaufman placed his hand on the other's arm. "Please," he implored, "don't turn back."

Jack Warner of Hollywood, holding forth to young Randolph Churchill concerning the art of producing, was exasperated by the irrepressible Churchill's interjected suggestions for improving Warner Brothers' output. Finally he exclaimed, "Young man, when you are my age. . . ."

"You'll be 80," finished Churchill.

Joe LaGore of Paducah, Kentucky, tells about the fellow who swaggered into a hotel elevator, and as it moved upward, started trying to impress the pretty young operator. "I'll bet all these stops and starts make you mighty tired," he cooed.

"I really don't mind the stops and starts," she said icily. "But I do get tired of all the jerks!"

My commanding officer at an Army base in the South was the son of a well-known senator—a fact that he never let anyone forget. He was bawling out a lanky mountaineer one day, and in the course of his tirade asked, "Do you know who my father is?"

The mountain lad looked him straight in the eye. "Why, no, suh," he replied. "Don't you?"

At a dinner attended by Charles de Gaulle during World War II, a French general was telling the story of his escape from Germany. It was his moment of glory, and he went into minute detail. The narration lasted from the soup right through the dessert. At last he was finished. De Gaulle said quietly, "And now, *mon général*, tell us how you were captured."

The bus was already crowded when an enormously fat woman entered. She stood for a moment glaring at the seated passengers. Then she asked, "Isn't some gentleman going to offer me his seat?"

At this a little wisp of a man rose. "Well," he said timidly, "I'm ready to make a small contribution."

Lady Nancy Astor once got annoyed at Churchill. "Winston," she said sharply, "if you were my husband, I'd put poison in your coffee."

"And if I were your husband, Nancy," said Churchill, "I'd drink it."

A notorious puffed-head was supping with Oscar Levant in Hollywood's Brown Derby when the fellow soliloquized: "I wonder if all my fans will love me when my acting days are over?"

"Of course they do," came Oscar's assurance.

In *The Vicious Circle* Margaret Case Harriman writes about her father, Frank Case: "He could not abide the grimy horrors of William Faulkner's books. Meeting Faulkner in the lobby of the Algonquin Hotel one day, he said, 'Hello, how are you?' and Faulkner replied that he wasn't feeling so well, he'd had kind of an upset stomach lately. 'Ah,' said Father, 'something you wrote, no doubt.'"

At a restaurant an elderly wolf had made several futile attempts to flirt with the pretty young waitress who was serving him. Finally, when she brought his dessert, he grew a little more bold. "My dear," he purred, "where have you been all my life?"

"Well," said the girl, "for the first 40 years anyway, I probably wasn't born."

John Barrymore, watching a tense football game, was distracted by the man next to him, who bragged, "When I was in college I helped Harvard beat Yale three times in succession."

"That so?" snapped Barrymore. "Which team were you playing on?"

Sir C. Aubrey Smith, grand old gentleman of stage and screen, liked to dine quietly. Consequently he was rather put out when, in a Hollywood restaurant, he happened to be seated near a noisy diner who kept yelling for the waiter. "What do you have to do," demanded the noisy one finally, "to get a glass of water in this dump?"

The sedate Sir Aubrey turned and quietly said: "Why don't you try setting yourself on fire?"

At the Stork Club, a bore was describing what happened to him on a trip to Grand Canyon. "There I stood," he orated, "drinking in the scene, with the giant abyss yawning before me."

"Was it yawning," interrupted his dinner partner, "before you got there?"

What a beautiful suit you're wearing," cooed one woman at a cocktail party. "I like it better every time I see it."

The other woman thanked her. Then, fingering the material of her friend's dress, she retaliated: "That's such lovely cloth, my dear. You really should have it made into a dress!"

Actress Beatric Lillie said to comedian Bob Hope: "I'm approaching the age of 30."

"Tell me, Bea," he queried, "from which direction?"

Cold Comfort

Really, Helen," he said when he saw her for the first time in five years, "you've changed so I would hardly have known you."

"That's a little ambiguous," she answered archly. "For better or worse?"

"Why," he said enthusiastically, "you could change only for the better, of course!"

The victim, a woman in her early 30s, told this one:

It had been several weeks since a prosperous farmer had been in the bank where she worked. "Miss Lee," he greeted her, "you seem to be getting a little stouter."

"Don't you know you musn't ever tell a woman she is getting fat?" she chided.

"Oh," he said with surprise, "I didn't think a woman your age would mind."

Frank Nye, brother of the well-known humorist Bill Nye, once innocently made a political speech in a town whose citizens were almost solidly on the opposite side of the fence. The audience joyously hissed and booed throughout the address. Afterward the auditorium janitor undertook to comfort the shaken campaigner. "Never mind, Mr. Nye," the old Irishman said. "This bunch is nothing but the rag-tag and bobtail of the town. Everyone with any sense stayed at home."

Madame de Stael, one of the most brilliant women of her time, was, physically, very unattractive. At one of her salons, all male guests, save one, deserted her upon the entrance of a celebrated beauty. With a cynical smile she turned to the man who stood by. "Prince, I want you to answer me honestly. Were you, the beauty, and I in a small boat in a storm, and it overturned, which would you save: the beauty or me?"

The Prince bowed, and answered: "Madame, you swim so well."

In a photography studio a society matron was looking at a new picture she'd had taken. "Why that picture's an outrage!" she stormed. "Now I ask you, does it look like me?"

The suave photographer was flustered for a moment, but quickly regained his composure. "Madam," he said, bowing slightly, "the answer is in the negative."

A salty Maine lobsterman, who made a tidy summer income hauling "trippers" in his small fishing boat, was known far and wide for the yarns he spun. One day a newcomer, an ample widow still sporting her city clothes and manners, raised her voice against the wind and shrilled, "Captain, they tell me you're the biggest liar on the Maine coast."

"Madame"—the battered straw hat came off in a sweep, the captain bowed in as courtly a gesture as the roll of the boat permitted—"Madame, you are the most beautiful woman I ever saw in my life!"

On his first trip to America, actor Robert Morley ran into Llewellyn Rees, a fellow actor and old friend from England. Rees seemed very pleased and said, "It's nice meeting old friends. A lot of people think I'm dead."

"Not if they look closely," Morley assured him.

A member of the Coolidge Cabinet with whom the President remonstrated became angry and said: "Sir, do you think I am a fool?"

"Why, no," returned Coolidge. "Of course, I might be mistaken."

Lord Beaverbrook, publisher of the London *Daily Express,* once printed a violently insulting editorial about a certain young Member of Parliament. A few days later he found himself face to face with the M.P. in the washroom of a London men's club. "My dear chap," Beaverbrook said, "I've been thinking it over, and I was wrong. Here and now, I wish to apologize."

"Very well," muttered the M.P. "But the next time, I wish you'd insult me in the washroom and apologize in your newspaper!"

I always wonder," said a friend to Anita Loos, "how you could write *Gentlemen Prefer Blondes* when you are a brunette."

"That's how I know," sighed Anita.

Parting Shots

When the naturalist Thoreau was near to death, a very pious aunt asked him in deep concern: "Henry, have you made your peace with God?"

"I didn't know that we had ever quarreled," was the reply.

The wife of a middle-aged business executive met him at his office late one afternoon. As they were going down in the elevator, it stopped and a high-octane secretary got on. Poking the executive in the ribs, she said gaily: "Hello, cutie pie!"

Unperturbed, the executive's wife leaned over with a smile and announced, "I'm Mrs. Pie."

After a dance at the University of North Carolina, one member came back to his fraternity house with tie askew, hair disheveled, shirt torn and face scratched. Asked what had happened, the chap drew himself up and said, "Sir, I have been fighting over the honor of a lady."

"Which side were you on?"

One rainy night in New York when there were no taxis to be had, actor Monty Woolley started down the stairs of the Times Square subway. Halfway down he slipped, a stout lady toppled against him, and they ended up on the bottom step with the lady sitting in Woolley's lap. He tapped her briskly on the shoulder. "I'm sorry, madam," he rasped, "but this is as far as I go."

How do you grow old so gracefully?" an admirer asked Alexandre Dumas.

"Madam, I give all my time to it."

A notorious pest, meeting James McNeill Whistler one afternoon, exclaimed familiarly, "Hello, Whistler, I passed your house today."

"Thank you," retorted the artist.

At a reception I was talking to a friendly stranger who had arrived late. "I don't know what's the matter with that tall man over there," I said rather querulously. "He was so attentive a while ago, but he won't look at me now."

"Perhaps he saw me come in," she replied. "He's my husband."

After a year's contract with a Hollywood studio, the famous French director René Clair was called into the front office and told that although his work was splendid it wasn't what the studio had in mind. Maybe it would be better if he found a new assignment. Clair agreed, and, in parting, said: "I want you to know that I've enjoyed every minute I've spent at 19th Century-Fox."

Pert, pretty and in a hurry, she sailed round a corner into New York's Fifth Avenue. Tall and in equal haste, he came in the opposite direction. They crashed head-on, stepped back to apologize, then started off again—directly in the other's path. Five times they blocked one another, first on this side, then that. Finally, his exasperated drawl brought her to a dead halt: "Just once more, honey, then I really have to go."

Out of This World:
THE DEAR DEPARTED

I T SEEMS TO BE a fact that death has stimulated about as much humor as any other subject except sex. Says the Chinese philosopher Lin Yutang: "A solemn funeral is inconceivable to the Chinese mind." An English detective-story writer (no Chinese blood, I believe) makes a similar observation: "Death seems to provide the minds of the Anglo-Saxon race with a greater fund of innocent amusement than any other single subject." And in our own country the great Broadway hit of some years ago, *Arsenic and Old Lace,* garnered its laughs largely from its cheerful view of human mortality. No matter how irrational it may be to think so, it remains true that there is something perennially funny about an undertaker. People even used to find diversion in the idea of a public hanging—or maybe it wasn't the idea so much as the execution: they all enjoyed a good choke. Shakespeare usually wrote beautifully or solemnly or terrifyingly about death. But on many occasions (the gravedigger scene in *Hamlet* was doubtless played for laughs) he got his effects by introducing humor. The lines

> *Golden lads and girls all must,*
> *As chimney-sweepers, come to Dust*

draw all their poignancy from the pathetic little pun. As for deathbed remarks, I know of only one that is perfect: Lady Mary Wortley Montagu's "It has all been very interesting."

The Quick and the Dead

A New Hampshire farmer had been urged to attend the funeral of his neighbor's third wife. "But I'm not goin'," he announced to his own wife.

"Goodness sakes, why not?" she asked.

"Well, Mary, I'm beginnin' to feel kinda awkward about goin' so often without anything of the sort to ask him back to."

The *Springfield Republican,* edited by Samuel Bowles, which rarely made a mistake, once reported the death of a citizen who was very much alive. He came into the editor's office later in the day to protest.

"I'm sorry, but if the *Republican* says you're dead, then you are dead," insisted Bowles. The only compromise he would make, after long discussion, was to print the man's name in the birth notices the next morning.

He was not a popular man, and the passing of the years did nothing to improve his disposition or increase his popularity. When he died, the few people who showed up at the funeral tried their best to say something nice about the deceased. Later, some of the mourners wound up in the barbershop, still trying to say something nice.

Finally the head barber came to their assistance. "You know," he said, "he was not a hard man to shave."

A certain sentimental bricklayer had, from the first, worked in the building of the National Cathedral at Washington. When his good wife died, the authorities at the Cathedral were embarrassed by his request that she be sealed in one of its crypts—along with Woodrow Wilson, Admiral Dewey, and the like. Tactfully they told him it might not be. But he seemed no whit offended when he returned to work after the funeral and cremation. He mixed his mortar and laid his bricks with his usual cheerfulness. On the way home from work that day, one of his fellow workmen tried to incite him to a decent resentment about the uppity refusal. The bricklayer's wife had a *right* to be buried in the Cathedral. The bricklayer responded with an enigmatic smile. "She's there, all right." he said..

A man went to Florida for his health, but, unfortunately, died there. His body was shipped back to New York, and as the widow was viewing the remains at the funeral parlor, a friend remarked, "Doesn't he look wonderful!"

"Yes," replied the widow. "I think those two weeks in Florida did him a world of good."

In the lower left corner of a page of the Cleveland *News* was a two-column patent medicine testimonial from a Mr. Alexander Kellough, of 2508 Morris Black Place, who rejoiced to find himself now rid of backache, insomnia, sour stomach and gas pains, and enthusiastically concluded: "Giljan is a wonderful medicine. Any person with trouble such as mine should lose no time in taking it."

In column seven of the same page appeared a briefer notice: "Kellough, Alexander . . . passed away at late residence, 2508 Morris Black Place."

Through a coincidence in published names, Louis Zucconi of California was thought by some of his friends to have died. A couple of weeks after the announcement, when he was walking down a street, he bumped into an old buddy. The latter paled slightly, then blurted, "Louie! Hey, I'm sorry I didn't make your funeral, but I did send flowers!"

Insurance companies often come across unique evasions on the forms applicants fill out. One man, in the space asking the cause of parental death, wrote, "Father was taking part in a public function and the platform gave way, ending his life." Subsequent investigation disclosed that his father had been hanged for cattle rustling.

Exit Laughing

Were you able to sell old MacTavish a grave?" asked the superintendent of the cemetery.

The secretary shook his head. "He was afraid he might not get the full value of it," he explained.

"But, hang it all, a man has got to die sometime!" exclaimed the superintendent.

"That's what I told him, but he only answered, 'Suppose I get lost at sea?' "

A certain chap has the craftiest business-expense dodge that we've come upon lately. As owner of a cemetery property, he daily records an expense-account item which he classifies as: "Lunch with prospect."

Cousin Bob," as he was affectionately known to everyone in the little Missouri town, had just passed his 70th year. "But, Cousin Bob," asked a neighbor commiseratingly, "don't you hate to get old?"

"Hell, no!" snapped Cousin Bob. "If I weren't old, I'd be dead!"

A dilemma occurred at the deathbed of one of the many millionaires who had moved from New York to sunny California. His family had to ask him an extremely sensitive question.

A son finally put the question to him: "Since you have a cemetery plot back in New York and a plot in California, where do you wish to be buried?"

The old man looked up and with a twinkle in his eye said, "Surprise me!"

The city of Kissimmee, Florida, sold its old parking meters for $5 each to any citizen who could think of a use for them. One woman bought one to set aside for eventual use as a tombstone. She felt it would be appropriate, since the flag bore the word "Expired."

Comedian Harry Hershfield told about the dictator in an oxygen tent who was sinking fast. By his bedside was his second in command, tears streaming down his face. The dictator feebly patted his aide's hand. "Do not grieve so, comrade," he whispered. "I want you to know that because of your loyalty I am leaving you my money, my cars, my plane, my country estate, my yacht—everything!"

"Thank you, thank you," cried his successor. "You're much too good to me. If there was only something I could do for *you!*"

The dying man boosted himself up a bit. "There is," he gasped. "Just take your foot off the oxygen tube!"

In Mansfield, Louisiana, a doctor running for election for coroner circulated this card: "Be 'Dead Right.' Vote for Dr. J. Segura, Jr., for coroner."

A friend's wife answered the doorbell and faced a young man selling plots in one of our large cemeteries. When she told him that they already had a plot in another cemetery, he seemed uncertain as to his next move. But he recovered to say politely, "I hope you'll be very happy there."

A Londoner found this note, written on a funeral parlor's letterhead, pinned to the windshield of his automobile: "You are parked in front of my driveway. I look forward to being of service to you soon."

A former undertaker, who applied for a job with a Charlotte, North Carolina, business firm, was asked: "What did you like most about your former job?"

To which he replied: "Working with people."

The prize of all radio announcements was heard in California. A plummy-voiced gentleman was pleading for his sponsor, who built mausoleums: "Ladies and gentlemen," said he, in organ tones, "is seepage disturbing your loved ones?"

Leave It to Them

My weakness is insurance policies, and fitting them all into the family budget is quite a problem. A few months ago, I told my wife about the agent's latest idea for increasing our insurance, and she blew her top. I hastened to explain that the policies were designed to take care of her and the children in case I died. "Yes, I know," she sighed. "But what will we do in case you live?"

A Boston bachelor bequeathed his fortune to the three girls who turned down his offer of marriage, because: "I owe them what peace and happiness I have enjoyed."

The poet Heinrich Heine bequeathed all his property to his wife on condition that she remarry immediately. "Because," said Heine, "there will then be at least one man to regret my death."

I had taken to my bed because of a bad cold. Feeling singularly sorry for myself and wanting sympathy, I began to work out how much my wife would be worth if I died. After I told her that she would collect around $40,000, she scolded me for having such awful thoughts, saying that I was the only thing she wanted.

After a pause, and in a milder tone, she said, "Does that include your GI insurance?"

The French novelist Honoré de Balzac loved the good things of life. So when an uncle, who was old and stingy, left him a sizable sum, Balzac wrote friends the good news in these words: "Yesterday, at five in the morning, my uncle and I passed on to a better life."

Six prominent Berkeley men were named as pallbearers in the will of a man who died penniless and owing them considerable sums. "They have been wonderful creditors," the will said, "and I would like to have them carry me to the end."

Several elderly church members were being asked to what they attributed their longevity. "And why do you think God has permitted you to reach the age of 92?" one wealthy old lady was asked.

Without hesitation she responded: "To test the patience of my relatives."

An elderly gentleman—wealthy and very deaf—came into our shop to purchase a much improved hearing aid. Two weeks later he returned to report that he could hear conversations quite easily, even in the next room.

"Your friends and relatives must be very happy that you can hear so much better," I said.

"Oh, I haven't told them," he chuckled. "I've been sitting around listening—and do you know what? I've changed my will twice!"

R. I. P.

EPITAPHS IN OLD CHURCHYARDS
FROM THE COLLECTION OF
CARL S. CLANCY

IN MEMORY OF ANNA HOPEWELL
Here lies the body of our Anna
Done to death by a banana
It wasn't the fruit that laid her low
But the skin of the thing that made her go.

SACRED TO THE MEMORY OF JARED BATES
Who died August the 6th, 1800.
His widow, aged 24, lives at 7 Elm Street,
Has every qualification for a good wife,
And yearns to be comforted.

IN MEMORY OF MR. PETER DANIELS
Born August 7, 1688. Died May 20, 1746.
Beneath this stone, a lump of clay,
Lies Uncle Peter Daniels,
Who too early in the month of May
Took off his winter flannels.

Here lies the body of Susan Lowder
Who burst while drinking Sedlitz Powder
Called from this world to her Heavenly rest
She should have waited till it effervesced.

Beneath this stone in hopes of Zion
Is laid the landlord of the Lion
Resigned unto the Heavenly Will
His son keeps on the business still.

A visitor to the 18th-century cemetery at Wiscasset, Maine, reports a tombstone over the grave of a farmer who out-lived two wives. He is buried between them. His epitaph reads: "Here I lie between two good wives, Tillie and Millie. I loved them both—but tilt me a little toward Tillie."

Self-Composed Epitaphs:
Don Herold: This is too deep for me.
Clive Brook: Excuse me for not rising.
Lionel Barrymore: Well, I've played everything but a harp.
Owen Davis: Here lies an author—as usual.
W. C. Fields: On the whole I'd rather be in Philadelphia.
Fontaine Fox: I had a hunch something like this would happen.
William Haines: Here's something I want to get off my chest.

The manager of a marble works was commissioned several weeks ago by a young widow to carve on her husband's monument: "My sorrow is more than I can bear." Then just the other day, the manager reports, the widow—wearing a new wedding band—returned and asked him to add the word "alone" to the epitaph.

Here lies Pierre Victor Fournier, inventor of the Everlasting Lamp, which consumes only one centime's worth of oil in one hour. He was a good father, son and husband. His inconsolable widow continues his business in the Rue aux Trois. Goods sent to all parts of the City. Do not mistake the opposite shop for this.

Clause in the will of Harriet Hartbyrne, who died a spinster at age 87: "I don't want anybody to put 'Miss' on my tombstone—I haven't missed as much as some people may think!"

Blithe Spirits

Medium at séance: "Please, Harry—if you didn't take it with you, where is it?"

When Lord Bessborough died some years ago, the London *Times* published in error the obituary of Lord Desborough. Somewhat taken aback, Desborough telephoned the *Times* to report that he had just read his own obituary. A grand voice replied, "I see, sir. And where are you speaking from?"

A certain country minister posted this notice on the church door: "Brother Smith departed for Heaven at 4:30 a.m."
    The next day he found written below: "Heaven, 9:00 a.m. Smith not in yet. Great anxiety."

In England, where ghosts abound, there are doughty souls who take them in their stride. For instance, a visiting missionary acknowledged cheerfully at breakfast that the family's ghost had paid him a bedside visit. "He didn't keep me awake," he added. "He vanished as soon as I asked him for a contribution."

Then there was the house guest, wandering lost in a maze of dark corridors, who was accosted by a ghost who declaimed that it had been pacing the halls, nightly, for seven centuries. "Good," was the guest's reaction, "then you can tell me the way to the bathroom?"

Did you hear about the ghost who was so shy he couldn't even spook for himself?

If two ghosts went to school together, would they be known as ghoulmates?

Rain lashed the windows of the old castle, and the wind howled mournfully as the timid guest was escorted to his room under the castle eaves. "Has anything unusual ever happened in this room?" he asked the sinister-looking butler.

"Not for 40 years."

Heaving a sigh of relief, the guest asked, "What happened then?"

The butler's eyes glittered ominously as he hissed, "A man who stayed here all night showed up in the morning."

Affairs of Moment:
OUR PUBLIC SERVANTS

THE MOST REMARKABLE thing about our political humor, from Mark Twain through Mr. Dooley to Art Buchwald, is that it often manages to be funny, even though politicians, merely by being themselves, generally do the job so much more effectively. "One must have a heart of stone," said Oscar Wilde, "to read the death of Little

Nell without laughing." Similarly, one must have the im-
mobility of a statue to read without writhing the jokes credited to most of our Presidents. The editors of this volume
have done their best, poor fellows, but one look at the
humor attributed here to Jackson, McKinley, Wilson,
Coolidge, Eisenhower, and F.D.R. will explain why when a
genuinely witty man, Adlai Stevenson, proposed himself
for the Presidency we rejected him in a panic. No aspirant
for high office since Stevenson has dared to be amusing—
even Eugene McCarthy is careful to curb his naturally witty
intelligence. We like our political representatives to be
dull fellows. If they weren't, perhaps we couldn't snicker at
politicking, surely one of the most undignified vocations
ever invented by man.

Vox Populi

When Ken Gray, Illinois Democrat, was running for a
third term in Congress, he spotted a farmer leaning on a
fence post and stopped to shake hands and introduce himself. "I'm Ken Gray, your congressman," he said.

The farmer, quite hard of hearing, said, "You're who?"

Gray replied, "I'm your congressman, Ken Gray." The
old man still looked puzzled.

Trying a new tack, Gray bellowed, "I'm Ken Gray, and
I'm running for Congress and would like to have your
vote."

The old farmer's face brightened and he said, "You'll
sure get my vote, son. That guy we've got in there now
isn't worth a damn."

POLITICAL POLL — 1776

ART BUCHWALD

THE POLLSTER has become such an important part of the American scene it's hard to imagine how this nation ever functioned without him. What would have happened, for example, if there'd been political pollsters in the early days of this country? This is how the results might have turned out:

Asked if they thought that the British were doing a good job in administering the Colonies, a cross section of the people responded:

British doing good job	63%
Not doing good job	22%
Don't know	15%

Next question: "Do you think that the dumping of tea in the Boston Harbor helped or hurt the taxation laws in the New World?"

Hurt the cause of taxation	9%
Helped the cause	12%
Didn't make any difference	9%

"Which of these two Georges can do more for the Colonies: George III or George Washington?"

George III	76%
George Washington	14%
Others	10%

It is interesting to note that 80 percent of the people questioned had never heard of George Washington.

"What do you think our image is in England after the Minute

Men attacked the British at Lexington?"

Minute Men hurt our image	83%
Gave British new respect for us	10%
Undecided	7%

"Do you think that the Declaration of Independence is a good —or bad—document?"

Good document	12%
Bad document	14%
No opinion	74%

A group of those polled felt that the Declaration of Independence had been written by radicals and that the publishing of it at this time would only bring harsher measures from the British.

"Do you think that Patrick Henry did the right thing in demanding liberty or death?"

Did a foolhardy thing, was a troublemaker	53%
Did a brave thing, made his point	23%
Should have gone through courts	16%
Don't know	8%

On the basis of the results, the militant Colonials decided they did not have enough popular support to foment a revolution and gave up the idea of creating a United States of America.

———— • ————

Not long ago I found myself in a small, mid-Kansas town and fell into conversation with a bright-eyed, 70-year-old farmer who asked, "Where you from, son?"

"Washington," I replied.

"Washington, D.C.?"

"That's right."

"You've got some pretty smart fellas back there, ain't ya?" he asked. I nodded. "You've got some that ain't so smart, too, ain't ya?" Again, I agreed. "Damn hard to tell the difference, ain't it?" he concluded.

———— • ————

An election candidate was making door-to-door visits. One door was opened by a stern-faced woman.

"Well?" she said.

"What party does your husband belong to, madam?" the candidate asked.

"Young man," replied the woman, bristling, "I'm the party he belongs to!"

Haughty dowager to public-opinion-poll investigator: "I never vote! It's quite a relief not to feel responsible for what goes on in Washington."

Asked what he thought of the two candidates for the election, an enlightened voter replied: "Well, when I look at them I'm thankful only one of them can get elected."

Wife to husband: "All I know about politics is that my vote usually cancels out yours."

One spring day in San Francisco, the announcer on KTVU's "Televote" said: "One of the major issues in Washington is retransigence. Senator Garred Zender says it should be part of our international dealings. Others, including most Republicans, say it shouldn't. So our question on Televote today is: Should the United States adopt retransigence in its foreign policy?" The phones immediately started ringing and when they had stopped, 62 votes had been recorded for retransigence, 38 against.

Don't bother to look up "retransigence" in your dictionary. There's no such word. It was the station's April Fool joke, but the response—completely serious—was a little frightening.

In Indianapolis, a young man circulated an open letter in the Indiana General Assembly suggesting a youth council to help keep teen-agers out of trouble. The letter concluded with the observation that "the juvenile deliquent of today is the senator or representative of tomorrow."

Overheard in a Washington, D.C., restaurant—one girl to another: "What I'm looking for is a man who will treat me as if I were a voter and he a candidate."

Housewife over telephone: "Hello, Mr. Gallup? I've changed my mind!"

Running Scared

When a certain Southerner announced that he was "a favorite son," one of his enemies roared: "That's the greatest unfinished sentence in the history of the Southland!"

After giving what he considered a stirring, fact-filled campaign speech, the candidate looked out at his audience and confidently asked, "Now, are there any questions?"

"Yes," came a voice from the rear. "Who else is running?"

In Alabama a veteran, discharged from a mental hospital, announced his candidacy for Congress with the slogan: "I'm the only politician in Alabama with papers to prove he's not crazy."

Most politicians have four speeches: what they have written down, what they actually say, what they wish they had said, and what they are quoted as saying.

Will Rogers covered several presidential campaigns. At one 1932 national convention, a reporter said to him, "I'm covering strictly the serious side of the convention, Mr. Rogers, so if I see anything humorous, I'll let you know."

"Thanks," said Rogers. "And if I see anything serious happen, I'll let *you* know!"

If you eliminate the names of Lincoln. Washington, Roosevelt, Jackson and Wilson," said Will Rogers, "both conventions would get out three days earlier."

The Democratic convention of 1924 cast 104 ballots before finally choosing John W. Davis as its candidate for the Presidency. As a result of the apparent deadlock the delegates were away from home longer than they had expected to be.

An old-timer recalls that at one point the Massachusetts chairman called his delegates together and said, "Gentlemen, we've got to make a choice. Either we pick a cheaper hotel or a more liberal candidate."

Are you going to take all this lying down?" boomed the election candidate. "No!" shouted a member of the audience. "The reporters are doing that."

The latest Martian story is about one who landed in Las Vegas. After watching a series of players pumping the arm of a slot machine, the Martian stepped up to the slot machine and whispered, "I don't know what office you're running for, buddy, but try to smile a little more when you shake those hands."

From the Burlington, Iowa, *Hawk-Eye Gazette:* "'I've never campaigned on anybody's shortcomings and I never will,' he declared. 'I try to get elected on my own.'"

Admirer to Senatorial candidate after speech: "Great speech, sir—I like the straightforward way you dodged those issues."

The politician's promises of yesterday are the taxes of today.

Brooks Hays, former Arkansas representative, tells of a Congressman whose primary came right in the middle of the session, making a difficult decision necessary. He put it like this in a stump speech when he finally got home for a brief visit: "My friends, I pondered long the question, should I stay in Washington and protect the taxpayers, or come down home to look after my petty political interests? In these meditations I drifted into the Capitol, where I paused in front of the statue of Thomas Jefferson to put the question to him. I could almost see his marble lips move, and his voice came crystal-clear: 'Stay here.'"

In a campaign speech the next day his opponent told the voters: "You'd better elect me instead of a fellow who goes around mumbling to statues."

A group of reporters waited outside the office of a senator campaigning for re-election. Suddenly the door flew open. "Quick!" the candidate shouted to his secretary. "Where's that list of people I call by their first names?"

During his first race for mayor of New York City in 1929, Fiorello La Guardia charged the popular Jimmy Walker with all sorts of corruption, and Walker never answered a single charge. "Why should I make his campaign for him?" he said to me. "I won't build him up. It would be fun, though, to ask him one question—what was he doing in Waterbury on July 16, 1928?"

"Was he there at that time?" I asked.

"I dunno," Walker replied. "But if I asked that question, he could deny he was there until he was blue in the face. A lot of suckers would still believe there was something very fishy about him and Waterbury."

Notice in the Waltham, Massachusetts, *News-Tribune:* "I want to thank the 300 voters of Ward 5 who endorsed my nomination for city councillor; also the 600 voters who said they would vote for me, the 400 who said they did, and especially the 92 who voted for me. Raymond A. Hayes."

Mr. President

A delegation from Kansas, calling upon Theodore Roosevelt at Oyster Bay, was met by the President with coat and collar off. "Ah, gentlemen," he said, mopping his brow, "I'm delighted to see you, but I'm very busy putting in my hay just now. Come down to the barn and we'll talk things over while I work."

When they reached the barn, there was no hay waiting to be thrown into the mow. "James!" shouted the President to his hired man in the loft. "Where's that hay?"

"I'm sorry, sir," admitted James, "but I just ain't had time to throw it back since you forked it up for yesterday's delegation."

President Roosevelt's favorite story was about the commuter from Westchester County, a Republican stronghold, who always walked into his station, handed the newsboy a quarter, picked up the New York *Herald Tribune,* glanced at the front page and then handed it back as he rushed out to catch his train. Finally the newsboy, unable to control his curiosity any longer, asked his customer why he only glanced at the front page.

"I'm interested in the obituary notices," said the customer.

"But they're way over on page 24, and you never look at them," the boy objected.

"Boy," said the tycoon, "the _____ _____ I'm interested in will be on page one, all right!"

Andrew Jackson, before he became President, was once making a stump speech in a small village. Just as he was finishing, a friend who sat near him whispered: "Tip 'em a little Latin, General; they won't be contented without it."

The man of the iron will thought upon the few phrases he knew, and in a voice of thunder wound up with "E pluribus unum, sine qua non, ne plus ultra, multum in parvo." The effect was tremendous, and the shouts of the Hoosiers could be heard for miles.

Coolidge had humor and sense enough to escape that exaggeration of the ego that afflicts a good many of our Presidents. He was once intercepted taking a nap in the middle of a presidential executive day. When he opened his eyes, he grinned and asked: "Is the country still here?"

When Mrs. Calvin Coolidge went abroad after her husband's death, she feared there would be unnecessary fuss made over the wife of an ex-President. But the friend with whom she was traveling said, "Don't worry. In the little places where we'll be stopping they don't know one President of the United States from another. People won't bother you." And no one did—until in a small Italian town they received word that reservations for them were made in the next town. This sounded ominous. When they reached the hotel in question they were received pompously by the manager. Bowing profoundly, he said, "We are proud to welcome the wife of the great President of the United States. Will you register, Mrs. Lincoln?"

President William McKinley, campaigning for re-election, once made a speech from the rear platform of his train at a whistle stop in Indiana. As the train pulled out and he waved to the crowd, he dropped a glove, one of an expensive pigskin pair. Whereupon, with the accuracy of a ballplayer, he tossed the other glove so that it came to rest beside its mate. "There is nothing more maddening than to find one glove," he explained to the man standing next to him.

Abraham Lincoln was resting with his managers in a hotel lobby. As usual the village dudes had congregated there, and one, bolder than the rest, remarked: "Mr. Lincoln, your speech was good but there were some points quite beyond my reach."

The simple Lincoln looked up and chuckled, "I'm sorry for you; I once had a dog that had the same trouble with fleas."

Harry Truman, talking politics with a group of Yale students, was asked by one earnest youth, "How do I start in politics, sir?"

Replied the former President, "You've already started. You're spending somebody else's money, aren't you?"

William Allen White, the famous editor of the Emporia *Gazette,* once asked Franklin D. Roosevelt for a picture of the President in one of his favorite seersucker suits. F.D.R. sent it in a letter which began: "Dear Bill: Here is the seersucker picture, duly inscribed by the sucker to the seer."

The White House was undergoing one of its periodic piecemeal repairs. President Calvin Coolidge found his way to the attic one day when the architect and the contractor were there looking at the roof rafters and girders. The architect pointed out to him the bad condition of the timbers charred from the fire the British had set in 1814. He insisted they be replaced. The question was, should it be done with wood or the more expensive steel beams?

The President carefully examined the charred wood, then turned to the contractor and said, "All right. Put in the steel beams and send the bill to the King of England."

When Woodrow Wilson was president of Princeton University the mother of one of the students urged him to make it a coeducational institution.

"Why?" he asked.

"To remove the false glamour with which the two sexes see each other," she replied.

"My dear madam," Wilson shot back, "that is the very thing we want to preserve at all costs."

When Truman returned to Independence, Missouri, to vote in the 1948 elections, a group of newspapermen were assigned to stay close to him at all times. They landed at the Kansas City airport and found that the President had already arrived and was on his way home. With a noisy police escort scattering traffic out of the way, they raced after him in a press car, but when they reached the house he was not there. He turned up some time later and a worried reporter asked him what had happened.

"Oh," said Truman, "we were stopped by a police car and had to pull over. Seems there were some very important people going through town."

A chap who played golf in a foursome with President Eisenhower at the Cherry Hills Club in Denver shanked an approach shot. To his horror, the errant pellet flew toward the President and hit him in the right rear pocket. The mortified player raced toward the Chief Executive, all apologies. "Mr. President," he exclaimed, "I hope you aren't hurt."

The President gingerly rubbed the place where the ball had hit.

"I carry my wallet back there," said Ike. "This is the first time I've been touched there without being hurt!"

An old Springfield friend of Lincoln's, after an evening at the White House, asked, "How does it feel to be President?"

"You have heard," said Lincoln, "about the man tarred and feathered and ridden out of town on a rail? A man in the crowd asked him how he liked it, and his reply was that, if it wasn't for the honor of the thing, he would rather walk."

Party Lines

Grandpa, reading to four-year-old: "Now the first little pig was a fuzzy-thinking liberal who built his house of straw supplied by the federal government."

A woman who no longer shares her parents' political views received this letter from her mother: "Much as we love you, dear, your father and I wish you wouldn't come home for a visit until after the election."

For twenty years two senators, one a Democrat, the other a Republican, quarreled every day. Finally a third party intervened. "Boys, this must stop," he said. "Let's have a drink together and make peace."

The senators agreed, and when the drinks were served the friend cried, "Now make a toast to each other."

Raising his glass, the first senator said, "Here's wishing for you what you're wishing for me."

"Oh, now you're starting in again!" yelled the other.

Chapel speaker urging students to think more deeply about politics: "Many of you are Republicans because your fathers were Republicans. And many of you are Democrats because your fathers were Republicans."

Referring to politicians who give lip service to American principles while smashing them in practice, former President Herbert Hoover once said: "All this reminds me of the small girl who said, 'Mother, you know that beautiful jug you said has been handed down to us from generation to generation?' Mother replied, 'Yes, Ann, what of it?' And Ann answered solemnly, 'This generation dropped it.'"

A political convention is a gathering at which factions speak louder than wards.

Dark-horse candidates seldom say nay.

Switchboard operators at the Democratic National Committee headquarters in Washington were harassed one day by a flood of calls on one of a block of 20 telephone lines into the office. The word had spread that if you dialed FED UP 68 you would be connected to the Democrats. More conventionally, the number was 333-8768.

Will Rogers: "I can remember way back when a liberal was one who was generous with his own money."

Physician to patient: "We do have a heart available to you, but it belonged to a Democrat."

At a cabinet meeting one day Franklin D. Roosevelt gleefully told this story: An American Marine, ordered home from Guadalcanal, was disconsolate because he hadn't killed even one of the enemy. He stated his case to his superior officer, who said, "Go up on that hill over there and shout: 'To hell with Hirohito!' That will bring the Japs out of hiding."

The Marine did as he was bidden. Immediately a Japanese soldier came out of the jungle, shouting, "To hell with Roosevelt!"

"And of course," said the Marine, "I couldn't kill a Republican."

Capital Offenses

The world was created in six days, no Senate confirmation being necessary.

A State Department press officer being questioned by newsmen on a Vietnam story said, "I'd like to be evasive on that, but I've been ordered not even to do that."

When reporters asked former Under Secretary of State Robert J. McCloskey about the art of decision making, he answered: "One thing you must keep in mind here: that all decisions aren't made until all decisions are made."

I was in Washington recently," claims comedian Stu Allen, "and thought I might go into politics. I talked to one of the big men there, and he asked me what I could do. I said, 'Nothing,' and he said, 'Wonderful. Then we won't have to break you in.'"

Former Secretary of State Dean Rusk was being gently chided by a senator for straying afield in answering one of his questions at a Senate Foreign Relations Committee hearing. "When I was young up here on Capitol Hill," Rusk explained, "I was told, 'If you can't answer the question, answer another one.'"

The late Senator Everett Dirksen was a storied word merchant who once took 99 words to say, "I don't know." The question, asked on September 25, 1963, was whether a civil-rights bill would pass that year.

Ev's answer: "Well, what's today? The 25th? That's almost October. Which reminds me, I'd better start picking my apples. They're approaching a state of ripeness. So already you're into November. As you know so well, with November comes Thanksgiving, and that takes a big chunk out of a man's life. Before you know it, we're into December and then the Yuletide begins. It begins coursing through our veins. Downtown they'll be hanging wreaths and soon they'll be singing, 'Hark! The Herald Angels Sing' and after that, 'O Little Town of Bethlehem.' Where are we now? Who knows? Who is to say?"

During the course of a long and wearing committee session, Senator Dirksen was interrupted time after time by a Democratic colleague. Each time he yielded, but at length he tired of the interruptions.

"My good friend," he said, in his most honeyed accents, "you are interrupting the man I most like to hear."

Government bureau: Where the taxpayer's shirt is kept.

One of the hardest things for a Government official to understand about money matters is that it does.

Statesmanship is more difficult than politics. Politics is the art of getting along with people, whereas statesmanship is the art of getting along with politicians.

Washington appears to be filled with two kinds of politicians—those trying to get an investigation started, and those trying to get one stopped.

They Represent You

The late Senator Styles Bridges of New Hampshire told the story about one of his predecessors who came storming into the White House during the administration of Calvin Coolidge to complain that a man under consideration for a Republican senatorial nomination was "an out-and-out s.o.b."

"That could be," Coolidge conceded, "But there's a lot of them in the country and I think they are entitled to representation in the Senate."

ALL IN FAVOR OF
A CLEAR DAY
COREY FORD

OW I see where the government is going to regulate rain.
The President has signed a bill creating an Advisory
Committee on Weather Control, and it ought to be quite
a relief to the weatherman. From now on, when it pours on Sunday, people can blame the Administration.

It seems that weather has been getting out of hand ever since
they started to make rain by seeding clouds with silver iodide.
A lot of clouds simply can't handle the stuff, and sometimes a
young cumulus-cloud formation will get loaded and stagger
aimlessly across the landscape, shooting off bolts of lightning
and dousing Sunday-school picnics. It's all very well for a farmer
to create a private rainstorm in order to sprinkle his lower forty,
but when he succeeds in washing out a couple of bridges in the
adjoining county it's high time the government stepped in.

The first thing Congress will have to figure out is what kind of
weather people want. This is going to be hard. I took a little poll
last night coming home on the train, and the man next to me said
he hoped it would be clear tomorrow because he had just washed
the car. The man across the aisle said he hoped it would rain,
because otherwise his wife was planning to drag him to a lawn
party. Another man said he didn't care what it did as long as it
stayed cool so he wouldn't have to put up the screens, and the
man beside him said that he was counting on a warm day to get in
some golf. The conductor said all he wanted was for the weather
to make up its mind one way or the other because his corns hurt,

and by the time the train got to the station nobody was speaking. So you can see what Congress is going to be up against.

Consider the pressure that a congressman will be under once weather gets into politics. His agricultural constituents will bombard him with demands for a wet growing season, while the summer-resort people will fight a rainy spell tooth and nail. A delegation of umbrella manufacturers will present a petition, signed also by the slicker people, urging him to vote wet. A rival lobby representing the bathing-suit industry, backed up by the makers of sunglasses, will threaten to bolt him in the coming election unless he votes dry.

A bill sponsoring ice and blizzards will win him the loyal support of the long-woolen-underwear industry, the ski and skate interests, not to mention the crutch people, the splint people and the younger members of the medical profession who are trying to build up a practice; but it is bound to antagonize elderly ladies and postmen. The kite people, supported by the manufacturers of straw hats, will demand wind, but they will be vigorously opposed by ladies with knock-knees, and garden-club members who don't want to see their peonies knocked flat.

About the only people who will be satisfied either way are wives. A wife doesn't care what the weather is like on a weekend. If it's clear, her husband can (a) mow the lawn, (b) take down the storm windows or (c) finish painting the garage that he started last week but it rained. If it rains, he can (a) straighten up the attic, (b) get at that mess in the cellar or (c) paint the kitchen that he didn't finish the week before because the sun came out so he started the garage instead.

One solution for Congress, of course, is to do away with weather entirely. Unfortunately this would also do away with virtually all conversation in this country. People wouldn't even say "Good morning" any more, because there wouldn't be any other kind. Newspapers would have to get along without those little feature stories about a freak twister in Kansas that blew backward, unwinding all the clocks and straightening spiral staircases, or a bolt of lightning in Texas that chased a farmer clear across his pasture and snipped every button off his suspenders. Golfers couldn't blame their score on the fact that the sun got in their eyes. Old folks would have nothing to predict with their rheumatism. Postmen would not be not halted on their accustomed rounds by snow nor hail nor sleet. Nobody would save up for a rainy day.

But there are other solutions that the Committee on Weather

Control might consider:

1. Substitute something else for weather.
2. Leave the weather the way it is, but arrange it a little differently, so that the summer months would fall in the middle of winter
when they'd do more good.
3. Bring everything indoors.

———————— • ————————

Two delegates to a political meeting were arguing the merits
of their respective states. "Well," said one, "in my state we
have the finest governor and best legislature that money
can buy."

Washington *Roll Call,* the Capitol Hill newspaper, uses the
following gambit to attract advertisers: "Congressmen (our
devoted readers) spend more than $90 billion a year."

Card addressed to Senator Kenneth Keating of New York:
"I was given this card to urge you to support a bill I know
nothing about. Since I have complete confidence in your
judgment, I will use it instead to wish you a Happy Birthday."

One woman to another in Senate visitors' gallery: "Sometimes, during these filibusters, they give out real good reci-
pes."

A Congressman sent out questionnaires to his constituents
asking: "What do you think is the most important thing that
Congress could do?" One reply that came back was: "Mind
its own business."

Representative Ross Bass, of Tennessee, broke his rule
against sending more than ten government publications to
any one person at one time. He sent 76 of the do-it-yourself
pamphlets to a Tennessee man who pleaded: "Recently
married, expecting, just moved into new home and broke. I
do not know anything about anything. Neither does my wife.
Thanks."

———————— • ————————

One Congressman denies that his is a "me too" stand. "Having been to night school," he thunders, "I think of myself as an 'I also.'"

The sunflower is the state flower of Kansas. The state bird of Iowa is the goldfinch. In a relaxed mood one day, the Iowa legislature passed a resolution declaring the sunflower to be a "noxious weed." Reciprocating in kind, the Kansas legislature declared the goldfinch to be a "public nuisance."

Father to teen-age boy: "You should run for Congress, Sheldon. You're very good at introducing new bills in the house!"

Gentlemen," begged the Republican chairman of a bipartisan Congressional committee, "permit me to tax your memories for a moment." "Golly," muttered a Democratic member to a crony, "why haven't *we* thought of that?"

The biggest job Congress has is how to get the money from the taxpayer without disturbing the voter.

After a lengthy, heated debate in Congress, one Representative stalked out of the House only to meet his tailor on the street.

"Excuse me, sir," said the tailor, "but did you get the bill I sent you last month?"

"Certainly I got it," came the dignified reply. "And it has already received its first reading."

Psychiatrist to patient: "I can't help you, Senator, if you're going to answer 'No comment' to all my questions."

The Red Tape
Tangle:
BUREAUCRACY IN ACTION

I ONCE READ a science-fiction story about a great war between Country A and Country B. A licked B without any blood being spilled. Its army used a secret weapon— a ray that destroyed only paper. All bureaucracies depend, as the jokes that follow demonstrate, on the constant circulation of pieces of paper. It is also essential that what is written on the pieces of paper be in a made-up language that will effectively prevent communication—for the survival of any bureaucracy depends on the systematic maintenance of confusion. (See "That Special Language," on page 223.) It's interesting that most of the funny stuff that follows was not made up by weary gag writers but is simply a transcript of what actually exists, especially among the greatest gobbledy-gookers in existence, the military. (The IRS runs a close second.) Gobbledygook and argot have somewhat similar origins. Argot is the special language used by thieves, crimi-nals, and outlaws to disguise their activities. Gobbledygook is the special language devised by bureaucrats to cover up the fact that most of what they do would be unacceptable in any reasonable society. It may well be that our unconscious desire for such a reasonable society surfaces in our laughter at bureaucrats.

Washington Runaround

A middle-aged woman wandered into the Senate Interstate and Foreign Commerce Committee one day and asked if a Mr. Sexauer worked there. A helpful employee thought she might be looking for the Banking and Currency Commit-tee and offered to check by telephone. When a feminine voice answered his ring, he inquired politely: "Do you have a Sexauer over there?"

"Listen," she snapped, "we don't even have a ten-minute coffee break any more."

Sending for a federal government publication, "Hand-book for Emergencies," Dr. John Ziegler of Cincinnati care-fully jotted down the number of the pamphlet—15,700.

Two weeks later 15,700 copies of the booklet arrived at his residence.

An employe of the U.S. National Bureau of Standards filled out a government form to have a new smock, size 20, issued to her. Instead she received two smocks, both size 10!

When promising U.S. soldiers were sent to colleges for engineering courses during World War II, the assignments were made alphabetically. The result: of 300 soldiers arriving at one small Southern school, 298 were named Brown.

An index of legislation published by the Washington State legislature includes House Bill No. 70, which would permit women to sit at bars in cocktail lounges. The bill is listed under "insects" in the index and described as: "Bar flies, female, HB 70."

Quip heard in Washington, D.C.: "If you're not confused, you're not well informed."

Two men working side by side in the War Production Board in Washington never spoke, but each watched the other. One man quit work daily at four o'clock, while the other always worked till six or later. Finally the harder worker approached the other. "I beg your pardon," he said. "Do you mind telling me how you clean up all your work every day at four o'clock?"

"Not at all. When I come to a tough piece of detail, I mark it 'Refer to Commander Smith.' I figure that in an outfit as large as this there is sure to be a Commander Smith and I must be right. None of those papers come back to me."

"Brother," said the hard worker, removing his coat, "prepare for action. I'm Commander Smith."

With the present emphasis on security, at least one Navy office, in need of something more superlative than "Top Secret," has started using "Cosmic Top Secret." And at the Pentagon, according to an officer, they have a new classification known as DBR—Destroy Before Reading.

A busy man forgot to file his income-tax return until a few days after the deadline. "I have no excuse," he confessed to the Government in an accompanying note. "I just forgot. I am enclosing the required five percent fine." Shortly, he received a ponderous and official letter. Would he be good enough to fill out the enclosed form, setting forth the reasons for his delinquency, and have it notarized? "No excuse," he wrote back. "Have paid fine."

Later he got another letter: No excuse, it said in essence, is not an excuse. "Please file notarized affidavit testifying that you had no excuse."

A veteran obtained a job in a Government bureau, only to have it discovered later that he had never taken a Civil Service examination to determine whether he was qualified for the job which he had been handling for a year and a half. So he was given the test. He failed because of "lack of experience." The problem was neatly resolved, however, by promoting him to be chief of his section.

The metal strips used to band birds are inscribed: "Notify Fish and Wild Life Service, Washington, D.C." They used to read "Washington Biological Survey," abbreviated to "Wash. Biol. Surv." This was changed after an Alberta farmer shot a crow and then disgustedly wrote the U.S. Government: "Dear Sirs: I shot one of your pet crows the other day and followed instruction attached to it. I washed it and biled it and surved it. It was terrible. You should stop trying to fool the people with things like this. . . ."

Labels seen on desk trays in a U.S. government office: "Urgent," "Frantic" and "Most Frantic."

One bureaucrat to another: "So we made a blunder! Don't just stand there—label it 'Top Secret' and file it away!"

State Department official to man at desk: "Jackson's sick today. Take over his crisis."

Overheard in Washington: "Yep—triplets. She was a government secretary for so long I guess she figures she's got to make three copies of everything."

The Post Office Department at Washington, searching the titles to post-office sites in Louisiana, was dissatisfied with one because it went back no farther than 1803. To the Department's request for earlier information, the attorney for the owners replied as follows:

> Please be advised that the Government of the United States acquired the Territory of Louisiana, including the tract to which your inquiry applies, by purchase from the Government of France, in the year 1803.
> The Government of France acquired title by conquest from the Government of Spain.
> The Government of Spain acquired title by discovery of Christopher Columbus, explorer, a resident of Genoa, Italy, who, by agreement concerning the acquisition of title to any land he discovered, traveled under the sponsorship and patronage of Her Majesty, the Queen of Spain.
> The Queen of Spain had received sanction of her title by consent of the Pope, a resident of Rome, Italy, and ex-officio representative and vicegerent of Jesus Christ.
> Jesus Christ was the son and heir apparent of God.
> God made Louisiana.
> I trust this complies with your request.

In a government building in Washington a conscientious lady employe, new to the job, broke her glasses. She requested permission from her immediate superior to run across the street to the optician's for a quick repair. He brooded for a moment, then sent her to his superior, who passed her along to *his*. Here, after she had stated her errand to a secretary and the secretary had searched the files for the lady's dossier, she was granted an interview. "This request places me in an awkward position," she was told. "You see, you haven't yet earned any sick leave." The lady groped her way back to her desk and, for all we know, is still waiting to accumulate enough sick leave to do her errand.

A somewhat bewildered new official in Washington described his position as being like that of the young Eastern potentate whose father presented him with 100 concubines on his coming of age. "It's not that I don't know what to do," he said. "The question is where to begin!"

In *Lying in State* Stanton Griffis, former Ambassador to Poland, to Egypt, to Argentina and to Spain, writes:

Probably the most amusing picture of the State Department at work is the comparison of its operations with the love life of elephants, attributed to Bob Lovett. The analogy falls into three phases of comparisons: the first, that all important business is done at a very high level; secondly, that any developments are accompanied by tremendous trumpeting; and thirdly, that if any results are accomplished, the period required is from 18 months to two years.

From the Union Station in Washington a man took a taxi to the offices of the Small Business Administration. A short while later he came out and found the same taxi waiting. He entered, and the driver started off immediately.

"But I haven't told you where I want to go," the man said.

"Senate Office Building," said the cabby.

"That's right, but how did you know?" asked the visitor.

"Well," the cabby explained, "whenever I take a fare to the Small Business Administration, I know that the first thing he'll want to do afterward is see his senator."

An efficiency expert stalked up to two clerks in a Government office in Washington. "What do you do here?" he asked one.

The clerk, fed up with red tape, buck-passing, forms, office politics and, above all, efficiency experts, growled: "I don't do a thing!"

The interrogator nodded, made a note, then turned to the other clerk. "And you, what's your job here?"

The second man, following his fellow worker's lead, replied, "I don't do a thing either."

The efficiency expert's face lighted up. "Hmmmm," he said knowingly, "duplication!"

During World War II, a Manhattan bank vice-president applied for a job at the Board of Economic Warfare. While he awaited the answer, a BEW official asked the bank to recommend someone for the job. The vice-president was suggested and hired on the spot.

Later, when the banker was hard at work in Washington, he got a letter on BEW stationery, forwarded from New York. It regretfully informed him that his application had been refused because he was unqualified for the job. Looking closer, he found the letter was signed with his own name.

All Clear?

WELFARE, IT'S WONDERFUL

M ARCH 28, 1960
OFFICE OF THE DIRECTOR,
Payroll Division, Redistribution Bureau, Washington, D.C.

DEAR SIR: After submitting it for my endorsement, my employer as usual sent my pay check to Washington last week to cover my participation in the federal-benefits program. But something must have happened to it.

Anyway, I haven't received my certificates of entitlement for this week. My wife needs an infected tooth pulled but cannot get an appointment with the United States dentistry office here without her certificate for this week. The Dry Gulch Valley Authority has threatened to shut off my electricity if I don't turn in my certificate showing I am a paid-up consumer.

Also, until I can show my entitlements for this week, my credit has been cut off at Brannan Memorial Delicatessen No. 82A, I can't get a pair of shoes my boy needs from the Federal Clothing Allotment Administration branch here, I can't make the next payment on my house to the Bureau of Low-Middle-Class Housing and I can't get credit for the second-quarter premium on my Government life insurance.

While I am writing you, I would like to take care of a couple of other matters. Since I have been authorized by the Bureau of Extra-Curricular Employment Assignment to raise a half-acre of black-eyed peas in my back yard, I would like to apply for the required 200 pounds of Government fertilizer.

THORNTON P. BLIVETT

Wet Rock, Ark.

THORNWALL T. BLIVETS,
Wet Rock, Ark.

DEAR MR. BLIVETS: Yours of the 28th instant received and noted.

However, you failed to submit your correspondence in octuplicate so as to provide copies for each of the organizations mentioned in your letter.

Kindly resubmit your letter thus in order that all items may be properly channeled.

QUAGMIRE K. GRAPHT,
Director, Payroll Division,
Redistribution Bureau

P.S.—You are cautioned to note closely the carbon-paper ration for your district for the current month and penalties for exceeding same.—Q. K. G.

DIRECTOR, PAYROLL DIVISION.

DEAR SIR: It's been two weeks since I resubmitted. I'm now missing certificates for three weeks. My family is starving. My electricity has been shut off. My wife's jaw is infected, my insurance has been canceled and the Government is threatening to foreclose on my house. Can't you do something? And my name is not Thornwall T. Blivets.

THORNTON P. BLIVETT

Wet Rock, Ark.

THORNWALL Z. BLIVENS,
Wet Rock, Ark.

DEAR MR. BLIVENS: In answer to your request of April 9, 1958, please find enclosed the Government manual on Sex Life of the Female Night Crawler in Lower Slobovia.

OLIVER H. RINGWORM,
Department of Animal Husbandry

DIRECTOR, PAYROLL DIVISION.

DEAR SIR: I'm now down to 103 pounds and barefoot. For goodness' sake, do something! Even if it's only getting my name right.

THORNTON P. BLIVETT

Wet Rock, Ark.

THORNLEY E. GLIVENS,
   Wet Rock, Ark.

DEAR MR. GLIVENS: As per your request, 103 pounds of fertilizer is being shipped to you express collect.

CROMWELL C. COMPOST,
Department of Utter Fertility

DIRECTOR, PAYROLL DIVISION.

DEAR SIR: What's the matter with you people? A month has passed since I wrote you. I'm now out of a job and living in a tent on the courthouse lawn. Can't even get unemployment compensation because you've got my records all tied up. I beg you, get this mess straightened out.

THORNTON P. BLIVETT

Wet Rock, Ark.

THORNY C. SPIVENS,
   Wet Rock, Ark.

DEAR MR. SPIVENS: After a thorough check of your records, we fail to understand your trouble.

According to our files, you died February 16 last year.

Such being the case, you will report immediately to the public embalming administration branch office nearest your home.

In your case, this office is located in Formaldehyde, Ariz.

We hope this takes care of your case. We have been happy to assist you, and assure you that any future business you may have with our department will be just as speedily consummated.

CLIFTON Q. BUNGSTARTER,
Federal Benefits Administration

———— • ————

On a U.N. questionnaire: "If your answer ·to the above question is *Yes,* explain why not."

———— • ————

Social Security administrators had trouble explaining this advice issued by one of their regional offices: "If you should die or retire after June 30, 1952, get in touch with your Social Security Office."

In a discussion of the water-pollution problem threatening a California beach, a County Flood Control District spokesman asked for a delay for further study, saying: "We don't want to be in favor of something we might be opposed to if we knew what it was."

The dean of the University of Miami has interceded in behalf of a student whose local draft board changed his classification to 1-A because "to keep your deferment you must be ranked in the top two thirds of your class, and you are only in the top one fourth."

Former U.S. AID Administrator David E. Bell told a press conference: "Our trade relations with Japan are really very good. They buy from us a great deal more than we sell to them."

For nearly a year, Laddie Marshack, a picture editor of *TV Guide,* had a runaway correspondence with the gas company. One month she would get a note informing her she had underpaid her bill, the next that she had overpaid it. Laddie blamed it all on that inscrutable way big companies have of getting tangled in red tape.

Finally the whole thing was cleared up. Laddie received a form card containing a number of standard reasons for the irregularities in accounts, such as "Signature incomplete" and "Payee not this company." None, however, applied to her. But on the back of the card was penciled in a patient but long-suffering hand: "You have been paying the date— *please* pay the amount."

The Federal Personnel Manual carries this revealing sentence: "The death of an employe automatically ends his employment."

In Georgia a young lady heard that the Government was making a loyalty check of its employes. But she apparently got a slightly garbled version, because she wrote the Treasury: "I understand the Government is to give loyalty checks to its employes. I worked for the War Department two years during the war and I had an excellent efficiency rating. Please don't overlook me when the Government starts to hand out those checks."

From a description of the physical requirements for a civil-service job at U.S. Naval Air Station, Quonset Point, Rhode Island: "Ability to distinguish basic colors without the use of a hearing aid is required."

A man filling out an application for duty in the Army's Counter-Intelligence Corps found himself stopped cold by this question: "Have you or any of your relatives ever committed suicide?"

The Committee Will Please Come to Order

Chancellor Roger Heyns of the University of California, explaining why his lovely house on the campus had beige draperies and rugs: "The house was decorated by a committee—and the only shade any committee can agree on is beige."

I have always cherished the story of the Detroit executive whose secretary burst into his office on May 21, 1927, and cried; "Mr. Murphy, a man has just flown from New York to Paris all by himself!" When he continued to work calmly, she cried out, "You don't understand! A man has just flown the Atlantic *all by himself!*"

Now Murphy looked up. "All by himself, a man can do anything," he said quietly. "When a committee flies the Atlantic, let me know."

In Britain, filling out endless bureaucratic forms is accepted as inevitable, but every so often the worm turns. One builder, Eric Neate, constructing a small factory at Andover in Hampshire, sent a blueprint to the County Planning Committee. Complying with committee orders that all factories must have flower beds, Neate's architect indicated a space for "shrubs." Back to Neate came the plan with a question: What kind of plants did Neate intend planting? Back to the committee went Neate's reply: he was planning to plant *Urtica dioca, Calystegia sepium, Rumex obtusifolius* and *Taraxacum officinale.* The county council stamped his application "approved."

Apparently none of the committee bureaucrats realized that what Neate proposed to plant were stinging nettles, bindweed, dock and dandelion.

A decision is what a man makes when he can't find anybody to serve on a committee.

A school board in Maryland decided their district needed a new school. After much discussion, the board passed this resolution:

Be it resolved that this school district shall have constructed a new school building, and be it further resolved that, in view of the increasing cost of materials, the new building shall be constructed of the materials now in the existing school building, and be it finally resolved that to avoid interruption of school functions the present school building shall be continued in use until the new school is ready for occupancy.

Some winters ago a small Pennsylvania town had a disastrous fire which could not be controlled because the fireplugs were frozen. The city council met to take measures to prevent a recurrence of the catastrophe.

After hours of hot debate one man jumped to his feet and shouted: "I move that the fireplugs be tested three days before every fire!"

Another member seconded the motion, and the resolution was passed.

A Midwest town council was in session during an earthquake one year. When the shock hit, everyone rushed out of the building. According to an item in *Party Line,* publication of the Republican State Central Committee, the clerk later wrote in his minutes: "On motion of the city hall, the council adjourned."

Senator Henry Cabot Lodge, commenting on the ineffectiveness of some Congressional investigating committees, remarked that they reminded him of a certain Si Hoskins. "Every day," he said, "Si sat near a dam with a gun on his knee. Seeing him one day, I asked, 'What are you doing, Si?'

"'I'm paid to shoot the muskrats, sir. They're undermining the dam.'

"'There goes one now!' I yelled. 'Why don't you shoot?'

"Si puffed a tranquil cloud from his pipe and said, 'Do you think I want to lose my job?'"

That Special Language

Government manuals with their inevitable amendments are always good in our office for at least a quizzical eyebrow. But an edition of instructions about preceding instructions topped them all. On the second page of the booklet a word was followed by an asterisk. Pursuing the asterisk to the bottom of the page, we read: "Ignore all asterisks in this edition."

Federalese," the term used to describe the tortuous terminology in which bureaucratic directives are written, knuckled under to Plain English when a New York City plumber wrote to the Bureau of Standards that he had found hydrochloric acid good for cleaning out clogged drainpipes. The bureau's response was: "The efficacy of hydrochloric acid is indisputable, but the corrosive residue is incompatible with metallic permanence." The plumber wrote back he was glad the bureau agreed with him.

To which the bureau replied: "We cannot assume responsibility for the production of toxic and noxious residue with hydrochloric acid and suggest you use an alternative procedure." By return mail, the plumber told how glad he was the Government thought his idea was O.K.

In desperation, the bureau broke down and wrote the plumber in plain Anglo-Saxon language: "Don't use hydrochloric acid. It eats hell out of the pipes."

A directive from the Office of the Secretary of Defense, giving instructions to the personnel of military installations on how and when to mow the grass, reads: "In general, vegetative areas shall be mowed at a maximum height consistent with their current use. Mowing schedules shall be regulated by the amount of growth."

A door in a government building in Washington, D.C., is labeled: "4156; General Services Administration; Region 3; Public Buildings Service; Buildings Management Division; Utility Room; Custodial."

What's behind the door? A broom closet.

One Congressman gave the Gobbledygook Award to the Bureau of Public Roads, which in a recent report used the term "impact attenuation devices." These turned out to be old oil drums used to block off highway-construction projects. The runner-up for the Congressman's salute went to the Air Force, which recently used "aerodynamic personnel decelerator." The Air Force was trying to say "parachute." And honorable mention went to the Defense Department, which once used the term "combat emplacement evacuator," which, in layman's terms, is a shovel.

When you spend $44,500 on the production of comic books—as the United States Information Agency did a few years ago for distribution overseas of the life story of President Kennedy—you can't call a comic book a comic book any longer. The USIA refers to it as "an illustrated continuity."

A District of Columbia engineer commissioner, defending a proposal for further study of a project, said,. "There will be no delay—merely a regression time-wise."

A government questionnaire to drug and cosmetic makers aroused the curiosity of a congressional committee, and thus we are permitted a glimpse into the mysteries of the bureaucratic system. The printed sheet was marked, at the top: 1-1071-P1OF5-NOBU-COS-WP. Translated it means that it came from the government agency which designates itself as No. 1; that it is order number 1071 of that agency; that it is page 1 of five pages; that the form is printed on one side of the paper only (no back up); that the pages are collated and stapled; that the questionnaires are wrapped in bundles.

A high-ranking State Department careerist handed down this admonition to speech and press-release writers: "Avoid clichés like the plague."

Who but a Washington economist would coin the phrase "negative saver" to describe a person who spends more than he makes?

Traveling Lightly:
AMERICANS ON THE MOVE

T RAVEL MAY BE DEFINED as the opposite of tourism. That's
why for a second or two I couldn't see the joke in the
story about Marge on page 246. She seemed to me to
be talking plain common sense. As G. K. Chesterton put it,
"The traveler sees what he sees; the tripper (tourist) sees

what he has come to see." Flying, of course, has turned travel into something archaic. In order to get from one depressing city (Los Angeles) to one even more depressing (New York), I fly 100,000 miles a year. Considered purely as travel, a slow, thoughtful walk the length of my living room is far more interesting. As for cars, the revival of the bicycle may point to some repressed sanity in us. On the whole, however, we still bow down before the highway engineer. His creed is simple. He believes that the ideal United States consists of a continually multiplying web of freeways intended for the benefit of those first-class citizens, the motorcars; and that for the second-class citizens, known as people, this web must unfortunately be broken and interrupted by a continually diminishing collection of increasingly blighted areas. Out of all this we manage somehow to extract quite a lot of innocent merriment.

Far from the Madding Crowd

GETTING AN EDGE IN WORDWISE
CORNELIA OTIS SKINNER

I AM in the happy state of having just returned from a vacation in Japan. But I'm not sure that the happiness is shared by my friends. I've noticed a certain bracing of their shoulders when we meet and they realize that they're going to have to ask me about my trip.

Actually it strikes me as incredible that they don't ask me

about it right off. Just this morning I drove out of my gate and all but ran headlong into my next-door neighbor coming out of *his* driveway. We slammed on respective brakes, paused to exchange blithe apologies, and to my wounded surprise he never said, "I hear you're just back from Japan." The only reason he didn't hear it then and there was the fact that I had heard *he* was just back from Scotland and, not feeling up to a panegyric on the beauties of the Hebrides, I hurried off before he could get started. But I still think it was unneighborly of him not to have asked me about Japan.

I know perfectly well that the last thing in the world anybody wants to hear is a detailed account of somebody else's holiday safari. The reaction of every listener is the same. To begin with, he doesn't listen. Then, as soon as possible, he changes the subject—to a second gratuitous travelogue describing his own recent holiday.

Only last week a friend whom I met on the commuter train felt duty-bound to inquire politely, "How was Japan?"—and before I could draw a deep breath she started telling me how Sweden was. Sweden lasted most of the way to her destination, and the Rising Sun of Japan barely peeped above the conversational horizon.

Another and more insidious type of listener is the travel snob, who appears to be paying rapt attention to your every word, then ruins your act by suddenly indicating a superior familiarity with the country you're describing. He drops the name of some oh-so-native restaurant or obscure little shop and adds with smiling condescension, "You went there often, of course." And of course you never went there once.

Curious the compulsion which makes one keep on, quite consciously, being a crashing bore. On the ship coming back from my vacation I shared a table with a couple who should be reported to the Hawaiian Chamber of Commerce for sabotaging tourist trade in the Islands. No topic came up at any meal which didn't lead them straight back to Oahu. They said "Aloha" on all occasions—in place of "Good morning," "Good night" and "Here's mud in your eye"—and their conversation was interspersed with a lot of words which it's doubtful that even Queen Liliuokalani ever knew. They drove me into making a vow to the waves: "When I get home, I will *not* talk about Japan!" Then, not to commit myself too far, I added ". . . unless, of course, the subject comes up in conversation."

It is frustrating to discover how seldom the subject does come up in conversation. People don't just throw out helpful openers like "What *is* the name of those sliding doors you see on Japanese houses?" But now and then some unsuspecting victim will bring up the subject obliquely.

The other day a taxi driver came out with, "Have you ever seen worse traffic?" and, quick as a flash, I had him with, "Yes! In Tokyo." At this the poor devil felt obliged to rejoin, "Yeah? Is it bad there?" It took a distance of 30 blocks to tell him just how bad. But the good man got an extra tip.

In the absence of such opportunities, the alternative is to depend upon native ingenuity to steer the conversation "into channels"—a feat I've rarely been able to manage with dexterity. The nearest I've come to it lately was to maneuver a person into talking about lawns, and from there I raised the problem of the Japanese beetle. But before I could launch with any logical grace into a short dissertation regarding the beetle's country of origin, some oaf had switched things into an animated causerie concerning the mating habits of the mud wasp. This naturally led to a reappraisal of the Kinsey report—after which who on earth wanted to hear my trip-to-Japan report?

One way for the returned voyager to bring up his pet topic is through the use of props. Especially in the home. Eye-catchers such as bright-colored brochures or illustrated magazines printed in the language of the recently visited country come in handy if left lying about with planned carelessness.

Little Oriental artifacts clutter my house. A Japanese match-box reposes in every ash tray (also Japanese). Guests who have drinks are obliged to set down their glasses on lacquered coasters and to spread over their laps quaint finger napkins "which," I explain as I hand them out, "are, of course, the sort of thing you'll find in your geisha-house." (Why I feel compelled to call it "*your* geisha-house" I wouldn't know, except that it sounds more author-itative. And of course I take care to pronounce it "gay-sha"—just as I admit to calling the traditional garment a "*kee*-mo-noh.") Not everyone rises to the bait, although now and then some patient soul will say resignedly, "Well, tell us about *our* geisha-houses," and I'm off in a cloud of cherry blossoms.

For a time I carried a ten-yen banknote in my purse. It proved a pretty good conversation piece when I'd start to hand it out, then in pretty confusion retract it, saying, "Look at me, giving you ten yen!" or "Mercy! I can't seem to get rid of my Japanese currency!" The conversation didn't always get going, however —particularly when the other person didn't know a yen from a farthing, and cared less.

Maybe the people who've made out so well with those telephone-answering services might go further and set up a listening service for the benefit of both the returned tourist who feels he can't bear it if he doesn't talk about his trip, and his friends who know they can't bear it if he does. When all else fails, the irrepressible traveloguer could be led gently to the telephone, there to unburden his soul to a sympathetic voice which would make appropriate responses, while the rest of the assembled company could go back to discussing the recent election.

———————— • ————————

Travel agent to customers: "I'm sorry—all the offbeat little destinations are booked solid."

Woman huddled under blanket on deserted, wind-swept beach, to husband: "Tell me again how much money we're saving by taking an off-season vacation."

Beat the Heat
The city heat's become a bane?
    The sun's too high in wattage?
You crave, perhaps, a week of rain?
    Then rent a summer cottage.

Travel agencies in Brussels have struck a bonanza with their sale of "Mystery Tours." Tourists have no idea where they're going, but look forward to the trip.

———————— • ————————

A Dutch travel agency advertises: "Take a plane trip over the North Pole on your honeymoon. The nights last 24 hours."

Woman to travel agent: "When you say it's a resort with old-world atmosphere, do you mean I'll have to look around for the bathroom?"

A story is told about a fellow who was driving to a mountain resort. A cop stopped him and said, "Did you know you're riding without taillights?" The driver got out of the car visibly disturbed by this piece of information. The officer sought to reassure him. "It's not too much of an infraction," he said. "Nothing to get upset about."

"It may not mean much to you," the driver replied. "But to me it means I've lost a trailer, a wife and four kids!"

A paragraph from a Swiss hotel's prospectus reads: "This place is known as the preferred resort of those wanting solitude. People searching for solitude are, in fact, flocking here from all corners of the globe."

From a tourist promotion folder of a small Italian mountain village: "We offer you peace and seclusion. The paths to our hills are passable only to asses. Therefore, you will certainly feel at home in our secluded spot."

Host to visiting couple: "We took one of those 'all-expense tours'—and that's just what it was."

Wife to husband on beach at luxurious tropical resort: "Just think—only last week at this time, we were sloshing through ice and snow to draw out our life's savings."

Change is what a person wants on a vacation—and a lot of currency, too.

After a week, at a hotel, of tipping doormen, bell boys, waiters, hat-check girls, ad infinitum, a traveler was completely fed up with the whole system. Then came a knock on his door. "Who is it?" he called.

"The bell boy, sir. Telegram for you."

A crafty gleam came into the eyes of the tip-tortured guest. "Just slip it under the door," he directed.

Barely a moment's hesitation, then, "I can't, sir."

"And why not?" snarled the unhappy guest.

"Because, sir," answered the determined bell boy, "it's on a tray."

I got up at dawn to see the sun rise," boasted a tourist.

"Well," commented his friend, "you couldn't have picked a better time!"

Little children shrieking
Little sleep for me
Is it merely August
Or Eternity?

Thornton Wilder: It's when you're safe at home that you wish you were having an adventure. When you're having an adventure you wish you were safe at home.

A traveler was telling of an adventure in New Mexico. "It was harrowing," he declared. "Indians to the right of me, Indians to the left of me, Indians in front, Indians everywhere."

"Whew!" exclaimed a listener. "What did you do?"

"What *could* I do? I bought a blanket."

A summer is divided into three parts: anticipation, vacation and recuperation.

On the Road

DETROIT, SPARE THAT WHEEL!

OGDEN NASH

THEY who make automobiles,
They hate wheels.
They look on wheels as limbs were looked on by Victorian
aunts,
They conceal them in skirts and pants.
Wheels are as hard to descry as bluebirds in lower Slobovia,
The only way you can see a wheel complete nowadays is to look
up at it while it is running ovia.
They who make automobiles,
They are ashamed of wheels,
Their minds are on higher things,
Their minds are on wings.
The concept of earthly vision is one that their designers stray
from;
Currently, a successful parking operation is one that you can
walk away from.
Unremittingly the manufacturers strive
To provide point-heads with cars that will do a hundred and
twenty miles an hour where the speed limit is fifty-five.
The station wagon that shuttles the children between home and
school is hopelessly kaput
Unless two hundred and thirty horses are tugging at the acceler-
ator under Mummy's foot.
I don't like wings, I like wheels;
I like automobiles.
I don't want to ride to the station or the office in jet-propelled
planes,
All I want is a windshield wiper that really wipes the windshield,
and some simple method of putting on chains.

———— • ————

Cars are here to stay, or as one wag put it: "Every time
you park one car next to another a new car is born."

———— • ————

On the outskirts of an Oklahoma town are six service stations in a row. Posted in front of the first is a large sign: "Last Chance to Buy Gas—the Next Five Stations Are Mirages."

Found on a piece of paper fastened by a rubber band to a defective parking meter in Dayton, Ohio:

"I put three nickels in this meter. License number: 95PQ.

"320PT also.

"So did I—532QD.

"I'm not going to pay a nickel to find out if these guys are lying. 884X."

On the outskirts of a small town out West, we saw a sign reading: "Slow Down—Speed 25 m.p.h. Rigidly Enforced."

I must have been slow to react because within a block we hit a deep, bone-shattering gap in the pavement, which left us wondering whether the car or the passengers would fall apart first. A few feet beyond was another sign, bearing just one word: "See?"

A mountain road on the island of Crete is labeled: "Secondary, but useful for goats."

Two friends were discussing their automobile troubles. "What model is your car?" asked one.

"It isn't a model," retorted the other. "It's a horrible example."

In the early days, people were flabbergasted when somebody drove 15 m.p.h.—they still are.

Garageman giving estimate to car owner: "First, the good news—your glove compartment and sun visor are in excellent condition!"

Road signs on the Atlanta freeway mirror the tempo of that surging Southern city. They say simply: "Don't poke."

On Route 68 in the village of West Liberty, Ohio, a small sign at an intersection reads: "Caution—Jogger crossing."

CHASING THE WILD MOTEL
ROBERT M. YODER

ONE NEGLECTED reason for the great popularity of motels and tourist courts today is that these bedding-down places, ranging from passable to exceptional, have turned the otherwise stodgy business of going to roost into the liveliest feature of a day on the highway. Around 5 p.m. travelers by the hundreds begin passing up spots that would do all right, in the hope of grabbing off something superior. The result is a stirring new game, something like musical chairs at 65 miles an hour.

This nervous roaming in the gloaming is a light variety of gambling, contains elements of bargain hunting and is a dandy form of self-inflicted anxiety. As the sun sinks to rest, and travelers figure on doing the same, the driver in any expedition says, "Keep your eyes peeled, now, for a good place to stop. What about that joint right there?" Nobody says no, but nobody is willing to say yes, either. The crafty decision is to look a little longer. The game is in full swing.

It is generally agreed that to accept the first place, however pleasant, is for weaklings. They submit meekly to their fate, like horses trudging into their appointed stalls. The bold, the venturesome and those who made a bad choice last night forge ahead.

For best results there ought to be two factions in every car, and nature, in her infinite wisdom, usually provides them. The conservatives' policy calls for stopping pretty soon, or we're going to end up in the crummiest joint on Route 202. It is the duty of the conservatives to remark, "That place would have been fine," just after the place is well passed. The progressives, secretly losing confidence as day fades, simply put on speed. The idea is that if there isn't much ahead we can at least get there fast.

The best motels on any route are always located at 1:30 p.m. This is mildly supernatural, but entirely true. At this hour, when Mount Vernon itself at two dollars a night would be no good to you, you run into a belt where there are good ones to the left and better ones to the right. At five o'clock, however, they vanish like taxis in the rain.

You can, of course, go to the extreme of making reservations in advance. This is the prudent thing to do, and in perhaps three cases out of a thousand somebody does it. It accomplishes one thing: it exercises a remarkable effect on weather, road surfaces and traffic. Yesterday you crawled along over pitted highways in dense traffic and spent two hours on detours and alternates. Today, in beautiful weather, you bowl along over superior roads through traffic so light that you reach your reserved stop at precisely 3:30 p.m. Stop, and you will have five or six hours of good driving time in which to bicker about whose idea this was, anyway. Or you can kill time watching the improvident grasshoppers show up at about 6 p.m. and get fine accommodations, on the spur of the moment, at the court across the road, a spot so new it wasn't in your guidebook.

———— • ————

License plate on a Manchester, New Hampshire, obstetrician's racy sports car: "STORK."

Mechanic to car owner: "Let me put it this way—if your car were a horse, it would have to be shot."

A large motor company made a survey of Volkswagen owners to ascertain the reason for their ardent devotion to their cars. One owner replied, "That's easy—because it *needs* me."

———— • ————

Driving his new Rolls-Royce through the Alps, an Englishman had his composure jolted when a front spring broke as he was making a tight curve at high speed. After limping into the nearest Swiss town, he explained his problem by phone to Rolls-Royce, Ltd., in England. The next day a company representative appeared, replaced the spring, and the Englishman purred on his way.

Back in England, realizing that no bill had come through from Rolls, he called to ask them to check their records for "Swiss repair of broken spring." A few minutes later, a most correct Rolls manager was on the phone. "There must be some mistake, sir. There is no such thing as a broken spring on a Rolls-Royce."

In King County, Washington, a hay-fever sufferer requested and got plates bearing the letters "ACH-OOO."

Actor Ernie Borgnine claims his car is so old the license bureau issues him both upper and lower plates.

Mechanic to owner of foreign car: "You'd be better off deporting it."

Hollywood was amused when an enthusiastic Democrat received his new license plate: "NXN."

A California department of motor vehicles examiner stepped into a car halted at the curb in a line for the driving test. He went through the usual safety checks with the driver —brakes, lights, turn indicators. The driver obeyed each instruction without a word. They pulled into traffic. "Turn right," ordered the examiner. "Turn left ... stop ... go ... back up. ..."

Each order met with silent obedience. Finally, the driver asked, "Do you mind telling me what this is all about? I'm from out of town and I just pulled to the curb to check my road map."

A couple stationed in Europe bought two identical fire-engine-red Karmann Ghias. One day they took both cars to a service station for an oil change. The French mechanic on duty looked from one car to the other and inquired, "Is *monsieur* planning to mate them?"

YOU CAN'T HELP BUT MISS IT!
H. ALLEN SMITH

ARLY ON a May morning in 1927 Charles A. Lindbergh, flying solo from New York to Paris, saw a fishing boat in the Atlantic below him. Uncertain of his location, he throttled down, dipped his plane close to the vessel and yelled to the fishermen, "Which way is Ireland?" Later he wrote of the incident: "They just stared. Maybe they didn't hear me. Or maybe they thought I was just a crazy fool."

In my opinion Lindbergh was fortunate. If those fishermen were anything like the people I encounter from day to day, and if they had signaled directions to him, he might well have landed in Fort Lauderdale, Florida.

For all the other qualities of mind they may possess, most people, male or female, cannot properly direct a motorist or a pedestrian—or a Lindbergh in an airplane—to his destination. Several years ago my wife and I were invited to visit friends in rural Connecticut. I telephoned the lady of the house for directions. The portion of her monologue that I remember most vividly went this way: "You keep going quite a ways and finally you'll come to a three-story gray house that is burned down."

The stumbling block in that sentence would appear to be the gray house that is burned down. But there is an equally insidious semantic monstrosity: the phrase, "quite a ways." There could be a difference of 40 miles between what *she* considers "quite a ways" and what *I* consider "quite a ways." How am I to know what a farmer means when he says the next town is "a fur piece off"? Or "not very fur"? In Latin-American countries every destination is "just beyond the next hill, *Señor.*" The "beyond" involved here may turn out to be 20 miles or 80 or 140.

The citizens of England have a charming but no less frustrating variation. There, when you inquire of an English countryman how to get to Popskull-on-the-Rilleragh, he will respond, "Proceed stryte ahead to the second roundabout and take the turning to the right and soon you will arrive at a cluster of small shops. Stop there, sir, and ask agayne." So you stop at the cluster of small shops and ask agayne and they send you along another few miles, advising you to stop at a certain public house and ask agayne.

The chief fault of the average direction-giver is an over-devotion to detail. "Go straight out Gutteridge," I was told in Los Angeles recently, "and finally you'll come to Division Street. Cross Division, stay right on Gutteridge. After a while you'll come to Killjoy. Cross Killjoy, keep going, stay on Gutteridge. Soon you'll see a big cemetery on a hill, then you'll come to a light—that'll be Cumshaw Boulevard. Cross Cumshaw, stay right on Gutteridge, go past a big supermarket with a red tower, just keep on going." All this drivel about cemeteries and Cumshaws and supermarkets and Killjoys could have been covered in three words: "Stay on Gutteridge." As it was, I got fouled up somewhere along the way and ended up in Oxnard.

Then there is the person, usually male and proud of his efficiency, who showers you with fractions. "Turn right at the second traffic light," he will say, "and go $7\frac{3}{10}$ miles to Hardscrabble Road. Then turn left, go $3\frac{3}{10}$ miles to Douglas, and turn left. Our house is exactly one tenth of a mile from that intersection." This sort of precision is likely to be the death of me: I've come within

$1\frac{2}{10}$ inches of annihilation through keeping my attention fastened on the mileage dial rather than on the road.

Another specialist direction-giver might be called the highway-engineer type. "You go three miles on this paving block until you hit ferroconcrete," he says. "Turn left on the ferroconcrete, go four miles and then turn right on a tar job gritted with chippings. Go $2\frac{1}{2}$ miles to a fork, than take the grouted macadam instead of the bituminous clinker—the one with the steep camber—and you'll come to a washboard bearing left."

This man is about as helpful as the rural nature boy who instructs the driver from the city to "keep goin' till you come to a grove of hemlocks. . . ." The city driver wouldn't know a grove of hemlocks from a pride of lions or a hand of bananas. Still, he would never confess that ignorance, and so he probably ends up in a wilderness of hemlocks.

Masculine pride shows up in another way. Men will make inquiries at a filling station when lost, but they refuse to stop along the highway and ask directions of a stranger. This stubbornness has long been a source of irritation between husbands and wives. Humorist Robert Benchley once undertook to explain the wife's point of view. It is based on experience, he said, "which has taught her that *anyone* knows more about things in general than her husband."

I know of a man whose business takes him by car all over the country and who would prefer death in a deep canyon to asking a stranger for directions. To this problem, however, he has found a solution. When he drives into a strange town where he has a business engagement, he finds a taxi and says to the driver, "Go to 1594 Hickory Street." Then he simply trails along after the cab.

In the art of direction-giving I would naturally like to point to myself as a paragon of efficiency. I know how it should be done. If you live in a difficult locality and find it necessary to tell people how to get to your place, rehearse your speech. Make it simple, and make it crystal-clear. Don't clutter it up with bituminous clinkers or three-story gray houses that are burned down.

But will mankind profit by this hard-earned advice? Of course not. We'll all blunder along like the woman I know who asked an Iowa farmer how to get to a certain town. He gave her a long routine of turn rights and bear lefts and finished off by saying, "You can't help but miss it!"

On the Rails

Robert Benchley: Probably the most common of all antagonisms arises from a man's taking a seat beside you on a train, a seat to which he is completely entitled.

A waiter in the diner of a Canadian Pacific train approached a regal-looking woman and bent over her solicitously. "Pardon me," he asked, "are you the cold salmon?"

Commuter railroads have never lacked for critics, one of the latest of these being a Cherokee Indian. A reporter from the New Britain, Connecticut, *Herald,* interviewing passengers aboard a short run of the New Haven, got this reply from Harry Stone of Silverton, Colorado: "My ancestors used to attack trains like this."

Jim Crowder, a midwestern book magnate, got a seat in a railroad diner one day. "Do you like split-pea soup?" asked the waiter.
"No," said Jim.
"Chicken croquettes?"
"No."
"Prune pie?"
"No."
The waiter took the napkin off the table. "Good-day," he said. "You have had your lunch."

A railroad engineer got up on the wrong side of the bed one morning. The water for his shower was cold. His shoelace broke. At breakfast his toast was burned. His car wouldn't start and he had to taxi to the yards. He was late, so when he started his train he speeded it up to 90 miles an hour. . . . Just as he swung around a curve he saw another train coming straight at him — on the *same* track. He heaved a big sigh and, turning to the fireman, said, "Did you ever have one of those days when just everything goes wrong?"

On a fishing trip I was attempting to board a train in Mexico when my interpreter and the Mexican conductor got into a terrific argument. "What's the uproar all about?" I asked.

"He says," explained the interpreter, "that this is yesterday's train. Our tickets are for today's train which isn't due until tomorrow!"

The luggage-laden husband stared miserably down the platform at the departing train. "If you hadn't taken so long getting ready," he admonished his wife, "we would have caught it."

"Yes," the little woman rejoined, "and if you hadn't hurried me so, we wouldn't have so long to wait for the next one!"

An indignant commuter wrote: "I take your 9:35 a.m. train daily. I cannot get a seat near the front of the train and sometimes have to stand all the way. Several coaches on this train near the rear end carry very few passengers. Will you please advise me why those coaches cannot be put on the front of the train so we won't be so crowded?"

The Pullman porter had just roused me and, still half-asleep, I was sitting on the edge of my lower berth, unshaven and tousled. A mother and daughter passed by on their way to the diner and I got up and followed toward the men's lounge.

"Don't worry, dear," I heard the older woman say encouragingly, "they *all* look like that in the morning."

The train was pulling out of the station when a young man threw his bag onto the observation platform and swung himself up over the handrail. He stood panting but triumphant as the train gathered speed.

An elderly party on the platform observed him with some scorn. "You young fellows don't keep yourselves in condition," he snorted. "Why, when I was your age I could carry a cup of coffee in one hand, run half a mile, catch the 8:15 by the skin of my teeth, and still be fresh as a daisy."

"You don't understand, pop," puffed the young man. "I missed this train at the *last* station."

An American was seated opposite a nice old lady in the compartment of an English railway car. For some minutes he chewed his gum in silence, then the old lady leaned forward. "It's so nice of you to try to make conversation," she said, "but I must tell you that I'm terribly deaf."

Each Friday evening I drove my wife to the station for the train to Weimar, California, so she could visit her sister who was ill. Ten minutes later, my sister arrived by train from Sacramento to manage our household over the weekend. On Sundays this procedure worked in reverse, with my sister departing by train ten minutes before my wife arrived.

One evening after my sister had left and while I awaited my wife's arrival, a porter sauntered over.

"Mister," he said, "you're sure some man! But one of these days you're gonna get caught."

———— • ————

YOU BET TRAVEL IS BROADENING
OGDEN NASH

DOCTORS tell me that some people wonder who they are, they don't know if they are Peter Pumpkin-eater or Priam, But I know who I am.
My identity is no mystery to unravel,
Because I know who I am, especially when I travel.
I am he who lies either over or under the inevitable snores,
I am he who the air conditioning is in conflict with whose pores,
I am he whom the dear little old ladies who have left their pocketbooks on the bureau at home invariably approach,
And he whom the argumentative tippler oozes in beside though there are thirty empty seats in the coach.
I am he who finds himself reading comics to somebody else's children while the harassed mother attends to the youngest's needs,
Ending up with candy bar on the lapel of whose previously faultless tweeds.
I am he in the car full of students celebrating victory with

instruments saxophonic and ukulelean,
And he who, speaking only English, is turned to for aid by the
non-English-speaking alien.
I am he who, finding himself the occupant of one Pullman space
that has been sold twice, next finds himself playing Santa,
Because it was sold the second time to an elderly invalid, so
there is no question about who is going to sit in the washroom
from Philadelphia to Atlanta.
I guess I am he who if he had his own private car
Would be jockeyed into sharing the master bedroom with a man
with a five-cent cigar.

Winging It

Woman explaining husband's hangover to friend: "The
champagne flight was stuck in a holding pattern over the airport for two hours."

Always apprehensive about flying, I boarded the plane
and chose a seat next to a solid-looking citizen. I tried to
settle back to endure the six hours ahead of me but found my
eyes glued to the engine within my view.

After an hour or so my fellow passenger turned to me with
a kindly smile. "Miss," he said, "if you would like to rest
for a while, I'd be glad to watch that engine for you."

When airlines were young and people were wary of flying,
a promotion man suggested to one of the lines that they
permit wives of businessmen to accompany their husbands
free, just to prove that flying was safe. The idea was quickly
adopted, and a record kept of the names of those who accepted the proposition. In due time the airline sent a letter to
those wives, asking how they enjoyed the trip. From 90 percent of them came back a baffled reply: "*What* airplane
trip?"

An airline, priding itself on the executive treatment ac-
corded its passengers, advertises: "Our steaks are prepared
with the president of U.S. Rubber in mind."

Airline passenger to stewardess: "I know this is the economy section—but showing the co-pilot's home movies is carrying it a bit too far!"

Stewardess, as passengers leave plane: "Please do not reveal the ending of the movie to passengers awaiting departure."

Attendant meeting jet-liner with stretcher: "It's another ten-countries-in-11-days case, Doc!"

It happened on one of those huge jets that wing across the continent. A businessman with a wry sense of the incongruous boarded the plane in New York. When airborne, he unfastened his seat belt and looked around. There were two or three stewardesses, a purser, and through the open door of the flight deck he could see a co-pilot and a flight engineer. Otherwise, he was the only person aboard. There were 100 empty seats! He walked back to the pantry, picked up the intercom microphone, pressed the button and growled, "Good morning. This is your passenger speaking."

Marge, where did you go on your holiday?" an English girl asked her friend.
    "Majorca," replied Marge.
    "Majorca, where's that?"
    "I don't know," replied Marge. "I flew."

A former U.S. Secretary of Commerce used to tell about a planeload of people flying across the Atlantic. A voice comes on the intercom: "We are now flying at 35,000 feet. If you will notice, out the right window, the two engines on that side are on fire. Looking out the left window, you will see that those engines had to be stopped. If you look directly below, there is a yellow sea-recovery raft with six small dots on it. The dots are the pilot, co-pilot, flight engineer, navigator and two hostesses. This is a recording."

A reservation clerk for TWA in Phoenix had an inquiry from a man about a tour, part of which involved use of Hawaiian Airlines. Since the latter company demands to know the weight of its passengers, she asked him, "How much do you weigh, sir?"

"With or without clothes?" the passenger asked.

"Well," she replied, "how do you intend to travel?"

Lady traveling with friend to airline pilot: "Now don't start going faster than sound. We want to talk."

Young stewardess to pilot on her first flight over the Grand Canyon: "Could this have been prevented by contour plowing?"

Columnist Frank Scully says he has been eyeing his suitcases with great respect ever since he packed them for a flight abroad. Because the overweight charges were so steep, Scully decided to weigh his luggage before going to the airport. He hauled his bags to a drugstore, piled them on a scale and dropped a penny in the slot. Out shot a card reading: "You weigh 65 pounds. Your keen analytical mind and sound judgment are of the greatest assistance in solving the problems of others."

Passengers on one of the transatlantic airlines are given a pamphlet called "Your Safety Is Our First Consideration." In the pamphlet are explicit instructions on what to do in case the plane is forced to ditch. The last one reads: "Avoid getting unnecessarily wet."

On a recent night flight I sat next to an elderly woman who kept peering out of the window at the blinking wing-tip light. Finally she rang for the stewardess. "I'm sorry to bother you," she said, "but I think you ought to tell the pilot that he's left his turn indicator on."

One stormy day at the New Orleans airport a man sitting in the waiting room overheard two women discussing the flying conditions. They were uneasy about their trip north, so they decided to take out flight insurance. At first they couldn't decide whom to name as their beneficiaries, but finally each named the other, and a moment later they happily boarded the plane together.

Rushing up to a large airline's ticket counter, a man gasped, "Miss, please help me. I have to get to Chicago in the worst way!"

The clerk calmly pointed to her left and said, "Sir, that would be the competing airline next to us."

Innocents Abroad

SEX, HONOR AND
THE ITALIAN DRIVER
JACKSON BURGESS

BEFORE you start your car in Italy for the first time, sit in the driver's seat, hold the steering wheel and think: *I am the only driver on the road, and mine is the only car.* This may be hard to believe, especially after you have seen Rome in July or Milan during rush hour, but millions of Italian drivers believe it, and so can you. And you'd better. You won't have a chance unless you can match this faith. Remember, your car is THE CAR. All the others are aberrations in the divine scheme.

As elsewhere, there are laws about stop streets, maximum speeds and so forth. But in Italy these laws exist only as tests of character and self-esteem. Stopping at a stop sign, for example, is *prima facie* evidence that the driver is, if male, cuckold, or if female, frigid and barren. Contrarily, running a stop sign is proof that you are a Person of Consequence. This is why the Italian driver who gets a ticket goes red in the face, wrings his hands and beats his forehead with his fists. It isn't the fine, or the inconvenience. It's the implication that he is, after all, not quite important enough to drive the wrong way down a one-way street.

The basic rule in cities is: force your car as far as it will go into any opening in the traffic. It is this rule which produces the famous Sicilian Four-Way Deadlock.

It would appear that the Deadlock can be broken if any one backs up. But you can't back up; there is another car right behind you. Anyway, if you could and did, you would become an Object of Ridicule. For this would suggest a want of spirit.

The impossibility of backing up accounts for some of the difficulty in parking. You will find that when you stop just beyond a vacant space and try backing into it, you can't—because that fellow is still right behind you, blowing his horn. You can give up and drive on, or you can get out, go back and try to persuade him to let you park. This you do by shouting Personal Abuse into his window. One of three things will happen: he may stare sullenly straight ahead and go on blowing his horn; he may shout Personal Abuse back at you; or he may get out of his car and kill you, subsequently pleading *delitto d'onore* (crime of honor), which automatically wins in southern Italian courts.

Since Italians usually drive head-first into parking spaces, every third or fourth parked car has its tail end sticking out. Driving is further complicated by double-parked cars—and the Italian style of entering from a side street by driving halfway into the near lane of traffic and then looking. The way to deal with these hazards is to blow your horn and accelerate around them. (All Italian drivers accept the axiom that anything you do while blowing the horn is sacred.) If you make a careful, in-line stop, you not only expose your social and sexual inadequacies but you may never get moving again, since you also mark yourself as a weakling whom anyone can challenge with impunity.

The thing to remember about one-way streets in Italy is that they are not one-way. A driver who has a block or less to go automatically realizes at once that when the authorities put up the signs, they were not thinking of cases like his. He drives it the wrong way, going full throttle to get it over with quickly, and to prove that he really is in a terrible hurry.

Similarly, the traffic circle, with its minuet-like formality of movement, is to an Italian driver just so much exhilarating open space. You do not go around it; you go across it, at high speed, taking the shortest path from your point of entrance to your intended exit, while sounding your horn.

In Italian cities, four-lane streets usually become, after four or five blocks, two-lane and then one-lane streets. Since most cities are force-fed with automobiles by an excellent turnpike system, this produces the Funnel Effect.

The Funnel Effect can be unnerving. The unwary motorist may get trapped against one side or the other and have to stay there until traffic slacks off around one or two o'clock in the morning.

But the Reverse Funnel Effect is even more dangerous. Imagine the effect of bottling a number of prideful and excitable Italian drivers in a narrow street for a half-mile or more and then suddenly releasing them. It's like dumping out a sack of white rats. As each car emerges, it tries at once to pass the car ahead of it — and, if possible, two or three more. The car ahead is passing the car ahead of it, and so on. Thus the first hundred yards of the Reverse Funnel, before the cars shake down, is a maelstrom of screaming engines, spinning tires and blaring horns.

The word *sorpassare* means both "to pass with an automobile" and "to surpass or excel" — socially, morally, sexually and politically. To be *sorpassato,* then, is to lose status, dignity, reputation. Thus, it is not where you arrive that counts, but what (or whom) you pass on the way. The procedure is to floor your accelerator and leave it there until you come up on something you can pass. (Passing becomes possible, in the Italian theory, whenever there is not actually a car to your immediate left.)

When an Italian driver sees the car ahead of him on the highway slow up or stop, he knows there can be but two causes: the driver ahead has died at the wheel, or else he has suddenly become a Person of No Consequence, which is roughly the same thing. He therefore accelerates at once and passes at full speed. If the driver ahead has, in fact, stopped for a yawning chasm, the passer is done for, of course.

When you are involved in an automobile collision, the Italian word for it is *l'investimento.* (Notice that I do not say "if" but "when.") The aftermath of *l'investimento,* provided there is no serious injury, is as formal as a quadrille. First, all drivers and passengers spring from their cars shouting Personal Abuse. Passers-by spring from *their* cars. Pedestrians act as if they have been principals in the crash. Stores empty as shoppers join the crowd. Invalids rise from their beds for blocks around to totter to the scene, shouting and gesticulating.

Do not be afraid of this crowd, even if you are absolutely in the wrong. Half of the people are on your side. If a priest has blamed you, the communists become your partisans. If a rich man should point out that you were, after all, dead drunk and driving up the sidewalk with your eyes closed, any man with callused hands will swear that he has known you for years at a teetotaler.

All this, however, is mere rhetoric. In an *investimento,* blame has nothing to do with the actions of the drivers. It is entirely a matter of status and virility. The driver of the newer, more expensive car is automatically in the right. He is, in fact, an Injured Party. If one driver is in a suit and tie and the other is not, he raises the rank of his car by one grade. If one has a calling card, the balance can shift in an instant. If both have cards, it becomes a contest of titles.

Who cares what happened? That's over. What matters is what is happening now—the battle of dignity and manhood. You are being watched by hundreds of eyes alert to the slightest loss of poise, the first retreat from savage indignation. But you can win. As you stand there in your wilted sport shirt, comprehending nothing, groggy with cross-country driving, remember—you can win! Just keep telling yourself: "I am a Person of Consequence. I am, I *am!*"

———— • ————

In preparing for a recent trip to Japan we used the services of a travel bureau in that country but specified dates, methods of travel and hotels. Most of our suggestions were followed, but in one city the travel bureau reserved a room in an inn other than the one we had requested, offering this explanation: "Our company has never sent our clients to this inn. The inn is likely to be a sort of rest house for an instant couple."

———— • ————

Even a California driver is stunned by his first taste of European traffic. Pedestrians walk in the middle of the street, drivers triple-park, U-turn and in general carry on as they please. Since the gutters are not piled high with bodies, I have always suspected that there was an unwritten code which governed the relationship between driver and pedestrian. One evening in Rome I discovered what it was.

A pedestrian was crossing the street in the middle of the block and directly in the path of an oncoming car. The driver swerved and the pedestrian jumped—both in the same direction. Again the pedestrian moved, and so did the driver. The distance between them was shortening. The pedestrian reversed his direction, only to find himself once more in the path of the approaching car.

This was the last straw. The pedestrian raised his hand in the universal gesture meaning STOP. His Italian temperament now long past the boiling point, he strode toward the driver. "Idiot!" he screamed. "You don't dodge me—I dodge *you!*"

I often recall the story of an American who made a grand tour of Europe on a plan which allowed 48 hours at the most for each of the great capitals. When he returned to "God's country," a neighbor asked him if he had seen Venice.

"Yes," he replied, "but when we got there they were in the midst of a terrible flood. All the streets were under water and all the people were traveling around in boats, so we didn't stay."

The party of American tourists viewing the ruins of Pompeii were told by their guide: "This is the city which, you may remember, was destroyed by an eruption in 79."

"My goodness," exclaimed a woman from the Middle West, "just eight years after the Chicago fire!"

Translated, one of China's road signs reads as follows: "Go soothingly on the greasy mud, for therein lurks the skid demon."

———— • ——

While driving through the southern island of Japan, Kyushu, I came upon a road-construction crew at work. They had posted a large detour sign. Underneath the Japanese word for detour, the message in English announced: "Stop—Drive Sideways."

Foot-weary husband in Café Venezia: "Besides, the longer we sit here, the older the Ponte Vecchio will be when we finally *do* see it."

While traveling in Africa a friend of mine was invited to go on a safari. She was delighted until she learned that part of the itinerary lay through cannibal country. Knowing that the safari cook was a member of one of the cannibal tribes, she decided to consult him. He proved to be a pleasant, civilized man.

"You need have no fear of my people," he told her. "It would never enter their minds to harm anyone on a safari." My friend was just beginning to be reassured when his glance passed lightly over her short plump figure. "Of course," he added, "if you happened to meet with an accident and be killed, you wouldn't be *wasted.*"

———— • ——

THE DEVIOUS ART OF PLACE DROPPING

COREY FORD

THERE'S an indoor game that is bound to be very popular at social gatherings this winter, what with practically everybody traveling abroad.

It's called Place Dropping, and the object is to work into your table conversation (very casually; that's the whole game) the name of somewhere you've been. If nobody else has been there, it counts ten and you can talk without interruption through the rest of the dinner.

The trick is to sort of slip in the fact that you've been to a Place without coming right out and stating so. You never say to your dinner partner, "We went to Yurrop," for instance. Instead you glance at your watch and remark: "Well, right now it would be one o'clock back in Paris."

Or else you observe with a rueful shake of your head: "I just can't get used to these modern airplanes; this time yesterday we were having lunch in Wien—or, as you probably call it, Vienna." (Part of the game is to use a foreign name and then explain that München is really Munich, you know.)

There are various ways to maneuver into a good scoring position. One Place Dropper I know hits the basket every time by referring to his weight. "I bet I put on ten pounds this summer—that good old German *dunkles Bier*."

Another Dropper shoots a consistently high score by bringing up the international date line. "I never can remember whether you gain a day or lose it; let's see, this would be Monday in Nippon. Japan, that is."

Water is usually a good opening—"I got the worst case of dysentery in Chile"—and food is always surefire. "Did you ever eat baby squid? We found the quaintest little restaurant in Athens. . . ." "I never thought I'd like fried seaweed, but in Hong Kong. . . ."

As a rule, female Droppers prefer the underhand toss. "What a pretty tablecloth, dear; did you get it in Portugal? Oh, really?" with a condescending smile. "You ought to go to Lisbon sometime. They have the most beautiful linen."

On the other hand, male Droppers like to try a direct shot from the center of the floor. "Pretty good stuff, hah? Brought it back from Scotland myself."

Sometimes a successful Drop can be achieved without mentioning the Place at all. A skillful player just pulls a matchbox out of his pocket with "Air France" or "The Raffles Hotel, Singapore" on the cover, or absently hands the taxi driver a couple of drachmas or maybe an Indian rupee. A direct hit can be scored by simply carrying a tweed topcoat inside out so the Glasgow label shows.

Dropsmanship is a highly competitive sport. Topping another Dropper counts double, and the strategy is to steal the opponent's play. The other night at dinner the lady beside me said she simply adored Fraunts (Place Droppers are also Accent Droppers) and oh! to be back in la belle Paree, sipping a glass of shabley on the Shonz L S A.

The man on her right said that speaking of wine, they had a coconut drink in Ind-juh that would knock your hat off, and the lady beside him wondered if it was anything like the distilled cactus juice she had in May-heeco. A man sitting opposite said quickly that in Iceland he once drank fermented seal blubber, and the hostess inquired triumphantly whether anyone had ever tried Mongolian yak milk.

I didn't hear how the game came out, because I ducked around the corner for a glass of beer. The bartender said it wasn't like the stuff you get in Dublin, though.

———————— • ————————

A Detroit businessman recently flew to Abaco, a small island in the Bahamas, to spend a couple of weeks. There was no formal entry procedure awaiting passengers at the airport on this piece of British territory, but there was a small customs shanty, padlocked, with this notice on the door: "If someone comes and no one is here, wait until someone comes here."

A professor, his wife and their two dogs had just landed in Japan and were going through customs. "What kind of dogs, please?" asked the customs official.

"Boston Bull," was the reply.

An examination of the customs declaration later showed that the entry "2 dogs" had been changed to read: "1 Boston Bull, 1 Boston Cow."

A woman we know who spent some time in Egypt was telling us of a bazaar she visited in one of the side streets of Cairo. As a special attraction, the proprietor was exhibiting at one end of the room "The Skull of Cleopatra." Beside it was a smaller skull, and this one piqued our friend's curiosity. She asked the proprietor whose skull that was.

"That is Cleopatra's too," he explained kindly, *"as a child."*

Language handbooks and lessons are anticipating a traveler's every need these days. One of the Vista Books tells how to say in Polish: "If you please, I asked for some coffee half an hour ago. If I don't have my coffee in five minutes, I shall set fire to the hotel."

———————— • ————————

Woman to customs man going through her suitcase: "Once you've made the chalk mark, does that mean I've won?"

Sign in Amman, Jordan, tailor shop: "Order now your summer suit. Because in big rush we will execute all customers in the strict rotation."

"THE ENGLISH:
HOW SHE IS TALKED"
H. ALLEN SMITH

I'M QUITE certain that Mrs. Mardsley was paved with good intentions when she gave me the little book. The moment she found out I was contemplating an Italian journey, she insisted that I have it.

She hastened to explain that this was no ordinary language guidebook of the type customarily carried by American tourists. It was a guide written for Italians, a *Manuale di Conversazione Italiano-Inglese* or, in my own smooth translation, "The English: How She Is Talked."

"With this little volume," Mrs. Mardsley told me, "you will learn to talk about the things that Italians talk about among themselves."

I flipped open the book, and my eye fell on this exchange: "What was the loud noise?"

"Oh, nothing. Just an explosion."

I looked at Mrs. Mardsley, who said, "Not there. Let me show you how. Just open it at random."

Pretending continental insouciance, I turned a few leaves and, using the hatpin system of picking horses, jabbed my finger at the righthand page. It said: "*Non potete insegnare alla nonna a bere le uova.* Don't try to teach your grandmother to suck eggs."

Mrs. Mardsley bent over and inspected the lines and then scowled at me, as if *I* had written them.

"How about *that?*" I said. "Am I going around the streets of Rome and Venice and Naples saying *that* to the Italian people?"

"Please," she protested. "Turn to some place in the middle—hotels and railroads and the post office." I did, and arrived at a section dealing with signs: "Beware of the dog! Beware of sheep! Beware of pickpockets!" And my eye fell on a startling line: "My collarbones are broken."

I closed my eyes and shook my head briskly and pondered the preoccupations of Italian small talk. A loud noise that was nothing, just an explosion, brought me out of my reflections—it was Mrs. Mardsley urging me to try another section of the little book.

I went to work and quickly discovered that if I am to enjoy myself to the fullest in Italy, I should be able to convey such light-hearted sentiments as: "I am cold. I am hot. I am hungry. I am tired. I am ill. Can you help me? It was not my fault. I cannot find my hotel. I have lost my friends. I forgot my money. I have lost my keys. I have missed the train. They are bothering me. Go away. I have been robbed. Where is the Lost and Found desk? That razor scratches. No, I part my hair on the other side."

I was getting into a state of nerves. It had been my aim to *noleggiare automobili* in Italy and let them put me in the driver's seat, so I feverishly flipped to the appropriate section and found, "Excuse me, I was confused by the traffic; I am a stranger here," quickly followed by the question, "How much is the fine?" Same as everywhere else—you can't win. And then: "My tire has collapsed. It is a slow leak. My engine skips. There is a grinding. There is a diminution of power. It stops. You must change the bush of the engine, register the tappets." A bit further on, I found: "I came in from your left and so I had the precedence. It was your fault."

Maybe, I thought, I had better not rent a car. How about, instead, a nice boat trip in the lovely Adriatic? I hopefully turned to matters *marittime* and there it was, the same dirge, Italian-style: "I am sick. Please show me the quickest way to my cabin. Are you sure we are on course? Where are the pills? Go away." Cruising the Adriatic—*out.*

Remembering my customary concern for my health when traveling, I turned with morbid fascination to the medical section. Pretty soon I was suffering maladies I had never known before, for the spirited *conversazione* went: "I have a pain in my back, in my stomach, in my head, in my kidneys, in some bones. Taxi, be quick! I feel these pains before eating. When riding. When I walk fast. Sitting down. I suffer from headaches, dizziness, nausea, colics of the liver, nettle-rash, *morbillo* (measles) and *orecchioni* (mumps)." I fled right out of that chapter, like a startled gazelle.

By this time I was feeling pretty glum *(sconsolato)*. It seemed unreasonable to me that a vacation in sunny Italy should be so fraught with disaster, unprogrammed interruptions such as colics of the liver, unregistered tappets, collarbones cracking in pairs, man-eating sheep and withered grandmothers sitting around sucking eggs.

"It may be," I said to Mrs. Mardsley, "that I'll postpone my trip to Italy."

Then suddenly the truth hit me. The little book was not about Italy at all. The dangers and disasters described were not endemic to Rome or Florence. They were put into print for the benefit of Italians getting ready to travel among *us* . . . in the United States! A great oppression lifted from my spirit, a heady eagerness seized me. I wanted to head out for Italy *immediatamente*. After all, it is good for the soul to get away from one's own kind for a while, away from one's own barber who can't even locate the part in one's hair, from where even *I* can't locate the Lost and Found desk.

————————— • —————————

One afternoon a rickety old car drew up to a café on Madrid's Gran Via. Its canvas top hung in flounces, its metal was rusty and a heavy cloud of steam issued from the radiator where the cap was missing.

The driver stepped up to a man lounging nearby and asked: "Will you keep an eye on my car while I make a phone call?" The other agreed. When the driver returned he asked the man how much he owed.

"Fifty pesetas," was the reply.

"But that's robbery! I was only gone five minutes."

"I know," the man answered. "But it wasn't the time—it was the embarrassment. Everyone thought the car was mine."

————————— • —————————

------- • -------

At rush hour, the Etoile, the circle that runs around the Arc de Triomphe, is a terrifying place for a driver who is unfamiliar with Paris traffic. Private cars, taxis, motorcycles, bicycles and other assorted vehicles roar around it at breakneck speed. Driving down a boulevard, I made a wrong turn, was caught up in the maelstrom and was promptly maneuvered into the inner circle. Round and round I drove, unable to extricate the car.

I was utterly frustrated and on the verge of tears when the *agent de police,* whom I must have passed a dozen times, hopped onto my running board. Raising his hand, he stopped the rushing traffic and steered me over to a side street.

"I should really have liked to see more of you, mademoiselle. It's been charming," he said. "But with all these people about. . . ." He gave a Gallic shrug, bowed gallantly and departed.

------- • -------

BON VOYAGE!
ART BUCHWALD

As ONE who has made a close study of tourism, I believe I have isolated a type of tourist that is becoming more and more prevalent. I recently met an American couple who had been touring Europe for a month and were on the home stretch in Paris. In line with my theory, their reactions were predictable. "Jane," the man said, "didn't like Rome, but I still thought it was better than Venice."

Jane said: "That's because Harry didn't have the experiences I had. I still maintain I'd rather spend four days in Venice than two in Rome."

"It was that bad, huh?"

Harry said: "Well it wasn't as bad as Zurich."

Jane agreed: "We both hated Zurich. We didn't have any fun in Zurich at all. It was almost as bad as Copenhagen."

"You didn't like Copenhagen?" I asked.

"Does *anyone* like Copenhagen?" Harry wanted to know.

"We were almost as disappointed in it as we were in London."

"Which," said Jane, "turned out to be dreadful."

"The funny thing," said Harry, "I hated London, but I thought Jane liked it, so I said I liked it."

"And," said Jane, "I thought Harry liked it so I didn't tell him I hated it. If we had known, we would have left right away."

"But where would you have gone?" I asked.

"Not to Monte Carlo, that's for sure," Harry said.

"I don't see what Princess Grace sees in *that place,*" Jane said.

"Well, what about Paris?" I foolishly asked.

"The worst," said Jane. "The people are so unfriendly and the prices are high, and I don't see what there is that's so special about Paris."

"There's no doubt about it," Harry said. "Europe's overrated."

I left them on the Champs Elysees. Harry was explaining to Jane why he didn't like the Arc de Triomphe, and Jane was telling Harry why she didn't like the Place de la Concorde. You couldn't find two happier people.

Taxi!

A taxi was creeping slowly through the New York rush-hour traffic and the passenger was in a hurry. "Please," he said to the driver, "can't you go any faster?"

"Sure I can," the cabby replied. "But I ain't allowed to leave the taxi."

Wife to husband hailing taxi: "Now don't fraternize yourself into a big tip."

An embittered cabby, jammed in Manhattan's garment-center traffic, turned to his fare and grimly told him: "I've got the only solution for New York's traffic snafu. I'd have the mayor call out every car and truck in New York one day, and when they've got everything locked tight, pour concrete over the lot, and start from there."

A New York taxi driver had his own explanation for an excessively rainy week end: "You throw things at the moon, you gotta expect they'll throw something back."

In Washington two D.A.R. ladies hailed a cab and asked to be taken to the convention of the Daughters of the American Revolution.

The cab driver looked them over dubiously and said: "If it's all the same to you, ladies, take some other cab. I'm not driving for any revolutionists."

When a man who wears a hearing aid got into a Washington taxi the driver displayed great interest. "Must be tough to be hard of hearing," sympathized the hackie. "But then, nearly all of us have something the matter, one way or another. Take me, for instance, I can hardly see."

In Paris we took a taxi one day at the peak of the rush hour. It seemed as if every car was determined to push ahead of the others, and when a space opened in front of us, our driver rushed to get in. But another taxi edged us out. Whereupon our driver lifted his hat and without a change of expression said to the other driver, "My compliments to Ma'm'selle, your mother."

Visitors to Beirut, frightened by the speed and nonchalance of Lebanon's cab drivers, are surprised to learn that the accident rate is low. "It shouldn't surprise anybody," explained a cabby. "All the bad drivers are now dead."

Our taxi driver was darting in and out of heavy traffic with complete abandon. After a few harrowing blocks, my friend leaned forward. "Would you please be careful? I have eight children at home," she said.

To which the driver replied, "Lady! You're telling *me* to be careful?"

As my taxi left New York's Penn Station, the driver slammed on the brakes to avoid a pedestrian who darted into our path. When the driver leaned out the window and hurled a string of uncomplimentary epithets, the pedestrian snarled, "Drop dead!"

This set my driver off on another round of verbal fireworks. "Don't you think you'd better calm down?" I said finally. "Just think what this is doing to your blood pressure!"

At this, he turned around. "You got it all wrong, Mac," he said. "I got no cause to worry about hypertension. I know how to release my aggressions."

A cab pulled up to a curb in San Francisco and the driver said, "That'll be $4."

"Oh, no, it won't," sniffed the customer, turning his pockets inside out. "I'm broke, and y'know what they say. You can't get blood out of a turnip!"

"Look, mister," said the cabbie, grabbing him. "You ain't no turnip, and your blood is worth $4 a pint." And he hustled him into the nearby blood-donor center, stood by while a pint was extracted, and collected his four smackers.

Traffic Tangles

The Fort Pitt Bridge in Pittsburgh is a magnificent specimen of engineered chaos. Leaving the city, six lanes merge into four, which in turn become two exits—one going south through a tunnel, the other leading west along the Ohio River. At peak commuter hours, one is reminded of an anthill, with cars constantly changing lanes at high speed, the drivers determined to get across the bridge as quickly as possible.

It was a hot and humid afternoon at the height of the rush hour, when my son's car stalled in the middle of the bridge. As he stood there bewildered and frustrated, cars screeched around him, horns blaring, drivers shouting. Over this babel of animosity came a friendly, compassionate voice offering the only logical advice: "Jump!"

The sage who said "Go West" never had to figure out how to do it on a cloverleaf intersection.

Wherever the place,
Whatever the time,
Every lane moves
But the one where I'm.

Lane borders lane and you haven't much leeway
In the land of the brave and the home of the freeway.

Midtown conversation: "The only way to get around in city traffic is to follow a demonstration."

On his TV show, Jack Paar commented on the traffic problems in Manhattan, complaining that it sometimes takes 15 minutes to go only a couple of blocks. He told about an exasperated fellow motorist who had been delayed for some time in one of these traffic jams. In desperation he rolled down his car window and hollered, "Let me through, will you! I've got important news for President Cleveland!"

City traffic is so bad that most of the streets that intersect are sorry afterward.

Among nature's mysteries is the way she arranges it so that the fellow who doesn't know how to drive in snow and ice is always first in a line of 100 stalled cars.

The woman driving the car in front of us gave a distinct righthand-turn signal. However, her male companion in the front seat put his arm out of the window and over the top of the car and pointed vigorously—indicating she was going to turn left. She did.

Friends of mine were planning to attend a meeting in downtown Miami. One woman offered to drive her car, but said they would have to go via the old route, as she couldn't drive on the expressway. Asked why, she replied, "I can't merge."

Wife to husband as they sit in car trapped in bumper-to-bumper traffic: "I *told* you it was too nice a day to go to the beach!"

Man to family climbing out of car: "Well, we finally found a parking space. Does anybody remember why we're here?"

A man stood on a street corner waiting in vain for the heavy traffic to thin out so he could cross. Finally, as he was about to take his chances, he spied a man on the other side and called to him, "Say, how did you get over there?"

The other cupped his hands about his mouth. "Easy," he shouted. "I was *born* over here!"

A crosstown bus, caught in a midtown Manhattan traffic jam, was barely creeping through an ever-tightening truck tangle between Seventh and Eighth avenues. Finally the bus driver saw an opening at the curb. Swinging his bus in, he flung open the door and called out the stop: "Seven and seven-eighths!"

Man, in traffic tie-up, to passenger: "I've got a job with a real challenge—getting to and from work."

A woman inching through the traffic in downtown Atlanta one morning struck up a conversation with a fellow in the adjacent car. Noting that it was 9:30, she remarked, "Well, I'm glad I wasn't in that 8:30 traffic."

"I hate to tell you this, lady," the man replied, "but this *is* the 8:30 traffic."

Another woman driver!" my husband growled as a car cut us off on a busy freeway. Later we drew abreast of the offender and saw that it was a man. Unrepentant, my husband observed, "His mother probably taught him to drive."

An announcer for station KELP, El Paso, Texas, ended his commercial announcement with: "You can get all these bargains at Meyers, located midway between the downtown traffic mess and the Five Points traffic-circle bottleneck."

It was late afternoon in a large, crowded shopping center near Oak Park, Michigan, when a distraught-looking young housewife dashed into a phone booth. Then she stood outside until a taxi drove up. "Where to, lady?" the driver asked.

"Just drive around the parking lot," she answered. "I've lost my car!"

Driving is like baseball, in a way: it's the number of times you reach home safely that counts.

It was on a narrow country lane. A man driver was about to blow his top; for an hour he had been traveling slowly behind a woman driver. The woman seemed to have a set of hand signals of her own invention, because when she speeded up, slowed down, turned right or left, she would hold a languid hand from the car and wiggle her fingers. Finally, when they approached a wide place in the road and the woman's limp hand appeared with the fingers downward, the bewildered man pulled up alongside and called out, "Madam, do I understand your signal right? You're going underground?"

It's a Mad, Mad World:

DILEMMAS OF MODERN MAN

T HIS SECTION might well have been enlarged to the dimensions of the *Encyclopaedia Britannica*. To NASA, ours may be the Space Age, but for us ordinary earthbound people it is pre-eminently the Age of Friction—a fact that humorists have exploited with energy. It is the small matters of daily living that are the hardest to handle. It is easier to find a suitable marriage partner than to find parking space. It is easier to make $50,000 a year than to get a decent restaurant meal. In fact, many of us are beginning to think that the latter half of our century should be marked "Opened by Mistake." At least that's the impression one gets from the cheerfully despairing jokes and japeries below. Particularly funny is Art Buchwald on transatlantic telephoning. That selection recalls a story told about the great French painter Degas. Degas was dining at a friend's house in which the then new-fangled invention, the telephone, had just been installed. The bell rang. The excited host dropped his knife and fork and proudly rushed to the phone. Degas looked up in horror and amazement, crying out: "Good God! *It* calls and *you* answer?" This little anecdote points up one of the "dilemmas of modern man": As between man and the machine, which is boss?

Separate Tables

Peeved patron in restaurant: "You say you're the same waiter I gave my order to? Somehow I expected a much older man."

French waiter to American couple: "Monsieur, we have an American-tourist special—ten percent off if you *don't* try to order in French."

Man in restaurant, trying to cut tough steak, to wife: "I see what the waiter meant when he recommended their *pièce de résistance.*"

Duncan Hines appraising new eatery: "If the soup had been as warm as the wine; if the wine had been as old as the turkey; and if the turkey had had a breast like the waitress, it would have been a splendid dinner."

A friend indeed is one who takes you to lunch even though you are non-deductible.

Man to business associate in restaurant: "You've bought lunch the last five times. Let's flip for this one!"

Penciled on the wall of a run-down restaurant: "Duncan Hines wept here."

A plump gentleman ate a fine meal at an expensive New York restaurant, topped it off with some rare Napoleon brandy, then summoned the headwaiter. "Do you recall," he asked pleasantly, "how a year ago I ate just such a repast here and then, because I couldn't pay for it, you had me thrown into the gutter like a veritable bum?"

"I'm very sorry," began the contrite headwaiter.

"It's quite all right," said the guest, "but I'm afraid I'll have to trouble you again."

He ordered *Poulet à la Ferrari,* and it turned out to be a chicken that had been run over by a sports car.

New York restaurateur Toots Shor boarded a taxicab and asked the driver, "Know of a decent restaurant? I'm a stranger here."

"Yes, sir," said the cabby. "One of the greatest eating places in this whole world is Toots Shor's on 51st Street. I'll drive you straight there."

At the end of the journey Toots was so pleased that he slipped the cabby a ten-spot, saying, "Keep the change."

"T'anks," said the driver. "T'anks a lot, Mr. Shor!"

An American newspaperman was attracted to a dancer in a Madrid night club. Advised by the headwaiter that he could take her away from the job for the rest of the evening if he paid for her time, the correspondent proceeded to write out a check. This the headwaiter was obliged to refuse. But, on learning that the patron had a Diners' Club card, he gravely agreed to charge the lady as dessert.

A well-known comedian was in Pittsburgh for a one-week stand. On Monday he picked out a restaurant that looked attractive, and liked everything except the bread. "I always eat whole wheat," he told the waitress, but she brought white. On Tuesday, he reminded her about the whole wheat, but was served white bread again. Wednesday she made the same mistake, not to mention Thursday and Friday. Finally on Saturday when she took his order, the actor said, "Just for the heck of it, I think I'll take white bread today."

"That's funny," said the waitress, "Aren't you the party who always orders whole wheat?"

When somebody phoned Mike Romanoff's restaurant in Hollywood and asked, "How much is dinner?" Joe, the maître d'hôtel, replied with sympathy: "If you have to ask, believe me, you can't afford it."

One woman to another in tearoom: "The service here is terrible, but you don't mind waiting, because the food's so poor."

Matron, hesitating in door of restaurant, to headwaiter: "Do your waitresses have everything on?"

Man in restaurant to waiter: "What's our offense? We've been on bread and water for almost an hour."

Age of Affluence

THE LIFE ABUNDANT
WILL STANTON

I T WAS Robert Louis Stevenson who first observed that the world was full of a number of things. But the fact is, in his day the world wasn't even half-full. It just seemed full to him. Today there are more things than R. L. S. ever dreamed of.

For instance, there are more people. And they have more children, and the children have more things, and the things have more parts that fall off and get stepped on when you get out of bed to answer the phone. And, of course, there are more phones. More people making calls, too. But not so many people answering. The ones who don't answer have recordings telling you the doctor is out.

There are more weeks in the year—Use More Lard Week, Learn to Play the Guitar Week, Be Kind to Stepmother Week. . . . And through Daylight Saving Time we even have more hours in the day. I suspect someday our grandchildren will be expected to pay it all back, the same as the National Debt.

There are more new cars today. There are also more old cars. In addition, there are more highways where people can drive their new cars and look at the piles of old cars.

There are more comedians. There's still the same number of jokes—but they get told more often.

There are more books, and there is more interest in sex, and the relationship is the same as the chicken and the egg. From best-sellers to comic books, any child who hasn't acquired an extensive sex education by the age of 12 belongs in remedial reading.

There are more rich people and more poor people. There are more politicians who were formerly poor people and are now rich people and consequently understand the problems of both sides.

There are more diseases for doctors to diagnose, more laws for attorneys to find loopholes in. There is more sin for the clergy to think about. In fact, it wouldn't do the rest of us any harm to think a little more about sin, now that we have more leisure.

There is more insecurity, bird watching, incompatibility, tomato paste, nagging backache, outdoor living and sonic boom—to name a few. I don't know how it balances out, whether it's good or bad. I do know that Stevenson was dead wrong. By our standards his world was practically empty.

———— • ————

In supermarket, one man with overloaded cart to another: I'm caught between the population explosion and the abundant life."

Wife to husband in restaurant: "Heavens, if you're going to keep worrying about prices, what was the point in getting the Diners' Club card?"

Wife to husband: "This affluent society I keep hearing about—when are we going to join it?"

Budget-balancing husband to wife: "I don't know how it's possible, but we seem to be in the middle-income, upper-outgo group."

———— • ————

A San Diego physician with a boat, a big house, lots of insurance and three kids in college put it this way: "For my family to go on living in the way they are living now, I can't just die. I've got to die accidentally."

Overheard at a party: "The reason I know I'll never be rich is that my wife thinks we have to create the impression that we already are."

In plushy restaurant, wife to husband: "Can I order anything I want, dear, or is this coming out of our house money?"

At bus stop: "My family doesn't need comsumer education—they're natural-born consumers."

Noticing how eagerly my teen-age daughter fights down every obstacle in her path to answer the telephone on the first ring, I told her that in my day girls used to wait for the third or fourth ring so they wouldn't appear too anxious.

"Good gosh, Mom!" she retorted. "That was before the age of status symbols. Do you want everyone to think I live in an underphoned home?"

City Blights

Playwright Arthur Kober once stayed in a Hollywood hotel with thin walls. He was awakened in the middle of the night by a sleepy voice saying, "Would you get me a drink of water, dear?"

He got up, stumbled to the bathroom and came back with a glass of water before he realized he was sleeping alone.

Man, trying on suit, to salesman: "Do you mind if I step outside and look at it in the smog?"

Mother to child lunching at outdoor city restaurant: "Finish your soup, dear, before it gets dirty."

THE PEOPLE UPSTAIRS

CHESTER T. CROWELL

THE TIME has come to give some attention to the weirdest of all tribes, those strangers whom you never meet but whose goings-on defy reason—The-People-Who-Live-in-the-Apartment-Above. Your only acquaintance with them comes through the medium of unexplained, often alarming, sounds. Perhaps more data would promote understanding and good will.

During 20 years I have seen only one important factual contribution about such people. It was an item in the New York *Times* under a Los Angeles date line:

> *For 10 years Mrs. Frances Jebb has lived at 1036 West Washington Boulevard, and never complained to her landlord, but when another tenant, Richard Godfrey, 18, started taking a draft horse upstairs of an evening she called the police. The officers found Tuffie, a 350-pound midget draft horse, enjoying all the comforts of a furnished apartment.*
>
> *"I've never let Tuffie out of my sight," the horse-fancier is reported to have explained.*

That the New York *Times* should have had to reach all the way across the continent for this testimony is beyond my understanding.

I have lived in New York City; I am certain that The-People-Who-

Lived-in-the-Apartment-Above often harbored draft horses; I think they also had moose, mice, deer, psychoses and delirium tremens. One family certainly had nine cats; another, six dogs.

The subject should be examined on a broad, scientific basis. For example, I should like to know why the pair who live above me go to bed four, five and even six times every night. I am sure they do this because I hear them pull out the lower drawer of the couch, thus turning it into a bed. The sound is unmistakable. They grab it first at one end and then at the other, worrying it out inch by inch. Then they close it and start over, sometimes immediately, sometimes after an interval of five minutes to half an hour.

When they have made up enough beds to retire for the night, they open the window. They have their own peculiar technique. One of them rushes at the window, leaps into the air, and strikes the lower panel with both feet. While the wood is quivering the other attacks with tooth and claw. Evidently they are under the impression that a window, unless overwhelmed, will fight back.

Sometimes they go in for sports during the long winter evenings. Each takes an article of furniture with little rollers under it, and they push these the length of the apartment and back again. They are not rearranging the furniture, unless by rearranging is meant massing all of it first at one end of the apartment and then at the other. There are no halfway stops and the pace is appalling.

There is other evidence that they are fond of athletics. Every morning they run, and run, and run. They sprint into the kitchen and put on the coffee pot, then tear back to the bathroom. But their running form is not good: instead of being poised on the ball of the foot they run on the heel, and I predict a flock of Grade A bone bruises. They must be very hardy or they would have them now. To see them getting dressed must be a wonderful sight. I have to stand still, at least for a moment, to get into my pants; socks also slow me down. They never stop. I wonder how they manage to drink their coffee.

Saturday evenings they always have guests in, and insane laughter, without audible cause, comes cascading down the ventilating shaft until midnight.

Every morning, except Sundays, The-People-Who-Live-in-the-Apartment-Above slam the door at half after eight o'clock and go galloping along the corridor as though they were going to work. My guess is that they have to report to a psychopathic clinic.

---•---

When my wife and I moved into our new apartment I discovered a convenience men expect to find only in hotels: a slot in the medicine cabinet for the disposal of used razor blades. But about two weeks later the woman in the apartment next to ours asked my wife to please tell me to stop using the slot.

The used blades were dropping into her medicine cabinet.

Apartment—a place where you start to turn off the radio and find you've been listening to your neighbor's.

A couple who recently moved to New York are just beginning to learn how wary city people are. The other day, for example, when the wife found that she needed some boxes to store winter clothes in, the husband went to the corner supermarket to get them. "May I have a few empty cartons?" he asked the manager.

The manager of the store stared at him suspiciously. "Empty cartons of what?" he demanded.

Number, Please

YES, I DON'T HAVE YOUR PARTY NOW

ART BUCHWALD

A RECENT advertisement in an American magazine caught my eye. The headline said: "HEADING FOR EUROPE? PLAN AHEAD BY PHONE." The copy, underneath a picture of a very contented man, read: "A good way to smooth your business trip abroad is to call ahead. You can *talk* to the people you want to see, find out when they're available, decide where and when to meet. . . . It's easy. Just give the operator your call."

The reason the advertisement caught my eye was that I had received a call from the West Coast on the previous evening and

I marveled at the way it was all made to sound so simple. It was midnight, Paris time, when the call came through. An English-speaking operator with a heavy French accent, said, "Monsieur Buchwald, you have a call from America. Can you take it?"

I assured the operator I could.

"Then we will call you back," and she hung up.

A half hour later the phone rang again. "Monsieur Buchwald, we have a call from America for you. Are you ready to take it?"

I said I was.

"Thank you. We will call back."

Fifteen minutes later the phone rang again. "Monsieur Buchwald, America is calling you."

"I know," I said.

"Please do not hang up," she warned me.

I promised her I wouldn't.

Then I heard the French operator say, "Hello, New York? We have Monsieur Buchwald on the phone."

A voice with a heavy New York accent said, "All right, Paris! I will connect you with Beverly Hills."

There was a pause and then I heard the New York operator say, "Hello, Beverly Hills?"

The Beverly Hills operator said, "Yes, New York."

The New York operator said, "I have Mr. Buchwald on the phone."

"Just a minute, New York," the Beverly Hills operator said.

There was a pause, and then I heard her talk to someone on the other end of the line. "We have Mr. Buchwald on the line from Paris."

The person at the end of the line said, "Just a minute. We're trying to find the party who made the call."

The Beverly Hills operator said, "Hello, New York. We're trying to find the party." The New York operator said, "Hello, Paris, Beverly Hills is trying to find your party." The Paris operator said to me, *"Ne quittez pas."*

I promised I wouldn't *quitter.* Then I heard a man's voice. "Hello, Art?"

"Just a minute," the Beverly Hills operator said. "Hello, New York, we have the party on the phone."

"Thank you, Beverly Hills," the New York operator said. "Hello, Paris. Is Mr. Buchwald there?"

The Paris operator said, "Monsieur Buchwald, are you there?"

I said I was.

The Paris operator said, "Monsieur Buchwald is there."

"Thank you, Paris," the New York operator said. "Hello, Beverly Hills. You can go ahead."

"Hello, Art," a man said. "This is Dave."

"Dave who?"

"Dave . . . ."

"I can't hear you."

"Can you hear me now?"

"Yes, I can hear you now."

"Okay! This is Dave . . . ."

"I'm sorry, I can't get the last name."

"Operator, operator," I heard him say. "What's the matter with this connection?"

"Just a minute," I heard the Beverly Hills operator say. "Hello, New York, can you hear me?"

"Yes, Beverly Hills. Hello, Paris, can you hear us?"

"Yes, New York, we hear you."

Then New York said, "They hear you now."

The Beverly Hills operator said, "Go ahead now. Paris can hear you."

"Art . . . Dave . . . want . . . Bardot. . . . Can you do it?"

"I'm sorry, but I can't hear you. Why don't you send me a letter?"

"Send you a what?"

The Paris operator said, "A letter."

The New York operator said, "A letter."

The Beverly Hills operator said, "A letter."

Dave said, "A letter?"

"That's right," I said. "SEND ME A LETTER."

"Okay," said Dave. "I'll send you a letter."

"Thanks, Dave," I said. "It was swell talking with you."

The Beverly Hills operator said, "Are you finished talking?"

The New York operator said, "Hello, Paris. Are you finished talking?"

The Paris operator said, "Are you finished talking?"

"Finished?" I said. "How do I know? I don't even know who I was talking to."

———— • ————

Man to man, outside phone booth: "I'm afraid it will be quite a long conversation. She's just changed ears."

———— • ————

One of the most frustrating conversations in theatrical history is recorded by *Theatre Arts* magazine: A subscriber dialed "Information" for the magazine's number. "Sorry," drawled the lady, "but there is nobody listed by the name of 'Theodore Arts.'"

"It's not a person; it's a publication," insisted the subscriber. "I want *Theatre Arts.*"

The operator's voice rose a few decibels. "I told you," she repeated, "we have no listing for Theodore Arts."

"Confound it," hollered the subscriber, "the word is Theatre: T-H-E-A-T-R-E."

"That," said the operator with crushing finality, "is not the way to spell Theodore."

A fellow on producer Darryl Zanuck's crew spent several months in the Belgian Congo filming *The Roots of Heaven*. While he was there he collected a trunkful of shrunken heads. He decided they might be worth something; so when he returned to Hollywood he called up Saks Fifth Avenue, Beverly Hills.

"To whom do I speak about selling some shrunken heads?" he asked the switchboard operator.

She told him to wait a moment. Then there was a clicking sound and a firm, businesslike voice said, "This is the head buyer speaking."

We wanted to telephone one of my daughter's dancing-school classmates, about whom we knew nothing except that her name was Johnson. There were five Johnsons in the telephone book so we started down the list. Johnson number three was the first one at home. "Is this the Johnson where the little girl goes to dancing school?" I asked.

"No," came the answer. "This is the Johnson where the man was in the bathtub."

The voice on the telephone told me I must have dialed the wrong number.

"Are you sure?" I insisted.

The stranger replied, "Have I ever lied to you before?"

Workers in a Wichita, Kansas, auto-repair garage have stopped saying "Body shop" when they answer the phone. A number of long silences, gasps and indignant disconnections led to the discovery that their phone number was just one digit away from that of a local funeral home.

One monk to another: "They switched to all-digit dialing. It's IV VII VII IX III V."

A man has a phone number that seems to attract a lot of misdialers. He routinely asks what number they dialed, then suggests that they dial it again, more carefully.

But one day, when he asked a woman what number she had dialed she replied, "Well, I guess I must have dialed yours, whatever that is."

Having dialed a wrong long-distance number, a woman frantically demanded, "Is June there?"

A man's deep voice replied, "No, madam. I don't know where *you* are, but it's still April here."

Wakened out of deep sleep, man answering phone: "You have the wrong idiot, you number!"

Science
Stumbles On:
THE AGE OF TECHNOLOGY

A COUPLE OF PAGES BACK, we popped this question:
Which is boss, man or machine? The pages following
give the answer, at any rate the humorists' answer.
Good old machine wins, hands down. The mutilation of the
IBM card is sinful; the mutilation of the human spirit is
only to be expected. If you feel like communicating with

anything other than a tape recording, talk to yourself. (Even this may disappear; we'll be programmed from birth, so that all we human tapeworms can do is listen to the recording of ourselves.) In a few paragraphs of hollow laughter Corey Ford's "Carry Me Back to Old Yesterday!" sums up our forlorn case against technology. It's probably too late for anything *more* than laughter—our ancestors should have brained Ug-glug just before he invented the wheel. On the other hand, as someone once remarked, it's a good thing the wheel was invented before the automobile. Otherwise just think of the awful screeching!

Computer Complaints

"R U THERE, MADAM?"
CONSTANCE L. MELARO

August 17

DEAR MADAM:

Our records show an outstanding balance of $2.98 on your account. If you have already remitted this amount, kindly disregard this notice.

THIS IS A BUSINESS MACHINE CARD.

PLEASE DO NOT SPINDLE OR MUTILATE.

August 19

Gentlemen:

I do *not* have an outstanding balance. I attached a note with my payment advising you that I had been billed *twice* for the same amount: once under my first name, middle initial and last name; and then under my two first initials and my last name. (The former is correct.) Please check your records.

September 17

Dear Madam:

Our records show a delinquent balance of $2.98 on your account. Please remit $3.40. This includes a handling charge.
THIS IS A BUSINESS MACHINE CARD.
PLEASE DO NOT SPINDLE OR MUTILATE.

September 19

Dear Machine:

You're not paying attention! I am NOT delinquent. I do *not* owe this money. I was billed TWICE for the same purchase. PLEASE look into this.

October 17

Dear Madam:

Our records show you to be delinquent for three months. Please remit the new charges of $13.46, plus $4.10. (This includes a handling charge.) May we have your immediate attention in this matter.
THIS IS A BUSINESS MACHINE CARD.
PLEASE DO NOT SPINDLE OR MUTILATE.

October 19

Dear Machine:

My attention! You want MY attention! Listen here, YOU ARE WRONG!!! I DON'T owe you $4.10. CAN YOU UNDERSTAND THAT? I also DON'T owe you the new charge of $13.46. You billed ME for my MOTHER'S purchase. Please correct this statement AT ONCE!

November 17

Dear Madam:

Our records now show you to be delinquent for four months in the total amount of $17.56, plus $1.87 handling charges.

283

Please remit in full in ten days or your account will be turned over to our Auditing Department for collection.

THIS IS A BUSINESS MACHINE CARD.

PLEASE DO NOT SPINDLE OR MUTILATE.

November 19

Dear Human Machine Programmer—
Dear ANYONE Human:

WILL YOU PLEASE TAKE YOUR HEAD OUT OF THE COMPUTER LONG ENOUGH TO READ THIS? I DON'T OWE YOU THIS MONEY!!! I DON'T OWE YOU *any* MONEY. *None.*

December 17

Dear Madam:

Is there some question about your statement? Our records show no payments on your account since August. Please call DI 7-9601 and ask for Miss Gilbert at your earliest convenience.

THIS IS A BUSINESS MACHINE CARD.

PLEASE DO NOT SPINDLE OR MUTILATE.

December 18

. . . Deck the hall with boughs of holly . . . "Good afternoon. Carver's hopes you have enjoyed its recorded program of carols. May I help you?"

"Hello. Yes . . . My bill is . . . should I wait for a 'beep' before I talk?"

"About your bill?"

"Yes. Yes, it's my bill. There's a mistake. . . ."

"One moment, please. I'll connect you with Adjustments!"

Good afternoon and Merry Christmas. This is a recorded message. All our lines are in service now. If you will please be patient, one of our adjusters will be with you as soon as the line is free. Meanwhile, Carver's hopes you will enjoy its program of Christmas carols. . . . Deck the halls with boughs of holly. . . ."

December 26

Dear Machine:

I tried to call you on December 18. Also the 19th, 20th, 21st, 22nd, the 23rd and the 24th. But all I got was a recorded message and those Christmas carols. Please, oh, please, won't you turn me over to a human? *Any* human?

January 17

Dear Madam:

Our Credit Department has turned your delinquent account over to us for collection. Won't you please remit this amount now? We wish to coöperate with you in every way possible, but this is considerably past due. May we have your check at this time.

Very truly yours,
HENRY J. HOOPER, Auditor

January 19

Dear Mr. Hooper:

YOU DOLL! You gorgeous HUMAN doll! I refer you to letters I sent to your department, dated the 19th of September, October, November, December, which should clarify the fact that I owe you nothing.

February 17

Dear Madam:

According to our microfilm records, our billing was in error. Your account is clear; you have no balance.

We hope there will be no further inconvenience to you. This was our fault.

Very truly yours,
HENRY J. HOOPER, Auditor

February 19

Dear Mr. Hooper:
Thank you! Oh, thank you, thank you, thank you!

March 17

Dear Madam:

Our records show you to be delinquent in the amount of $2.98, erroneously posted last August to a nonexistent account. May we have your remittance at this time?

THIS IS A BUSINESS MACHINE CARD.
PLEASE DO NOT SPINDLE OR MUTILATE.

March 19

Dear Machine:

I give up. You win. Here's a check for $2.98. Enjoy yourself.

285

April 17

Dear Madam:

Our records show an overpayment on your part of $2.98. We are crediting this amount to your account.

THIS IS A BUSINESS MACHINE CARD.

PLEASE DO NOT SPINDLE OR MUTILATE.

———— • ————

Computer operator to office mate: "If it writes 'To err is human' once more, I'm going to cut off its electricity."

A large computer-oriented Dallas corporation has the following entry in one of its ledgers: "This correcting entry is to correct an incorrect correction made incorrectly in January."

At a meeting of air scientists and pilots, the scientists made it clear that they would like to replace the pilot in the aircraft with instruments and servo-mechanisms. Scott Crossfield, a U.S. test pilot, rejoined by asking: "Where can you find another non-linear servo-mechanism weighing only 150 pounds and having great adaptability that can be produced so cheaply by completely unskilled labor?"

A store owner, telling one of his employes why he need not worry about being replaced by automation, said, "They haven't invented a machine yet that does absolutely nothing."

At the University of Illinois, where students number about 30,000, the College of Fine and Applied Arts has tried to find a way of humanizing the trend to computerization. Early in the semester the administration sends out a card to check the student's program. It begins: "Dear 344-28-0430: We have a personal interest in you."

———— • ————

One unemployed man to another: "What hurts was that I wasn't replaced by a whole computer—just a transistor."

Man to boss: "Computer No. 14 isn't working properly—at least that's the information Computer No. 13 is putting out."

Boasting that his electronic brain could do anything, the designer told a skeptical friend to ask any question.

"Where is my father right now?" the friend asked.

Out popped the answer: "Your father is fishing in Nova Scotia."

The friend delightedly disagreed: "My father, Robert Brewster III, is in San Francisco. I just talked to him on the phone."

Retorted the machine: "Robert Brewster III is in San Francisco. Your father is fishing in Nova Scotia."

Small boy presenting report card to father: "The teaching machine doesn't like me!"

In a regional Health, Education and Welfare office, a stack of punch-cards was placed in a sorting machine, and the machine was set to divide the cards according to the sex of the person named on the card. The outcome was five stacks of cards.

This Is a Recording

A New York artist has tape-recorded the following message for his phone-answering device: "I'm not at my studio at the present time, but if you care to leave a message, please do so now. On the other hand, if you are a machine, I'm glad we could get together."

"WHEN YOU HEAR THE TONE . . ."

BILL VAUGHAN

Hello, Sutforth's Dry Goods?"
This is Sutforth's Dry Goods, your wish our command. This is a recording. When you hear the tone please wait one second then place your order. (Blap . . . followed by several seconds of silence.) Thank you for calling Sutforth's. This is a recording.

"Will you say that again, please?"
This is Sutforth's Dry Goods, your wish our command. This is a recording. When you hear the tone please wait one second then place your order. (Blap . . . followed by several seconds of silence.) Thank you for calling Sutforth's. This is a recording.

"You're not a recording. Instead of saying, 'This *is* Sutforth's,' the second time you emphasized the *this.* I ought to know a recording when I hear one; it's all I ever get. You are a real, live person."
This is Sutforth's. . . .

"Shut up. (Aside) Hey, Francine, come listen to this. I've got a real, live person on the telephone. I am not kidding. It is not another of my jokes. Listen. . . ."
This is Sutforth's Dry Goods, your wish our command. This is a recording. When you hear the tone please wait one second then place your order. (Blap . . . followed by several seconds of silence.) Thank you for calling Sutforth's. This is a recording.

"You are a person. A human being with dandruff and gallstones and who-knows-what-all, like everybody else. I can hear you breathing. (Aside) Francine, couldn't you hear the breathing? What do you mean, you're not sure? It was huh-huh-huh. Breathing, like I haven't heard on a telephone in five years. I tell you there is a human hand holding that phone! Listen again."

This is Sutforth's Dry Goods, your wish our command. This is a recording. When you hear the tone please wait one second. . . .

"I know you. You're old man Sutforth and you're drunk. Or you're too cheap to fix your recorder. What's the matter with you, Sutforth? (Aside) What do you mean it doesn't sound like old man Sutforth? I go bowling with him every week and he breathes just that way—huh-huh-huh."

This is Sutforth's. . . .

"Cut it out, Sutforth. If I wanted to talk to you I'd see you at the bowling alley. Why don't you admit that you are just pretending to be a recording. Speak up like a man."

. . . Thank you for calling Sutforth's. This is a recording.

"All right, Sutforth, you've gone too far this time."

Click.

"Hello, police department? I want to report a fiendish scheme by old man Sutforth, trying to drive me as batty as he is by pretending to be a recording."

This is your police department. When you hear the tone, state the nature of your complaint. This is a recording.

"Clancy? Sergeant Clancy. That's you. I can hear you breathing. Pretending to be a recording. It's a plot to unhinge my mind. Real people answering telephones. (Aside) Call the psychiatrist, Francine. You already have? What did he say? A *recording* answered? You fool. It wasn't a recording. It was the doctor pretending to be a recording."

Click.

"Lie down? A cool cloth? The green-and-white capsule? Thank you, dear."

———— • ————

To executive picking up desk phone: "You have dialed a nonworking number. Please hang up and dial again, and next time don't be so clumsy. This is a recorded announcement."

Angry man on phone: "What do you mean you're a recording? You called me!"

———— • ————

Recently I installed an electronic telephone-answering machine to take my business calls while I am away. I soon realized, however, that the electronic age has gone too far—another machine keeps calling my machine. It drones on for its allotted time about the virtues of some product while my machine obediently gives it instructions on how to leave a message. Then come the tone signals from each machine and silence while each waits for an incoming message. There is none. The operators of the machine on the other end have obviously chalked me up as a "no response" and have programmed their machine to call me again.

At least that's what I think has happened. Or could it be that the machines are attracted to one another? You see, my machine has a male voice recording, theirs has a female.

Secretary on phone: "Our automatic answering device is away for repair. This is a person speaking."

Man in elevator hears voice from loudspeaker: "This is your automated elevator wishing you a Merry Christmas."

Voice over telephone: "This is a recording. You have been dialing the wrong recording."

Space Shots

It's Astronomical
Twinkle, twinkle, little star,
I don't wonder what you are;
I surmised your spot in space
When you left your missile base.
Any wondering I do
Centers on the price of you,
And I shudder when I think
What you're costing us per twink.

Several of us waiting at a bus stop were listening to reports of a space flight on the transistor radio carried by one commuter. After a while one woman remarked, "Well, they've been around the world once, and we're still waiting for the bus."

The young son of a Cape Kennedy missiles engineer was attending his first day at kindergarten. When the teacher announced that the children were going to learn to count, the boy said proudly that he already knew how and he started to demonstrate: "10-9-8-7-6-5-4-3-2-1—Nuts!"

Breathless scientist, to returning spaceman: "Is there any life on Mars?"

Spaceman: "Well, there's a little on Saturday night, but it's awfully dead the rest of the week."

A Gainesville, Texas, woman has applied for space-flight training. "I weigh only 95 pounds," she explains, "and I also play the harp."

Salesgirl showing toy rocket to prospective customer: "This is a very realistic space toy—half the time it doesn't work."

Woman running toward launching pad where space ship has just lifted off: "The car keys, Arthur—you've got the car keys!"

At missile site: "Out to launch."

Boss to operator of space-rocket lever: "Just a simple 10-9-8-7 countdown, Chalmers—never mind the little Indians!"

At launching site, woman to astronaut: "What's a mother for unless it's to see that they've checked your retros, packed your drogue chute, checked your oxygen. . .?"

A space-agency psychologist asked one of the astronauts what he was thinking about as he strapped himself into his craft atop the rocket which was to hurl him into space.

"All I keep thinking," he replied, "is that everything that makes this thing go was supplied by the lowest bidder!"

Machine Aged

During the afternoon coffee break at our plant, a fellow put his dime in the coffee machine, pushed the button labeled "Coffee, Sugar and Double Cream" and waited expectantly. There was the usual whir but no cup. And then the two jets went into action. Sweet cream poured out of one, and black coffee came from the other. They splashed onto the grill where the cup should have been and drizzled down the drain. The man stood there bug-eyed until the measured amount had been dispensed. Then he proclaimed philosophically, "That's real automation. This thing even drinks it for you!"

An auto manufacturer claims to have a finish that'll outlast the car. A friend says he bought one and finds himself with only the paint and six payments left.

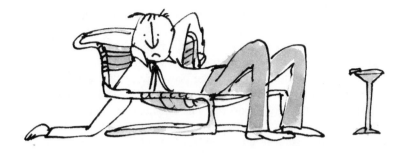

CARRY ME BACK TO OLD YESTERDAY!

COREY FORD

S OMETIMES I think science has gone too far. All these efforts
to make life more efficient only make mine more complicated. Each shiny new push-button invention is designed
to save time, but the time I save is spent trying to figure out which
button to push.

I admit I'm a complete inefficiency expert when it comes to
things mechanical. Recently I bought a fire extinguisher with
directions reading, "To operate, turn bottom up and bump head on
floor." Which pretty well describes my own frustration.

I can remember when you opened a door by turning a knob.
Today a door slides into the wall, or folds in the middle like an
accordion and pinches my fingers. Or the door is concealed in a
row of identical glass panels, along which I move helplessly like
a goldfish in a tank, looking for the one that opens. Most confusing of all is the furtive type which operates with a photoelectric
eye. It always catches me unawares. I shift my bundles to one
arm, extend my free hand and give the door a hard shove just as
it parts silently in front of me, causing me to lose my balance and
land on my momentum.

I wouldn't object to home improvements if I could see what
they improve. All the windows in the House of Tomorrow are her-
metically sealed, and an air conditioner blows an icy draft down
the back of my neck during the night. Instead of a down-filled
comforter, there is an electric blanket which can be turned up if
the temperature drops while I'm asleep. By the time I've switched

293

on the light and located my glasses in order to adjust the controls, I'm wide awake.

The dependable coal stove has been replaced by an eleborate electric model with an instrument panel like the console in a missile-launching station, but if the power fails I have to cook in the fireplace. The old gooseneck lamp has yielded to a fluorescent ceiling light that I can't read by. The garbage pail has given way to an automatic-disposal unit, which gives way in turn whenever I fail to remove such indigestible items as olive pits or demitasse spoons. Two thousand years of scientific achievement, and still I'm sorting garbage!

They can't even leave furniture alone. Form follows function, the edict states, but the function doesn't follow *my* form. Metal chairs with crisscrossed leather thongs may be the *dernier cri* in fashion, but I feel as if I were staging a sitdown strike on a sidewalk grating. Back when I was a boy we had a porch hammock in which I could creak back and forth contentedly while reading the Sunday papers. Try to find one today. Now my lawn furniture is made of bent aluminum tubing, supporting a plastic seat shaped like a bedpan, which is hard to sit in and harder still to get out of.

The trouble with modern conveniences is that they're so inconvenient. The paper towels in a public washroom are locked inside a metal receptacle which bears the cryptic instructions, "Pull down and pull up to pull out." After pawing over the bolts and rivets of the box, trying to find the release, I reach inside the slot and pinch off a quarter-inch of protruding towel, which promptly turns to dough in my fingers.

The fad for concealment, in the interest of design, has spread all the way to Detroit. The streamlined dashboard of the latest model car is a masterpiece of obscurity. All the gadgets look alike, and I'm always pulling out the air intake to turn on the lights. The emergency brake is tucked away slyly beneath my feet, and in a crisis I yank the lever where the brake used to be and release the hood instead. At least I can't see the accident when it happens.

Each forward step that science takes leaves me two steps further behind. A few years ago they installed the dial system in my New Hampshire town. Previously I could ring the local operator, chat pleasantly about the weather and ask her for a name instead of a number. She knew everyone in town and would inform me that the party I was calling had just strolled past the telephone office and should be home for lunch in a few minutes. Now on long-distance calls I have to memorize an access code plus an area code plus seven digits, and if I make a mistake all I get is a jeering whine or a blatant Bronx cheer.

The worst part of self-operating devices is that I can't operate them myself. When my dishwasher has finished its cycle and I try to open it, it just starts up again. If anything goes wrong with my television set, I have to call a repairman. "It's your own fault," he tells me sternly. "You've been fooling with them dials again."

My electric typewriter goes so fast that allthewordsruntogether, and if I rest my finger on a key for a moment, trying to compose my thoughts, it keeps typing the same letter over and overrrrrrrr. I'd use a pencil, but I've just bought an electric pencil sharpener.

Everything is faster these days, but it takes you longer to get there. Jet airplanes span the continent in a flash, but you have to wait a long time at both terminals and then spend two hours more driving into town. Cars zoom along a superhighway without a traffic light, but if you miss your turnoff you have to go another 50 miles to the next exit.

In short, science has taken such gigantic strides that we're almost back where we started. Take a friend in Connecticut who has built a fallout shelter beneath his house and spends all his time down there. I asked him if he was afraid of a nuclear attack.

"Oh, it isn't that," he replied with a happy smile. "My wife didn't want to buy new furniture for the shelter, so we lugged down some things we'd stored away in the attic. There's an overstuffed sofa that's long enough to stretch out on, and an old-fashioned Morris chair I can adjust by hand and a music box that winds up with a key. I don't even have a phone. I haven't been so comfortable in years."

I'm starting a fallout shelter tomorrow. It's the only answer to survival in our Efficient Age.

———— • ————

We've developed a coin machine guaranteed to give the customer satisfaction," the salesman told the storekeeper.

"You mean it's built so the customer can't lose his coin?"

"No," replied the salesman. "But when he kicks it, it groans."

Garage mechanic to car owner: "My advice is to keep the oil and change the car."

———— • ————

---•---

Man, on hands and knees, looking under car: "It's rejected the new carburetor."

---•---

TECHNICALLY SPEAKING —
I CAN'T

CORNELIA OTIS SKINNER

AMONG THE people who have my admiration are those who know the correct terminology for mechanical devices which are not necessarily up their alley. Take, for example, the car owner who, though no expert on automobiles, can drive into a garage and give the mechanic an accurate diagnosis of what's wrong.

I, who wouldn't know a gasket from a tisket or a tasket, am forced to employ my own limited powers of description when confronted by a misbehaving motor. Not long ago I was obliged to seek help, not from our local garage, where they know me as a somewhat simple-minded customer and never ask me to explain, but at a busy garage in a small New England town along the highway on which my motor had started doing peculiar things.

A mechanic approached with the kindly attitude of a doctor ready to hear the patient's complaints. I smiled and said, "She's acting up."

I used the feminine pronoun to give an impression of automotive knowledge. It would never occur to me to call an automobile a "she," as though it were an ocean liner or a hurricane, but for some curious reason nearly all men do.

"How 'acting up'?" the mechanic asked.

"Well," I explained, "every now and then, she sort of goes *bloomp.*"

"Bloomp? I see," he said, although it was quite obvious that he didn't.

"It is really more of a *chunk.*"

"A chunk? Do you mean you've got a chunk of foreign matter in your manifold?"

"I have no idea," I replied. I also had no idea that I possessed a manifold. It sounded biblical. I tried to assume the expression of someone who knew all about manifolds.

"Is she missing?" he asked.

"No, she's not missing. It's just that every once in a while there'll be this *flonk,* and then she'll shudder."

The mechanic was silent.

"Let me take you for a little ride," I said. "Jump in beside me and I think you'll get what I mean."

Unfortunately, to the mechanic, who was obviously a God-fearing, happily married man, it must have sounded archly coy, and the idea he got wasn't exactly what I had in mind.

"All I'm asking you to do is listen!" I said impatiently.

With cautious dignity he got in, and I drove down Main Street. The car, need I say it, ran with the smooth performance of a Rolls-Royce. I varied the speed, but it neither bloomped nor chunked nor did it so much as flonk, and never once did it shudder. As a matter of fact, "she" behaved like a perfect lady, which was highly infuriating.

My passenger tersely suggested that we return to the garage. When we got there, he made the further suggestion that I leave the car, do any errands I had in town and come back in an hour. Meanwhile he'd try to locate the trouble. I said okay.

When I returned, the trouble had been located and cured. It seems that what had gone haywire was . . . oh, well, why should anyone want to know? Besides, I wasn't really listening to the explanation.

———————— • ————————

In this day of almost total dependence on mechanical gadgets, a Minneapolis supermarket has found it necessary to put this warning on its entrance: "Caution. No Automatic Door."

Editorial in the Arlington *Northern Virginia Sun:*

Who might be taken as the symbolic representative of Western man at this stage of civilization? Some astronaut? Scientist? Movie star? Statesman? Soldier? Poet? Engineer? We nominate the 29-year-old Chicagoan who, during a recent visit to New Orleans, was knocked into Bourbon Street during a scuffle and sucked up by a street-sweeping machine and carried for three blocks before the device ejected him.

———————— • ————————

The Price of Progress

TINKER'S ITCH

CLIFTON FADIMAN

THE IMPROVEMENT mania, known medically as Tinker's Itch, is part of the progress of modern design. Our gullible great-grandfathers believed in the Perfectibility of Man. Today, faced with considerable contrary evidence, we have replaced this doctrine with a belief in the Perfectibility of Things. If we cannot make a better man, we feel, let us make a better mousetrap. But this commitment entails its own dangers.

The Perfectibility-minded designers are guided by one or more sacred dogmas. I list a few:

1. *Never let well enough alone.* This is the basic commandment. I offer an example. Before me lie two nutcrackers. One is a stone-age implement that will do nothing but crack nuts. It consists of two homely movable straight legs, connected at one end and evenly corrugated so as to grip any conceivable nut. The other nutcracker is a chrome beauty, streamlined so as to offer no resistance to the air, a property of untold value should you desire to propel a nutcracker into space. Its Dietrichian legs boast three beautifully scalloped curves, for large, medium and small nuts. Unfortunately, only a very few nuts of exactly the right size can be gripped at all, much less cracked.

2. *Make it inaccessible.* The Law of Inaccessibility operates with machine-turned precision in the case of many common objects: sardine cans, flip-top cigarette boxes, and any number of things mummified in cellophane. I hold in my hand two con-

tainers designed to hold books. The new one is a nifty patent job. It boasts two main features: (1) staples that yield only to the fingers of Hercules; (2) soft sides stuffed with dirty shredded paper. The book corners usually penetrate the shredded paper, or the struggle to dislodge the staples will accomplish a similar result: even, universal shred distribution.

The second container, the old-fashioned one, is a simple cardboard box, openable at once by the pulling out of a small tab. It is entirely without ingenuity. It merely permits you to get at the book.

3. *The right size is the size too small.* To illustrate, I point to the exits of our railroad cars, so designed as to divide a commuter's trip into two equal time intervals: 45 minutes from Blankville to the city and 45 minutes from interior of car to platform of station; or taxicabs that involve a struggle for emergence.

Most wallets are devised on the assumption that modern man never carries about in his billfold anything more than a single bill, or perhaps two. But the truth is that modern man, uncertain of his own identity, is compelled to bear with him whatever scraps of evidence he can rake up that he is someone. I, for example, have in my wallet a commutation-ticket book, a Social Security card, two hospitalization identification cards, two small checks I've meant to cash for eight months, an assortment of business cards of acquaintances now quite unrecallable, and a moderate quantity of fuzz.

Also, why are return envelopes from banks and department stores *just* large enough for a single enclosure, but not sealable if you wish to add another? Why are men's wooden pants hangers devised so that the pants at the fold are always too wide to be draped over the horizontal bar?

4. *The complex is preferable to the simple.* The fountain pen I am now writing with is 13 years old. It is terribly old-fashioned. You unscrew the top half and then pump in the ink by alternately squeezing and releasing a rubber sack that must cost about one tenth of a cent. It has no springs, levers, hydraulic motors, streamlining, irium, barium, thorium; it cannot be dropped from a plane without breakage; it comes unjeweled and only in black. All it does is write. This is more than can be said for some of its complex competitors.

The doctrine of the Perfectibility of Things stems from a delusion suggesting infantile behavior. The infant moves his hands and arms, not on purpose, but simply because to his delight he finds he can move them. Similarly when we ingenious "grown-ups" discover that our marvelous new tools can change almost any object, we conclude that therefore we *should* change it. I believe that some of the more baffling experiments in modern design are the result of the desire to apply power just because power is available.

My garage doors are electrically operated. A miracle. But when power fails (as it does in the country), I'm stuck. Are power-worked car windows *true* improvements? Or are they the consequences of the free operation of the play instinct, about on a level with thumb-sucking? Do tail fins really make for a better car? Or are they the consequences of gleefully fooling around with a billion-dollar Meccano set?

And—to bring us up to date—are satellites the issue of a basic scientific curiosity? Or is this attempt to communicate with the nonhumanity of outer space merely a confession of our failure to communicate with each other?

———————— ● ————————

Our forefathers used to wait days for a stagecoach; today our patience wears thin if we miss one section of a revolving door.

Asked what changes we could expect by the year 2000, a scientist pondered a moment, then replied, "Well, Brigitte Bardot will be 70."

It isn't progress that is hurting us so much today—it's the side effects.

Chairman of woolen-company board: "Good news, gentlemen! Our research department has developed a moth that will eat synthetics."

Man, brooding, to bartender: "Right now, someone, somewhere, is putting my name on a mailing list."

———————— ● ————————

---・---

Perhaps it's true that modern-day America is getting overmechanized. Recently I called a friend whose house has a telephone in the kitchen and an extension upstairs. The phone rang, two receivers clicked, two voices said, "I've got it"—and then, simultaneously, two people hung up.

Now I Set Me
Now I lay me down to sleep,
  And from the nightstand buttons peep:
Electric blanket set on cutoff,
  Electric clock on delay shutoff,
Sleep-maker set on medium tension,
  Radio set on voice suspension,
Burglar alarm on activate,
  Carport light for son who's late,
Coffeepot on percolate,
  Furnace on at ten of eight.

Bless our all-electric castle;
Let no errant fuse defile it.
I'm wide-awake from such a hassle;
I have mate, but need copilot.

My husband thoughtfully bought me an electric blanket, since I always complain about cold sheets. I was a little reluctant to sleep under all that electric wiring, but he assured me it was safe, and in minutes I was dozing off contentedly.

What my husband did not know was that I had put a ham in the oven to bake all night at low heat. When he awakened in the night and smelled something cooking, he reached over and shook me. "Dot, Dot, honey!" he cried. "Are you all right?"

Airman to officer: "Our anti-anti-missile missile just shot itself down, sir!"

---・---

Doctor, Doctor:
THE
MEDICAL WHIRL

I LEARNED A NEW WORD the other day while I was getting a medical checkup. The doctor told me I had idiopathic something-or-other. Alarmed, I asked him what "idiopathic" meant. He said, "Oh, it means we don't know a damn thing about the cause of the disease—indeed we don't really know anything about it." This reassured me. While on the subject of medical vocabulary, I might add a new phobia to Robert Benchley's list below: Santa Claustrophobia, or fear of Christmas. And to the gags about head shrinkers, add this succinct one by Lord Webb-Johnson, British surgeon: "A neurotic is the man who builds a castle in the air. A psychotic is the man who lives in it. And a psychiatrist is the man who collects the rent." The jokes about psychiatrists in this section seem to me among the wittiest in the book. Even the oldies (that one about elephants, for example) are delightful to revisit. Sometimes I think the father of all the psychiatry jokes must be a lovely cartoon given to me by Jim Thurber. It used to hang on my office wall as a continual warning to me. The psychiatrist is shown asking the patient: "And just when did you begin having this obsession about seeing rabbits everywhere?" The psychiatrist, of course, is a rabbit. Many other jokes about psychiatry turn on the idea of adjustment. That's because most normal folks seem to feel vaguely that there's something weird about being encouraged to adjust to a completely balled-up world. Maybe the maladjusted are the sane ones. The thought has occurred to most of us. Best not to think of it too often. It'll drive you nuts.

Case Histories

A man who stuttered badly went to a specialist and after ten difficult weeks learned to say quite distinctly: "Peter Piper picked a peck of pickled peppers." His friends congratulated him on his achievement.

"Yes," said the man doubtfully, "b-but it's s-s-such a d-difficult remark to w-w-work into an ordinary c-c-conversation, d-don't y'know!"

One stomach specialist I know has a simple formula for disposing of patients with nervous indigestion. He asks them if they play golf. If they say, "Yes," he orders them to stop. If they say, "No," he orders them to start.

A Dallas man had a thorough physical exam. Afterward the doctor told him that he was in good shape but that his blood pressure and cholesterol count were a little high. This opinion cost money, of course, but the patient was glad to get the verdict. He then called a cab to get back to work and got one of those friendly, talkative drivers. "Been to the doctor?" asked the cabbie. The man said he had been in for a checkup. "Well," said the cabbie reassuringly, "you look like a healthy businessman to me, except you probably have high blood pressure and your cholesterol count is too high."

An elderly woman in a drugstore, groping to remember the name of a medicine, said, "It's named after a type of bad woman." The clerk finally figured out what she wanted—cortisone.

A man went to his doctor and complained of a pain in his ankle. After a careful examination, the doctor inquired, "How long have you been walking around like this?"

"Two weeks."

"Say, man, your ankle is broken! Why didn't you come to me sooner?"

"Well, doctor, every time I say something is wrong with me, my wife declares, 'Now, you'll *have* to stop smoking.'"

A high-powered insurance agent talked an aging and over-worked book publisher into taking out a new policy. The publisher submitted to a physical examination and then waited in vain for a call from the agent. Finally he called the agent and asked the reason for his silence. In an embarrassed tone the agent explained, "You may have noticed that our company doctor makes out a chart of the applicant's body and punches a hole in it wherever he finds something that isn't just right."

"I noticed, all right," said the publisher. "What did he do with my chart?"

"I am sorry to inform you," said the agent, "that the doctor took your chart home with him and tried it out on his player piano. The tune that came out was 'Nearer My God to Thee.'"

Two elderly women were trying to outdo each other in discussing their ailments and medications. Finally one announced triumphantly, "I'm taking a pill that has nothing but side effects."

A lawyer in our city noted for his tightness had to undergo a course of treatment for an ailment. Outraged by the doctor's bill, he bellowed, "Great Scott, Doc! All that for one week's treatment?"

"My dear fellow," replied the doctor, "if you knew what an interesting case yours was, and how strongly I was tempted to let it go to a post-mortem, you wouldn't grumble!"

Specialist to patient: "Medicine has made great progress, Mrs. Smedley. We used to think your trouble was caused by teeth. Now we've progressed to the point where we don't know what's causing it!"

During my first week of medical practice in a country town there was a knock on the door about 4:30 a.m. I rushed downstairs ready to cope with an emergency. "My wife's in the car," the farmer on the porch told me. Hurrying after him, I found a cheerful young woman sitting calmly in the car. When I asked what I could do for her, she looked surprised.

"Why," she said, "you told me to come in for a blood test before breakfast."

Dr. Joe R. Brown of Rochester, Minnesota, tells of trying to get a physical history of a patient. The man's wife answered every question the doctor asked. Finally Dr. Brown requested that she leave the room, but after she left he found her husband couldn't speak. Calling the wife back, Dr. Brown apologized for not realizing the man had aphasia—loss of speech—and couldn't speak a word.

The wife was astonished. She didn't know it either.

A friend of mine was thoroughly examined by an oral surgeon who prescribed a simple operation to relieve his ailment. Asked if he wanted this operation performed immediately, my friend replied, "How will this affect my hobby?"

Puzzled, the doctor inquired, "What is your hobby?"

"Saving money," was the reply.

During our introduction to the stethoscope, in the first year of medical school, our instructor told us of an experience with a previous group of students.

When they were sufficiently familiar with the variations in normal heartbeats, they were taken to the surgery ward to learn to recognize the peculiar lubbs and hiccuping dupps of malfunctioning hearts.

The first patient was a beautiful blonde, who appeared far less anxious about being examined by the entire group than the students felt about creating a favorable impression on her. The first student approached her calmly, placed the stethoscope on her chest and proceeded to listen intently. The room was silent. For a moment the girl hesitated, then looked sympathetically into his eyes. Reaching up, she gently placed the earpieces in his ears.

Id Bits

Man to psychiatrist: "I have neither illusions nor delusions, Doctor. My problem is that I exist day after day in a world of grim reality."

YOU, TOO,
CAN HAVE
A PHOBIA

ROBERT BENCHLEY

THE discovery of phobias by the psychiatrists has done much to clear the atmosphere. Whereas in the old days a person would say, "Let's get the heck out of here!" today he says, "Let's get the heck out of here! I've got claustrophobia!"

Most everybody knows the name of the phobia that he has personally, and it is a great comfort to him. If he is afraid of high places, he just says, "Oh, it's just my old acrophobia," and jumps.

If he is afraid of being alone, he knows that he has monophobia and has the satisfaction of knowing that he is a pathological case. If he keeps worrying about the possibility of being buried alive, he can flatter himself that he has taphephobia, and that it is no worse than a bad cold.

But there are some honeys among the phobias that don't get much publicity. There is, for example, kemophobia, or the fear of sitting too close to the edge of a chair and falling off. People with kemophobia are constantly hitching themselves back in their chairs until they tip themselves over backward, which gives the same general effect as falling off the chair frontward.

Then there is goctophobia, or the fear of raising the hand too far and striking oneself in the face, with the possibility of putting an eye out. These patients keep their hands in their pockets all the time and have to be fed by paid attendants. A nasty complication arises when they also have nictophobia, or fear of paid attendants.

Some of the other little-known phobias are octophobia, or fear of the figure 8; kneebophobia, or the fear that one knee is going to bend backward instead of forward someday; and optophobia, or the dread of opening the eyes for fear of what they will see.

Tell us your phobias, and we will tell you what you are afraid of.

————— • —————

Psychiatrist to patient: "Maybe you don't have a complex—maybe you *are* inferior."

Classified ad: "Dr. Vincent Halter, psychiatrist. Positive cure in two years or your mania back."

Child to psychiatrist: "It's about my father, actually—he's got this fixation that a *cow* can orbit the moon!"

A teacher noticed that one little boy was drawing everything in heavy black crayon. He drew black horses, black cows and black barns. Disturbed about what was going on in his mind, she called a meeting of the little boy's parents, the principal of the school and a psychiatrist.

They finally got at the root of the trouble—it was the only crayon he had.

A patient was brought to a psychiatrist by friends, who informed the doctor that the man was suffering from delusions that a huge fortune was awaiting him. He was expecting two letters which would give him details involving the deeds to a rubber plantation in Sumatra and the titles to some mines in South America.

"It was a difficult case and I worked hard on it," the psychiatrist told some colleagues. "And just when I had the man cured—the two letters arrived!"

————— • —————

A New York psychiatrist ran into one of his patients at a restaurant. "Doctor," the woman said, introducing her spouse, "this is my husband—one of the men I've been telling you about."

Psychiatrist to Internal Revenue agent on couch: "Nonsense! The whole world isn't against you. The people of the United States, perhaps, but not the whole world."

Her husband's odd habit was becoming unbearable: he just couldn't say a sentence without snapping his fingers. So the wife finally prevailed upon him to go to see a psychiatrist.

While the psychiatrist interviewed him, the exasperating quirk asserted itself.

"Are you happily married? Ever quarrel with your wife?"

"Oh, (snap) never. She's the finest woman a (snap) man could wish for."

"Get along with your boss?"

"Marvelously (snap). He's probably (snap) the most congenial (snap) boss in the city of New (snap) York."

"How about your father or mother?"

"No (snap) question about it; they were (snap) ideal parents."

Desperate, the doctor asked, "Then why this compulsion to snap your fingers?"

"Oh, (snap)," the patient replied, "I do that to keep the (snap) elephants away."

"But there isn't an elephant loose within 2000 miles of here!"

"You (snap) see?" said the patient, beaming. "Damned (snap) effective, what?"

One woman to another: "I must say that after three years of analysis he's not so fussy about having the yolks right in the middle of his fried eggs any more."

Members toasting guest of honor at psychoanalysts' society dinner: "For he's an adequate fellow, for he's an adequate fellow. . . ."

On psychiatrist's door: "Merry Christmas and a well-adjusted New Year."

Psychiatrist to patient on couch: "There *is* a man following you. He's trying to collect my bill."

Overheard in a psychiatrist's waiting room: "I can't help it, doctor. I keep thinking my inferiority complex is bigger and better than anybody else's."

A psychologist was giving a young man some personality tests. He drew a vertical line and asked, "What does this make you think of?"

"Sex," said the young man.

Next the psychologist drew a circle. "And what does this make you think of?"

"Sex," said the young man again.

The psychologist drew a star. "And this?" he asked.

"Why, sex, of course," the young man said.

The psychologist put down his pencil. "In my opinion," he said, "you have an obsession about sex."

"*I* have an obsession!" protested the young man. "Who's been drawing all those off-color pictures?"

Psychiatrist to voluptuous blond patient leaving office: "That about winds things up. Any inhibitions you have left you're going to need."

I hope you won't mind," a girl sighed to her friend, "but I'm feeling a little schizophrenic today."

"Well," replied the friend, "that makes four of us."

Know the difference between a psychotic and a neurotic? The psychotic thinks that two plus two is five. The neurotic knows that two plus two is four—but he *hates* it!

Drill We Must

"Open wide," demanded the dentist as he began his examination of a new patient. "Good grief!" he said. "You've got the biggest cavity I've ever seen—*the biggest cavity I've ever seen!*"

"You didn't have to repeat it," snapped the patient.

"I didn't," said the dentist. "That was the echo!"

And there I sat in the dentist's chair," exclaimed one woman to another, "with my mouth propped open and feeling as if every moment would be my next!"

While I was waiting to see the dentist, a woman came out of his office smiling. Nodding to me, she said, "Thank goodness, my work is completed. I'm so glad to have found a painless dentist, and he's so nice too."

When seated in the dentist chair, I told the doctor, "I have a compliment for you," and related what the last patient had said. He laughed and explained, "Oh, that was my mother."

Distraught dentist to mother of small boy: "Two fillings. Don't let him bite anyone for at least an hour."

I came in to make an appointment with the dentist," said the man to the receptionist.

"He's out just now," said the receptionist, "but . . ."

"Thank you," interrupted the prospective patient. "When will he be out again?"

Heard about the dentist who found a badly decayed cavity in the tooth of a glamorous female patient?

"My dear," he murmured, "what's a place like this doing in a nice girl like you?"

---●---

Patrick, suffering from toothache, got up enough nerve to visit his dentist, but lost it again when he was about to get into the chair. The dentist told his assistant to give Pat a tot of whisky. "Got your courage back now?" he asked.

"No," replied Pat. So a second tot was brought, and a third.

"*Now* have you got your courage?" asked the dentist.

Pat squared his shoulders. "I'd like to see the man," he said, "who'd dare to touch me teeth now!"

With some difficulty the dentist persuaded my friend to have an abscessed tooth pulled. When the ordeal was over the dentist wrapped the tooth in a napkin and put it in his patient's coat pocket, saying, "There, you haven't lost the tooth after all."

The incident was forgotten until some time later when my friend, putting on a suit fresh from the dry cleaners, discovered something in his pocket. It was the napkin. And within its folds, in place of the tooth, was a shiny new dime!

From Here to Maternity

A doctor examined a pretty new patient carefully, then beamed, "Mrs. Atherton, I've got good news for you."

The patient said, "Pardon me, it's *Miss* Atherton."

"Oh," said the doctor. "Well, Miss Atherton, I've got bad news for you."

A London doctor lecturing at Yale speculated that Mona Lisa's enigmatic smile was due to her pregnant state. Another possibility, however, was offered in a letter to the *New England Journal of Medicine.* "To one unencumbered by the sophistication of the obstetricians and historians," wrote a doctor, "that smug, sly smile can have only one explanation: Mona Lisa has just discovered that she is *not* pregnant."

---●---

Doctor to prospective father: "As a theater manager, Mr. Wilson, you will be interested to know that your wife's X ray showed a preview of two coming attractions."

When my doctor's wife answered the telephone, the frantic voice of a young prospective father asked for the doctor, saying that his wife was having labor pains. Trying to determine if the situation was urgent enough to communicate with her husband, who was on another call, she asked how far apart the pains were. After a second's silence, the young man blurted, "I think they're all in just about the same place!"

While in the hospital for the birth of our son, I shared a room with a young mother whose obstetrician was very reserved and businesslike. On one of his visits, trying to make conversation, she said, "Doctor, they certainly keep you busy, don't they?"

"Yes," he said quietly, without looking up from his notes. "I have too many men working for me."

Two nurses were wearily folding diapers in the maternity ward. "You know," observed one, looking over the room of squealing infants, "I just can't *believe* they're only 80 percent water!"

The day I was to bring my first-born home from the hospital our doctor, realizing how jittery I was, said reassuringly: "You'll do fine if you just remember two thing—keep one end full and the other end dry."

When my son was born, my father-in-law, whose first grandchild it was, phoned the hospital to see how mother and baby were. On hearing his name, the nurse assured him that his wife and child were fine.

"Oh, dear, no," stammered Dad. "I'm not the husband—just the father!"

Nurse to expectant father: "Just because you've been kept waiting so long, it doesn't necessarily mean the baby will be a girl."

Doctors' Dilemmas

The doctor's new secretary, a conscientious girl, was puzzled by an entry in the doctor's notes on an emergency case: "Shot in the lumbar region," it read. After a moment she brightened and, in the interest of clarity, typed into the record: "Shot in the woods."

My husband, a lawyer, often refuses to accompany me to parties because so many people spoil his evening by asking him for advice. I asked a doctor if this happened to him. "All the time!" he said.

"Then how do you get rid of these people?"

"I have a wonderful remedy," the doctor grinned. "When someone begins telling me his ailments, I stop him with one word, 'Undress!'"

At the peak of the cold and virus season last winter, our family doctor was giving a record number of penicillin injections. Tacked to the door of his inner office one afternoon was this notice: "To Save Time, Please Back Into the Office."

Patient to doctor: "No, I don't feel listless. If I felt that good I wouldn't be here."

Two specialists were off on a holiday. "These girls in Florida certainly have beautiful legs, don't they?" said the orthopedist, after an appreciative look around the beach.

"I hadn't noticed," said his companion. "I'm a chest man, myself."

Nurse to doctor: "Better take a tranquilizer—40-24-35 is here for her physical."

Overheard at a doctor's office, as the doctor was giving a seven-year-old boy a vaccination: "Johnny we prefer to call this a vaccination rather than a 'fix.'"

Woman, in doctor's waiting room, to friends: "Boy, have I got a symptom to throw at him."

Doctor reading resolution at medical meeting: "All in favor stick out your tongue and say, 'Ah.'"

Meek little man to doctor: "I think what's really bothering me is a pain in the neck. But I don't suppose there's anything I can do about *her.*"

The doctor was trying to encourage a gloomy patient. "You're in no real danger," he said. "Why, I've had the same complaint myself."

"Yes," the patient moaned, "but you didn't have the same doctor!"

Patient to doctor: "I've lost my will to live—except on weekends."

---•---

Sign in a doctor's waiting room: "Please do not remove magazines from the office. The nurse will tell you the end of the story."

One doctor to another in hospital corridor: "I usually take two aspirin every four or five patients."

Office nurse to doctor: "Somebody wants to know if you will make a house call—whatever that is."

Hospital Blues

HOSPITALS CAN BE FUN
EDDIE CANTOR

IT ISN'T OFTEN that I go to hospitals, unless you want to count those visits to the maternity wards. Those times had nothing to do with me—or did they?

But I am convinced that hospitals can be a lot of fun if you are not too sick—as in my case recently. All I had was a ruptured blood vessel around my vocal cords. This happened during a television show. It seems one of my jokes backfired.

Let me put down what happened after the doctor saw me to bed and told me to shut up. I was told that anything I wanted should be written on a pad. Now, my handwriting is a cross between a doctor's prescription and Egyptian hieroglyphics. I can recall once when I left a note for my wife, Ida. She picked it up, took it to a Chinese laundry, and came back with two shirts and a half dozen pairs of socks. But the doctor said, "Use the pad," and I did.

My second morning I pushed the button for the nurse and handed her a slip on which I had written "breakfast." She nodded and returned five minutes later with the barber. (I'm probably the only man living who has had two haircuts in two days.) I still wanted breakfast and pointed to my mouth. The nurse smiled knowingly, left the room, and returned with a toothbrush. I finally solved the problem by waiting three hours and writing "lunch." This, I discovered, is the only legible word I write. From then on I had "lunch" for breakfast, dinner and supper.

In the hospital they took so many X-ray pictures that my friend John Gunther borrowed half of them for his new book, *Inside Eddie Cantor.* And I'll never get over those involved blood tests. The nurse pricked my finger—oh, at least three or four fingers— then my ear lobes—then took some out of my arm. I don't think that all this blood was necessary; I have a feeling she was keeping an anemic friend.

I quizzed the doctor about his findings. "First of all," he said, "while your blood pressure is high, I'm not worried about that."

I said, "Look, Doc, if your blood pressure was high, I wouldn't worry about it, either."

The doctor continued, "Your tests showed 30 percent albumin, 25 percent calcium, 30 percent cholesterol and 20 percent sugar."

I said, "What, no blood?"

The fellow's a pretty good heart man, but one test I could not understand. He had me get off the bed and jump on one foot for what seemed like a long time. He listened to my heart through his stethoscope and didn't like what he heard. I'm sure I was all right before I started jumping. At 59 one doesn't all of a sudden get up from a bed and start jumping on one foot. It's pretty silly.

I believe doctors are all right, but they specialize too much. I'll never forget the medical man to whom I said, "There's something wrong with my eye." He asked me which eye, and I told him, "The left one." He replied, "I'm sorry, I'm a right-eye specialist."

I'm not knocking doctors. If you're not feeling well, you should see one, because he must live. And when the doctor gives you a prescription, have it filled because the druggist must live, but when you get the medicine, don't take it, because you must live, too!

I don't know why people think hospital food is not good enough and so they bring you your favorite dishes. I happen to like chicken-noodle soup. My relatives and friends brought me enough noodle soup to eat, bathe in and take care of my laundry. I got so I saw noodles everywhere. Even the chairs looked noodle-point.

One thing that burns me up in a hospital is when several doctors get together in a corner of your room for a consultation. They mumble—look at you—turn away—take another look—and go into a huddle again. One day when this happened, I stared at them, and you know I've got something to stare with. They left the room and continued their talking in the hall. I got out of bed, tiptoed over to the door and listened. You know something? They were planning a big party for the following Saturday night, and I have a feeling that I'm the party who was paying for the party.

A hospital is a good place to see your friends. Jimmy Durante visited me and recommended a new doctor. "Sweetheart," Durante'd Jimmy, "ya gotta have dis doctor I know. He's really a great N.D. Y'know, some doctors could treat ya for pneumonia and ya could die of appendicitis, but not dis doc. Whatever he treats ya for, ya die from!"

P.S. Just learned from my doctors that I must have some surgery. They've discovered that I have something called "S.L.A.T." They're determined to rid me of it. You never heard of "S.L.A.T."? "Something Left After Taxes."

———•———

Have you heard about the fellow who underwent major stomach surgery? When his midriff was opened up, out flew a flock of butterflies. "Well," exclaimed his doc, stepping back, "I'll be hanged—the guy was right!"

Voice heard from surgical team at start of operation: "Who opens?"

Two little boys in a children's ward were discussing their hospital experiences. "Are you medical or surgical?" asked one.

"I don't know what you mean," the other answered.

The first boy, who had been a patient in the ward for some time, looked scornfully at the newcomer. "Were you sick when you got here," he explained, "or did they make you sick after you came?"

Wife sitting by husband's hospital bed reading his mail: "This card says 'Get Well Quick.' It's from our hospitalization plan."

———•———

With only a local anesthetic I was fully conscious during my recent operation, and even able to watch some of the proceedings. I noticed four doctors keeping busy, plus a few nurses. One doctor was making notes as the head surgeon dictated. "This is like a business meeting," I said. "You seem to be the secretary: Dr. G. there is evidently the chairman, and I guess those two other fellows are vice presidents. But what am I?"

"You, Mr. McMillen," came the prompt answer, "are chairman of the finance committee!"

Woman watching movie of surgeons operating: "The *prices* they charge—I don't wonder they wear masks!"

Comedian Ernie Kovacs once spent 15 months in the hospital. His illness was critical, but he never lost his manic sense of humor. One doctor recalls the day they brought Ernie to the X-ray laboratory on a stretcher, draped in a sheet: "When we looked at him through the fluoroscope we were startled to see a sign that read OUT TO LUNCH. Ernie had cut it out of aluminum foil and pasted it on his stomach."

Convalescent explaining why he left his Jello untouched, "I don't want to eat anything that's more nervous than I am."

Recuperating from an operation I began to wonder if the young doctor who was looking after me was competent. He always had such a dreamy, faraway look in his eyes. But when the day came for him to remove my stitches he attacked the job with unusual concentration. And as each stitch came out he whispered something under his breath. When he got to the last one he held it up and beamed at me. "She loves me!" he confided gleefully.

Legal
Entanglements:

AMERICANS AND THE LAW

I T'S HARD TO UNDERSTAND why lawyers from time imme-
morial have been subjected to such merciless satire.
After all, they aren't much worse than the rest of us.
Indeed, I have known one or two who might even have been
better than some of us. But, as any lawyer would say, that's
arguable. One can easily imagine the audience at the Globe

Theatre yelling their approval when in Shakespeare's *Henry VI, Part II,* one raffish character, mixed up in a subversive movement, cries out, "The first thing we do, let's kill all the lawyers." Rather should we be charitable and think kindly of lawyers, and think kindly also of criminals, without whom we would have no lawyers; and when we think of criminals let us remember W. S. Gilbert's tender lines:

> *When a felon's not engaged in his employment,*
> *Or maturing his felonious little plans,*
> *His capacity for innocent enjoyment*
> *Is just as great as any honest man's.*

Attorneys' Trials

A favorite joke among San Francisco lawyers concerns the phony who fakes an injury in an auto crash, comes to court in a wheel chair and is awarded $100,000. When the verdict is announced, the insurance company's lawyer snaps, "You're going to be tailed by a private eye wherever you go from now on, and as soon as you take one step out of that wheel chair, we'll throw you in jail."

"Don't go to all that trouble," advises the phony pleasantly. "I'm going from here to the Waldorf in New York, then to the Savoy in London, then to the Ritz in Paris, then to the French Riviera—and after that to Lourdes for the miracle!"

Albert Blinder, former New York City assistant D.A., was cross-examining a witness. After getting her name, he asked, "Occupation?"

"Housewife," she answered.

"Your husband's occupation?"

"Manufacturer."

Blinder continued, "Children?"

"No," replied the witness. "Ladies' handbags."

The belligerent prosecutor was almost insulting as he questioned the young pugilist on trial for assault and battery. And under the verbal onslaught, the fighter finally admitted he'd given the plaintiff "a little push."

"A little push, eh?" repeated the prosecutor, as he hit upon an idea that would certainly incriminate the boxer. "Show me exactly what you did."

"Y'mean," asked the pug, "that you want me to show you just how hard I pushed him?"

"That's right," nodded the prosecutor.

The fighter's eyes gleamed. He leaped from his chair and landed against the prosecutor with all his force, knocking the prosecutor cold. "Gentlemen," said the fighter, turning to the jury with a smile, "about one tenth that hard!"

In Richmond, the Assistant District Attorney was questioning a witness. The man was exceedingly cooperative but he kept addressing his answers directly to the attorney. "Speak to the jury," directed the Assistant D.A.

The witness looked the jury over, nodded affably, and said, "Howdy."

A. S. Trude, the famed trial lawyer, and the distinguished Dr. Frank Billings lived next door to each other in Chicago. One day Billings testified as a medical expert against Trude. Trude's cross-examination of his eminent neighbor was brief. "Was Marshall Field one of your patients?" he began.

"Yes."

Trude asked, "Where is Mr. Field now?" and the doctor said, "Dead." Trude named other patients of Billings — Mr. Armour, Mr. Pullman, Mr. Cudahy, all of whom had died natural deaths. Each time Trude asked: "Where is he now?" and each time Dr. Billings had to answer: "Dead."

"That's all, thank you," the lawyer concluded, and won his case.

A wealthy woman was being sued for a fat sum by a maid who had fallen off a small stepladder. There before the jury's eyes stood the plaintiff's prize exhibit, the ladder itself, alleged to be rickety and unsafe. Lloyd Stryker, the attorney for the defense, a rugged, big-shouldered hulk of a man, was extolling the ladder's sound construction. To prove his point he climbed its four steps and stood on top. To clinch his case, he jumped on the ladder. It practically exploded all over the courtroom.

Stryker picked himself up. "You see, gentlemen," he said quietly, as though he had planned it that way, "you see how solidly that stepladder was built? A big fellow like me had to jump on it with all his weight to break it."

A lawyer of the old school had a way with a jury. His voice would make the courthouse windows rattle, his flailing arms stirred up a breeze like an electric fan. One day, defending a damage suit, he put on a long, loud and impressive show. When he finally sat down, exhausted, his opponent rose to reply.

He loosened his collar, waved his arms, pounded with his fist and jumped up and down in front of the jury a full two minutes — never uttering a word. Then he buttoned his collar, smoothed his hair and said quietly: "Gentlemen of the jury. Now that I have fully and completely answered the arguments of my learned opponent, I would like to discuss with you the facts in this case."

A Seattle lawyer broke a lengthy cross-examination of a witness to exclaim: "Your Honor, one of the jurors is asleep."

"You put him to sleep," replied the judge. "Suppose you wake him up."

Order in the Court

A young lady was asked by the prosecuting attorney, "What gear were you in when the crash took place?"

She replied quickly, "A beret, two-tone shoes and a gray flannel suit."

The prisoner was being tried for horse-stealing. The prosecuting attorney read the indictment sternly, then asked, "Are you guilty, or not guilty?"

The culprit wriggled perplexedly, then said, "Why, ain't that exactly the thing we come here to find out?"

Willie Johnson, a sawed-off, beaten-down little man, was arraigned in a Texas district court on a felony charge.

The clerk intoned: "The State of Texas versus Willie Johnson!"

Before he could read further, Willie almost broke up the meeting by solemnly declaring: "Lawd Gawd! What a majority!"

Judge Kenesaw Mountain Landis once sentenced an old offender to five years in prison.

"But, Your Honor," the felon protested, "I'll be dead long before that! I'm a sick man—I can't do five years!"

Landis glared at him. "You can try, can't you?"

The woman called to the stand was handsome but no longer young. The judge gallantly instructed, "Let the witness state her age, after which she may be sworn."

It was the first case for most members of the jury in a little New England town, and they debated for hours. At last they came back, and the foreman solemnly voiced the verdict. "The jury don't think that he done it, for we allow he wasn't there; but we think he would have done it if he'd had the chanst!"

At a trial in a Detroit court, a young woman who had accused the defendant of making an improper proposal was asked to state the question that allegedly had been asked. It embarrassed her to repeat it, so she was permitted to write it on a piece of paper. After the judge, prosecutor and defense counsel had read it, it was passed to the jury. Each juror read it, and gave it to the next juror.

After an attractive female juror had read it, she attempted to pass it to the man on her right, but found him dozing. Without comment, she nudged him and gave him the slip of paper. The awakened juror read the note, smiled at her, nodded, and put the note in his pocket!

A woman on trial for murdering her husband was acquitted because of the efforts of one little old lady on the jury. After the trial the latter explained her attitude: "I guess I just felt sorry for her. After all, she's a widow."

A New York man, forced to take a day off from work to appear in court in answer to a minor traffic summons, grew increasingly restless as he waited hour after hour for his case to be heard. Late in the afternoon, he stood before the judge only to hear that court was adjourned and he would have to return the next day. "Why?" he snapped at the judge.

His Honor, equally irked, roared, "Twenty dollars—contempt of court. That's why!" Then, noticing that the man was checking his wallet, the judge relented. "That's all right. You don't have to pay the fine right now."

Replied the young man, "I'm just seeing if I have enough to say two more words."

A jury in Jackson County, Texas, impressed with the polite expressions of the legal profession, returned this verdict on a murder trial: "We, the gentlemen of the jury, find the defendant not quite guilty."

Parting of the Ways

A Las Cruces, New Mexico, lawyer was sitting in his office one day when a woman entered unannounced and, without preliminaries, declared that she wanted a divorce.

"On what grounds?" the attorney asked.

She replied that she did not think her husband was faithful.

"And what makes you think that he isn't faithful?"

"Well," the lady replied, "I don't think he's the father of my child."

When Mrs. Pierre Riendeau, 79 years old, asked for a legal separation from her 86-year-old husband, the judge asked how long they had been married. "Sixty years," she replied.

"Why are you seeking a separation after all this time?" the court asked.

"Enough's enough," she said.

The court agreed to hear suit.

After a lengthy conference with the estranged husband, the lawyer reported to his client: "Mrs. Blake, I have succeeded in making a settlement with your husband that is eminently fair to both of you."

"Fair to both," exploded Mrs. Blake. "I could have done that myself! What do you think I hired a lawyer for?"

An irate woman, seeking a divorce, told the judge: "My husband never thinks of anything but horse racing. That's all he talks. The track is the only place he goes. From morning till night it's horses, horses, horses. Why, he doesn't even remember our wedding date."

"That's a lie, judge!" shouted the husband. "We were married the day Twenty Grand won the Kentucky Derby."

During a divorce proceeding, the wife was testifying as to beatings her husband had given her. Citing one specific instance, she stated that she and her husband had been sitting in their living room, quietly reading, when he suddenly put down his book, crossed the room and started hitting her.

Cross-examining her about this, one of the attorneys, as an afterthought, asked, "Do you know what he was reading?"

Her reply: *"The Power of Positive Thinking."*

A woman in Chicago got a divorce after charging that her husband played poker for high stakes with the boys but put on a three-cent limit when he played at home with her. "All I wanted," she complained, "was the same chance his pals had to win his money."

A Los Angeles woman won a divorce when she charged that her husband made her unscrew the light bulbs to save wear and tear on the switches.

A Texarkana husband sued his 15-year-old wife for divorce on the grounds that she acted like a child.

A Lansing, Michigan, man, wed only four weeks, asked for a divorce on the grounds that his eyeglasses were out of focus when he married.

Testifying that her husband had knocked her out by hitting her on the head with a live chicken and then, finding that the impact had killed the chicken, revived her and ordered her to cook it, Mrs. Viola Beck sued for divorce.

Samuel Hoffenstein, scenarist and poet, of Hollywood, was divorced by his wife, who objected to jingles he dedicated to her:

When you're away, I'm restless, lonely,
Wretched, bored, dejected;
But here's the rub, my darling dear,
I feel the same when you are here.

On the Beat

Two snowy-haired old ladies jouncing along in an antiquated automobile through York, Pennsylvania, made an illegal turn. The traffic cop had to blow his whistle vigorously and repeatedly before they came to a stop. "Didn't you hear my whistle, lady?" he asked.

Wide-eyed and innocent, the little lady looked at him. "Yes, indeed," she said, "but I never flirt while driving."

Ticket-writing motorcycle policeman to sports-car driver: "Perhaps you weren't doing a hundred. However, I'm going to reward you for trying."

A fellow stopped for doing 70 told the traffic cop: "I can't understand it. I must have had a 20-mile-an-hour tailwind."

Houstonians, who insist their drivers are the world's worst, tell of a policeman who asked an injured pedestrian if he had noticed the license number of the driver who struck him.

"No," was the reply, "but I'd remember his laugh anywhere."

A Detroit motorist, charged with driving through an intersection without due caution, explained, "I always hurry through intersections to get out of the way of reckless drivers."

Woman driver to traffic officer who has stopped her: "Are you supposed to warn me of my constitutional rights, or am I supposed to warn you that my nephew is on the police commission?"

A Cleveland policeman stepped into the precinct station and told his superior that there was a dead horse on Kosciusko Street. The officer said, "Well, make out your report."

The policeman, a poor speller, disappeared. After an hour he came back, disheveled and out of breath. His superior demanded to know where he had been. The policeman replied, "I was moving the horse to 79th Street."

In Paris a motorcycle officer stopped a driver who had been sampling the grape too freely and escorted the man to the nearest station. The official sobriety tests were given, including a drunkometer test. Later, making out his report, the officer came to the column listing the results of the breath test and carefully entered: "Saint-Emilion 1953."

It's true that I've driven through a number of red lights," confessed Glenn Gould, the eccentric Canadian concert pianist. "But, on the other hand, I've stopped at a lot of green ones I've never gotten credit for."

Driver to highway patrolman: "I was speeding to get off the radar screen."

The meek little man approached a policeman on the street corner.

"Excuse me, officer," he said, "but I've been waiting here for my wife for over an hour. Would you be kind enough to order me to move on?"

On his first day out, a rookie policeman in Chicago was having trouble with a bum. He had got him as far as a patrol call box when the derelict swung at him and knocked him down. Another policeman, seeing the commotion from across the street, started over to help. But as he approached, the rookie scrambled to his feet and started to run. The other officer finally caught him and demanded: "What's the matter with you anyway?"

"Holy suffering!" panted the new recruit. "I forgot I was a policeman. In the neighborhood where I come from, we always ran from cops!"

A police officer told a motorist parked in a commercial loading zone to move on, but the driver replied that he had to park there because he was getting a 175-pound package from the side door of the store. And sure enough, as the officer watched, the motorist's wife came out the side door and got into the car.

The policeman was still scratching his head as they drove off.

Woman driver to traffic cop: "Does this ticket cancel the one I got this morning, Officer?"

During a downpour, the policeman directing traffic near a popular Dallas restaurant was wearing a bright-yellow slicker heavily labeled with the insignia of the Dallas Police Department. At a particularly busy moment, a woman ran up. "Are you a policeman?" she said.

"No, lady," said the officer patiently. "I am a giant canary."

In Brighton, Colorado, a drunk, obviously in no condition to take the wheel, was getting into his automobile when a sheriff's deputy halted him and asked: "You're not going to drive that car, are you?"

"Certainly I'm going to drive," the man replied. "I'm in no condition to walk."

The policeman presiding over the traffic from his tower at Harvard Square in Cambridge was shouting instructions to pedestrians and motorists over a loudspeaker. The driver of a car with Missouri plates, trying to navigate the maze of one-way signs and flashing lights, started to turn the wrong way into a one-way street. "You can't turn that way, lady," boomed the officer.

She rolled the window down and called desperately, "But how will I ever get back to that street?"

Back came the answer: "The world is round, lady. The world is round."

Criminal Tendencies

The FBI agent in a Western state was hot on the trail of a fugitive. When word came that he was heading for a small town, the G-man called the local sheriff. "You send me a pitcher of that guy and I'll git him good," the sheriff promised. That night the Government agent mailed the sheriff not one but a dozen pictures of the wanted man—profiles, fullface, standing, sitting, and in various costumes. Within 24 hours he received a telephone call: "We got 11 of those crooks locked up already," the sheriff boasted. "And I guarantee to jug the last one before morning!"

Can you describe your assailant?" the officer asked as he helped the bruised man up from the pavement.

"That," said the man, "is just what I was doing when he hit me."

Suspect at police station: "On the night of March 2, I was sitting right here telling you where I was on the night of February 18."

FBI secretary to visitor: "He's not in—care to leave your fingerprints?"

A Vancouver, B. C., man was sentenced to jail for breaking into a café, despite his protestations that he had stumbled against the window, breaking two panes, had entered to leave his name and address, and was looking in the till for a pencil when caught.

A Chicago man admitted in court that he stole 75 checks, worth $600, from mailboxes, but asserted he always sent $5 from every stolen check he cashed to the chaplain of the Federal Penitentiary at Terre Haute "for the betterment of prison conditions."

Because safecracking and housebreaking had become too difficult for him, an 85-year-old man, arrested in New York, was earning a living by renting out his kit of burglar tools.

Returning from a vacation, a writer of detective stories found his apartment rifled by burglars. On his desk was a note, written on his own typewriter: "Figure this one out in your spare time, brother."

On a column in a newspaper published at the Wyoming State Penitentiary: "HERE TODAY, HERE TOMORROW."

Shirley Jackson, in her book *Come Along With Me,* told about a letter she got from one of her readers: "He clearly expected me to recognize his name and reputation, which I didn't. Finally I decided on a carefully complimentary and noncommittal answer. Later, I showed his letter to friends. They identified him as a man who had just been barely acquitted of murdering his wife with an ax. I looked up the carbon of my answer to him. 'Thank you for your kind letter about my story,' I had written. 'I admire *your* work, too.'"

William Howard Taft was a Federal Circuit Judge in Ohio, when he found himself in a barber's chair one morning. "You're Judge Taft, aren't you?" asked the barber as he lathered the Justice's face.

"Yes, I am," Taft replied, comfortably settling his considerable bulk.

"Remember a man by the name of Stebbins? You gave him 20 years." The barber was stropping a razor with unusual care.

"Yes, I remember Stebbins," answered the justice. "A bad boy."

"He's my brother," said the barber as he laid his razor to the judicial neck. Judge Taft felt himself begin to sweat as the sharp steel was drawn back and forth over his jaw and throat. He shut his eyes, contemplated the life eternal, and waited.

Finally the barber stepped back, closed his razor with a snap. "Well, Judge," he said. "You did right. My brother is a no good bum. Belongs in jail anyhow."

A gangster rushed into a saloon, shooting right and left, yelling, "All you dirty skunks get outta here."

The customers fled in a hail of bullets—all except an Englishman, who stood at the bar calmly finishing his drink. "Well?" snapped the gangster, waving his smoking gun.

"Well," remarked the Englishman, "there certainly were a lot of them, weren't there!"

---•---

While in New York, a man had his wallet stolen in the subway. The following morning he received a letter reading: "Sir, I stoal youre munny. Remauss is noring me, so I send sum of it back to you. Wen it nors again I will send sum more."

One counterfeiter to another: "People are getting suspicious of cash. We're gonna switch to credit cards."

John Carmichael, the Chicago baseball writer, tells the story about a woman who divorced her husband and obtained custody of their 12-year-old son. When she remarried after a year or so, her ex-husband was somewhat concerned about the boy. "How do you get along with your stepfather?" he asked the lad the first chance he got.

"Fine," said the youngster. "He takes me swimming every morning. We go out to the lake, and he rows me out to the middle, and then I swim back in."

"Isn't that a pretty long swim for a boy your age?" asked the father.

"Not too bad. Really, the only tough part of it is getting out of the sack."

A committee was appointed by the magazine *Redbook* to study the question of how best to hold a wife, and a selected list of husbands was written to. The only reply received was from a certain western penitentiary. It stated briefly: "I found the best way was around the neck, but it should not be overdone. Please note change of address."

Police chief to painter: "We'd like the interrogation room painted tattletale gray."

---•---

Stop
the Presses:
PUBLISHERS' ROW

W E COULDN'T LIVE WITHOUT NEWSPAPERS, I suppose. Many newspapermen, pressed to defend their interesting trade, will sooner or later solemnly quote Jefferson's famous remark: "Were it left for me to decide whether we should have a government without newspapers or newspapers without government, I should not hesitate a moment to prefer the latter." We should keep in mind, however, that in Jefferson's time the newspaper was easily liftable by a small child. Today the proper handling of the Sunday *New York Times* is a team project. One recalls an observation of Henry Fielding, author of *Tom Jones.* He said something to the effect that newspapers would continue to consist of the same number of words whether there was any news in them or not. I am grateful to newspapers. Without them the headline—one of the most useful inventions since the wheel—would never have existed.

The newspaper business is rich in humorous lore, as we can see from the collection that follows. The editors must have rejected, as too ancient, the story of the cub reporter who, sent out to cover the Johnstown flood, wired back: "All is excitement. Can learn nothing." I still like it.

The Newspaper Game

"THE LORD HELPS THOSE . . ."
MARK TWAIN

ONCE WHEN William Swinton and I were poor young cub reporters, a frightful financial shortage occurred. We had to have three dollars that very day. Swinton maintained with simple confidence, "The Lord will provide." I wandered into a hotel lobby, trying to think of some way to get the money. Presently a handsome dog came along and rested his jaw on my knee. General Miles passed by and stopped to pat him.

"He is a wonder. Would you sell him?"

I was greatly moved; it was marvelous the way Swinton's prediction had come true. "Yes," I said, "his price is three dollars."

The general was surprised. "Only three dollars? Why, I wouldn't take $100 for him. You must reconsider."

"No, three dollars," I said firmly. The general led the dog away.

In a few minutes a sad-faced man came along, looking anxiously about. I asked, "Are you looking for a dog?"

His face lit up. "Yes. Have you seen him?"

"Yes, I think I could find him for you."

I have seldom seen a person look so grateful. I said I hoped he would not mind paying me three dollars for my trouble.

"Dear me! That is nothing! I will pay you $10 willingly!"

I said, "No, three is the price," and started off. Swinton had said that that was the amount the Lord would provide; it would be sacrilege to ask more. I went up to the general's room and explained I was sorry but I had to take the dog again; that I had only sold him in the spirit of accommodation. I gave him back his three dollars and returned the dog to his owner.

I went away then with good conscience, because I had acted honorably. I never could have used the three that I had sold the dog for; it was not rightly my own, but the three I got for restoring him was properly mine. That man might never have gotten that dog back at all if it hadn't been for me.

———————— • ————————

Mark Twain, in his reporting days, was instructed by an editor never to state anything as a fact that he could not verify from personal knowledge. Sent out to cover an important social event soon afterward, he turned in the following story: "A woman giving the name of Mrs. James Jones, who is reported to be one of the society leaders of the city, is said to have given what purported to be a party yesterday to a number of alleged ladies. The hostess claims to be the wife of a reputed attorney."

A note from the editor in the McLean County, Kentucky, News: "This is another of those weeks when we didn't publish nearly all we knew. For which many may be thankful."

———————— • ————————

A British fledgling reporter had been reprimanded for his overlong accounts and told to be brief. His next story was turned in as follows:

"A shocking incident occurred last night. Sir Reggy Blank, a guest at Lady Briny's ball, complained of feeling ill, took his hat, his coat, his departure, no notice of his friends, a taxi, a pistol from his pocket and, finally, his life. Nice chap. Regrets and all that."

The sweetly cynical managing editor of the Boston *Advertiser* once gave me a valuable lesson in reporting. Some too-sweeping condemnation in my copy attracted his notice. "That won't do," he said. "You may believe, and it may be true, that every member of the Umteenth Ward Young Men's Political Reform Association is an incurable ass, but don't write it. Say: 'Every member, with one solitary exception, is an incurable ass.' Then no member of the Association will feel personally offended."

The fierce competition between London newspapers is illustrated by the cable sent from the *Daily Express* to its Congo correspondent during an uprising: "Today's *Daily Mail* reports their correspondent shot at yesterday stop Why you not shot at?"

In Garber, Oklahoma, the editors of the *Free Press,* who had moved to a new office, apologized for a rash of misspellings in recent editions of the newspaper: "Please excuse. Most of the words we use frequently and cannot spell are written correctly on the wall in our old location."

A Chicago news photographer was assigned to cover a reunion of the nuclear physicists who achieved the first self-sustaining chain reaction. "Now, fellows," said the cameraman to Vannevar Bush, Enrico Fermi, Arthur H. Compton and Harold C. Urey, "I got three pictures in mind. First, you guys putting the atom in the machine. Then splitting the atom. And finally all of you grouped looking at the pieces."

A fair young graduate of the School of Journalism got a job as cub reporter on a Long Island daily. Her first story won the editor's approval, but he pointed out a few minor inaccuracies.

"Remember," he concluded, "it was Joseph Pulitzer, founder of the School of Journalism, who declared that accuracy is to a newspaper what virtue is to a woman."

"That in itself is not entirely accurate," said the girl triumphantly. "A newspaper can always print a retraction!"

A copyreader on an Illinois newspaper couldn't believe it when he read a reporter's story about the theft of 2025 pigs. "That's a lot of pigs," he growled, and called the farmer to check the copy. "Is it true that you lost 2025 pigs?" he asked.

"Yeth," lisped the farmer.

"Thanks," said the copyreader and corrected the copy to read "two sows and 25 pigs."

Walter Winchell's favorite story, which may be apocryphal, is about an editorial feud between the old New York *Sun* and *Post,* when both were conservative papers. One day the very proper and staid *Post* lost its temper and editorially called the *Sun* a yellow dog. The *Sun* replied in its starchiest manner: "The *Post* calls the *Sun* a yellow dog. The attitude of the *Sun,* however, will continue to be that of *any* dog toward *any* post."

The New York *Mirror* once published a picture of Representative Hamilton Fish on the same page as a picture of a tropical fish, and inadvertently the captions were transposed. George Dixon of the rival *Daily News* promptly summoned some boon companions and telephoned the *Mirror*'s editor. He announced himself as Fish, and began denouncing the editor for the error, which he said had held him up to all kinds of ridicule. "You'll hear from my lawyer!" he threatened.

"But, Congressman Fish," the distressed editor protested, "we corrected the mistake in the second edition."

"Congressman Fish, hell!" Dixon roared. "This is Tropical Fish!"

When James Thurber was a rewrite man on the New York *Post* he did his colleagues a service by pointing up the absurdity of an office demand for short leads. Thurber's contribution: "Dead. That's what the man was the police found in an alleyway yesterday."

News-slanting is as ancient as newspapers themselves. The classic illustration is a Paris paper's successive headlines reporting Napoleon's escape from his exile in Elba:

"The Corsican Monster Has Landed in the Gulf of Juan."

"The Cannibal Is Marching Toward Grasse."

"The Usurper Has Entered Grenoble."

"Bonaparte Has Entered Lyons."

"Napoleon Is Marching Toward Fontainebleau."

"His Imperial Majesty Is Expected Tomorrow in Paris."

Bill Vaughan, of the Kansas City *Star,* feels that the public underestimates a columnist's labors. When he met a wealthy obstetrician he hadn't seen in years, the medical man asked patronizingly, "Are you still writing those little squibs for the paper?"

"Yes," Bill answered. "And are you still delivering those little people?"

H. Allen Smith in his reportorial days once phoned the office and said he couldn't come to work because he'd slipped on the ice.

"Yeah?" said his city editor. "How'd you ever get your foot in a highball glass?"

William Allen White, famous editor of the Emporia, Kansas, *Gazette,* once described his war against the staff's overuse of the word *very* this way:

"If you feel you must write *very*, write *damn.* So, when the urge for emphasis is on him, the reporter writes, 'It was a damn fine victory. I am damn tired but damn well—and damn excited.' Then, because it is the Emporia *Gazette,* the copy desk deletes the profanity and the quotation reads: 'It was a fine victory. I am tired but well—and excited.' That's how the *Gazette* attains its restrained, simple and forceful style. Very simple."

When James Gordon Bennett, Jr., was guiding the destinies of the New York *Herald,* he issued an edict that under no circumstances should the name "Herald" appear except in italics.

One printer really showed his unflinching obedience to the order when, during the holiday season, he set up a Christmas program announcement with the following item: "Hark the *Herald* Angels Sing."

In *The Years With Ross,* James Thurber tells about Harold Ross's dislike for the thoughtless use of the words "pretty" and "little" in *The New Yorker.* For a column in the magazine, Thurber wrote, deadpan, the sentence: "The building is pretty ugly and a little big for its surroundings."

Horace Greeley, who always insisted that the word "news" was plural, once wired to a reporter: "Are there any news?"

The reply came back by wire: "Not a new."

Correction sent out to newspapers by the Associated Press: "On food page mailed July 8, add to blueberry-muffins ingredients, for release July 27, 1 cup blueberries."

A famous story among *Wall Street Journal* staffers concerns a note that Bernard Kilgore, the late chairman of Dow Jones & Co., wrote to one of his editors: "If I see 'upcoming' in the paper again, I'll be downcoming and someone will be outgoing."

Headliners

A Catholic writer, who went to Rome to interview scores of priests, monsignors, bishops and cardinals on their feelings about birth control, titled his report: "The Pill's Grim Progress."

On Utica, New York, *Observer-Dispatch* story of a gangster's disappearance: "JOE BANANAS WITH BUNCH IN NORTH AFRICA."

The New York *Daily Mirror* headed a story that America was supplying false teeth to Europeans under the Marshall Plan: "PUTTING BITE ON U.S."

The weather in the Southwest was so bad one winter that when the sun finally shone for a few consecutive hours the El Paso, Texas, *Herald-Post* splattered the front page with this headline: "PRODIGAL SUN RETURNS."

When the star of a traveling Shakespearean company playing *Hamlet* at the University of Wisconsin was visibly intoxicated, the student newspaper, *The Daily Cardinal,* headlined its review: "HAM LIT."

Charles Chapin, city editor of the old New York *World,* once ordered Frank Ward O'Malley: "Go to New Jersey and visit the town of Hohokus. Come back with a story we can run under the headline: "HOKUS POKUS IN HOHOKUS."

Lord Moran once told his patient, Winston Churchill, that he should not accept an invitation to the Kentucky Derby. Churchill was disappointed, for he had hoped to supply the following caption for news photos: "CHURCHILL UP AT CHURCHILL DOWNS."

On a Washington *Post* story about a government investigation of the contents of the frankfurter: "HOT DOG FACES GRILLING."

On a Gettysburg, Pennsylvania, *Times* story about the labor shortage in Adams County: "SHORT SUPPLY OF LABOR FOR HARVESTING ADAMS APPLES."

On a story of the marriage of John Lennon and Yoko Ono in the Utica, New York, *Press:* "LENNON TURNS YOKO INTO JAPANESE BEATLE."

On a Dallas *Times Herald* story of the theft of a church organ: "ORGAN TRANSPLANTED."

Headline in the Victoria, B. C., *Daily Colonist:* "PULP HEAD TO SPEAK."

Headline in a San Diego paper: "BEAUTY UNVEILS BUST AT CEREMONY."

Headline in Oakland, California, *Tribune:* "TWO CONVICTS EVADE NOOSE: JURY HUNG!"

When Senator Frederick G. Payne was defeated in Maine, the *Manchester Guardian* headed the story: "THE PAYNE IN MAINE IS PLAINLY ON THE WANE."

The Marietta, Ohio, *Times* headed a picture of two members of the Czech legation leaving Stockholm after being declared *persona non grata* in a spy investigation: "SWEDEN BOUNCES BAD CZECHS."

An Ohio Protestant group owns the Real Form Girdle Company. This fact was revealed by *Women's Wear Daily* under the headline: "ROCK OF AGES ON FIRM FOUNDATION."

Headline in Canton, Ohio, *Repository:* "KEY WITNESS TAKES FIFTH IN LIQUOR PROBE."

On a New York *Times* story about a musical program in New York's Fulton Fish Market: "FISH MARKET CONCERT FLOUNDERS A BIT."

Jack Mann, former sports editor of Garden City, New York, *Newsday,* headlined a story on the men who hold the stopwatches at a track meet: THESE ARE THE SOULS WHO TIME MEN'S TRIES."

Publish or Perish

Publisher Richard Simon decided to include a half dozen adhesives in a juvenile called *Dr. Dan the Bandage Man,* and wired to a friend at the Johnson & Johnson Co., "Please ship two million Band-Aids immediately."

Back came a telegram reading, "Band-Aids on the way. What the hell happened to you?"

A favorite story at Doubleday is about the conscientious proofreader working on a Kathleen Norris novel. On galley 96 was the line, "She laid her cool lips against his." At this point the proofreader, ever laboring for consistency, raised the question. "Okay? Hot on galley 10."

Edna St. Vincent Millay, in a letter to Harper's Cass Canfield, rejected a proposition by the publisher designed to step up sales of her books. "Trusting, however," she wrote in closing, "that it may be said of me by Harper & Brothers that although I reject their proposals, I welcome their advances."

When *The Bookseller,* in London, expressed some puzzlement over the phrase "uncensored abridgement" used by an American publishing house, a full explanation came from Frederic J. Warburg, chairman of Secker & Warburg, British publishers:

"To a publisher the explanation is simple. 'Uncensored' means 'We have left the dirty bits in'; 'abridgement' implies 'We have left the dull bits out.'"

The iron-clad rule that there must never be an off-color situation, an indecent word or suggestion in the old *Saturday Evening Post* was broken when Katharine Brush's *Red-Headed Woman* began its serial run. The end of the first installment found the secretary-heroine having a drink with her boss at his home, the boss's wife away and night drawing on. To the profound shock of numerous readers, the second installment began with the two having breakfast. Editor George Horace Lorimer prepared a form letter to answer the indignant mail. "The *Post,*" he said, "cannot be responsible for what the characters in its serials do between installments."

Switchboard operator: "Acme Publishing Company— good morning, she said with a flashing smile. . . ."

A friend of mine went to work for an editor in a New York publishing house. The editor's reputation for attention to detail was formidable. After a few weeks, I asked my friend what it was like working for someone so thorough. She replied, "The only way I can describe him is to tell you that if he were publishing a dictionary, it would have an index."

In his autobiography Mark Twain concluded a tirade against a publisher, who had once swindled him outrageously, on a note of forgiveness. "He has been dead a quarter of a century now," Twain wrote. "I feel only compassion for him and if I could send him a fan, I would."

All the News . . .

Item in the London *Times*: "The Clairvoyant Society will not have its usual meeting this week, due to unforeseen circumstances."

Concert note in the Redwood Falls, Minnesota, *Gazette:* "Only in his third number was there a hint of exhibitionism. Played entirely on the G string, it was a difficult and entertaining feat."

From the Columbus, Ohio, *Citizen:* "A study by three physicians showed that perhaps two out of three births in the U.S. result from pregnancies."

Announcement by the Procrastination Club of America: "Last week was National Procrastination Week."

From the Van Wert, Ohio, *Times-Bulletin:* "The Garden Study Club will meet Thursday. The study topic, 'My Potted Friends,' will be given by Mrs. Gene Kintz."

From the Newport, New Hampshire, *Argus-Champion:* "Mr. and Mrs. Evan Hill had Mr. and Mrs. Frank Sarles for Thanksgiving dinner. They were delicious."

From an advertisement in the Ketchikan *Progressive Alaskan:* "Spend your Saturday Nights at the Hacienda and your Sunday mornings in bed with a Progressive Alaskan."

From the Grand Rapids, Michigan, *Herald:* "Reporting to police the loss of $20, she said the money was concealed in her stocking, and the loss was discovered soon after the departure of a vacuum-cleaner salesman who had been demonstrating his line."

From the Des Moines, Iowa, *Register:* "Myrtle French is staging a vigorous fight for a public rest room for this city of 35,000 persons. The Women's Relief Corps has been backing Myrtle."

Correction in the Plymouth, Indiana, *Pilot-News:* "Mrs. Rebecca Robinson, 99, recites poetry as a hobby. One of her favorites is 'There Are No Sects in Heaven,' not 'There Is No Sex in Heaven' as stated incorrectly in the Wednesday edition of the *Pilot-News.*"

Social note in the Tarpon Springs, Florida, *Leader:* "Mr. and Mrs. Sidney Bomberg entertained Mr. and Mrs. Thomas Flynn and their eight-year-old son at dinner Friday night. A good time was had by all, except Sidney, Jr., who stated that he did not have a good time."

From the *Home Furnishings Daily:* "He also received the first national bedding award from the National Association of Bedding Manufacturers. He is married and has nine children."

From the Clarkston, Michigan, *News:* "We have been fortunate, indeed, to have Mr. Kalinke visit us and when he leaves we will be more than thankful."

From the Tujunga, California, *Record-Ledger:* "Rev. Hammond was congratulated on being able to get his parish plastered."

From the Jenkintown, Pennsylvania, *Times Chronicle:* "Girl wanted to assist magician in cutting-off-head illusion. Blue Cross and salary. Phone The Wizard."

Notice in the Baton Rouge *State-Times:* "To the bank robbers who broke into our Jefferson Highway Branch: City National Bank offers complete banking service at all of our offices. Next time you have a financial problem let one of our trained loan officers assist you."

From the San Francisco *Chronicle:* "Warning! to person who removed two antique gold rings from our gallery. These are Berber Fertility Rings and have been most effective in the past. You are on your own!"

From the Calgary, Alberta, *Herald:* "Rented room on April 18 in East Calgary. Couldn't find way back. Could landlord please phone me at this number. . . ."

From a Klamath Falls, Oregon, paper: "Joe W. Get in touch with me at once. Bring three rings. Engagement, wedding and teething. Have news for you. Betty."

From the Springer, New Mexico, *Tribune:* "Mr. and Mrs. Dennis have purchased a home adjacent to the Springer cemetery, where they plan to make their future home."

The Throes of Creation:
ARTS AND LETTERS

O UR APPARENT INABILITY to teach the young how to write may have its happy aspect. The balance may swing so widely to the side of cheerful illiteracy that fewer bad books will be written and published. One should never give up hoping. There's the story of the young author who made his way to the editor's sanctum in a state of considerable agitation and burst out with the question: "Sir, can you tell me how long a novel is?" The editor hesitated; then, "Well, lengths differ, but you might say something over seventy-five thousand words." The young man's face cleared as he exclaimed, "Thank God! I'm through!" Yes, authorship is a wearing vocation, to be recommended only to the tough of skin. When Edward Gibbon, creator of the monumental *Decline and Fall of the Roman Empire,* presented a quarto copy of Volume III to the Duke of Gloucester, the Duke remarked pleasantly: "Another damned thick, square book! Always scribble, scribble, scribble! Eh, Mr. Gibbon?" We poor typewriter drudges need occasionally to remind ourselves that neither Jesus nor Socrates left a word in writing.

Author, Author

Astronaut Edward H. White II made a lady author very happy at a Houston reception. "Ma'am," he told her, "I was reading your book while we were in orbit—and I just couldn't put it down!"

To illustrate an anachronism, Louis Nizer in his book *My Life in Court* uses this anecdote: An amateur playwright has a French obstetrician leave home at dawn to attend a delivery. When he returns home exhausted, his sympathetic wife inquires, "Did all go well?"

"It was a very difficult delivery," the doctor says, "but it was worth it. You know who was born today? Victor Hugo!"

GENIUS
AT MIDNIGHT
H. ALLEN SMITH

ONE NIGHT a few weeks ago I awoke from a deep sleep with the most brilliant idea that ever passed through the mind of mortal being. I groped for the light, found my pad and pencil and wrote it down, convinced that this was a concept which would shake the earth.

Next morning at breakfast I suddenly remembered that I had committed a soul-stirring idea to paper during the night, though I couldn't recall a thing about it. I rushed to get it, and this is what I found:

> this at time Roosevelt died
> see in clips—Times broch
> not understandable to me—to us—
> examine intellectual rot
> they mean well—maybe
> the plumber
> the $5 gardner
> do something about it.

There wasn't anything I could do about it. There was vast meaning and significance in it somewhere, but it eluded me. It eludes me still.

This happens to me all the time. And I've found that it happens to others who write memos in the night. The things we scribble down are almost always pure nonsense. Perhaps the most famous example is that of Mrs. Amos Pinchot. Out of the blackness came a poem so beautiful and so filled with wisdom that she felt she would be acclaimed as the greatest poet and the most profound thinker in history. In the morning this is how it looked:

Hogamus Higamus
Men are Polygamous,
Higamus Hogamus
Women Monogamous.

A neighbor of mine, in a period of sleeplessness, arrived at an idea he believed would be of enormous benefit, so he wrote it down. The next day he was unable to make any sense out of it: "German doctor—lines patients up in a circle—checks 'em from his bicycle seat."

When Fred Beck of Los Angeles was associated with the famous Farmers Market he had a night thought designed to bring the market a flood of publicity. He wrote down: "Arrange have Capistrano swallows switch to F.M." Unhappily he didn't write down the part in which he had figured out how to convince the swallows.

Hugh Troy, who lives in Washington, D.C., is—in the Brooklyn phrase—a man of many facets, all turned on. Many lovely philosophical concepts come to him during the night. One of them turned up on his note pad as follows:

Call State dept.
All energy is state of mind. Going
    uphill
is state of mind. Climb Everest—
    think
downhill while climbing. You'll
    really be
going downhill. Important.

For some years I have preserved a thing which had me convinced, at the time I put it down, that I would be the first man in history to win *two* Nobel Prizes in the same year—the prize for literature and the prize for peace. I dozed off, thinking of my trip to Sweden and the fame that would be mine. The next morning I found on my scratchpad:

insomnia for poor people
think of something downstairs
think of something in bathroom
(powdered alum)

think of something in bedroom
                        RETRACE!!!!

There is a story about Oliver Wendell Holmes the Elder. As a doctor he was interested in the use of ether and once had a dose administered to himself. While he was going under, a great thought framed itself in his mind—he believed that he had grasped the key to all the mysteries of philosophy. When he regained consciousness he was unable to recapture it. It was of vital importance to mankind, so he arranged to have himself given ether again and determined that he would speak the great thought so that a stenographer could write it down. Just before the anesthetic took full effect he had the vision again, and he spoke as follows:

The entire universe is permeated
   with a
strong odor of turpentine.

I am an admirer of a poem that Ann Maulsby, a neighbor of mine, composed in the night and couldn't even remember writing down. She simply found it and recognized her own handwriting. Here it is:

Stuck with the stuff of gardeners'
   dolls—
One-half man and one-half woman.
Little Mary Ott on her blot-stained
   cot,
Plagued by austerer values than
   ours.

In my opinion it's as good as anything T. S. Eliot ever wrote.

———— • ————

At a Washington party photographers were busy snapping pictures of Dame Edith Sitwell, the English poetess. During the workout one cameraman was seen shaking his head and muttering to himself. "What's the matter?" asked a pal.

"I just don't like it," he said. "People shouldn't call a dignified broad like that a dame."

———— • ————

George Bernard Shaw was poring over a second-hand bookstall of volumes much marked down, when he came across a volume containing his own plays. The book was inscribed, moreover, to a friend, beneath whose name on the fly leaf G. B. S. saw, written in his own hand, "With the compliments of George Bernard Shaw." Buying the book, Mr. Shaw wrote under the inscription: "With renewed compliments. G. B. S.," and sent it back to the early recipient.

My first literary burglary was committed at the tender age of 14. The Boston *Transcript* has a page of Notes and Queries—a sort of literary quiz. One day I sat down and wrote the editor. "Sir: Will you please give me the name of the author of the poem beginning: 'The dismal day, with dreary pace, hath dragged its tortuous length along.'" I signed it "Maxfield Newman."

The letter was duly published. The following week I again wrote the editor. "Sir: The author of the poem beginning, 'The dismal day,' is Gelett Burgess. The whole poem is as follows:

> *The dismal day, with dreary pace,*
> *Hath dragged its tortuous length along;*
> *The gravestones black, and funeral vase*
> *Cast horrid shadows long—"*

But I guess that's enough of it—it had three stanzas. That was my first appearance in print.

A U.S. publisher, discussing an author's latest novel, announced: "As far as we can see, the book has everything in it that made its predecessor sell: horror, sex, madness and depravity—all handled with dignity and restraint."

Like most prominent authors, Sir James Barrie received frequent requests from aspiring writers to read their efforts. A would-be novelist once handed him a 1500-page manuscript, asking him to read it and suggest a title. Barrie handed it back. "Tell me, young man," he said, "are there any drums or trumpets in your novel?"

"Why, no, Sir James," the young man protested. "It isn't that kind of book at all."

"Good!" said Barrie. "Then call it *No Drums, No Trumpets.*"

George Bernard Shaw once got a letter addressed to George Bernard Shawm. In a beard-tossing fury, Shaw roared to his wife that his correspondent could not even spell the name of the world's greatest man. Moreover, fumed G. B. S., there was no such word as "shawm."

Shaw's wife, one of the world's most martyred women, quietly disagreed, led Shaw to a dictionary and pointed to "shawm . . . an old-fashioned wind instrument."

A society woman came up to Michael Arlen and gushed about how she wanted to be a writer. What, she wanted to know, was the best way to start in writing?

"From left to right," the author answered brusquely.

"We Regret . . ."

A writer for a national magazine was cajoled into reading a manuscript written by his dentist. He found it hopelessly dull. Returning the manuscript to the dentist, he carefully began his criticism: "This may hurt a little. . . ."

The best rejection slip I ever heard of," Russel Crouse told a group of authors, "was an editor's note attached to a heavy manuscript. It read: 'I'm returning this paper—someone wrote on it.'"

A young English writer sent a number of his manuscripts to a celebrated newspaper columnist, asking his advice as to the best channel for marketing the writings. The manuscripts came back with this note: "The one channel I can conscientiously recommend as the greatest outlet for articles of this type is the English Channel."

A young author sent a manuscript to an editor with a letter in which he stated, "The characters in this story are purely fictional and bear no resemblance to any person, living or dead."

A few days later he received his manuscript with the penciled notation: "That's what's wrong with it."

John K. Williamson, American author, received the prize rejection slip of his writing career from a firm of Chinese publishers.

"We read your manuscripts with boundless delight," wrote the Chinese firm. "By the sacred ashes of our ancestors we swear that we have never dipped into a book of such overwhelming mastery. If we were to publish this book it would be impossible in the future to issue any book of a lower standard. As it is unthinkable that within the next 10,000 years we shall find its equal, we are, to our great regret, compelled to return this too divine work and beg you a thousand times to forgive our action."

Editors of *Collier's* received a letter from an aspiring contributor: "I am enclosing another of my masterpieces which I have been sending you since 1930. You never paid me for any of them though I know you took ideas from all of them, even from the ones I never mailed to you. Please attend to this matter as soon as possible."

Hearing nothing concerning a story she had sent a magazine, a woman wrote an indignant letter asking the editor kindly to read and publish the story immediately, or return it, as she had other irons in the fire. The script came back at once with a note: "I have read your story and advise you to put it with the other irons."

Actor-manager Sir Herbert Beerbohm Tree broke the news to an author this way: "My dear sir: I have read your play. Oh, my dear sir!"

In analyzing why a religious publication had rejected her manuscript, Helen Topping Miller thought perhaps it was because one of her characters used the word "darn." She rewrote the story, cut out the offensive word and sent it back to the editor with this note: "I have cut the 'darn' out of my story. I hope you can use it now."

Once again the story was returned. This time there was a message scribbled on the margin of the rejection slip: "We do not wish to appear irreverent, but if you cut the hell out of this story we still could not use it."

Eugene Field disposed of a would-be poet who had submitted a verse entitled, "Why Do I Live?" by writing on the rejection slip: "Because you sent your poem by mail."

Picture That

The proprietor of an art gallery in London, showing pictures to a customer who didn't know what he liked, tried out a landscape, a still life, a portrait, and a floral piece, all without results. "Would you be interested in a nude?" he finally asked.

"Good heavens, no," said the visitor. "I'm a physician."

POP ART, SHMOP ART,
LEAVE ME ALONE
LEO ROSTEN

DEAR LEFTY—
Well, pal, I just have to tell you what has transpired, even altho you won't hardly believe it. I might not believe it my self if I did not actually see it with my own 2 eyes and ears.

Well, last Saturd. in the p.m. I am strolling up Madison Av with a new dish, a classy blond I am soffening up for the finals—when I spot this parked sportscar, a gordgeous red Convertable job with zebra seats.

Man, O man, I xclaim, tho addressing a member of the opposing sex. How would you like to take a zoomeroo in that?

I do not prefer my tresses blown in my face whilst proceeding down a thruway, says Marcia. Are you per chance interested in Music, Lit or the Finer Arts?

Me? I retort, Why I am a real artist at heart—on acct. my old lady was a sculpter! She was? amazed Marcia. Sure, I say, she used to carve Easter Bunnies out of chocolate.

You are pulling my leg, says Marcia. Not yet, I say, but that is a good idea.

O see what is in that shopwindow! she hastens.

And here, Lefty, is where you have to start believing and not wondering if maybe your old pal has lost so many marbles they have put him on the paper-doll squad in Group Therape. Because in that window is a gaɪoadge pail, full of Custard, and across the pail in pukey purple letters is the word—BEING. And in the goo are maybe 100 popsikles covered by a Fish-net, in which a U.S. *flag* is planted! And across our Stars & Strips is pasted—NOTH-INGNESS. So help me, Lefty, I am not slipping you no baloney.

Marcia is regarding this mish-mosh with Rapture, and asks— What do you think of the artist?

I wish him a speedy recovery, say I.

He is trying to make a Personal Statement about Our Times! she xplains.

The statement is: You can blow bubbles in my head without even inserting soap, I answer.

This artist has a Committment! she cries.

They ought to parole him, say I.

You have no sympathy for Pop Art, she mones.

Pop Art? I ecko, Why baby, you suprise me. Pop Art is Out, to anyone who is In, of who I happen to be 1 of the select few.

O, then you prefer *Op* art? she asks.

Op Art is dead, say I.

Then what school *do* you espouse? she throws me.

Mop Art, I bunt.

Mop Art? she asks, What is that?

That is where you apply the paint with a Mop made of chicken feathers dipped in Yogurt, I reply.

A look of pain from some old ailment occupys dear Marcias features. Let us go in, she strangles.

So we go into the establishment, wich I see is Very Chic. A place is very Chic when the broads are very skinny and the mens legs are held together by tight pants instead of skin. Lefty, the noise there is like Shraffts before a Wedn. Matinee if Maurice Chevrolet happened to drop in. I never heard such a gaggel of babbel and giggel from the Kooks who are trying to prove they are xcstatic Art Lovers in the Avon Gard. And whilst me and Marcia squeeze our way to and fro, I catch words like Kinnetic Action and Vibrant Validity and Fluid Drive.

What is creating all these $1.00 words? The stuff on the walls —the work of ½ wits who would not pass an Insanity Test given by Casey Stengel. 1 so-called picture is actually a chunk of Burlap, dripping oatmeal. That is called *Farewell to Brer Rabbi.* Another is a big white Square with a gold cornflake in the middle, named *Cerebral Cereal.* I also observe a big red Circle with a blue circle inside it, with a red circle inside the blue, with a blue circle inside etc until by the time you come down to the teeny center you can check in at the nearest Eye Bank. This master-pizza is called *Litany for Hopheads,* wich I do not dout.

But in the meanwhile where is Marcia? I find her, allright— yakking away with the joker who runs the joint, wich I can tell because he has a Caranation in his button-hole, plus wavy pink hair. They are both gushing over a bunch of Oil cans wich have been mashed together into 1 wrinkled blob of metal, like pressed prunes in armor.

So spontan-eous throbs Mr. Clean, A form of axidental design!

Assthetics victory over Materialism! says Marcia.

It stinks on ice, says a voice from a nearby broad who is xtreme-ly well-stacked. She grabs my arm, xclaiming, My name is Leila La Mont.

Its not your fault, I say.

You are a scream, she screams.

Observe *A Soul in Torment,* says Mr. Goldilox, Step back sos you can xperience its full impact.

All I see are a lot of straight lines in squares, I protest.

But are they not *xciting?* asks Marcia.

Sure, I say, If you are a ruler.

Marcia hands me a look you can cut into ice-cubes.

Suddenly, wham! Without warning an earthquake attacks the joint with a terrific CRASH—SKREESHMRRRR!!!! from outside, 1 and all rush to the front door, where Caranation Charlie omits a cry of anguish—O, he hollers, My car! What have they done to my beautiful little dream?

The snazzy red Convertable is *pancacked,* since a Moving Van has backed up, squashing it against whats parked behind—wich is meerly the Derrick for the xcavation of next door. Lefty, that sports job looks like an accordion made out of Marashino Cherrys.

Mr. Clean is moning and groning in the throws of despair, My baby! My Minnesota-Fascisti, 1922! It is roond! Roond!

Up steps Miss Leila La Mont with a Florence Nightandale smile. No, no, regarday it this way! she coos, It is a personal *statement.* The victory of Assthetics over Materialism. You are now the own-er of a new masterpiece of Axidental Design!

Well, boy, that about raps it up. I have given Marcia back to the Bronx and I am making time with Miss Leila La Mont, who I will escort to see the Mets play this Frid. night. She does not give me no ringing in the ears, between BEING and NOTHINGNESS. Hoping you are the same,   Your old pal,

                                                    Vern

A zealous art student went to a gallery and spent a bewildered hour looking over abstract and cubist works. She was finally attracted to a painting consisting of a black dot on a field of white and framed in brass. "How much for this?" she asked.

"That's the light switch," she was told.

A prizefighter, visiting the studio of James Montgomery Flagg, asked if the artist thought he had inherited his ability.

"I doubt it," said Flagg. "Now you take the Spanish painter Velázquez. Did you ever hear of Velázquez's father?"

"No," the prizefighter said.

"Did you ever hear of Velázquez's mother?"

"No."

"Well," Flagg said, "you see what I mean."

"Not exactly," the fighter said. "I never heard of Velázquez, either."

At a Montgomery, Alabama, art show the pictures were tagged by the artists with title and comments. Underneath one abstract the tag read: "Sure, you could do it too, but *would* you?"

When a certain well-known artist arrived at his studio, his model, who had been posing for his unfinished study of a nude, started toward the screen to disrobe. "Don't undress," the artist told her. "I shan't be painting today. I have a bad headache, and I'm just going to make myself a cup of tea and go home."

"Oh, please let me make it for you," the model said. The artist thanked her and told her to make one for herself, too. Just as they began to drink, however, the artist heard familiar footsteps in the hall.

"Good heavens!" he exclaimed. "Here comes my wife! Get those clothes off—quick!"

Man to wife as they gaze at huge abstract painting: "I know what he's trying to say—he's trying to say that he can't paint worth a damn!"

A man who purchased a small piece of abstract sculpture from an art gallery later received a letter from the gallery. It began: "Dear Sir or Madman."

Comedian Joe Smith tells of a banker who sat for his portrait, then refused to pay the $3000 fee, insisting, "It's not *me.*" Later the portrait was exhibited, titled "Thief," and the banker phoned the artist to complain. "But it's not you," said the artist. "You said so yourself." He finally sold the portrait to the banker, for $5000, changing the title to "The Philanthropist."

Painter Yves Klein used "living brushes"—he had his nude models smear themselves with paint, then let them hurl themselves at a blank canvas while he shouted directions from a stepladder. After *Time* published an article about Klein, reader Don Hunt wrote this letter to the editor: "Keep the paintings, but please send me some of his used brushes."

Critic's Choice

Editor and author Russell Lynes: "Every good journalist has a good novel in him—which is an excellent place for it."

A little boy stopped in front of an abstract painting in an exhibition of local talent in Arizona. "What's *that?*" he asked his mother.

"It's supposed to be a cowhand and his horse," she explained.

"Well," asked the boy, "why ain't it?"

From a book review: "It is not a book to be lightly thrown aside. It should be thrown with great force."

At an exhibit of abstract art at the Jewish Museum in New York City, I was standing before a large blob of plastic. Two Jewish matrons came up. After a moment of silence, one turned to the other and said in a distressed tone, "That's Jewish?"

When the question of an official state crest arose during a session of the Iowa legislature, an artist submitted a sample design, and columnist Donald Kaul of the Des Moines *Register* commented: "Thus far, sentiment seems to be leaning toward a dinosaur rampant on a field of trivia."

A New Yorker who had bought an old canvas in Rome lugged it to a 57th Street dealer to ascertain its true worth. "At first glance," opined the dealer, "I'd say it's either a Titian or a repetition."

Of an exhibition of D. H. Lawrence's paintings, largely nudes, Rebecca West once noted: "Mr. Lawrence has very pink friends."

Honor Tracy, witty Irish author, was not too pleased with the looks of the English edition of her newest book. She sent the London publisher a copy of the ever-so-much handsomer American edition with a note reading: "As the cock said to the hens when he showed them an ostrich egg, 'I am not disparaging; I am not criticizing. I merely bring to your attention what is being done elsewhere.'"

In one of his books novelist James Branch Cabell mentions a Texas judge who had said unfriendly things about him. After the judge's name is an asterisk, and—at the bottom of the page—the footnote reads: "Nothing whatever is known of him."

A young writer was being torn to shreds *in absentia* by a group of self-styled literary critics in the presence of a well-known French author. "It isn't right to talk of him that way," said the good-natured celebrity. "I like him very much."

"What do you like about him?" he was asked.

"He doesn't show off," the author replied. "That's very unusual for a man without talent."

Mark Twain, answering a letter from a would-be author, wrote: "Yes, Agassiz *does* recommend authors to eat fish, because the phosphorus in it makes brain. So far you are correct. But I cannot help you to a decision about the amount you need to eat—at least not with certainty. If the specimen composition is about your fair usual average, I suggest that perhaps a couple of whales would be all you would want for the present. Not the largest kind, but simply good middling-sized whales."

At a recent exhibit of work by the modern sculptor Henry Moore, I saw two youths standing before a figure that bore a somewhat far-out resemblance to a woman.

One of them bent close to the tag that gave the title and date of the sculpture and read aloud, "Reclining Woman, no date."

Eyeing the oddly twisted form, the other commented, "And no wonder!"

Staring hard at a surrealist painting, a woman remarked, "I have often felt migraine. Now I'm seeing it."

Samuel F. B. Morse, who was an eminent painter before he invented telegraphy, once asked a physician friend to look at his painting of a man in death agony. "Well," Morse inquired after the doctor had scrutinized it carefully, "what is your opinion?"

"Malaria," said the doctor.

Nicholas Chamfort, 18th-century French writer, commenting on a couplet: "Excellent, were it not for its length."

Man, reading novel, to wife: "If there's a hero in this book, he should kill the author!"

Articles of Faith:

RELIGION ON
THE LIGHTER SIDE

O UR AMERICAN JOKING about religion and churchgoing
(two things often associated in our minds though not
necessarily connected in fact) tells us something
about ourselves as a people. For one thing, the joking is
never really satirical, as Voltaire was satirical. It does not
aim at ridicule in any basic sense. Rather it seems an indirect

method of dealing with our embarrassment in the face of something that is truly serious. We Americans are not terribly good at making appropriate remarks when encountering the awesome or the transcendent. And so we sidestep the challenge with jokes and puns turning on miscomprehensions of the Bible. Or, put off by the uncomfortable fact that men of God *are* (or at least *should be*) different and apart from the rest of us, we make mild fun of preachers. Or, not quite having the courage to joke about religion ourselves, we ascribe the jokes to children, whose innocence exempts them from reproof. Our laughter at the institutions of religion is always mild and even timid, as if we wanted everyone to know that we don't really mean it. There's the old gag about the two soothsayers of ancient Rome who, as they passed in the Forum, always winked at each other.

And Gladly Preach

A minister who always read his sermons placed his text on the pulpit about half an hour before the service. One Sunday a young member of his congregation surreptitiously removed the last page of the manuscript.

Preaching vigorously, the minister came to the words, "So Adam said to Eve. . . ." Turning the page, he was horrified to discover the final page was missing. As he riffled through the other pages, he gained a little time by repeating, "So Adam said to Eve. . . ." Then in a low voice, but one which the amplifying system carried to every part of the church, he added, ". . . there seems to be a leaf missing."

Pastor at the offering: "And now, brethren, let us all give in accordance with what we reported on Form 1040."

On Sunday, the first day of daylight-saving time, a sleepy-eyed congregation watched the young priest ascend the pulpit in a Washington church. Not looking too wide-awake himself, he began, "As you all know, we lost an hour last night because of daylight-saving time. I don't know which hour *you* lost, but I lost the hour in which I usually write my sermon."

He returned to the altar and continued the service.

At Southampton's fashionable St. Andrew's Dune Church, after a week of steaming hot weather, guest minister Rev. William Henry Wagner told the congregation he would preach the shortest sermon ever. It consisted of the following words: "If you think it's hot here—just *wait!*"

We are all responsible for our own sins," said the preacher. "It's no use trying to put the blame for them on someone else: Adam blamed Eve, Eve blamed the serpent and the serpent hadn't a leg to stand on."

The order of service of the Congregational-Christian Church of Red Cloud, Nebraska, listed the sermon topic "Gossip." Immediately following was the hymn "I Love to Tell the Story."

The minister of a church in Wyckoff, New Jersey, told the sexton to put on the bulletin board his sermon topic for the following Sunday: "Are Ministers Cracking Up?" The sexton looked puzzled but did as he was told and put up the letters to announce: "Our Minister's Cracking Up."

An elderly minister was holding forth at a local bus stop, his small audience enthralled by his interesting monologue. Suddenly he broke off and turned to gaze at a smartly dressed young lady with an eye-catching figure who walked gracefully past. As the girl turned the corner, the spell was finally broken and the minister resumed his talk. "You know," he said, "I just never tire of admiring the work of the Lord."

A young minister delivering his first sermon to a new congregation quoted the parable of the loaves and the fishes. "Now," he said dramatically, "consider the scene where the Master with 5000 loaves and 2000 fishes fed five people." A murmur of amusement ran through the church and one old man up in front laughed out loud.

The poor young minister was so humiliated that the following Sunday he decided to regain the ground he'd lost by using the same parable in another sermon. "Now consider the scene where the Master with five loaves and two fishes fed 5000 people," he said. Then, having regained his confidence, he leaned over the pulpit and spoke to the old man who had laughed at him, "You couldn't do that, brother."

"Oh, yes, I could," said the old gentleman, "if I had what was left over from last week!"

When I was holding the 9:30 service one Sunday, I noticed that one parishioner was very late. To my surprise, he was at the 11 o'clock service as well. But when the congregation rose to sing the hymn before the sermon, he left, murmuring to the usher: "This is where I came in."

A visiting bishop delivered a speech at a banquet on the night of his arrival in a large city. Because he wanted to repeat some of his stories at meetings the next day, he requested reporters to omit them from their accounts of his speech. A rookie reporter, commenting on the speech, finished with the line: "And he told a number of stories that cannot be published."

A minister illustrated a point in his sermon by saying that a beneficent wisdom knows which of us grows best in sunlight and which of us must have shade. "You know you plant roses in the sunlight," he said, "but if you want your fuchsias to grow, they must be kept in a shady nook."

Afterward a woman came up to him, her face radiant. "Dr. Smith," she said clasping his hand, "I'm so grateful for your splendid sermon." His heart glowed for a moment. But then she went on fervently, "Yes, I never knew before just what was the matter with my fuchsias!"

A minister, preaching on the danger of compromise, was condemning the attitude of so many Christians who believe certain things concerning their faith, but in actual practice will say, "Yes, but . . . ." At the climax of the sermon, he said, "Yes, there are millions of Christians who are sliding straight to Hell on their buts."

The congregation went into gales of laughter, and the minister promptly closed the service with a benediction.

Sunday Scholars

FAITH, HOPE AND HILARITY

DICK VAN DYKE

WANTED: Teacher. Must have the wisdom of Solomon, the patience of Job and the courage of David."

That's the ad I'd run if I wanted to find the ideal Sunday-school teacher. I tried the job myself for three years at a Dutch Reformed church on Long Island. And from experience I'd say it also helps if a teacher has Jonah's ability to bob up smiling, the faith of the early Christians on Lion's Day at the Colosseum and the confidence of Noah that the whole trip is worth the trouble.

But if it was demanding, it was also a delight. My experiences and those of Sunday-school-teaching friends show the wondrous insights of children when confronted with the mysteries of faith.

Children have an uncanny way of reducing the unexplainable to their own terms. Witness the child explaining how God creates people: "He draws us first, then cuts us out." Or the child describing what a halo is: "They have this circle over their heads, and they always try to walk carefully so they stay right underneath it. It lights up."

Sometimes you can't beat them for aptness, as in the case of a child describing the difference between Protestants, Catholics and Jews:

"They're all just different ways of voting for God."

Clear-eyed, indisputable logic is children's stock in trade. Take the child who, when asked what one must do before obtaining forgiveness for sin, replied, "Sin."

Or take the child who heard the story of the Prodigal Son for the first time. "In the midst of all the celebration for the Prodigal," said the teacher, "there was one for whom the feast brought no happiness, only bitterness. Can you tell me who this was?" "The fatted calf?" suggested a sad little voice.

A reverse logic seems to apply in the case of a child who had just heard the story of the Good Samaritan. "What does it teach you?" she was asked. "That when I'm in trouble," said the child, "someone should help me."

Quite logically, too, children relate Bible allusions to the world they live in. If they don't have the answer to a question, one soon comes bubbling up from their imagination. One boy, when asked why there are no longer burnt offerings to God, suggested, "Air pollution." Another, answering a question, described the "multitude that loafs and fishes."

Among my favorites in the "inner logic" department is the story of a minister showing a painting of Christ to a child. It's not really Jesus, he explained, just an artist's conception of him. "Well, it sure *looks* like him," said the child.

Anyone who has listened to kids saying prayers knows that these moments are full of surprises, family bulletins and glimpses of what goes on in a child's mind. One little boy, smarting after punishment, finished his prayers with the usual blessings for all the family members but one. Then, turning to his daddy, he said, "I suppose you noticed you wasn't in it."

Children's prayers have an amazing intimacy and directness. One child, told by his mother that he might go on a picnic she had previously vetoed, sighed, "It's too late, Mom. I've already prayed for rain."

As Sunday-school teachers we face questions that for centuries have made doctors of divinity tear at their beards, such as, "If God made us all in his own image, why are some people bad and ugly?" The children's answers are often better than our own. To the query, "Why is there but one God?" a child answered, "Because God fills every place, and there's no room for another one." Asked to explain the difference between the role of the Creator and that of the Saviour, one boy did it with breathtaking brevity: "God puts us down and Jesus takes us up."

The faith of children has an innocence—a kind of trust and openness—that the Bible surely meant when we were told, "Whosoever shall not receive the kingdom of God as a little child, he shall not enter therein."

———— • ————

The Lord's Prayer has had to withstand considerable abuse, especially from children trying to learn it from poor enunciators or from mumbling congregations.

One little boy was heard to pray, "Harold be Thy name." Another begged, "Give us this day our jelly bread." A New York child petitioned, "Lead us not into Penn station."

A little boy, aged five, was playing with the small daughter of new neighbors. They had been wading at the lake, and finally decided the only way to keep their clothes dry was to take them off.

As they were going back into the water, the little boy looked the little girl over. "Gosh," he remarked, "I didn't know there was *that* much difference between Catholics and Protestants!"

In Denver, the members of a Sunday-school class were asked to set down their favorite Biblical truths. One youngster laboriously printed: "Do one to others as others do one to you."

A Naval officer asked his small daughter what she had learned at Sunday school. "We studied about the ten commanders," she reported. "We learned they are always broke."

———— • ————

Each week a New York youngster would bring home from Sunday school an illustrated card that dramatized one of the Ten Commandments. The first week showed people worshiping at church. Another week, to illustrate "Thou shalt not kill," the picture showed Cain in the act of slaying Abel.

"I waited with considerable alarm for the seventh week," reports the child's father. "But fortunately, tact and delicacy prevailed. Under the caption 'Thou shalt not commit adultery' was a picture of a dairyman, leering villainously as he poured a huge pail of water into a can of milk!"

The Sunday-school teacher was describing how Lot's wife looked back and turned into a pillar of salt, when little Jimmy interrupted. "My mother looked back once while she was driving," he announced triumphantly, "and *she* turned into a telephone pole!"

In her book *Smile Please,* Mildred Spurrier Topp recalls the day she and her sister decided to send a valentine, supposedly from their widowed mother, to a prominent judge who had shown marked, if discreet, signs of interest. Mildred wanted to use a new word she had heard in Sunday school. "I'm not sure what it means," she confessed to her sister, "But it's in the Bible, so it must be OK. Besides, it was used about King Solomon, so it's bound to be romancy enough for a valentine."

That's how the judge came to receive a gaudy, lace-bedecked valentine that read:

> *If you will be my valentine,*
> *I will be your concubine. . . .*

The first-graders at an Episcopal Sunday school in San Diego were told to draw their conceptions of the Flight into Egypt. One little girl turned in a picture of an airplane with three people in the back, all with halos, and a fourth up front without one. Perplexed about the fourth person, the teacher asked the little girl who it was.

"Oh," replied the youngster, "that's Pontius, the pilot."

While the art class was setting up a Christmas scene on the school lawn, one of the boys asked uncertainly, "Where shall I put the three wise guys?"

Mommy," chirped my four-year-old, "don't you think it was nice of the shepherds to get all cleaned up before they went to see the baby Jesus?"

"What do you mean?"

"Well, you know that song, 'While shepherds washed their socks by night.'"

After the Sunday-school class had sung "Silent Night" and been told the Christmas story, the teacher suggested that her pupils draw the Nativity scene. A little boy finished first. The teacher praised his drawing of the manger, of Joseph, of Mary and the infant. But she was puzzled by a roly-poly figure off to one side and asked who it was.

"That's Round John Virgin," explained the youngster.

Two youngsters were walking home from Sunday school after having been taught a lesson on the devil. One little boy was overheard saying to the other, "What do you think about all this devil business?"

The other youngster replied thoughtfully, "Well, you know how Santa Claus turned out. It's probably just your dad."

———— • ————

HARK, THE SHRIEKING ANGELS!
CATHERINE B. HOFFMAN

EVERY YEAR at the end of the Christmas pageant in the candlelit church, with the little angels and shepherds grouped around the Holy Family looking like a Raphael painting, and the boy soprano singing "O Holy Night," and the magic of Christmas everywhere, the rector eases over to you and whispers, "Of course you'll take charge of the pageant again next year?" And you, completely undone, murmur, "Of course."

Fifteen minutes later, untying the wings of shrieking angels and ducking shepherds' crooks, you cry in anguish, "What have I done?" But your word is given, and you are in for it again.

The big rehearsal for this undertaking always seems to be held on the coldest Saturday morning the weather bureau can manage, and usually on a day the sexton has trouble "getting her to heat up." This is no problem for the shepherds, who have been working up a fine lather for an hour hooking one another by the neck with their crooks, but it is a chilly outlook for the leggy little angels who stand around red-nosed and shivering in their under-shirts, waiting to be measured for their cherub wings.

The pageant director will find that the Sunday school has gained miraculously in membership. Investigation reveals that several of the little shepherd boys are bona-fide members of the Sunday school, but weren't instantly recognized because they show up only when we give out the Christmas candy and the Easter plants. Twice a year is perhaps better than not at all, however, so each is fitted with a multicolored sack dress, circa 2 B.C. (Our costumes were designed and "run up" in 1920, but angel styles are fairly classic, and shepherds' gowns, like a good polo coat, never change.)

You now study a group of uncomfortable teen-agers. With a keen eye you can separate those who came only because Dad is a vestryman from those who are really dying to put on gold crowns and beards and wow the girls from Young People's. So it is fairly easy to get some impressive kings and a protective-looking St. Joseph (especially since Mary was chosen with an eye to her pretty little face and long blond hair).

After hours of rehearsing, the youngsters string out of the parish house nodding numbly to the shouted instructions: "Joseph, remember not to wear saddle shoes!" "All angels must wear either white dresses or a white petticoat!" "Frankincense king, remember your bicycle pump to get the incense going!" "Three o'clock sharp now!"

"Three o'clock sharp now" comes fast enough when you have spent most of the final day doing such things as striving for indirect lighting in the manger without setting the hay on fire. You can bank on it that the two lead angels will arrive in dark-blue velvet jumpers ("We were at Grandma's for dinner and didn't have time to change"). This is solved by stripping petticoats off two little girls who have come in white dresses *and* white slips. You can also be sure that Joseph will appear in saddle shoes, but he will cheerfully agree that he goofed and offer to walk in his stocking feet. You are lucky if his socks have no holes. If they do, simply blacken his feet with the burnt cork for the Wise Men's beards.

By 3:30 the parish house is jumping with shepherds again crooking one another, Wise Men trying to light the frankincense (which is damp after a summer in the cellar), and angels playing "Silent Night" and "Chopsticks" on one piano. Mary arrives with her blond tresses chopped off in a brand-new pixy cut, and there is a minor crisis while her headdress is rearranged to hide her un-Aramaic hairdo.

A shepherd whips back from the hall to announce loudly, "The whole church is full—I'm scared to death!" This sends the angels into a tizzy, and several of them decide that a visit to the girls' room is imperative. This means that a mother must be taken off halo-pinning to help the girls'-room contingent with their wings. Balthasar cannot get his sash tied, and Melchior says he thinks he is allergic to burnt cork because his face hurts. (That cork *was* a little warm.)

A pale-looking shepherd retires to a corner, moaning, "I think I'm going to throw up."

"Nonsense!" you say briskly. "They never heard of the virus in Bethlehem."

The organ is now playing "O Little Town of Bethlehem." At last all the giggling and pushing is over, and the children are standing hushed and wide-eyed, ready to enter. Under cover of the advancing choir, Mary and Joseph glide into position on either side of the manger.

The frankincense king, with a last mighty effort on the bicycle pump, has got the incense going, and clouds of smoke are seeping out into the church. There his little brother, bursting with excitement, whispers shrilly, "Mommy, I smell Harold!"

The angels progress through the church murmuring, "Three pews apart, she said, and don't back your wings into the candles!" The shepherds have made it up the chancel steps in their long gowns, and are peering into the darkness for the approach of the Magi.

O come, all ye faithful, joyful and triumphant! Surely this is not a little neighborhood church full of ordinary children re-enacting the Nativity in homemade costumes. On these little faces are the awe and the wonder that must have marked those faces long ago at the manger in Bethlehem. Who cares about the holiday rush and the bustle? This is the why and the wherefore. This is truly Christmas!

Clerical Notes

After hearing his first confession, the young curate went to the older priest and asked, "Well, Father, how did I make out?"

"My son," said the priest, "you did very well. But one suggestion: When you hear the confessions of these pretty young women, it would be a bit more seemly if you went *'tsk! 'tsk! 'tsk!* and not 'WHEE!'"

Church Sign: "This Is a Ch—ch. What Is Missing?"

The pompous young minister, who had been appointed to help the pastor of a large New York church, was annoyed that he was to be called "assistant minister." He felt that "associate minister" was a title more befitting his ability. He aired his grievance to an older colleague, who listened attentively, then said, "My dear boy, what does it matter either way? They'll both be abbreviated into ASS."

Asked to buy a ticket to a church benefit, a man said, "Sorry, I won't be able to attend. But my spirit will be there with you."

"Good," said his friend. "I have $2, $3 and $5 tickets. Where would you like your spirit to sit?"

Back in the days when Brooklyn had a baseball team, Francis Cardinal Spellman was watching a World Series game at Ebbets Field. During the course of the game, a high foul was hit toward his box seat. Catcher Roy Campanella tried to reach it but missed, and the ball hit the cardinal's knee. Campanella quickly asked whether he had been hurt.

"Don't worry about it, Roy," the cardinal said. "A priest's knees are the toughest part of his anatomy."

On his way to London to assume his post as executive officer of the Anglican Communion, Bishop Stephen F. Bayne, Jr., was asked how he felt about his new duties. "Well," he said, "I am rather like a mosquito in a nudist camp. I know what I ought to do, but I don't know where to begin."

At a faculty-student reception, Yale's chaplain, the Rev. William Sloane Coffin, Jr., met an intense sophomore with the light of battle in his eye. "Sir," said the boy belligerently, "religion is a crutch!"

"Sure it is," agreed Coffin, "but who isn't limping?"

Fund-raising sign in front of a Boston synagogue: "You Can't Take It With You, But You *Can* Send It on Ahead."

Where have you been for the last two hours?" demanded the minister's wife.

"I met Mrs. Brown on the street and asked her how she was feeling," sighed the weary pastor.

On a church bulletin board in Fairbury, Illinois: "Even moderation ought not to be practiced to excess."

Faith Lifts

A young California couple took a visiting aunt for a drive, and pointed out a fig tree as one of the sights.

"Fig tree!" exclaimed the elderly woman. "That can't be a fig tree."

"Certainly is," said her niece. "What makes you think different?"

"Well," said the aunt, subsiding a little, "I just thought . . . surely . . . the leaves must be bigger that that?"

A certain pastor, burdened by the importance of his work, went into the sanctuary to pray. Falling to his knees, he lamented, "O Lord, I am nothing! I am nothing!"

The minister of education passed by, and overhearing the prayer, was moved to join the pastor on his knees. Shortly he too was crying aloud, "O Lord, I too am nothing. I am nothing."

The janitor of the church, awed by the sight of the two men praying, joined them, crying, "O Lord, I also am nothing. I am nothing."

At this, the minister of education nudged the pastor and said, "Now look who thinks *he's* nothing!"

One medieval monk, transcribing scripture, to another: "Somebody's going to get a break. I skipped a couple of commandments."

A man who survived the Johnstown flood talked about it endlessly all his life. When he finally died and went to heaven, St. Peter greeted him and said, "If you think of anything that will make you happier here you have only to mention it."

"Well, there is *one* thing," replied the man. "I'd like to tell a group of people here about my terrible experiences in the Johnstown flood."

"There must be a number who would be interested," replied St. Peter. "It will be arranged."

The following evening a large group gathered. As the flood survivor was about to speak, St. Peter touched him on the shoulder and whispered, "Perhaps I should tell you that Noah is in the audience."

A woman tourist visiting the Holy Land went to a tourist office for information on roads. Told that it was now possible to go by car all the way from Dan to Beersheba, she confessed, "Do you know, I never knew that Dan and Beersheba were places. I always thought they were husband and wife, like Sodom and Gomorrah."

Three Monks of the Trappist order, which has a rule of silence, asked the abbot's permission to speak with one another. The abbot granted the oldest monk privilege to speak one sentence that year on a coming feast day. He granted the youngest the right to speak one sentence on that feast day one year later. The third brother was to wait still another year for his feast-day privilege.

Following breakfast the first year the oldest monk said, "I hate oatmeal."

A year went by and after breakfast the youngest brother said, "I like oatmeal."

Another year passed and the third monk said, "Listen, I'm getting awfully tired of this constant bickering."

From Northern Ireland comes the story of the nun who ran out of gas and walked to a filling station. The owner gave her enough gas to get her car started—in the only container he had available, a beer bottle.

She returned to the car and was pouring the contents of the beer bottle into the tank when a leader of the Protestant extremists drove by. He watched in amazement, then exclaimed, "We may have our differences, Sister, but I've got to admire your faith!"

A young couple bought a parakeet which would say only, "Let's neck." A preacher suggested that they put his bird, which always said, "Let us pray," in the same cage with the delinquent bird so that the latter might learn the more uplifting phrase.

When the two were put together, the couple's bird said, as usual, "Let's neck." Whereupon the preacher's bird said, "My prayers have been answered!"

The minister was whaling away with his niblick, trying to get out of the sand trap. Finally he lofted the ball, only to have it go over the green into a trap on the far side. Red-faced and exasperated, he turned to the other members of the foursome and said, "Won't one of you laymen please say a few appropriate words?"

Woman to husband, as they leave church: "Bob, I noticed you put ten dollars in the collection. *Now* what have you got on your conscience?"

Unaccustomed As I Am . . . :
THE SPEECHMAKERS

THE WITTIEST TOASTMASTER I have ever heard was without a doubt Clarence Budington Kelland. An excellent example of his inimitable style may be found in this chapter. I can add another. At one of the Dutch Treat Club's weekly luncheons, with Bud presiding, the scheduled speaker was the then president of Columbia

University, the formidable and famous Dr. Nicholas Murray Butler. There were few matters on which Nicholas Miraculous, as his detractors called him, did not have decided opinions. Kelland introduced him thus: "Friends, for years hundreds — perhaps thousands — of institutions, societies and organizations all over the country have been beseeching Dr. Butler to address them — with, I may add, remarkable success." There are lots of stories (see "Briefly Speaking," below) about short, witty speeches. The classic one is about H. G. Wells, who, on being introduced, was received with a tumultuous ovation. When it ceased he said, in his thin piping voice, "Ladies and gentlemen, your reception leaves me speechless," and sat down.

Toast Masterers

A toastmaster is a man who eats a meal he doesn't want so he can get up and tell a lot of stories he doesn't remember to people who've already heard them.

Master of ceremonies at banquet: "Let's have a round of applause for the wonderful job the program committee did in not being able to obtain a speaker."

My father was asked to introduce the speakers at a Methodist evening church affair in Martinsville, Virginia. Because of inclement weather the audience consisted of only a handful of people, but my father was equal to the occasion.

"I have been asked to introduce our speaker to you this evening," he began. "This I am very glad to do. Ladies and gentlemen, this is Mr. John Brown. Mr. Brown, meet Mr. and Mrs. Rucker, Mr. and Mrs. Witten, Mr. Stovall, Miss Stovall. . . ."

Author-lecturer Emily Kimbrough was introduced by a ladies'-club chairman with: "Miss Kimbrough is our only speaker today. The rest of the program is entertainment."

Hiram Fong, U.S. Senator from Hawaii, was being introduced by the late Senator Everett Dirksen. Dirksen's speech was excessively flowery and complimentary. When it was over Fong stood up. "Now," he said, "I know how a pancake feels after syrup has been poured over it."

The American novelist Clarence Budington Kelland was acting as master of ceremonies at a huge dinner party. The speakers' table was distressingly populous. Mr. Kelland got up, a slip of paper in his hand.

"Gentlemen," he began, "the obvious duty of a toastmaster is to be so infernally dull that the succeeding speakers will appear brilliant by contrast." The succeeding speakers began to chuckle heartily.

"I've looked over this list, however," added Kelland, "and I don't believe I can do it."

The speakers stopped chuckling and the diners bellowed.

The Perfect Preface

André Maurois, France's distinguished man of letters, opened his speech at the American Club of Paris: "Gentlemen, I unfortunately have been asked to speak today in English, and as a result, the language you will hear will be neither yours nor mine."

In preparation for a banquet at Radcliffe College, the chairs had been given a new coat of varnish. The evening was hot and humid, and as the after-dinner speaker started to rise, he found himself stuck to the seat. However, he was unabashed. "Ladies and gentlemen," he said, "I had expected to bring you a plain and unvarnished tale, but circumstances make it impossible."

Called upon to address the guests at a Thanksgiving dinner, William M. Evarts, Secretary of State under Hayes, began: "You have been giving your attention to turkey stuffed with sage; you are now about to consider a sage stuffed with turkey!"

After-dinner speaker's remark: "Now before I start I want to say something."

The late Rabbi Stephen S. Wise, a dynamic speaker, opened a talk one day with: "When I make a speech, I actually make three speeches. The first is the one I prepare before I even see my audience, and let me tell you it's an excellent speech. Then I face the audience, and I somehow feel that this is not the right speech for this audience. So I tear up my first speech and deliver an impromptu one. There again it's a wonderful speech. Then comes the time for me to go home and think of what I *should* have said. That is the best speech of all. So, if you want to hear a good speech, walk home with me tonight."

During his campaign for governor of New Jersey in 1940, Charles Edison, son of the inventor, introduced himself by explaining: "People will inevitably associate me with my father, but I would not have anyone believe that I am trading on the name Edison. I would rather have you know me merely as the result of one of my father's earlier experiments."

Playwright Jerome Lawrence began his address to the American Library Association convention with something he'd wanted to say to librarians for years: "Shhh!"

When a sudden storm blew up at sea a young woman, leaning against the ship's rail, lost her balance and was thrown overboard. Immediately another figure plunged into the waves beside her and held her up until a lifeboat rescued them. To everyone's astonishment the hero was the oldest man on the voyage—an octogenarian. That evening he was given a party in honor of his bravery. "Speech! Speech!" the other passengers cried.

The old gentleman rose slowly and looked around at the enthusiastic gathering. "There's just one thing I'd like to know," he said testily. "Who pushed me?"

Briefly Speaking

A curmudgeon in British publishing finally decided to retire at age 70. He was given the usual dinner. Associates, joyous at the prospect of his leaving, vied in elaborate praise. When the time came to respond, the old gentleman got up and said, "I had no idea I was held in such esteem. I shall stay on."

I have discontinued long talks on account of my throat," the speaker remarked. "Several people have threatened to cut it."

At an annual meeting of a sociological society the toastmaster said, "We are now coming to the evening's principal event. We have persuaded Lord Thistlebottom, the distinguished sociologist, to address us. He is going to talk to us on the subject of sex. I am sure Lord Thistlebottom will not think me rude if I suggest that we have had many speakers and the hour is getting late. Perhaps he would be willing to make his remarks briefer than usual. I now give you Lord Thistlebottom."

Lord Thistlebottom stood up and cleared his throat. "Sex. Ladies and gentlemen: it gives me *great* pleasure. Thank you very much."

Wilton Lackaye was on the program for a speech at a gathering in Chicago. It was late in the evening, and everyone had been bored by the other speakers.

When the toastmaster announced, "Wilton Lackaye, the famous actor, will now give you his address," Lackaye arose and said, "Toastmaster and gentlemen, my address is the Lambs Club, New York City." He sat down to tremendous applause.

At a luncheon in honor of Spyros Skouras, the introductions seemed interminable. When the movie magnate was finally introduced and stood up clutching a bulky prepared speech, the guests could hardly conceal their restlessness. But Skouras endeared himself to all of them. "Friends," he said, "it's so late I've decided just to mail each of you a copy of this speech." Then he bowed and sat down.

Dr. George Harris, former president of Amherst College, rose in chapel to address the students at the first assembly of the year, but after a sentence or two he stopped and broke into a smile: "I intended to give you some advice, but now I remember how much is left over from last year unused."

With that he took his hat and walked out.

Rising to the Occasion

PLATFORM PERFORMANCE
CORNELIA OTIS SKINNER

ONCE to nearly everybody comes the time when he must sit passively on a platform for a couple of hours facing a large audience and taking no more part in the events than one of the potted ferns or the draped American flag. You may be a delegate to something or a faculty member at commencement, or just a music-lover who discovers that the only way to hear the singer is to sit on a collapsible chair directly behind his back. The experience is the same.

You start out being acutely aware of what is commonly known as a sea of faces but what looks more like a collection of upturned, empty plates. For the first few moments you suffer the uncomfortable delusion that the eyes staring from the centers of these plates are focused directly on you. But as a matter of fact they aren't focused on anything. Only a few indicate they're even aware someone is addressing them. Some study their programs, some gaze with rapture at the ceiling and some glare accusingly at the chair before them.

You are in all probability doing some of these things yourself so you pull yourself together and attempt to concentrate on the speaker. This is difficult. There is something about staring at the back of a neck that is conducive to anything but absorption in what is coming from the front of it. Instead of pondering on World Peace or Higher Education, you speculate on just how much the rough edge of the speaker's collar is cutting into that roll of flesh that juts out over it, or why there should be a white thread dangling from under his coat.

It is nigh to impossible to concentrate when a couple of flies land alternately on the pages of the address or the orator's nose. And sitting where you are, you can't resist counting those pages and figuring out just how much longer it is all going to last. Gradually, in a state of reverie, you turn back to survey the audience.

391

For no apparent reason you find you have singled out one particular face and are riveting it with an unwavering gaze. The owner of the face begins to fidget, straighten his tie and give general indications of wondering what in the world's the matter with him. With a twinge of remorse you look quickly away, then before you know it there you are watching him again intently, with a stare that would have done credit to Mesmer.

You realize that certain members of the audience are doing just that same thing back at you. So you try to look intently at nothing, a proceeding that in time has a curious effect on the eyes. Not only do they become incapable of focusing; they experience an irresistible impulse to cross. If you're oversensitive you come to the panic-stricken conclusion that they have and that that's why the adenoidal youth in the second row is watching you with such fascinated amazement.

This brings you back with a jolt, and with an expression of rapt attention you again face the speaker . . . that is, you turn your face in the direction of his rear. He may have just cracked a joke which you didn't hear but which, to judge by the forced laughter, has been about average, so you beam with animated appreciation.

When I was a girl it was drilled into us that whoever crossed her legs was no lady. Try sitting for an hour or more without crossing your legs and you'd just as soon be a hussy. The effort of holding your knees together may produce a case of trembling that is viewed by your platform neighbor as an indication of either extreme emotion or the beginning of a fit. Sooner or later you think to hell with being a lady and cross your legs. But soon some muscle starts mysteriously twitching and you look as if you were testing your own knee jerks.

Among other horrors are the recurrent attacks of surprising and idiotic impulses. These start, casually enough, by wondering quite harmless things, such as what would happen if you were to kick off your shoes, or stick your tongue out at some benign old lady in front, or rise suddenly and kiss the speaker. Such playful speculations are amusing until it occurs to you that they may become irresistible obsessions that you won't be able to control.

Thus the time goes by. You continue to woolgather, to nod and smile vague approval. You develop itches that you don't dare scratch. Then you do when you think nobody's looking—but somebody always is. Eventually the words "in conclusion" come like music to the ear and you actually listen to the last two minutes of the address. You join the rest in applause which, in your relief, is rather overdone. Then you rise and, except for a brief and painful moment when you discover your feet have gone to sleep, your agony is over.

———— • ————

In a letter sent by an American Legion Post: "You are invited to be one of the speakers at our Memorial Day meeting. The program will include a talk by the mayor, recitation of Lincoln's Gettysburg Address by a high-school pupil, your talk and then the firing squad."

Upon entering a room in a Washington hotel, a woman recognized a well-known government official pacing up and down and asked what he was doing there. "I am going to deliver a speech," he said.

"Do you usually get very nervous before addressing a large audience?"

"Nervous?" he replied. "No, I never get nervous."

"In that case," demanded the lady, "what are you doing in the Ladies' Room?"

Talking to a group of California teachers about the problem of school facilities for the children of tomorrow, a speaker quoted statistics on the rising birth rate. "Teachers," he emphasized, "just try to *conceive* that number of babies!"

There is a story at the U.N. about the delegate who left his notes on the rostrum of the General Assembly. Written on the margin beside one passage was this admonition to himself: "Weak point. Shout."

A lecturer of some renown was asked to speak at a nudist camp. He was greeted by ladies and gentlemen with no more on than nature saw fit to bestow upon them. They suggested that he would probably like to get ready for dinner. He went upstairs realizing that he must disrobe like the rest of them. He paced the floor in an agonized panic of indecision. The dinner bell rang. With the courage of utter desperation he stripped, and in Adamite splendor descended the staircase— only to find that all the guests had put on evening clothes to do him honor.

———— • ————

Audience Participation

After being subjected to a particularly boring political speech, British writer Dame Rebecca West commented to an equally bored reporter sitting next to her, "I feel I can now say with perfect truth that we have slept together."

The banquet speaker droned on and on. Finally one trapped listener, who had had all he could take, put his napkin over his left arm, picked up his half-filled water glass and slipped out—as a waiter.

Owen Wister, in a foreword to *The Family Mark Twain,* recounts a yarn that the humorist once told him:

It was on a Sunday up at Hartford some years ago, and a missionary preached that morning. His voice was beautiful. He told of the sufferings of the natives; he pleaded for help with such moving simplicity that Twain mentally doubled the 50 cents he had intended to put in the plate. As the address proceeded, describing so pitifully the misery of the savages, the dollar in his mind gradually rose to five. A little farther along, the missionary had him crying. He felt that all the cash he carried about him would be insufficient and decided to write a large check.

"And then that preacher went on," said Mark Twain, falling into a drawl, "went on about the dreadful state of those natives. I abandoned the idea of the check. And he went on. And I got back to five dollars, four, two, one. But he went on. And when the plate came around—I took ten cents out of it."

I love a finished speaker,
   I really, truly do.
I don't mean one who's polished,
   I just mean one who's through.

Delegate at the closing session of an Oregon PTA convention: "The thing that left the strongest impression during this convention was the folding chairs."

An attorney for the local gas and electric company was addressing a town meeting in Roxbury, Massachusetts. "Think of the good this company has done for all the people of Boston," he exhorted the audience. "If you would permit a pun, I would say in the words of the immortal poet Lord Tennyson, 'Honor the Light Brigade.'"

From the rear of the hall came a clear small voice, "Oh, what a charge they made!"

One of the major embarrassments to which lecturers are submitted is the audience's looking at their watches. I once asked John Erskine if he found the ordeal particularly trying. "No," he replied, "not until they start shaking them!"

A young English author was due to deliver the first speech of his American lecture tour. "I am such a miserable speaker," he confessed to his American agent, "that I know they'll all walk out on me before I finish."

"Nonsense!" retorted the agent. "You are an excellent speaker and will keep the audience glued to their seats."

"Oh, I say," cried the author, "that is a wonderful idea! But do we dare?"

I've heard a million conversations,
A thousand speeches, talks, orations;
Though often "I" and "you" occur,
The word most popular is "er."

A young author about to give his first talk before a literary group went to Tristan Bernard, French wit and playwright, for advice. He asked how he should wind up his lecture.

"It's very simple," said Tristan. "You pick up your papers, you bow to the audience and then go off on tiptoe."

"Why on tiptoe?"

"So as not to wake them up!" said Bernard.

A speaker talked loud and long, then asked brightly, "Are there any questions?" A hand shot up. The speaker nodded. "What time is it?" the listener inquired.

It was an interminable speech, but finally he wound up, "I want land reform, I want housing reform, I want educational reform, I want—" Just then a bored voice in the audience interrupted: "Chloroform."

Perpetrating
Outrages:

BAD JOKES
AND OTHER
GROANERS

U NDER THE HEADING "The Merry Prankster," below,
you will find a splendid example of the talents of
Horace De Vere Cole, who devoted a well-spent
life to the creation of practical jokes. On the highest level
this kind of endeavor is an example of art for art's sake.
Mr. Cole once spent a furtive night filling the enormous
St. Mark's Square in Venice with incontrovertible evidence

of the recent visitation of innumerable horses. As the square is almost entirely surrounded by canals, it naturally presented to the tourists next morning a truly baffling problem. . . . It is sometimes hard to distinguish the practical joker from the inspired eccentric. The English naturalist Charles Waterton (1782–1865) spent his life doing things so lovably odd that he may in a way have been said to be playing practical jokes *on himself.* He used to give a semiannual dinner (in a grotto) for one hundred lunatics drawn from a nearby asylum. In his eighties he greeted a guest by barking at him from underneath a table, and then biting him on the leg. Once, during a stay in our country, he was told that dripping water would help his sprained ankle. He held it for a time under Niagara Falls. Men such as Waterton are the ornaments of mankind. There are too few of them.

Apun My Word

THE LOWEST FORM OF HUMOR

LOUIS UNTERMEYER

PUNNING, like poetry, is something every person belittles and everyone attempts. A pun, we are told, is "the lowest form of humor," and "he who will make a pun will pick a pocket." Oliver Wendell Holmes condemned the punning habit but was a terrific punner himself, and apparently his house served as a sort of pun exchange, for Longfellow had occasion to observe that there was no place like Holmes'.

Franklin P. Adams, who has done a bit of punning in his time, feels that often a pun is perishable in transit; that, being mostly oral, some of its appositeness is lost in print. Certainly the best puns, when removed from the situations that gave rise to them, often become virtually meaningless. For example, one must remember the Spanish Civil War to appreciate what somebody said when the Barcelonians were moving through a narrow corridor, that it was foolish to put all your Basques in one exit. Mr. Adams himself has been credited with asserting that, in any case, Spain is merely a snare Andalusian.

Punning, for all its detractors, has a long history and an honorable lineage. Shakespeare used puns not merely to amuse the low-brows (or, as he called them, "groundlings") but to lighten the tension of his almost overpowering dramas. He knew that a flash of wit would be welcome against the murky violence of death and disaster. In *Romeo and Juliet,* for example, Mercutio, who has been stabbed, expires with the pun: "Ask for me tomorrow, and you shall find me a grave man."

It is no accident that the best punsters have been poets. A pun is a kind of rhyme; it plays with a word not only for its sense but for its sound—a good rhyme, like a good pun, has the trick of seeming both accidental and inevitable. When reproached for not writing more serious poetry, Thomas Hood replied: "If I would earn my livelihood I have to be a lively Hood."

Hood is credited with the immortal pun made on a famous romantic verse. To the lines: "The light that lies in women's eyes . . ." Hood added, "and lies and lies and lies!"

Perhaps the best puns are those that embody not only a twist in meaning but a trick of idea. No one ever has surpassed the critical remark by Eugene Field, who ridiculed the actor McCulloch's performance of King Richard III: "He played the king as if he were afraid somebody else might play the ace."

And there was Artemus Ward's classic appraisal of Brigham Young and his ever-growing collection of Mormon wives. "Pretty girls in Utah," said the humorist, "mostly marry Young."

Hollywood has sent its quota of puns across the country, such as this Marx brothers' zany dialogue: *Groucho:* Now let us take up the matter of taxes. *Chico:* Dat'sa where my brother lives. *Groucho:* Your brother lives where? *Chico:* In Texas. *Groucho:* No, no. I'm talking of taxes—money, dollars. *Chico:* Dat'sa right. Dallas, Texas.

Such a confusion in sounds is made plausible by the absurd

mispronunciation and idiotic sequence of thought. But another Marx pun is memorable without dialect. "Look at X," said someone to Groucho. "The fatter he gets the more irresistible he acts. Is he really such a wolf?" "A wolf?" echoed Groucho. "He's *all* wolf—and a yard wide."

In Hollywood a certain screen writer decided to change her features, that were markedly Semitic. "Ah," said one of her friends when the plastic surgeon had finished, "I see you've cut off your nose to spite your race." "Yes," replied the writer imperturbably, "now I'm a thing of beauty and a *goy* forever." Here one does not have to know the Jewish word for Gentile to appreciate the double twist of the pun.

One does not have to be a French scholar to relish the story of the exchange of courtesies between two of the world's great department stores. When the head of Macy's visited Paris, he went to the Galeries Lafayette, where a committee received him. As he entered, the American said, "Galeries Lafayette, we are here!" Whereupon his French colleague, not to be outdone, murmured, "Macy beaucoup."

Such witticisms have not saved the pun from the scorn of its detractors. The reason for their condemnation is obvious: envy. The punster's reward is a jeer of disapproval, a universal groan. But the groan is really a tribute; it conceals the true reaction of the listener: "I wish I had said that."

I wish (to make it strictly personal) I had been the first to think of the one about the dog who chased his tail trying to make both ends meet; or the one about the girl who never had her ears pierced but often had them bored; or the one about the Turk who, meeting another Turk, said he couldn't remember his name but his fez was familiar.

But my favorite hero is the mythical jester who annoyed the king by punning on every subject except his royal self—the king, said the jester, was not a subject. So the exasperated monarch ordered his execution. As the poor fellow stood upon the gallows, a messenger arrived with the king's pardon, on one condition: that the jester promise never to commit another pun. Looking at the rope coiled about his neck, the jester smiled. "No noose is good noose," he said, and died gladly.

The pun is the lowest form of humor—when you don't think of it first.

Author Max Shulman found croquet a great game for venting frustrations—"pure hostility on the lawn. But of course," he added, lining up a malevolent shot, "I play with mallets toward none."

An editor, meeting Sir James M. Barrie, author of *Peter Pan,* at a dinner, asked him how his plays were doing. Barrie's reply: "Some Peter out, others Pan out."

Robert Benchley once sent his bank a foreign check with the added endorsement on the back: "Having a wonderful time. Wish you would clear!"

Max Beerbohm one declined to be lured into a hike to the summit of a Swiss Alp. "Put me down," he said firmly, "as an anti-climb Max."

A professor of ancient history took a long, disapproving look at his newborn son and told the doctor, "We'll name him Theophilus."

"Why wish a name like that on the poor tyke?" asked the doctor.

"Because," said the professor, "he's Theophilus looking baby I ever saw."

In a Minnesota State Legislature debate on the merits of front or rear license plates, a senator argued that the rear plate was more help to pursuing police and clinched his point with: "After all, most pinches are made from the rear."

When noisy chess kibitzers were thrown out of the hotel lobby where the contest was being held, the management explained, "We're just pulling our chess nuts out of the foyer."

When a woman explained coyly that she had had her female dog "adjusted," her friend remarked, "Why don't you call a spayed a spayed!"

An article in *This Week Magazine* described the dress of an Indian Maharanee as a sarong instead of a sari. The copy chief, who allowed the error to slip past him, wrote to the editor: "All I can say is I'm sari I was sarong."

A hard-working editor warned an underling: "Not another murmur about your indigestion—I've got enough of my own without worrying about anybody ulcers."

On the door of a Chicago photographer's studio destroyed by fire: "Good Night Sweet Prints."

Cavewoman to mate: "Don't just stand there, slay something."

A well-known comedian protests that he is always being told one of his own stories. A clear case of the tale dogging the wag.

Then there was the chap who fell into the lens grinder and made a spectacle of himself.

---•---

Groucho Marx inadvertently opening a drawer in a friend's home found a Colt automatic pistol and several small pearl-handled revolvers. "This gat," announced Groucho, "has had gittens."

It was rush hour and the subway car was jammed. A big blond giant of a man, hanging carelessly onto a strap, lost his balance when the car jerked, landing squarely in a forbidding-looking woman's lap. Before he could apologize, she blurted indignantly, "You! You big Swede!"

"Lady, I'm not a Swede," he replied. "I'm a Laplander!"

A story going the rounds concerns three pregnant squaws who slept on animal skins—one, on an elk skin; another, on a buffalo skin; the third, on a hippopotamus skin. The first squaw had a son; the second, a son; and the third, twin boys.

Which proves: The squaw of the hippopotamus is equal to the sons of the squaws on the other two hides.

How about the two podiatrists who became arch rivals?

And the hospital orderly who was drafted into the Army as a semi-private.

A professor of Greek tore his suit and took it to a tailor named Acidopolus, from Athens. Mr. Acidopolus examined the suit and asked, "Euripides?"

"Yes," said the professor. "Eumenides?"

On door of a Carmel, California, music store: "Bach at 2. Offenbach sooner."

Ruth rode on my motorbike directly back of me. I hit a bump at 65 and rode on ruthlessly.

---•---

The Shaggy Dog

At a college dinner a renowned professor was introduced by the chairman, who poured on compliment after compliment. The embarrassed professor said the introduction reminded him of the story of the three bulls—a big bull, a medium-sized bull and a little bull. As they trotted down a road together they passed a green field full of Conover model cows. After one look at these beauties, the big bull said "Good-bye" and jumped over the fence. The middle-sized bull and the little bull kept going until they reached another field full of Powers model cows. The middle-sized bull shouted "Farewell" and jumped over the fence. Then the little bull went on and on and on and on. . . .

The moral of this tale, the professor explained, is that a little bull goes a long way.

Bob Burns used to tell a story about his scientific uncle, who went up on a mountain back of Van Buren and found a huge rock poised on a cliff. He worked for hours and finally dislodged the monster, and it went bounding down the mountainside, headed straight for the town. Behind it, running as hard as he could, was Bob's uncle. The big boulder crashed through a livery stable, shot down the main street, went through the First National Bank and finally came to rest in the rear of that institution. The townspeople were gathering from all sides when Bob's uncle arrived on the run, shoved everyone aside and approached the rock, which he scrutinized carefully on all sides. Finally he straightened up and said: "Nope. No moss."

A tourist was introduced at Albuquerque to an Indian with a reputedly perfect memory. Skeptical, the tourist asked: "What did you have for breakfast on October 4, 1913?" The Indian answered, "Eggs." The man scoffed, "Everyone eats eggs for breakfast. He's a fraud."

Eight years later the traveler's train stopped again at Albuquerque, and he saw the same Indian lounging on the platform. The tourist went up to him and said jovially, "How!"

The Indian answered, "Scrambled."

A man went to a baker and asked him to bake a cake in the form of the letter S. The baker said he would need a week to prepare the necessary tins. The customer agreed, and returned a week later. Proudly the baker showed him the cake.

"Oh, but you misunderstood me," the customer said. "You have made it a block letter and I wanted script."

"Well," said the baker, "if you can wait another week I can make one in script."

A week later the customer came back, and was delighted with the cake. "Exactly what I wanted," he said.

"Will you take it with you," asked the baker, "or shall I send it to your house?"

"Don't bother," said the customer. "If you'll just give me a knife and fork I'll eat it right here."

Once upon a time two large turtles and a little one went to a bar to quench their thirst with a mug of sarsaparilla. As they began to drink it, one of the large turtles commented that it was raining. After a lively discussion, it was decided that the little turtle should go home for their umbrella. The little turtle demurred, afraid that if he went the big turtles would drink his sarsaparilla. But they convinced the little fellow they would leave his sarsaparilla alone, and he started after the umbrella.

Three weeks passed, and finally one of the big turtles said: "Let's drink the little guy's sarsaparilla."

"I've been thinking the same thing," said the other, "so let's do it."

From down at the end of the bar near the door, a shrill voice cried: "If you do, I won't go after that umbrella."

A man who had gambled away his last cent in Las Vegas had to beg a dime from another patron in order to use the rest room. The stall he approached, however, had not been locked, so he used the dime to play a slot machine —and he hit the jackpot. With the proceeds, he tried a more expensive machine, and won again. His run of luck continued, and he went on to play the roulette wheels and crap tables until he won a million dollars.

Rich and famous, he went on a lecture tour, telling his remarkable story, expressing gratitude to his benefactor and declaring that if he ever found the man, he would split the million with him. After many appearances, a man jumped up in one audience and cried, "I'm the man who gave you the dime!"

"You're not the one I'm looking for," the lucky man replied. "I mean the guy who left the door open!"

An American tourist went into a dimly lit bar in South Africa. When his eyes adjusted to the darkness, he saw on a stool beside him a perfectly formed human being in military uniform—only six inches high. Incredulous, the tourist stared until the bartender spoke up in broad cockney accents. "Don't you know the Myjor, sir?" he asked, reaching across the bar, picking the little fellow up and placing him on the bar. The tourist shook his head.

"Speak up, Myjor," the bartender said. "Tell the Yank about the time you called the witch doctor a bloody damned fool."

A thirsty gentleman wandered into a corner saloon and ordered a dry Martini. He drank it with relish, and allowed as how it was the best darn Martini he had ever tasted. The barkeeper whipped up another, and the customer declared it was even better than the first. "Such genius deserves a reward," he said. He reached into his pocket and produced a live lobster. "Here! Take this with my compliments," he said.

The barkeeper held the live crustacean gingerly at arm's length. "Thanks," he said dubiously. "I suppose I can take it home for dinner."

"No, no," objected the customer. "He's already had his dinner. Take him to a movie."

The Merry Prankster

SMITH'S PRIME RIBS
H. ALLEN SMITH

S EVERAL years ago I wrote a series of articles for the New
York *World-Telegram* dealing with famous practical
jokes. As soon as the articles appeared, a cascade of
mail descended on the newspaper. The letters fell into two
categories. One group denounced me for a cur and a cad. The
majority, however, sent in additional practical jokes, and these
letters I placed in a large red envelope. In succeeding years I
added to my collection. These are some of the best of them.

In World War II, Hugh Troy, artist, writer and accomplished
practical joker, was sent to a southern Army camp. He was
soon in rebellion against paperwork. Reports, reports, reports
and more reports on the most trivial details went to the Pentagon.
One day Troy devised a special report blank and had it mimeographed. It was in re the number of flies trapped during each
24-hour period on the 20 flypaper ribbons that hung in the mess
hall. The report included a sketch plan of the mess hall, showing
the location of each ribbon in relation to entrances, tables,
lights, windows and kitchen. Each ribbon was identified by
code number. Troy's first flypaper report showed that during
a 24-hour period Flypaper Ribbon X-5 trapped and retained 49
flies. Ribbon Y-2 did even better—63 flies. And so on. He sent
the report off to Washington. Every day he sent in a report.
About a week after he sent in the first one, two fellow officers
called on him. "You been catching any hell from Washington,"
they asked, "about some kind of goofy flypaper reports?"
"Why, no," said Hugh.
"It's about a daily report on flypaper in the mess halls. We've
been getting Pentagon queries, wanting to know why we haven't
been sending them in."
"Oh," said Troy. "I send *mine* in every day."
They protested that nobody had told *them* about any flypaper
reports, so Troy gave them copies of the mimeographed blank.

407

After that every bundle that went in to Washington included a census of dead flies. Troy thinks it's possible that the daily fly-paper report became standard Army procedure.

Hanging some paintings in his London house, Horace De Vere Cole, the celebrated British practical joker, ran out of twine. He walked to the nearest stringmonger's shop for another ball. On his way home he saw an elegant stranger approaching. The man was so stiffish, so splendidly dressed, that Cole could not pass him by. He whipped out his ball of twine and stepped up to the gentleman. "I say," he said, "I'm in a bit of a spot. We're surveying this area in order to realign the curb, and my assistant has vanished. I wonder if I could prevail upon your time for just a few moments?"

"To be sure," said the stranger, ever the proper Englishman.

"If," said Cole, "you'd be so kind as to hold the end of this string. Just stand where you are and keep a tight hold on it, and we'll be finished in a few moments."

The splendid gentleman took hold of the end of the string and Cole began backing away from him, unwinding the ball. He continued all the way to the corner, turned the corner and disappeared. Halfway up the block, the string gave out. He was about to tie it to a doorknob when Providence sent him a second gentleman, fully as elegant as the first. Cole stopped him. Would the good sir be so kind as to assist him in an engineering project? Certainly! Cole handed him the string and asked him to hold it. Then Cole hastened through an alleyway to the shop for another ball of twine and returned home. How long the two men stood there holding the string he never knew.

An extremely serious young Englishman who worked at the Disney Studio made a habit of bringing his lunch. Each noon he'd go to a nearby grocery store and buy a bottle of milk and a can of fruit. Some of his colleagues went to the grocery and bought some canned fruit and some canned vegetables and then switched the labels. They bribed the grocer to use this disguised stock whenever their victim made a purchase.

Soon the Englishman began finding string beans or corn instead of fruit in the cans. He asked his associates what he ought to do about it. They said it was truly a phenomenon and that he ought to write to Ripley, who conducted a "Believe It or Not" column. So he sat down, composed a long letter and mailed it to Ripley. Then, since it was lunchtime, he walked to the store, bought his bottle of milk and a can of pears, then returned to his office and got out his can opener. This time there was no fruit in the can, and no vegetables—only a small test tube, tightly corked. Inside the test tube was a piece of paper which said:

Dear Sir:
I don't believe a damned word of it.

Robert Ripley

I want it understood that I am not a practical joker. I have been involved in them, usually as a victim, but I'm not a practitioner. I can remember having played only one joke in the last ten years. A letter came from a man in the Middle West who had been reading some of my books. He insulted me at the outset by saying he knew I wouldn't even read his letter. My secretary would read it, but I wouldn't. The remainder of his impertinence was addressed to my secretary, and as he warmed to his task, he expressed the hope that she was young and redheaded and beautiful.

I have never had a secretary, but I invented one now. I wrote to this worm. I pretended I was my secretary. I told him he must have psychic powers, for I was young and redheaded and people thought I was not bad to look at. I said he sounded like a real interesting fellow, the kind of masculine man I (the redheaded secretary) was just dying to meet. If he ever got to New York, please let me know—I'd ask the boss to let me off work for a day *and a night* and meet him in New York and we'd have dinner and go places and do things. I signed the letter "Eunice Wagstaff." And mailed it.

Two days later Western Union phoned my house and asked if we had a Eunice Wagstaff around the place. Fortunately I remembered the letter and took the message. The telegram said: "LEAVING FOR NEW YORK AND YOU TONIGHT. MEET ME TOMORROW HOTEL B——."

I debated with myself about stopping him. Then I decided that he had it coming.

Brian G. Hughes, a wealthy New York businessman, was a renowned practical joker. On rainy days he often would enter a saloon, have a drink or two, and leave his handsome umbrella hanging on the bar. Then he'd retire to a corner and watch the eventual, inevitable theft. It delighted him to follow the culprit to the street, where, on being opened, the umbrella discharged posters proclaiming: "THIS UMBRELLA STOLEN FROM BRIAN G. HUGHES."

Lucius Beebe, having met an expert ventriloquist, asked the man to dress in somber clothes and then introduced him to the Yale chaplain as a celebrated preacher of the Far West. The chaplain invited the visitor to preach in the Yale Chapel. The impostor acquitted himself well, working up to a pitch of excitement. Suddenly he paused, threw back his head, cupped his hands to his mouth and shouted toward the ceiling: "Am I right, Lord?"

Back from the rafters came the faint but audible response: "You are right, my son!"

Franklin D. Roosevelt once decided to test the theory that people at social functions pay no attention to the murmured words sometimes required. He chose a big White House party, where there was a long reception line. As each guest came up and took his hand, the President flashed his celebrated smile and murmured, "I murdered my grandmother this morning." Only one guest was conscious of what he said. This man, a banker, heard the words, "I murdered my grandmother this morning," and promptly replied, "She certainly had it coming."

The late Frank Tinney, the actor, employed a gag to startle his acquaintances along Broadway. He would engage an open, horse-drawn cab, and get into the driver's seat with a live pony. When Tinney spotted one of his friends he would yell out, "Hey, Bill!" at the same time dropping out of sight on the floor and grasping his companion's halter. Bill would look up to see a pony sitting in a cab and bowing in his direction.

———————— • ————————

Once James Thurber was served with a summons intended for his brother, John. In court Jim had to prove that he was Jim and not John. Benchley was to identify him. Jim took the stand and offered his driver's license and letters addressed to him. At that moment, Benchley entered the room and called to Jim: "Har'ya, John!"

———————— • ————————

A woman visiting in Florida one winter was taken by friends to a plush night club. When she entered the rest room she discovered a large mural of Adam, wearing only a fig leaf. A sign warned customers: "Do Not Lift the Fig Leaf." But the visitor's feminine curiosity got the better of her, and she upped the leaf.

Bells began to ring, sirens sounded, plaster fell and bedlam set in. She turned and ran out the rest room door—only to be blinded by a giant spotlight, while the orchestra blared fanfares.

Mark Twain met a friend at the races one day in England. This friend came up to him and said, "I'm broke, I wish you would buy me a ticket back to London."

"Well," Mark said, "I'm nearly broke myself, but I will tell you what I'll do. You can hide under my seat and I'll hide you with my legs."

The friend agreed to this.

Then Mark Twain went down to the ticket office and bought two tickets. When the train pulled out his friend was safely under the seat. The inspector came around for the tickets and Mark gave him two. The inspector said, "Where is the other one?"

Tapping his head the humorist said in a loud voice, "That is my friend's ticket! He is a little eccentric and likes to ride under the seat."

Alexander Woollcott once asked Moss Hart to drive him to Newark to fulfill a lecture date. "I'll do it," the playwright agreed, "if you'll let me sit on the platform and be introduced to the audience. I once clerked in a bookstore in Newark and I'd like to show them I'm a big shot now."

Woollcott delivered his lecture without making the slightest reference to Hart, who fidgeted in his chair beside the speaker's table. At the end of the speech, Woollcott said: "Tonight I'll dispense with my usual question period. I'm sure you all want to know the same thing: Who is this foolish-looking young man here on the platform?"

With that he retired, leaving Hart to get out of the hall as best he could.

The author of a famous book on economics received a phone call from a stranger. "I question your statistics on the high cost of living today," said the stranger. "My wife and I eat everything our hearts desire and we get it for exactly sixty-eight cents a week."

"Sixty-eight cents a week!" echoed the economist. "I can't believe it! Won't you tell me how? And to make sure I get your story straight, please speak louder."

"I can't speak louder," said the stranger. "I'm a goldfish."

One of the assistant editors on a national magazine wore a new hat to the office one day. While he was in conference with his boss, a writer on the staff inspected the hat. then went down to the store it came from and bought an exact duplicate, complete even to the monogrammed initials on the sweatband. There was only one difference—it was three sizes larger than the original. Back at the office, he switched the hats. At the end of the day when the editor put on his hat, it fell over his ears. Thoroughly mystified, he took it off and examined it. There were his initials—it must be his hat.

The next day, he was again wearing the hat, which now seemed to fit pretty well. As soon as he went out of the room, the writer inspected the hat. He found the sweatband was stuffed with tissue paper; so he took the paper out, stuffed it in the original hat, and put that on the rack. At the end of the day, when the editor put on his hat, it just sat on the top of his head. Again he looked inside— and immediately went off to Bellevue Hospital for an examination.

Sense and Nonsense

At the circus in Chicago last year a man was observed near the camels. He picked up a straw, placed it squarely on a camel's back and waited. Nothing happened. "Wrong straw," he muttered, and hurried off.

A man was pegging along the street with a walking stick several inches too tall for comfort. A solicitous friend said, "That's a nice stick, but you better have somebody cut a few inches off that end."

"That wouldn't help," the owner answered. "It's this end that's too high."

A lady gave a moonlight party for 500 ostriches on a California beach. At a very late hour only 499 had shown up. Embarrassed by the rudeness of the 500th, all the others stuck their heads in the sand. Presently the 500th came galloping up to the gathering, looked about, and asked, "Where is everybody?"

Man slogging along in an April shower: "Boy, what a crude way to bring May flowers!"

Deep in the African jungle two cannibals were wending their way—a mother and her youngster. Suddenly there was a frightening noise in the sky, and the child ran to his mother for protection. "Ooh, Mummy, what's that?" he whimpered.

"It's all right, dear," said the mother, looking up through the trees. "It's just an airplane."

"Airplane? What's that?"

"It's a little like lobster. There's an awful lot you have to throw away, but the insides are delicious!"

Space Breaks

A Martian lands on earth, hops up to a gas pump and demands: "Take me to your leader." . . . A Martian lands in Paris, spots Brigitte Bardot and, electric-bulb eyeball flashing furiously, demands: "Take me to your leader—later." . . . A couple of Martians land in Washington, D.C., and one asks a nearby fire hydrant: "Which way to the White House?" "Good heavens," snorts the other Martian, "don't ask him. He's only a little boy." . . . A rocket-shot earthmouse lands on the moon, made as it is of green cheese, and orders: "Take me to your Liederkranz." . . . A Martian lands in a small, quiet town in dead of night, enters a near-empty eatery, goes up to the juke box with flashing lights and iridescent bubbles, demands: "Say, what's a slick chick like you doin' in a nothin' town like this?"

I wish I had enough money to buy an elephant."
"What on earth do you need an elephant for?"
"I don't. I just need the money."

Mama Skunk was worried because she could never keep track of her two children. They were named In and Out, and whenever In was in, Out was out; and if Out was in, In was out. One day she called Out in to her and told him to go out and bring In in. So Out went out and in no time at all he brought In in.

"Wonderful!" said Mama Skunk. "How, in all that great forest, could you find him in so short a time?"

"It was easy," said Out. "In stinct."

Two cavemen were huddled close to their fire. Outside it was raining and sleeting, thundering and lightning. One of the prehistoric guys turned to the other. "You know," he grumbled, "we never had this crazy weather before they started using bows and arrows."

We just received a new cookbook from deepest Africa. It's called *How to Serve Your Fellow Men.*

Noah, after the flood subsided, opened the doors of the Ark and released the animals. All living things rushed to freedom, except two snakes who lingered in a corner. "Why don't you go forth and multiply?" asked Noah in a stern voice.

"We can't," moaned one. "We're adders!"

Two friends were telling each other the dreams they'd had the night before. One of them said he'd dreamed he was in Coney Island having a wonderful time on the roller coaster.

"I can top that," said the other. "I dreamed I was alone in a room with Sophia Loren. And, as if that weren't enough, who should walk in but Marilyn Monroe!"

"Well, a fine pal you are," said the first man indignantly. "Why didn't you telephone me?"

"Oh, I did," said the friend. "I telephoned you in my dream. But your wife said you were in Coney Island."

GOOD OLD LIMERICKS
LOUIS UNTERMEYER

I T may surprise you to know that the most popular English verse form is the limerick, which has been and still is being composed by all kinds of people, from erudite writers to the humblest schoolboy or the busy housewife who snatches a moment to enter a soap contest. The origins of the form are dim; the name itself is a mystery, but is presumed to have derived from a song about the Irish town of that name. Although several examples existed before 1830, the limerick did not acquire fame until that odd ornithologist and landscape painter Edward Lear set the fashion with such irresponsible lines as:

There was an old man with a beard,
Who said, "It is just as I feared.
　Two owls and a hen,
　Four larks and a wren,
Have all built their nests in my beard!"

Almost immediately after publication of Lear's *Book of Nonsense* the brisk little stanzas caught the imagination of writers. They were imitated, varied, burlesqued, until today more than a million limericks have come into existence—many of them unprintable, but nonetheless popular. Great poets have vied with multitudes of the unknown to sharpen the point of their five-line absurdities. Rudyard Kipling wrote:

There once was a boy in Quebec
Who was buried in snow to his neck.
　When asked, "Are you friz?"
　He replied, "Yes, I is,
But we don't call this cold in Quebec."

Oliver Wendell Holmes, that irrepressible punster, wrote one of the most quoted of all limericks:

The Reverend Henry Ward Beecher
Called a hen a most elegant creature.
　The hen, pleased with that,
　Laid an egg in his hat—
And thus did the hen reward Beecher.

Langford Reed, compiler of *The Complete Limerick Book,* created a limerick that is collected continually (and misquoted) without credit:

An indolent vicar of Bray
His roses allowed to decay.
　His wife, more alert,
　Bought a powerful squirt
And said to her spouse, "Let us spray."

Another that has gone round the world, usually credited to Anonymous, was written by a witty Englishman, Cosmo

Monkhouse:

There was a young lady of Niger,
Who smiled as she rode on a tiger.
They returned from the ride
With the lady inside—
And the smile on the face of the tiger!

Woodrow Wilson was so fond of one limerick, written by a forgotten poet named Anthony Euwer, that he was thought to be the author:

As a beauty I'm not a great star;
Others are handsomer far;
But my face—I don't mind it,
Because I'm behind it;
It's the folks out in front that I jar!

Most limerick-makers seek a last line that will come like a climax, a surprise, a comic whiplash:

There was an old man from Peru,
Who dreamt he was eating his shoe.
He awoke in the night
In a terrible fright—
And found it was perfectly true!

There was a young lady named Banker,
Who slept while her ship lay at anchor.
She awoke in dismay
When she heard the mate say,
"Hi! Hoist up the top-sheet and spanker!"

There was a young wife from Antigua
What remarked to her spouse, "What a pigua!"
He retorted, "My queen,
Is it manners you mean?
Or do you refer to my figua?"

The last example suggested a new variation: limericks that were tricks of pronunciation and spelling. The late Carolyn Wells excelled in such accomplished word-scrambling and tongue-twisting as:

There was a young fellow named Tate
Who dined with his girl at 8:08.

But I'd hate to relate
What that fellow named Tate
And his tête-à-tête ate at 8:08.

The inconsistencies in English pronunciation were seized upon and exploited to the point of confusion:

She frowned and called him Mr.
Because in sport he kr.
*   And so in spite*
*   That very nite*
This Mr. kr. sr.

A girl who weighed many an oz.
Used language I dare not pronoz.
*   For a fellow unkind*
*   Pulled her chair out behind*
Just to see (so he said) if she'd boz.

In an effort to establish a difference in humor between American and British readers, H. J. Eysenck, the psychologist, reported his conclusions in *Character and Personality*. Among a group of limericks, the Americans chose this as the funniest:

There was a young man of Laconia,
Whose mother-in-law had pneumonia.
*   He hoped for the worst—*
*   And after March first*
They buried her 'neath a begonia.

The British preferred the following:

There was a young girl of Asturias,
Whose temper was frantic and furious.
*   She used to throw eggs*
*   At her grandmother's legs—*
A habit unpleasant, but curious.

Such choices may not be conclusive. But they prove that the limerick is a test of humor, a favorite medium for millions, and an international lure.

Higher Education:
CAMPUS LIFE

HESE JOKES are enjoyable enough, but campuses are not as comical as they used to be, and even athletes are no longer quite the figures of fun that tradition makes them out (many are quite literate). Jokes about coeds date badly (so do some coeds), though we can still take pleasure in a story Dr. Hutchins likes to tell about

419

the girl student in a small Texas college who was failing badly in her work and in general seemed in a state of extreme
depression. The dean tried to find out the cause of her
trouble. She replied, "It's this way, sir: I come here to be
went with, and I ain't."

What with demonstrating, cop-outs, opt-outs, and all kinds
of experimental curricula, even the Ivy League colleges
are not what they used to be. Which lends new point to an
old story. It seems that the students of a brand-new, modern
small midwestern college were surprised one morning to
find the following notice on the central bulletin: "There
is a tradition in this college that students may not cross the
grass-covered areas of the campus diagonally. This tradition
goes into effect next Monday morning at 9 A.M."

Getting Disoriented

As a freshman at Louisiana State University, I was filling
out one of the endless questionnaires during orientation
week. Evidently the pace was too much for the boy sitting
next to me. When he came to the question, "Do you believe
in college marriages?" he shrugged his shoulders and oblig-
ingly wrote: "Yes, if the colleges really love each other."

Among the forms to be filled out in applying for admission
to the University of Wisconsin is a personal-data sheet. In
response to the request "List your personal strengths," one
18-year-old applicant wrote: "Sometimes I am trustworthy,
loyal, helpful, friendly, courteous, kind, obedient, cheerful,
thrifty, brave, clean and reverent." Where the form said,
"List your weaknesses," he wrote: "Sometimes I am *not*
trustworthy, loyal, helpful, friendly, courteous, kind, obedient, cheerful, thrifty, brave, clean and reverent."

Sign in the administration office of a Colorado college: "Freshman English Spoken Here."

The president of our college was giving his annual welcoming address to the freshman class. In achieving academic success, he pointed out, there is no substitute for hard work. "You may have heard it said," he told the freshmen, "that all work and no play makes Jack a dull boy, but I shall also remind you that all play and no work will put Jack into the Army."

Verbatim howlers from high-school students' college application folders collected by an admissions officer of an Eastern university:

One boy wrote: "You informed me you were sending me a copy of your catalogue. By some insight, it was never sent to me."

The principal of a military academy, recommending an applicant: "His interests are scholastic, which has a tendency to set him apart."

From the endorsement of a Korean boy by his principal: ". . . he has an extinguished ability in math and science."

A young man tells exactly where he stands: "I neither like not dislike any language, except French."

From an alumnus' report on an interview with a girl applicant: "She is at present very much of a young lady. However, she might adapt herself to our college community very well."

When a girl applies for admission to Vassar, a questionnaire is sent to her parents. A father in a Boston suburb, filling out one of these blanks, came to the question, "Is she a leader?" He hesitated, then wrote, "I am not sure about this, but I know she is an excellent follower."

A few days later he received this letter from the president of the college: "As our freshman group next fall is to contain several hundred leaders, we congratulate ourselves that your daughter will also be a member of the class. We shall thus be assured of one good follower."

Making the Grade

A chemistry professor asked his class what they considered the most outstanding contribution chemistry had made to the world. The first student to answer shouted: "Blondes."

On a college birdwalk our instructor identified the first birdcall. When the next call was heard, he asked, "What was that?"

"A chipmunk," one of the girls volunteered.

"No," the instructor said patiently. "That's a tufted titmouse."

"Well," said the girl proudly, "at least I knew it wasn't a bird!"

What steps," a question in a college exam read, "would you take in determining the height of a building, using an aneroid barometer?"

One student, short on knowledge but long on ingenuity, replied: "I would lower the barometer on a string and measure the string."

A law professor at the University of Utah, known for his acid tongue, asked a woman student to recite on a case involving an expectant mother. Each time she came to the word "pregnant" the girl prissily substituted the word "ill." After the third substitution, the professor said, "She was what, Miss Jones?"

"She was expecting."

"The word is *pregnant,* Miss Jones—p-r-e-g-n-a-n-t, pregnant. Your mother was pregnant, your grandmother was pregnant, and, by the grace of God and the help of some young man, you too will be pregnant someday."

Miss Jones fled from the classroom in tears, and that evening her mother phoned the professor and asked for a public apology to her daughter. The next day the professor ambled in and sat down at his lecture table. "Well, fellahs," he said, "to clear the record, I want to say that I don't think Miss Jones will ever be pregnant."

In a science-course discussion on the structure of the atom, our instructor noticed a coed who apparently hadn't read the assignment, as she had difficulty understanding what was said. His suspicions were confirmed when he asked her what a neutrino was. She gave him a guilty, wistful look, then suggested hopefully, "An Italian neutron?"

A college professor outlined, at length, the nature of a rather brutal final examination. He concluded his remarks by asking the class if anyone had any question regarding the exam. The class sat in stunned silence.

Finally one brave soul asked, "Do you accept bribes?"

On an examination, a student was asked to name the various rooms in a Spanish *hacienda*. To his dismay, he discovered that he could not recall the Spanish word for bathroom. Last-minute ingenuity saved the day for him. In the appropriate area, he printed neatly: *"Juan."*

Being struck by a wordy muse, a friend of mine concluded her paper for a Shakespeare course with the statement: "Pusillanimity was, to the end, his downfall."

When the paper was returned, her professor had added: "As obfuscation is thine."

A University of Virginia mathematics professor was amazed, when he arrived at a neighboring woman's college to lecture on "Convex Sets and Inequalities," to find the auditorium filled to capacity. A glance at the campus newspaper gave him the answer. His subject was announced as "Convicts, Sex and Inequalities."

When a student at the University of Tennessee received a report card with four F's and one D, he was called before the dean and asked if there could be any explanation for *four* failing grades. "I guess I just spent too much time on the other subject," he replied.

---●---

The professor of political economy asked his class, "Give me an example of unremunerative outlay of capital."

"Taking one's sister out on a date," answered a youth in the back row.

A student government officer at the University of San Francisco wrote to the University of California concerning the use of the honor system during exams. He received this reply: "The University of California abandoned the honor system several years ago when it became evident that the professors had the honor and the students had the system."

At Amherst, Robert Frost's method of teaching his course in English Literature was to give informal talks at his home in the evening. The poet detested semester examinations, but since they were compulsory he obeyed. "But I made them as simple as I could," he said in a talk. "Once I asked only one question, 'What good did my course do you?' and requested brief replies. The answer I liked best was 'Not a damn bit!'"

"Did you pass him?"

"Yes, I gave him a 90."

"Why not 100?" he was asked.

"He left the 'n' off damn."

---●---

SEEING CELLS

JAMES THURBER

I PASSED all the other courses that I took at my university, but I could never pass botany. This was because all botany students had to spend several hours a week looking through a microscope at plant cells, and I could never see through a microscope. This used to enrage my instructor. He would wander around the laboratory, pleased with the progress all the students were making in drawing the involved and, so I am told, interesting structure of flower cells, until he came to me. I would just be standing there. "I can't see anything," I would say. He would begin patiently enough, explaining how anybody can see through a microscope, but he would always end up in a fury, claiming that I could *too* see through a microscope. "Try it just once again," he'd say, and I would put my eye to the microscope and see nothing at all, except now and again a nebulous milky substance. "I see what looks like a lot of milk," I would tell him. This, he claimed, was the result of my not having adjusted the microscope properly, so he would readjust it for me, or rather, for himself. And I would look again and see milk.

I finally took a deferred pass and waited a year and tried again. The professor had come back from vacation brown as a berry, bright-eyed, and eager to explain cell structure again to his classes. "Well," he said to me cheerily, the first laboratory hour, "we're going to see cells this time, aren't we?" "Yes, sir," I said. Students to right of me and to left of me were seeing cells; what's more, they were quietly drawing pictures of them. Of course, I didn't see anything.

"We'll try it," the professor said to me, grimly, "with every adjustment of the microscope known to man. As God is my witness, I'll arrange this glass so that you see cells through it or I'll give up teaching. In 22 years of botany, I—" He cut off abruptly for he was beginning to quiver all over.

So we tried it with every adjustment of the microscope known to man. With only one of them did I see anything and that time I saw, to my pleasure and amazement, a variegated constellation of flecks, specks and dots. These I hastily drew. The instructor, noting my activity, came back, a smile on his lips and his eyebrows high in hope. He looked at my cell drawing. "What's this?" he demanded, with a hint of a squeal in his voice. "That's what I saw," I said. "You didn't, you didn't, you didn't!" he screamed. He bent over and squinted into the microscope. His head snapped up. "That's your eye!" he shouted. "You've fixed the lens so that it reflects! You've drawn your eye!"

Halls of Ivy

Tiny tot to toy-department Santa: "Can you get me into Yale?"

A Boston brokerage house advertised for "a young Harvard graduate or the equivalent." Among the answers was one from a Yale man: "When you speak of an equivalent," he wrote, "do you mean two Princeton men or a Yale man half time?"

An instructor at Massachusetts Institute of Technology tells about a student in a Boston supermarket who came to the "Ten-Items-or-Under" checkout lane with a heavily loaded grocery cart. The clerk glanced at the over-the-limit contents of the cart and remarked, "I don't know whether you're from M.I.T. and can't read, or from Harvard and can't count."

Fred Allen liked to tell about the young man who took so long to get through Harvard that he had ivy growing up his left leg.

Oh, My Aching Baccalaureate

The month of June approaches,
    And soon across the land
The graduation speakers
    Will tell us where we stand.

We stand at Armageddon,
    In the vanguard of the press;
We're standing at the crossroads,
    At the gateway to success.

We stand upon the threshold
    Of careers all brightly lit.
In the midst of all this standing,
    We sit and sit and sit.

A Nieman Fellow at Harvard, upon first entering the Adams House gallery of portraits, where every important Adams since the Revolution is portrayed, said: "What this house needs is a good portrait of Eve!"

Graffiti on a washroom wall at M.I.T.:
And God said:

$$\frac{mv^2}{r} = \frac{Ze^2}{r^2}$$

$$mvr = n\frac{h}{2\pi}$$

$$r = \frac{r^2 h^2}{(2\pi)^2 mZe^2}$$

$$E = \frac{1}{2}mv^2 - \frac{Ze^2}{r}$$

$$E = \frac{2\pi^2 mZ^2 e^4}{n^2 h^2} = R$$

and there was light.

Overheard on a Milwaukee bus: "Oh, no, darling, don't send him to Harvard! *Everybody* goes there."

Betty Coed

At Fairleigh-Dickinson College in New Jersey a shapely coed, who wore her sweaters much tighter than necessary, was called up to the front of the room to give a report. But her uproarious classmates never gave her a chance to get beyond her opening words: "Now there are just two points I'd like to bring out. . . ."

To announce their presence in our girls' dormitory, it is customary for the maintenance men to yell: "Man aboard!"

When asked by the bursar's office to pay a $20 incidental fee, a University of Minnesota coed replied, "How many incidents does that entitle me to?"

After a big campus dance where the dates were arranged by a computer, I asked a friend what it was like.

"It's a frightening experience," she answered, "finding out just what you deserve."

College girls are of two strata — girls with dates and girls with data.

During sorority rushing at the University of Omaha, prospects are asked to fill out a questionnaire. Opposite "List any personal attributes which would be beneficial to the sorority," one hopeful rushee wrote: "35-23-34."

College glamour girl to suitor: "By 'secret engagement' I suppose you mean no ring."

A soft whistle came from the rear of the chemistry lab as a curvaceous coed in a close-fitting sheath walked across the front of the room. "Relax," said the whistler's partner. "She's three-fourths water."

"Right!" came the enthusiastic reply. "But what surface tension!"

Coed to date: "There's no one else, Sheldon — or I'd be out with him right now!"

Toronto psychology professor's sheepish confession: "I thought I was quite a debonair success with my coeds until I received a Christmas card from one of them addressed 'To my favorite father figure.'"

The wife of the poet Louis Untermeyer told this story about her talented spouse: "We went to a costume party one night. Louis was looking his silliest in a paper hat, tooting a horn for nobody's particular benefit, when a young college girl walked up to him, looked him up and down and turned on her heel with: 'Huh! And you're Required Reading!'"

Grid Irony

Michigan State's football coach Duffy Daugherty received a letter addressed to "Duffy the Dope."

"Didn't that make you mad?" he was asked.

"I didn't mind getting the card," he said. "It was pretty funny. The thing that bothered me was that the East Lansing post office knew exactly where to deliver it."

A coach was being congratulated on having a lifetime contract. "I guess it's all right," he said. "But I remember another guy with a lifetime contract. Had a bad year, and the president called him in, pronounced him dead and fired him."

Girl to friend seated on other side of her football-star date: "A great kicker, runner and passer, but has difficulty with the c-u-r-r-i-c-u-l-u-m."

Coach to football giant: "You're out of condition, Cooper. Whatta you been doing, studying?"

Football coach to player as shapely blonde walks past bench: "There goes the school's leading pass receiver!"

We know a kid who goes to an extremely progressive school —he plays avant-garde on the football team.

The coach at a midwestern university was discussing the loss of a key football player with a group of Monday-morning quarterbacks.

"He'll be a tough one to replace," said one alumnus. "What happened?"

"Well," the coach replied, "he could do absolutely everything with a football—except autograph it."

A football coach explained to his Monday-morning quarterbacks: "Well, that's the way the rookie fumbles."

Basketball coach to assistant coach: "What a wonderful dream I had! I meet this beautiful blonde, she invites me up to her flat and she has a brother eight feet tall!"

Football coach, giving his team a pre-game pep talk: "Well, here we are, unbeaten, untied and unscored upon—and getting ready for our first game."

Campus Candids

At the end of a college art class, a young instructor was returning a woman's skeleton, used as an anatomical model, to a storeroom. As he walked down the hall, carefully holding "her," he met a girl who fixed him and the skeleton with a curious stare. He shrugged apologetically. "Well," he said, "you know how it is with these blind dates."

In a contest sponsored by the campus literary magazine for the best original poem written by a student and dealing with a philosopher or philosophic theme, one entrant wrote: "Nietzsche is Pietzsche."

At Pomona College, Claremont, California, I was standing near the door of the girls' dormitory, saying good-night to my date, when I overheard an interchange between the couple near us.

The girl said haughtily, "I'm sorry, but I don't kiss on the first date."

"Oh," the boy said cheerily. "Well, how about on the last one?"

Professor to colleague: "I love the campus in the early autumn—before the demonstrations start."

College officials sorting through blanks filled out by Auburn students found the usual number of Baptists, Methodists, Presbyterians, and so on, listed under "Church Preference." But the neatly lettered card filled in by a college senior majoring in Architecture stopped them. His Church Preference was "Gothic."

At commencement exercises of a California university, the usual groups from the various colleges trooped up for their diplomas, but when the College of Forestry was called, only one graduate arose. "Look," exclaimed a spectator, "the Lone Ranger!"

Wife to husband: "Obviously you were laying it on pretty thick at your class reunion—here's a letter from your alma mater suggesting you endow the school!"

As a college freshman, I cajoled and nagged my dad for an inexpensive secondhand car. He assured me that there was no such thing: the extra unforeseen costs would make car ownership prohibitive. I didn't believe it, and kept on arguing until he finally stopped me by asking how old I was.

"Nineteen," I replied.

"Drew," he said, "if I'd had a car when I was your age, you would be 23 today."

There is much concern these days about bad spelling by the younger generation. For instance, a certain college senior may well be a most bewildered young man. Finding that he had left his dungarees at home, he wrote: "Dear Mother, Please send me my genes."

She replied: "Dear Son, If you don't have them by now, there is nothing I can do about it."

While visiting my daughter in her college dormitory room I mentioned that her bed was very narrow, not more than 30 inches wide. Her startled reply: "Why it can't be, my hips are 36!"

When a large Midwest university asked its alumni if they preferred their life today to the good old days on campus, one married alumnus voted for his present life because "I have a cuter roommate."

A mathematics professor, specializing in geometry, was heard to mutter, "I love my wife, but oh, Euclid!"

Call to Colors:
LIFE IN THE SERVICE

IT IS A CREDIT (or is it?) to our American sense of humor that we can somehow extract laughs out of the most unhumorous trade conceivable—professional killing. That may be because—though this is changing—we are not really professionals in the war business. In the past Americans have generally responded well enough to a call to the colors, but secretly we must feel that there is something absurd about the whole affair. That is why our tradition of military humor is actually a very rich one, superior in most ways to that of other countries. Only in America could a truly great humorist of war, such as Bill Mauldin, be produced; or even books that, though perhaps not literature, are hilariously funny, such as *No Time for Sergeants.* And even when the humor is serious, as in *Catch-22,* it has a certain American extravagance and imaginative wit that are hard to match. Compulsory military service is traditional in other countries, but only in our own has so much wry, telling humor been generated by the draft. In general, however, it's a fair bet that whether war exterminates the human race or the human race exterminates war, funny stuff about the military way of life will in the future seem as difficult to create as jokes about chattel slavery.

Welcome Aboard

Young fellow in phone booth at Army induction center: "Hello, Mom? I got the job!"

Job-hunting college graduate to friend on Seattle bus: "Western Universal liked my Rorschach, United Consolidated was impressed with my Depth Interview percentile and General Amalgamated Products was pleased with my Washburne S-A Inventory. Unfortunately, though, United States Army liked my age."

One of the questions on a standard form to be filled out when entering the armed services is: "Did you ever have trouble with school, studies or teachers? If answer is Yes, give details." One conscientious recruit replied: "Yes. I was a pour reeder."

One of the tasks of our Marine Reserve unit was to visit high schools and explain the Reserve Program to the students. At one school a student who seemed quite interested asked: "When the planes are bombing the shore, and the ships are bombarding the coast, and small boats are going into the beach loaded with men, who are the men in the boats?"

"The Marines," he was told.

"That's what I thought," he said as he disappeared into the crowd.

Sign posted in an Army recruiting station after the announcement was made that married men would not be drafted: "Better for Two Years Than for Life."

Any physical defects?" asked the draft-board doctor.

"Yes, sir," replied the hopeful inductee. "No guts!"

One of the young men in our office recently reported to the draft center for his pre-induction physical. Ahead of him was another young fellow, fortified with endless pages of medical records, doctors' certifications and related documents. The induction officer flipped the pages nonchalantly, "Tell me, son," he inquired. "How did you *get* here—in an ambulance?"

Let Us Destroy Your Draft Card!" reads a notice in the window of a U.S. Coast Guard Recruiting Station.

Enlistment officer to recruit: "And another advantage in making the Army a career is that you avoid the constant worry of being called up as a reservist."

In its campaign to recruit paratroopers, the French army achieved notable success with a poster at one of the busiest thoroughfares of Paris reading: "Young men! Join the parachutist forces of France. It is more dangerous to cross this street than to jump with a parachute."

But the spell of the ad was broken when someone scribbled at the bottom: "I would gladly join, but the recruiting office is on the other side of the street!"

Down to Basics

A friend of mine recently reported to Fort Polk, Louisiana, for basic training. In his first letter home, he wrote: "It's sure a new experience having wall-to-wall brothers!"

U.S. airmen training in the British Royal Air Force Parachute and Jungle Survival School at Changi, Singapore, are wryly advised: "Try to crash in June, July or August, when there is more edible fruit about."

Watching a new cavalry recruit at work, I discovered that he not only knew nothing of handling horses but was deathly afraid of them. Knowing that the Army was making much to-do over placing men according to former civilian skills, I couldn't resist asking him how he could have been assigned to the cavalry.

"Well," said the recruit, "most of my life I've been a bookie."

When I finished basic training at Fort Bragg I had no idea what kind of job I'd be assigned to—for I had been a licensed funeral director and embalmer in civilian life. The Army Classification Officer came through in fine style— I was assigned to the Fort Bragg dead-letter office!

My first day as a recruit I was ordered to report to the cookhouse, where a sergeant issued me a knife and introduced me to a mountain of potatoes.

"But, Sarge," I said, "surely in this day and age the Army has machines to peel potatoes."

"We have," he replied. "And you're the latest model."

Our favorite instructor in basic training was the lively colonel who taught us strategy and tactics. "Gentlemen," he asked the first morning, "how many of you took a girl to the dance last night? Well," he continued, "to give you an idea of this course: how you went about asking her was strategy; what you did when you got her there was tactics."

One phase of our course on explosives at Lowry Air Force Base, Colorado, dealt with the exacting job of removing fuses from live bombs and other projectiles. After days of exhaustive study of many types of fuses, one troublesome and obnoxious student asked the instructor, "Isn't there an easier way to learn this?"

"Yes, son," the instructor replied. "In your case, I strongly recommend trial and error."

In spite of being urged to write frequent letters home, many airmen going through basic training at Lackland Air Force Base neglect to do so. I had to call one such airman into my office after receiving this letter from his mother: "Dear Sir: I have not heard from my son for three weeks. If he is dead, please send his body to Route 1, Hugo, Oklahoma."

It was late summer at Fort Bliss, Texas, and I was going through the final stages of basic training. One of the last maneuvers was a march across the desert with full field pack. As we marched along, the sun beating down on the sand made my pack grow heavier with each step. When we got a five-minute break 8354 steps later, I turned to a buddy and groaned, "This pack must weigh a ton!"

With a weary look he inquired, "What did you forget?"

The instructor in a basic-training course asked a sleepy private, "If you were on night sentry duty and saw a figure crawling toward camp, what procedure would you follow?"

"Well, sir," the private answered, "I'd help the officer to his quarters."

When we arrived at Parris Island, South Carolina, for Marine basic training, our drill instructor intimidated us thoroughly at the outset. "All right," he began. "Get this and get it straight. My name is Staff Sergeant Stone, and I'm even harder than my name. If anyone has any other ideas, he'd better run out now or he'll regret every minute of the three months he's going to spend here."

He then strutted down the line of stiffened boys and asked the name of each in turn. Upon reaching the smallest one with his question, there was no answer. In a voice that would shake Gibraltar, he roared, "Are you just going to ignore me, private? I said, 'What's your name?' "

We could barely hear the almost tearful voice that answered: "Stonebreaker, sir."

During primary training with the RCAF, I was flying a light trainer when I had an uncomfortably close shave with another plane. My instructor and I were still shaky when we landed, but I had almost forgotten the incident when I returned to the barracks that evening. There I found a neatly lettered card taped to the wall above my desk: "A mid-air collision could spoil your whole day."

Drill sergeant to recruit: "Wipe that opinion off your face!"

———— • ————

A class at the Chief Petty Officers Academy was discussing the semiannual evaluation of enlisted personnel by their superiors. To illustrate his point that there is always some good quality to emphasize, the instructor cited one inspired evaluation: "This man is not a complete loss. He can always be used as a bad example."

———— • ————

For the Record

JOE FYFFE
VS. THE NAVY
WILLIAM LEDERER

As the liner *Coolidge* steamed slowly up the Whangpoo River at Shanghai, Ensign Hymie O'Toole was my official welcoming party. Hymie had arrived in Shanghai a month before and was the communications officer on the U.S.S. *Dale*.

None of the passengers could disembark for two hours; Hymie and I sat in the bar talking. "You know," said Hymie, looking over the *Coolidge's* luxurious lounge, "it's pretty damned marvelous that the Navy sends you out this way. And all for free."

"It's nice, all right."

Hymie said, "It didn't used to be this way. Formerly, if you came by commercial, you paid your own way—and tried to collect later."

"This cost the Navy about $600; I never could have scraped up that much cash."

"Think of the old days though," said Hymie dreamily. "Every time an officer had orders, especially if he had a family, he put out a couple of thousand bucks. That's why officers were always in debt. A distant relative of mine, Commodore Joe Fyffe, was the first one to fight that system. In fact it was through his efforts that legislation finally got passed. He was always fighting with stuffed shirts."

Hymie's eyes misted with sentiment and he ordered a couple of neat whiskies. "To Commodore Joe Fyffe," he toasted "the

441

Paul Bunyan of all the oceans!" Then Hymie told me about Commodore Fyffe.

When, in August 1870, Lieutenant Commander Joseph P. Fyffe received orders to the Orient via San Francisco, he was a happy guy. It meant independent command of a fine frigate. The only leak in the bilges was that traveling to San Francisco cost money and Joe Fyffe didn't have any.

"The Navy should pay for my transportation," he said, and forthwith wrote to the paymaster at New London, Connecticut. The paymaster endorsed the request: "Custom and regulations have determined that the officer pay his own way and submit an expense account upon reaching his destination."

So Joe communicated with the Secretary of the Navy, requesting that the Navy either lay out the money or supply him with railroad tickets or transportation via naval vessel. The reply came from the Chief of the Bureau of Navigation:

TO: LIEUTENANT COMMANDER J. P. FYFFE.

IN REPLY TO YOUR LETTER OF THE 18TH. YOUR REQUEST IS CONTRARY TO NAVY REGULATIONS. CARRY OUT YOUR ORDERS.

Joe Fyffe cursed. Then he carefully studied his orders. They terminated with the normal paragraph, WHILE CARRYING OUT THESE ORDERS YOU WILL KEEP THE BUREAU OF NAVIGATION INFORMED OF YOUR WHEREABOUTS. There was nothing which stated when he was supposed to arrive in San Francisco or by what means.

Joe donned his best uniform and strapped his sword to his small handbag. At sunrise on the 25th of August he walked out of New London and headed westward for San Francisco. By sundown he reached East Haddam, where he sent the following telegram to the Chief of the Bureau in Washington:

25 AUGUST 1870

COMPLIANCE ORDERS NUMBER 1998 LT. COMDR. FYFFE EN ROUTE: NEW LONDON TO SAN FRANCISCO X ON FOOT X THIS TELEGRAM TO KEEP BUREAU INFORMED MY WHEREABOUTS X MADE GOOD 22 MILES THIS DATE X SPENDING EVENING IN HAYLOFT IN MT. PARNASSUS X VERY RESPECTFULLY FYFFE.

Every evening for the next few days he sent a telegram.

26 AUGUST 1870

EN ROUTE X ON FOOT X MADE GOOD 31 MILES THIS DATE X BY GRA-

CIOUS CONSENT MAYOR OF BRISTOL AM SPENDING NIGHT MAYOR'S STABLES X HAVE NOTICED HE HAS HYBRID MULES SPECIALLY BRED FOR TROPICS X SUGGEST NAVY INVESTIGATE.

27 AUGUST 1870

EN ROUTE X ON FOOT X MADE GOOD ONLY 15 MILES THIS DATE X RAINED ALL DAY X STAYING OVERNIGHT AT LITCHFIELD WITH MY FATHER'S FRIEND GENERAL HOLMES X I FIND STANDARD BOOTS WORN BY NAVAL OFFICERS INADEQUATE FOR PROLONGED WALKING X SUGGEST SURGEON GENERAL INVESTIGATE.

28 AUGUST 1870

EN ROUTE X ON FOOT X SPENDING NIGHT LAKEVILLE X LOVELY COUNTRY EXPECT BUY HOME HERE SOON AS GET REIMBURSED TRAVEL VOUCHER SUBMITTED BY ME TO NAVY THREE YEARS AGO X TOMORROW I ENTER NEW YORK STATE.

29 AUGUST 1870

EN ROUTE X ON FOOT X MADE 28 MILES THIS DATE DESPITE BADLY WORN SHOES X PEOPLE NOT FAMILIAR NAVY UNIFORMS THIS AREA X GREAT CROWD WALKED PART WAY WITH ME X I SANG THEM SEA CHANTIES X POPULACE THINKS IT GREAT SIGN DEMOCRACY FOR COMMANDING OFFICER OF SHIP TO WALK 3000 MILES TO NEW STATION X POLICE CHIEF HUDSON NEW YORK HAS GIVEN ME BEST CELL IN JAIL FOR OVERNIGHT.

30 AUGUST 1870

EN ROUTE X ON FOOT X ARRIVED ALBANY X REQUESTED RECRUITING OFFICER BE AUTHORIZED ISSUE ME NEW SHOES X SHOES FELL APART NOON TODAY X ENTERED ALBANY BAREFOOTED X WILL REMAIN SEWARD HOTEL TWO DAYS AWAITING ANSWER X EARNING MY KEEP AS BARTENDER X LOCAL RUM FAR SUPERIOR THAT SERVED IN NAVY X AM SENDING SAMPLE X VERY RESPECTFULLY FYFFE.

The next evening the recruiting officer sent a messenger requesting Lieutenant Commander Joe Fyffe's presence. In full uniform, wearing borrowed shoes, Joe went to the recruiting station.

"I have a telegram for you, sir," said the recruiting officer. "Here it is."

PASS FOLLOWING MESSAGE TO LT. COMDR. J. P. FYFFE USN NOW AT SEWARD HOTEL BAR QUOTE I STRIKE MY COLORS X SECRETARY OF NAVY AUTHORIZES RECRUITING OFFICER ALBANY ISSUE YOU SHOES AND PROVIDE YOU QUICKEST TRANSPORTATION FROM ALBANY TO

SAN FRANCISCO X EVEN CHIEF BUREAU NAVIGATION CAN LAUGH
WHEN OUTSMARTED X UNQUOTE X RESPECTFULLY BUREAU NAVI-
GATION X

Between hiccups Hymie O'Toole concluded, "And that's
how it is that guys like you have their first-class passage on the
Coolidge prepaid by the Navy."

———————— • ————————

From form enclosed in soldiers' allotment checks: "Class Q
allotments are based upon the number of dependents up to
a maximum of three, so, if the birth of a child will mean
your husband is entitled to more quarters allowance, notify
him to take the necessary action."

The Navy, like the other armed services, is constantly
issuing orders, instructions, memorandums, revisions etc.,
to clarify and simplify the already clarified and simplified.
These efforts culminated in a recent instruction from
the Navy. It read: "Classified material is considered lost
when it cannot be found."

While serving in the Navy, I was assigned to a department where the work was somewhat classified. But I did
not fully realize the scope of our security until one evening,
on my way out of the office, I noticed a sign above the
door that read: "You have been exposed to classified
material. Destroy yourself before leaving this building."

In a Navy office in the Pentagon: "If you can keep your
head when all about you are losing theirs, maybe you just
don't understand the situation!"

Modern war is a complicated business with orders trans-
mitted down through a long chain of command. But during
the Civil War the procedure was much simpler. An Arkansas
colonel with meager military training had his own method
for moving his cavalry troop.
First order: "Prepare to git onto your critters."
Second order: "Git."

———————— • ————————

During that part of the Naval War College course known as "Command and Decision," our instructor was stressing the importance and the difficulty of being able to make a sound decision under pressure. A visiting officer from a small foreign navy spoke up, "Decisions, you talk about decisions. I was 700 miles to sea in my destroyer when I received a dispatch from my country: "We have just had a revolution. Which side are you on?""

Once a year commanding officers throughout the military sharpen their pencils and compose "efficiency" reports on the officers in their command. You might imagine they'd be dull reading, but actually they often supply intentional— and unintentional—humor. Here are examples from Army files:

This officer has talents but has kept them well hidden.

Can express a sentence in two paragraphs any time.

A quiet, reticent officer. Industrious, tenacious, careful and neat. I do not wish to have this officer as a member of my command at any time.

His leadership is outstanding except for his lack of ability to get along with subordinates.

In any change in policy or procedure, he can be relied upon to produce the improbable, hypothetical situation in which the new policy cannot work.

Needs careful watching since he borders on the brilliant.

Open to suggestions but never follows same.

Is keenly analytical and his highly developed mentality could best be utilized in the research and development field. He lacks common sense.

Never makes the same mistakes twice but it seems to me he has made them all once.

Over There

While cruising a lonely stretch of the South Pacific on a little old minesweeper, we observed a new Australian cruiser coming up on our stern. We all admired the handsome ship, and our captain sent a blinker-light message: "YOU ARE BEAUTIFUL."

Less than 30 seconds later, her captain blinkered back: "I BET YOU SAY THAT TO ALL THE SHIPS."

To escape German shellfire, I was hiding two Australians behind a partly wrecked building. One of them, reading a book, asked, "I say, what does this mean—'category?'" "That's easy," the other Aussie said. "C-A-T spells cat, E—it is a 'e cat, and you know what GORY means. Blimey, it's a bloody TOMCAT."

During World War II, an American flier was shot down and remained in a coma until he regained consciousness in an English hospital. "Where am I?" he asked.

"You're in jolly old England," replied his nurse with a pronounced cockney accent.

"Oh, did I come here to die?" moaned the flier.

"No," said the nurse sympathetically, "you came here yesterdie."

Officers assigned to a military assistance advisory group on Taiwan were searching for a name for their new officers' club. The finally agreed on "TAI-WAN-ON."

At an airstrip in a remote section of Southeast Asia, two small British military aircraft landed to refuel. While fuel was being pumped by hand from drums into his airplane, the flight commander was confronted by the distraught youngster piloting the second craft.

"I'm flying a bomb," he announced. "There's something amiss with my petrol line, and the whole bloody cockpit is full of fumes. What shall I do?"

The flight commander, knowing that the little strip offered no repair facilities, replied calmly, "Don't smoke!"

When I was posted to Christmas Island, my friends warned me that the days would pass slowly in this isolated outpost. I began to appreciate what they meant the day I found a soldier staring out across the Pacific and casually asked him the time. "July," he replied mournfully.

Mail is a big morale booster for those of us in Vietnam. Recently my unit received several hundred letters addressed to "Any Marine, Vietnam." Everybody got at least one. Mine, from a third-grade boy, had this priceless greeting: "Dear War Victim."

As a newly arrived officer in Nuremberg, I was being escorted about the post by an old hand. En route to the bachelor officers' quarters, my friendly guide commented that he was sure I would like the classic Greek decor of my new quarters.

"Classic Greek?" I inquired. "What's that?"

"Spartan, brother."

A vintage U.S. submarine was laboring south through Macassar Strait at her best surface speed of about eight knots when a destroyer overhauled her. After an exchange of recognition signals the speeding destroyer winked from the signal bridge: "Am making 27 knots. Do you wish to accompany me?"

The submarine captain blinked back: "Preparing to submerge. Do you wish to accompany me?"

Rank Nonsense

ECLIPSE OF THE SUN
THE OPERATION OF THE CHAIN
OF COMMAND

The Colonel to the Executive: "At nine o'clock tomorrow there will be an eclipse of the sun, something which does not occur every day. Get the men to fall out in the company street in their fatigues so that they will see this rare phenomenon, and I will explain it to them. In case of rain, we will not be able to see anything, so take the men to the gym."

The Executive to the Captain: "By order of the Colonel, tomorrow at nine o'clock there will be an eclipse of the sun; if it rains you will not be able to see it from the company street, so then, in fatigues, the eclipse of the sun will take place in the gym, something that does not occur every day."

The Captain to the Lieutenant: "By order of the Colonel in fatigues tomorrow at nine o'clock in the morning the inauguration of the eclipse of the sun will take place in the gym. The Colonel will give the order if it should rain, something which occurs every day."

The Lieutenant to the Sergeant: "Tomorrow at nine the Colonel in fatigues will eclipse the sun in the gym, as it occurs every day if it is a nice day; if it rains, then in the company street."

The Sergeant to the Corporal: "Tomorrow at nine the eclipse of the Colonel in fatigues will take place by cause of the sun. If it rains in the gym, something which does not take place every day, you will fall out in the company street."

Comments among the Privates: "Tomorrow, if it rains, it looks as if the sun will eclipse the Colonel in the gym. It is a shame that this does not occur every day."

———— • ————

The day before Hyman G. Rickover was promoted to vice-admiral a horse named Rickover won the fifth race at New York's Belmont Park. Rickover commented: "No other admiral in history has ever had a whole horse named for him."

———— • ————

On patrol off Formosa, the Officer of the Deck of the U.S.S. *Brownson* asked the starboard lookout what he would do if a man fell overboard.

"I would yell, 'Man overboard!'"

The officer then asked what he would do if an officer fell overboard.

The lookout was silent for a moment, then asked, "Which one, sir?"

A group of us were sitting in the ready room of our hangar when a chief walked in with more hash marks adorning his sleeve than we had ever seen. One sailor remarked, "Gee, chief, you've sure been in the Navy a long time. What were you in civilian life?"

The chief, without hesitation, answered, "A baby."

A couple of National Guard recruits were bird hunting when one of them shouted to the other that he had found a dead animal on the road. "It's got three stripes!" he yelled.

"Leave him lay!" shouted back his partner. "It's either a skunk or a sergeant."

During an evening of intramural bowling competition, we had to draft a young airman to fill out our team. Nervous over bowling with a group of older men, the young man inadvertently used the colonel's ball, smoked two cigarettes the old boy had lighted and mistakenly drank his beer.

"Young man," the colonel thundered, "it's a good thing you don't know where I live!"

Mother to departing draftee: "Now remember—the more stripes they have the more you mind them."

The captain was a hardworking, conscientious Army officer, but he had not received a promotion in 12 years. Asked if he had an explanation for his failure to advance, he replied "Many years ago I had an argument with a general—and I won!"

---•---

Bragging about his uncle's promotion, a small boy said: "The longer he stays in the Army the ranker he gets!"

Nothing Like a Dame

An Air Force buddy visited me after an extended tour of duty on one of the remote bases of our Distant Early Warning radar system. Attempting to arrange a blind date for him, I told the girl that he had been working on the DEW line for six months. After a slight hesitation, she answered, "Oh, I don't think that will be any problem. I've been working on my 'don't line' for six years."

When I couldn't locate the book I wanted in a Sheppard Air Force Base library, I asked the pretty WAF librarian: "Have you *No Time for Sergeants?*"

"I try my best," she replied.

A fighter pilot and perennial bachelor made his position clear to one and all: "No matchmaking! I've flown high and wide for years. And that's the way it's going to stay. High and wide. And alone."

Then came the day he sent this telegraphed announcement to all his friends: "Got shot down at 5 p.m. Jerry."

Two young sailors who had just reported for duty in Hawaii were out on the town on their first liberty. At a local nightclub, as a bevy of attractive girls were performing the hula in their traditional grass skirts, one sailor leaned over and remarked to the other, "Man, what fringe benefits!"

I had recently been discharged from the Army when I met a buddy, still in uniform, who had served with me in the South Pacific. After a hearty exchange of greetings, I gestured toward the impressive row of ribbons on his chest. "What did your girl say about all your medals?" I asked.

"Well," he replied, "the first thing she said was 'Ouch!'"

---•---

A buddy of mine, spending the night at an Air Force base, went to the library to write letters. The assistant librarian was a gorgeous young WAF, and my friend made separate trips to her desk for stationery, pen, an envelope, so that he could look her over from stem to stern. On his fourth trip the WAF quickly handed him a stamp.

"You're a mind reader," he said.

"If I were," she replied, "you'd be court-martialed."

My buddy and I, wounded at the same time, arrived together at a South Pacific base evacuation hospital. Neither of us had seen a girl in more than two years and were delighted to be greeted by a pretty Army nurse. We drank in the beautiful sight, our eyes moving slowly upward from the trim ankles to the lovely face.

"Well," said the nurse, "is everything as you remembered it?"

Wise GIs

On one of my father's tours of duty in Japan with the Marines, my mother wrote and asked if he would send her a genuine Japanese back scratcher. "Sorry, darling," my father replied, "they wouldn't let her through customs."

An Air Force enlisted man stationed in Rhode Island had little difficulty hitching a ride when he stood at the side of the road with duffel bag in one hand and a huge banner tied across his chest reading: "To Mother for Christmas."

At a British naval barracks the enlisted men were being given their shots prior to going overseas. One cheerful Scottish lad, having received his series of injections, asked for a glass of water. "What's the matter, mate?" asked the sickbay attendant. "Do you feel faint?"

"No," replied Jock. "I just want to see if I'm still watertight."

A chaplain preached a forceful sermon on the Ten Commandments, leaving one private in a serious mood. But eventually he brightened up. "Anyway," he consoled himself, "I never made a graven image."

A mess sergeant was lecturing: "Men, there's too much food being wasted in our mess. You must make use of leftovers. For instance, what can we make with leftover carrots?" Getting no response, he went on, "Carrot pie—that's what you can make with leftover carrots." He paused to let the idea sink in. "Any questions?"

A hand waved in the rear of the room, and an enthusiastic private asked, "Sir, what do you make with leftover carrot pie?"

While my husband was attending to some business at the MP station, he overheard this accident report: "I was driving along, when all of a sudden a drunk came right down the road and smashed into me." Asked how he knew the other driver was intoxicated, the somewhat tipsy private replied, "He must have been, sir. He was driving a tree!"

The young soldier's first child, born in an Army hospital, was wrinkled, as newborn babies are likely to be. "Isn't that just like the Army," remarked the GI, "to issue him a birthday suit that doesn't fit?"

At the Nashville Air Defense Center, a soldier who had requested assignment to pilot training was asked by the psychologist why he desired such hazardous duty. "Because," answered the soldier, "it's the only branch of service I know where you can retreat at 500 miles per hour!"

The new Navy captain looked the crew over and said, "Men, before anything more is said, I would like to clear up one thing. This isn't my ship—this isn't your ship—it's *our* ship!"

A voice from the crew muttered, "Good! Let's *sell* it!"

At Kirtland Air Force Base, I work as a radio operator in a Military Affiliated Radio System station. One day I got a call and I answered it in the usual manner: "MARS Station, Airman Sullivan speaking, sir."

I heard a gasp on the other end, then a woman's meek little voice: "Good heavens! I didn't want long distance!" And she hung up.

At Johnson Air Force Housing Annex in Japan, there was a big campaign to put over Fire Prevention Week. Each office or service on the base was asked to produce a sign or display depicting some aspect of fire prevention. Outside the base chapel appeared a poster covered with orange and red flames which read: "Don't Get Burned Here or in the Hereafter."

An officer of the Army Engineers who was about to be reassigned to the United States had to account for all his equipment before he turned over his duties. He was staggered to discover that one of his tugboats was missing. Then he had an inspiration. He included in his report items missing from an officers' club and listed: "Ten spoons, soup. Twelve spoons, tea. One knife, carving. One boat, gravy. One boat, tug."

Civvy Snickers

On his first day of retirement, an ex-Navy chief was asked, "How do you feel now that you're out?"

His reply: "Fine, just great. When I joined the Navy, I had $19 in my pocket. Today I have $18. Now where else can you stay for over 20 years for a dollar?"

Smiling wife reading to disgruntled husband from his war-time letters: "And here's one from January, '45 . . . 'food awful . . . been raining for three weeks . . . if I ever get home I'll never complain about anything.' . . . Want me to read more?"

I had considerable state-side duty with the Marines during World War II, and later was with them in the assault phase at Iwo Jima. My rate was 2/C Storekeeper in the Seabees.

Upon discharge, I returned to my former employment as president of a corporation which I had founded and in which I was the majority stockholder. Within a few weeks, the Navy was kind enough to send the corporation my qualifications, stating that I should make a good file clerk.

Soon to finish my tour in Vietnam and hoping to go to college, I wrote to the university of my choice for information on the curriculum and school policies. I received a reply from the dean of men, stating: "As a prospective student at our large and rapidly growing university, you may be leaving home for the first time, may find yourself surrounded by strangers in an unfamiliar environment. . . ."

Secretary discussing her blind date: "He just got out of the service—sort of a post-naval drip."

Watching the floor show at a San Francisco bistro, a Marine just back from Vietnam observed wryly, "Here at least there's a definite front and a definite rear!"

While stationed in Germany in October 1945, I went to an Army field hospital for a dental checkup. The examining dental officer turned out to be my cousin, whom I had not seen in three years. After a brief scrutiny he pronounced my teeth free of cavities, and we went forth to celebrate our unexpected reunion.

Less than three months later, when we were both civilians again in the States, I went to his office, complaining of a toothache.

"Badly neglected cavity!" he tsk-tsked.

"How come?" I asked. "You checked me out as cavity-free less than three months ago in Germany!"

He shrugged his shoulders. "Oh, you know those Army dentists," he said.

An Army colonel is sometimes referred to as a "screaming eagle" by virtue of his insignia. My brother, recently retired with the rank of colonel, returned to this city with his wife and seven-year-old son. Soon after his arrival, I called him, and my nephew answered. "Let me speak to the screaming eagle," I asked gaily.

"Ma! Oh, Ma!" I heard the youngster shout. "Someone wants to talk to you."

A veteran who had served with the Military Police was trying to convince another vet of the merits of his branch of the service. "After all," said the ex-MP, "we suffered more casualties than any other branch."

"And why shouldn't you have," sniffed the other vet, "with enemies on both sides?"

Cupid's Quiver:
THE MATING GAME

I N THE GREAT circus of humor, sex of course will always remain the main event in the center ring. Nothing, including the inevitable and too-long-delayed victory of women's lib, will ever change the fact that the most exquisite of human pleasures is also somehow the funniest. If, as Freud tells us, erotic jokes represent our effort to outwit our repressions by expressing indirectly what is taboo—well, in that case there may be a certain danger in doing away with all inhibitions. A danger for humorists at any rate.

To the good collection of mildly lavender anecdotes that follow we might add the pleasant reply of the young lady who, invited by her boyfriend to come over to his apartment for a whiskey-and-sofa, said, "No, but I might come over for a gin-and-platonic." Of all the millions of pointed remarks about the mating game, for me the most profoundly true is W. C. Fields's brief but final statement. You'll find it under "Points of View."

Courting Disaster

Am I the first girl you ever kissed?" she whispered softly to her escort.

"It's quite possible," he admitted. "Were you in Atlantic City in 1971?"

After a friend became engaged, she remarked that she wished there were a ring to denote engaged males. A friend suggested that engaged men could be branded as horses are.

"But that wouldn't *show*," she lamented.

The other quipped, "It would if he were leaving the corral."

Father to daughter's beau: "She'll be right down. Care for a game of chess?"

The instructor in a YMCA charm course was urging her students to give their escorts every chance to be gallant.

"Remain seated in the car until he has had time to step around and open the door for you," she said. Then, bowing to reality, she added, "But if he's already in the restaurant and starting to order, don't wait any longer!"

One girl to another: "We had an awful time. I had on my new Angora sweater, and he was wearing a blue serge suit."

One chorus girl to another: "He likes my company and I simply love his. I think it's called the Fidelity Trust."

Ardent guy to gal: "Of course I've kissed girls before—you didn't think I'd use you as a guinea pig, did you?"

One girl to another: "He seems rather dull and uninteresting until you get to know him. After that he's downright boring."

A Texan, attending a masquerade ball, was dancing with a girl wearing the map of Texas for a costume. Suddenly she slapped him. "What happened?" asked a friend.

"I don't know. When she asked me where I was from, I put my finger on Amarillo and she let me have it."

Girl to suitor who has just proposed: "Let me hear that part again where you realize you're not half good enough for me."

Zsa Zsa Gabor once found time in her busy life to moderate a TV show devoted to husband-and-wife problems. The first guest on the show confessed, "I'm breaking my engagement to a very wealthy man who has already given me a sable coat, diamonds, a stove and a Rolls-Royce. Miss Gabor, what should I do?"

Zsa Zsa counseled: "Give back the stove."

Girl, looking at engagement ring, to fiancé: "I didn't say the stone was small. I just said not all my friends have 20/20 vision."

One girl to another, watching departing jalopy: "I *know* Alvin's been faithful—his seat belts never have to be readjusted!"

Cold Shoulders

THE WALTZ
DOROTHY PARKER

WHY, *thank you so much. I'd adore to.* I don't want to dance with him. I don't want to dance with anybody. And even if I did, it wouldn't be him. Just think, not a quarter of an hour ago, I was feeling so sorry for the poor girl he was dancing with. And now *I'm* going to be the poor girl.

Here I was, minding my own business, not doing a stitch of harm to any living soul. And then he comes into my life, all smiles and city manners, to sue me for the favor of one memorable mazurka. Why, he scarcely knows my name, let alone what it stands for. It stands for Despair, Bewilderment, Futility, Degradation and Premeditated Murder, but little does he wot. I don't wot his name either; I haven't any idea what it is. Jukes, would be my guess from the look in his eyes. How do you do, Mr. Jukes? And how is that dear little brother of yours with the two heads?

What can you say, when a man asks you to dance with him? I most certainly will *not* dance with you, I'll see you in hell first. Why, thank you, I'd like to awfully, but I'm having labor pains. No. There was nothing for me to do but say I'd adore to.

Why, I think it's more of a waltz, really. Isn't it? We might just listen to the music a second. Shall we? Oh, yes, it's a waltz. Mind? Why, I'm simply thrilled. I'd love to waltz with you.

I'd love to waltz with you. I'd love to waltz with you, I'd love to have my tonsils out, I'd love to be in a midnight fire at sea. Well, it's too late now. *Oh.* Oh, dear. Oh, this is even worse than I thought it would be.

I'm so glad I brought it to his attention that this is a waltz they're playing. Heaven knows what might have happened if he had thought it was something fast; we'd have blown the sides right out of the building. Why does he always want to be somewhere that he isn't? It's this constant rush, rush, rush, that's the curse of American life. That's the reason that we're all of us so—*Ow!* For God's sake, don't *kick,* you idiot; this is only second down. Oh, my shin. My poor, poor shin, that I've had ever since I was a little girl!

Oh, no, no, no. Goodness, no. It didn't hurt the least little bit. And anyway it was my fault. Really it was. Truly. Well, you're just being sweet, to say that. It really was all my fault.

I wonder what I'd better do—kill him this instant, with my naked hands, or wait and let him drop in his traces. Maybe it's best not to make a scene. I guess I'll just lie low, and watch the pace get him. He can't keep this up indefinitely—he's only flesh and blood. Die he must, and die he shall, for what he did to me. I don't want to be of the oversensitive type, but when it comes to kicking, I am Outraged Womanhood. When you kick me in the shin, *smile.*

Maybe he didn't do it maliciously. Maybe it's just his way of showing his high spirits. I suppose I ought to be glad that one of us is having such a good time. After all, the poor boy's doing the best he can. Probably he grew up in the hill country, and never had no larnin'. I bet they had to throw him on his back to get shoes on him.

Yes, it's lovely, isn't it? It's simply lovely. It's the loveliest waltz. Isn't it? Oh, I think it's lovely, too.

Why, I'm getting positively drawn to the Triple Threat here. He's my hero. Look at him—never a thought of the consequences, never afraid of his face, hurling himself into every scrimmage, eyes shining, cheeks ablaze. And shall it be said that I hung back? No, a thousand times no. What's it to me if I have to spend the next couple of years in a plaster cast? Come on, Butch, right through them! Who wants to live forever?

Oh. Oh, dear. Oh, he's all right, thank goodness. For a while I thought they'd have to carry him off the field. Ah, I couldn't bear to have anything happen to him. I love him. Look at the spirit he gets into a dreary commonplace waltz; how effete the other dancers seem, beside him. He is youth and vigor and courage, he is strength and gaiety and — *Ow!* Get off my instep, you hulking peasant! What do you think I am, anyway — a gangplank? *Ow!*

No, of course it didn't hurt. Why, it didn't a bit. Honestly. And it was all my fault. You see, that little step of yours — well, it's perfectly lovely, but it's just a tiny bit tricky to follow at first. Oh, did you work it up yourself? You really did? Well, aren't you amazing! Oh, I think it's lovely. I was watching you do it when you were dancing before. It's awfully effective when you look at it.

It's awfully effective when you look at it. I bet I'm awfully effective when you look at me. Hair hanging along my cheeks, skirt swaddled about me, and the cold damp on my brow. This sort of thing takes a fearful toll of a woman my age. And he worked up his little step himself, he with his degenerate cunning. And it was just a tiny bit tricky at first but now I think I've got it. Two stumbles, slip, and a 25-yard dash; yes, I've got it. I've got several other things, too, including a split shin and a bitter heart. I hate this creature I'm chained to. I hated him the moment I saw his leering bestial face. And here I've been locked in his noxious embrace for the 35 years this waltz has lasted. Is that orchestra never going to stop?

Oh, they're going to play another encore. Oh, goody. Oh, that's lovely. Tired? I should say I'm not tired. I'd like to go on like this forever.

I should say I'm not tired. I'm dead, that's all I am. Dead and in what a cause! And the music is never going to stop playing, and we're going on like this, Double-Time Charlie and I, throughout eternity. I suppose I won't care any more, after the first hundred thousand years. I suppose nothing will matter then, not heat nor pain nor broken heart nor cruel aching weariness. Well, it can't come too soon for me.

I wonder why I didn't tell him I was tired. I could have said let's just listen to the music. Yes, and if he would, that would be the first bit of attention he has given it all evening.

Still, if we were back at the table, I'd probably have to talk to him. Look at him — what could you say to a thing like that! Did you go to the circus this year, what's your favorite kind of ice cream, how do you spell cat? I guess I'm as well off here. As well off as if I were in a cement mixer in full action.

I'm past all feeling now. The only way I can tell when he steps on me is that I can hear the splintering of bones. And all the events of my life are passing before my eyes, the time I was in a hurricane in the West Indies, the day I got my head cut open in the taxi smash, the summer that the sailboat kept capsizing. Ah, what an easy, peaceful time was mine, until I fell in with Swifty, here. I didn't know what trouble was, before I got drawn into this *danse macabre*. I think my mind is beginning to wander. It almost seems to me as if the orchestra were stopping. It couldn't be, of course; it could never, never be. And yet in my ears there's a silence like the sound of angel voices.

Oh, they've stopped, the mean things. They're not going to play any more. Oh, darn. Oh, do you think they would? Do you really think so, if you gave them fifty dollars? Oh, that would be lovely. And look, do tell them to play this same thing. I'd simply adore to go on waltzing.

———— • ————

A young man about town took a glamorous girl out on a date. They were driving down a moonlit country lane when the engine suddenly coughed and the car came to a halt.

"That's funny," said the young man. "I wonder what that knocking was?"

"Well, I can tell you one thing for sure," the girl answered icily. "It wasn't opportunity."

Girl to her date in a night club: "I think I'll have another drink. It makes you so witty."

Girl to girl: "I *think* he proposed. He said he wants to finalize our friendship."

Girl to suitor: "Look—let's compromise. I won't return your ring and I won't keep it. Let's sell it and split the cash."

Sweet young thing to suitor: "If people ask what I see in you, Herbert, what shall I tell them?"

———— • ————

The Perfect Mismatch

"DEAR ABBY"
ABIGAIL VAN BUREN

D EAR ABBY" (Mrs. Abigail Van Buren of San Mateo, California) has captured the imagination of newspaper readers across the country with her pithy answers to letters from problem-beset correspondents. A collection of letters and answers from her syndicated columns, published by Prentice-Hall, has been a best-seller. Following are some excerpts:

DEAR ABBY: I know that boys will be boys, but my "boy" is 60 years old and he's still chasing women. Have you any suggestions? *Clara*

DEAR CLARA: Don't worry. My dog has been chasing cars for years, but if he ever caught one he wouldn't know what to do with it.

DEAR ABBY: I'm forced to admit that I am one guy who has everything. Women are always flocking around me and telling me how good-looking I am and what a marvelous personality I have. I'm beginning to find this extremely tiring. How can I dissuade these hopeful females? *C. W*

DEAR C. W.: Keep talking.

DEAR ABBY: I am 44 years old and would like to meet a man my age with no bad habits. *Rose*

DEAR ROSE: So would I.

DEAR ABBY: I am married and have seven children under 12 years of age. Recently I started to work in a hospital and my job brings me close to X-ray equipment. I have heard that this will sterilize me. Is this true? *Sylvia*

DEAR SYLVIA: I wouldn't count on it.

DEAR ABBY: Which is better? To go to a school dance with a creep or to sit at home? *All Shook Up*

DEAR SHOOK: Go with the creep and look over the crop.

DEAR ABBY: What do you think of a man who keeps you on the string for six years? I've taken four blood tests and we've had the marriage license for so long I'm not even sure if it's still good. Now he wants me to take another blood test and I don't know what to tell him. *Bevs*

DEAR BEVS: I'd give my blood to the Red Cross and find another fellow.

I heard about this young couple who wanted to get married after they had known each other just a few days. He asked, "Do you think you could learn to love me?"

"I think so," she said timidly. "I learned shorthand in three weeks."

A disc jockey took a poll over the air, asking listeners whom they would like to be stranded with on a desert island. A young bride surprised her husband by naming John Wayne. When her husband asked why she didn't choose him, she replied, "Could you fight off wild animals or build a hut for me from driftwood?"

After thinking it over, the young husband said, "Come to think of it, I guess I would choose John Wayne, too,"

First Nighters

A Houston rabbi received this thank-you letter from a bridegroom he'd married: "Dear Rabbi, I want to thank you for the beautiful way you brought my happiness to a conclusion."

British radio personality Kenneth Horne: "On my way here, my car bumped into one that had a 'Just Married' notice on it. There was no damage, but I apologized to the fellow inside anyway. He replied: 'Oh, it doesn't matter. It's been one of those days!'"

When the minister performing the wedding ceremony in a Reading, Pennsylvania, church asked, "Wilt thou take this woman as thy wedded wife?" the groom called out clearly, "I wilt."

Wedding guest to groom: "Congratulations! . . . You'll be hearing a great deal about me. . . . I'll be the fellow she should have married. . . ."

A young bride-to-be sent us this thank-you note: "Dear Agnes and Cecil: If there's anything we need most, it's sheets—and such lovely ones! I wish we didn't have to wait until after the wedding to use all our new things."

A man wrote to the Credit Bureau of Salem, Massachusetts: "Sorry this bill has remained unpaid for so long. I've been married and have been on my honeymoon. As soon as I get on my feet, I'll be in to make a payment."

Points of View

W. C. Fields: There may be some things better than sex, and some things may be worse. But there is nothing exactly like it.

In a crowded elevator a man standing in front of a Jayne-Mansfield-type passenger called back, "Would you please stop pushing?"

"I'm not pushing," the girl protested. "I'm breathing."

A quiz emcee asked a contestant to "name a great timesaver."

"Love at first sight," she replied.

Clerk describing men's after-shave lotion: "Women adore it. It smells like a charge plate."

Er-a, Dad," stammered the youth, "I'm in love with a girl, and—"

"Well," interrupted his blasé parent, "you couldn't have made a better choice."

An airline pilot getting a medical checkup was asked by the doctor, "When was your last sex experience?"

The pilot said, "1955."

"So long ago?" the doctor asked.

The pilot glanced at his watch and said, "Well, it's only 21:15 now."

Tribesman, about disconsolate Arab chieftain sitting in his harem: "He's sulking because he couldn't buy the Miss America Pageant."

After several mistakes by the crew filming a chamber-music concert for the British Broadcasting Corporation, the director was overheard whispering to the conductor, "Could the young lady in the miniskirt be persuaded to ride her cello sidesaddle?"

My elderly uncle and I were sitting on our front porch when a young woman in a revealing dress sauntered by. Noting the eager look in my uncle's eye, I said, "Now don't be entertaining evil thoughts."

"I'm not," he snapped. "They're entertaining me."

Girl at record player to boy friend on couch: "Now don't misunderstand. It isn't music to do anything by!"

One girl in low-cut dress to another at military ball: "Don't dance with the general—his medals are cold."

Royal messenger to two cannibals about to heave a luscious blonde into the kettle: "Hold it! The chief wants his breakfast in bed."

The director of an art museum, told that his office needed a new machine, had spent the morning in a salesroom watching demonstrations of equipment. Afterward, in the crowded elevator, a woman screeched as a young man pinched her.

"Thank goodness," said the director, "some things in America are still done by hand."

Just Looking

Customer to topless waitress: "A dozen oysters, please—one at a time."

At a neighborhood dance a young man was eying an attractive young lady. He looked her over from head to toe, evidently trying to decide whether to ask her to dance. Finally the girl swept by him and asked, "Well, did I pass my physical?"

A GI told Groucho Marx that he was looking for a girl who didn't drink, smoke, swear or have any bad habits.

"What for?" asked Groucho.

Father to small boy dragging top half of bikini bathing suit along beach: "Now show Daddy *exactly* where you found it. . . ."

A couple of young nuclear physicists from Cal Tech were sitting in a Hollywood night spot when a lavishly endowed starlet came in. As she walked past their table, one of them whistled and commented, "Now there's an arrangement of molecules for you!"

Men do make passes at girls who wear glasses. It depends on their frames.

At the beach, one bathing beauty to another bringing back refreshments: "Spot any *Wall Street Journals* on the way?"

You can always tell when a woman's looking for a husband—she's either single or married.

My guest from Japan commented on the attractive girl who took our order when we stopped for lunch in Rocky Mountain National Park. "All American girls are beautiful," he said.

"Japanese girls are very pretty, too," I said.

"Ah, but not so three-dimensional as American girls," was his fervent reply.

Host introducing man to woman wearing a strapless gown: "This is Professor Schmertz, authority on structural engineering. He wants to ask you something."

Evangelist Billy Graham told a Richmond, Virginia, audience that actress Elizabeth Taylor was more to be pitied than censured. He suggested that his followers pray for her.

From the back of the auditorium, a listener responded audibly. "I've been praying for her for years," he said, "—but I never get her."

Girl at cocktail party to middle-aged wolf: "All right, Mr. Jones, so you can read me like a book—but would you mind not thumbing the pages!"

Columnist Bill Gold claims that when Caesar first saw Cleopatra, he exclaimed: "Wow! A perfect XXXVI!"

When my brother gave a well-proportioned young thing the eye, his not-as-well-endowed girl friend began her familiar lamentation, "Oh, I wish I had a figure."

"But you do, dear," my brother reassured her. "You have a perfect figure one."

Wife, on beach, to husband who is supposedly reading but is slyly eying nearby bikini-clad lovelies: "Those *aren't* your reading glasses!"

This
Imperfect
Vessel:
HUMAN FRAILTY

A PROPOS of "Identity Crises" (see below), Franklin P.
Adams, after a long, grueling, all-night poker session
of the Thanatopsis Chowder and Marching Society,
tottered out into the gray light of early dawn. A little newsboy rushed up to sell him a morning paper. Frank looked at
him severely and said, "My boy, you're far too young to be
keeping such late hours." As for the perennial absent-
minded professor story, there's the old one about the learned

gentleman who kept lurching along the street with one foot on the curb, the other in the gutter. His face grew more and more worried. Finally he muttered: "I knew it would happen. Locomotor ataxia." Familiar as it may be, I'm glad the editors have included James Thurber's classic piece, "The Secret Life of Walter Mitty." It depicts, of course, the secret life of all of us, and utters at least one of the last words about the human ego. Another last word is W. S. Gilbert's "You've no idea what a poor opinion I have of myself—and how little I deserve it."

Absent in Mind Only

I NEVER REMEMBER A NAME BUT I ALWAYS FORGET A FACE
CORNELIA OTIS SKINNER

I AM CONTINUALLY amazed at the emphasis there is in this country on the desperate importance of knowing a person's name. Not merely knowing it, but showing off the fact by repeating it over and over in a manner both eagerly precocious and completely unnecessary. The way our bright business boys intersperse their conversations with "Yes, R.B.," "You're a card, R.B." is curiously reminiscent of the old vaudeville "That was

Elmer" telephone routine. If I sound somewhat sour on this subject, it's because I am. I am totally unable to remember names. And all too frequently I don't even remember a face. Or I remember it attached to the wrong body.

It isn't that people don't make an impression on me. They do, and sometimes it's a whale of an impression. Furthermore, once I've identified an individual, even someone I hardly know, I can carry on in a manner that would rate me a *summa cum laude* at any Dale Carnegie success school, giving forth with how lovely it is to see them *again,* and how I did enjoy that lobster Newburg, and how is that charming Mrs. Snooks. However, let Mrs. Snooks turn up sometime later in a locale other than the one in which she rightfully belongs and I wouldn't know her from Mrs. Doakes.

For an itinerant member of the theatrical profession, people are always turning up. Friends, relatives and chance acquaintances —particularly those chance acquaintances who don't take into account the passage of years. Persons whose hair was once raven shouldn't suddenly arrive with pure-white hair or, what's even worse, with no hair at all, and say "You know, you haven't changed a bit . . ." without risking the rejoinder of "Well, toots, *you* sure have!"

Such was the situation last winter in a Midwestern city when there burst into my dressing room a handsome, smartly dressed woman with the glad cry of *"Darling!* I'll bet you never expected to see me here!" She was so right. I never expected to see her anywhere, for I hadn't the remotest idea who she was. She did look vaguely familiar and I managed to force out a "For heaven's sake, hello!" and to assume an expression of delighted astonishment. Beaming with glee, she burbled "Can you *believe* it? After all these years?" I said no I couldn't, and hoping for an enlightening clue, added, "Just how many years *is* it?"

"Oh!" she cried in mock dismay. "Don't let's say!" We didn't. "All you have to do is look at this!" and she patted her chic hairdo. The color was gray with a dash of bluing. I wigged her mentally . . . blond, brown, red . . . with no resulting glimmer.

As we floundered along, she told me that I looked wonderful and I told her that she did too, on the likelihood that she probably did. She recalled what great old fun we'd had that time and I restrained the impulse to ask *what* time and *what* great old fun and who in heaven's name is *we?* Mercifully she had a commuters' train to catch, for suddenly she glanced at her watch, leapt to her feet, gave me a good-by hug and said, "George sends his love."

"Dear George!" I responded warmly. "Do give him mine!"

My stage manager, who overheard our parting words, asked me later who my good friend was and I had to admit that his guess was as good as mine. Ever since, he and I have adopted the phrase "George sends his love" as a code signal for situations of peculiar bafflement.

The persons who present the worst problems are those who refuse to stay in their associated setting and still expect one to know them. I once spent several delightful hours in the home of a charming lady from Princeton, Illinois. What her name is I couldn't possibly tell you. When one evening in New York she put in an appearance backstage, it was clear to me that her face had been forgotten, too. I am afraid this was all too clear to her, for after I had floundered vaguely about, the kindly lady came to my aid. "Princeton. Remember?"

I said, "Why of course!" and dutifully concentrated my thoughts on the Athens of New Jersey, the ivy-wreathed buildings of Old Nassau, the people there whom I knew—even those I never knew, Dr. Einstein and Woodrow Wilson. Not a glimmer. The visit was strained, and the poor lady left somewhat abruptly. One minute after her departure the light dawned and with a loud cry of "Princeton, Illin*ois*!!!" I rushed out after her to the stage door. But by then she was engulfed in the Broadway shuffle.

Once on an Italian train I ran into a distinguished-looking Frenchman who obviously knew me, for as I entered the compartment (first class) he jumped to his feet and bowed. I had the feeling that I knew him too so I bowed back. We uttered the French equivalent of "Fancy meeting you here," and thereupon entered into a sprightly conversation.

He was, it seemed, on his way to visit a cousin near Como. We talked of the beauties of northern Italy, of the international situation, and of the legs of Josephine Baker. That is, he talked. I was too distracted trying to think who he was to contribute more than monosyllabic responses. At lunch we shared the same table and I found myself accepting his offer of a liqueur. His attitude was one of punctilious decorum.

Where had I met this elegant monsieur? Crossing on the *Ile de France?* At the American Embassy in Paris? As the train pulled into Turin, I admitted with what I hoped was pretty confusion that I was *désolée* to be such an *imbécile,* I knew him well of course, but would he enlighten me as to where we'd last met? He said certainly, and mentioned the modest Left Bank hotel which I usually patronize. "I am the concierge there," he added, "and many times I have handed Madame her letters and messages."

Many persons in mufti, as it were, are somewhat of a shock. The hospital nurse whom one has seen only in starched uniform and cap suddenly emerging from a swimming pool with wet hair and bare midriff produces the impression of a renegade nun who has just jumped over the wall. And one night at the opera I nearly dropped in my tracks when I learned that the glorious creature in white tie and tails was the surgeon whom last I had beheld in white skullcap and butcher blouse, bending over my bed of pain to admire the fine needlework he had done on my abdomen. Truth to tell, he didn't know me either.

Sometimes I do remember a face and it proves to be that of someone I've never met in my life. This can be extremely disconcerting. There was that time I sat down at a dining-car table opposite a white-bearded gentleman whose magnificent features were strikingly familiar. I was saved from exclaiming "Well for the love of Mike, look who's here!" only by the timely arrival of the steward who bowed deferentially and asked "What will it be today, Mr. Chief Justice?" It was Charles Evans Hughes.

My faulty memory worries me, although I'm really not losing any sleep over it. What I am losing, I suppose, is friends, and I also suppose I should do something about it. There are those memory courses. But come to think of it, there are quite a few faces I'd prefer not to remember. So maybe, in spite of everything, I'm just as well off.

———— • ————

John Dewey was every bit as absent-minded as professors are supposed to be. He was walking across a college campus with a friend one day when a little boy came up and asked him for a nickel. Dewey gave him one, but afterward he said somewhat irritably to his friend, "The trouble with the boys in this city is that they're always asking you for money."

"But isn't that your son?" the friend asked.

Dewey looked around. "Why, yes," he said, "I guess it is."

———— • ————

Sunbathing at Laguna Beach, my friend and I saw an elderly man approach the water's edge and start to wade in. We noticed he was wearing an expensive-looking wrist watch and my friend called out to him. The man thanked us for the warning, took off his watch, put it in a small pocket in his trunks and waded on into the surf.

Dwight Morrow once got on a suburban train and could not find his ticket. The conductor recognized him and said, "That's all right, Mr. Morrow, you can give us the ticket some other time."

"It may be all right for you, young man, but how am I to know where I'm going?"

I never forget a face or a name;
The bothersome thing in my case is:
The names I remember are seldom the same
As those that belong with the faces.

The late Norbert Wiener, professor of mathematics at M.I.T., was crossing a Cambridge quadrangle one afternoon when a student stopped him to discuss a problem. The professor graciously answered the student's question and then asked, "Which way was I going when you stopped me?"

"You were walking *that* way, sir," said the student, pointing.

"Oh, then I've had lunch," Professor Wiener murmured and continued on his way.

———— • ————

"You must help me, doctor," said the patient to the psychiatrist. "I can't remember anything for more than a few minutes. It's driving me crazy."

The psychiatrist asked gently, "How long has this been going on?"

"How long has what been going on?" replied the man.

The new young butcher prided himself on remembering names, but for some reason "Dressler" seemed to give him trouble, and I always had to tell him my name before he could write out the slip. One day I told him just to remember "Dress" and add "ler" to it. Because I'm a large person and take a good-sized dress, I said jokingly, "Just remember that it's the biggest thing about me."

The next day, when I stepped up to the counter, he greeted me cheerily with: "Good afternoon, Mrs. Butler!"

Never Too Old

LET'S NOT CLIMB THE WASHINGTON MONUMENT TONIGHT
OGDEN NASH

LISTEN, children, if you'll only stop throwing peanuts and bananas into my cage,
I'll tell you the facts of middle age.
Middle age is when you've met so many people that every new person you meet reminds you of someone else,
And when golfers' stomachs escape either over or under their belts.
It is when you find all halfbacks anthropoidal
And all vocalists adenoidal.
It is when nobody will speak loud enough for you to hear,
And you go to the ball game and notice that even the umpires are getting younger every year.

It's when you gulp oysters without bothering to look for pearls,
And your offspring cannot but snicker when you refer to your
   classmates as boys and your bridge partners as girls.
It is when you wouldn't visit Fred Allen or the Aga Khan if it
   meant sleeping on a sofa or a cot,
And your most exciting moment is when your shoelace gets tan-
   gled and you wonder whether if you yank it, it will come clean
   or harden into a concrete knot.
Also, it seems simpler just to go to bed than to replace a fuse,
Because actually you'd rather wait for the morning paper than
   listen to the eleven o'clock news,
And Al Capone and Babe Ruth and Scott Fitzgerald are as remote
   as the Roman emperors,
And you spend your Saturday afternoons buying wedding presents
   for the daughters of your contemporers.
Well, who wants to be young anyhow, any idiot born in the last
   forty years can be young, and besides forty-five isn't really old,
   it's right on the border:
At least, unless the elevator's out of order.

——————— • ———————

The older I get the less I pine for
Things that I have to stand in line for.

Worried over what to give his girl for her birthday, my
grandson asked his mother for help. "Mom," he said, "if
you were going to be 16 years old tomorrow, what would
you want?"
   "Not another thing!" was her heartfelt reply.

My wife turned 50 last year, and for her birthday dinner
she arranged candles on the cake to form the numerals 5
and 0. This year the cake was decorated with a 4 and 9.
   "I've begun my countdown," she explained.

You'll always stay young if you live honestly, eat slowly,
sleep sufficiently, work industriously, worship faithfully—
and lie about your age.

——————— • ———————

A mother reports that as she was helping her blissful teen-age daughter get ready for her first formal dance, the girl turned to her and asked, "Mother, did they have parties like this when you were alive?"

The ones who usually manage to get the most out of middle age are the grandchildren.

Social Security agent to applicant: "*Feeling* 65 isn't enough. You must *be* 65."

Not-quite-so-young single woman to another: "At my age I no longer plan the future. I *plot* it."

It may be true that *life* begins at 40, but everything else starts to wear out, fall out or spread out.

The middle-aged man was shuffling along, bent over at the waist, as his wife helped him into the doctor's waiting room. A woman in the office viewed the scene in sympathy. "Arthritis with complications?" she asked.

The wife shook her head. "Do-it-yourself," she explained, "with concrete blocks."

One man to another: "I like the old days best—I was younger then."

Middle-aged husband to equally middle-aged wife, staring at siren surrounded by all the other men in the room: "I don't know what they see in her, either—think I'll take a closer look."

Maybe they call it middle age because that's where it shows first.

Matron, looking at modern outdoor furniture, to clerk: "Whatever happened to lawn furniture you could get up out of?"

Identity Crises

THE SECRET LIFE OF WALTER MITTY
JAMES THURBER

WE'RE GOING through!" The commander's voice was like thin ice breaking. He wore his full-dress uniform with the heavily braided cap pulled down rakishly over one cold gray eye. "We can't make it, sir. It's spoiling for a hurricane if you ask me." "I'm not asking you, Lieutenant Berg," said the commander. "Throw on the power lights! Rev her up to 8500! We're going through!" The pounding of the cylinders increased: ta-pocketa-pocketa-*pocketa-pocketa*. The commander stared at the ice forming on the pilot window. He walked over and twisted a row of complicated dials. "Switch on No. 8 auxiliary!" he shouted. "Full strength in No. 3 turret!" The crew, bending to their various tasks in the huge eight-engine Navy hydroplane, looked at each other and grinned. "The Old Man'll get us through," they said to one another. "The Old Man ain't afraid of hell!"

"Not so fast! You're driving too fast!" said Mrs. Mitty. "What are you driving so fast for?"

"Hmmm?" said Walter Mitty. He looked at his wife, in the seat beside him, with shocked astonishment. She seemed grossly unfamiliar, like a strange woman who had yelled at him in a crowd. "You were up to 55," she said. "You know I don't like to go more than 40. You were up to 55."

Walter Mitty drove on toward Waterbury in silence, the roaring of the SN202 through the worst storm in 20 years of Navy flying fading in the remote, intimate airways of his mind. "You're tensed up again," said Mrs. Mitty. "It's one of your days. I wish you'd let Dr. Renshaw look you over."

Walter Mitty stopped the car in front of the building where his wife went to have her hair done. "Remember to get those overshoes while I'm having my hair done," she said. "I don't need overshoes," said Mitty. She put the mirror back into her bag. "We've been through all that," she said, getting out of the car. "You're not a young man any longer." He raced the engine a little. "Why don't you wear your gloves? Have you lost your gloves?" Walter Mitty reached in a pocket and brought out the gloves. He put them on, but after she had gone into the building, he took them off again. He drove around the streets aimlessly for a time, and then drove past the hospital on his way to the parking lot.

. . ."It's the millionaire banker, Wellington McMillan," said the pretty nurse. "Yes?" said Walter Mitty, removing his gloves slowly. "Who has the case?" "Dr. Renshaw and Dr. Benbow, but there are two specialists here: Dr. Remington from New York and Dr. Pritchard-Mitford from London. He flew over." A door opened and Dr. Renshaw came out, distraught and haggard. "Hello, Mitty," he said. "We're having the devil's own time with McMillan, the millionaire banker and close personal friend of Roosevelt. Obstreosis of the ductal tract. Tertiary. Wish you'd take a look at him." "Glad to," said Mitty.

In the operating room there were whispered introductions: "I've read your book on streptothricosis," said Pritchard-Mitford, shaking hands. "A brilliant performance, sir." "Thank you," said Walter Mitty. "Didn't know you were in the States, Mitty," grumbled Remington. "Coals to Newcastle, bringing Mitford and me here for a tertiary." "You are very kind," said Mitty. A huge, complicated machine, connected to the operating table, began to go pocketa-pocketa-pocketa. "The new anesthetizer is giving way!" shouted an intern. "There's no one in the East who knows how to fix it!"

"Quiet, man," said Mitty, in a low, cool voice. He sprang to the machine, which was now going pocketa-pocketa-queep-pocketa-queep. He began fingering delicately a row of glistening dials. "Give me a fountain pen!" he snapped. Someone handed him a fountain pen. He pulled a faulty piston out of the machine and inserted the pen in its place. "That will hold for ten minutes," he said. "Get on with the operation."

A nurse hurried over and whispered to Renshaw. Mitty saw the man turn pale. "Coreopsis has set in," said Renshaw nervously. "If you would take over, Mitty?" Mitty looked at him, at the grave, uncertain faces of the two great specialists. "If you wish," he said. They slipped a white gown on him; he adjusted a mask and drew on thin gloves; nurses handed him shining. . . .

"Back it up, Mac! Look out for that Buick!" Walter Mitty jammed on the brakes. "Wrong lane, Mac," said the parking-lot attendant, looking at Mitty closely. "Gee. Yeh," muttered Mitty. He began cautiously to back out of the lane marked "Exit Only." "Leave her sit there," said the attendant. "I'll put her away." The attendant vaulted into the car, backed it up with insolent skill, and put it where it belonged.

They're so damned cocky, thought Walter Mitty, walking along Main Street; they think they know everything. Once he had tried to take his chains off, outside New Milford, and he had got them wound around the axles. A man had had to come out in a wrecking car and unwind them, a young, grinning garageman. Since then Mrs. Mitty always made him drive to a garage to have the chains taken off. Next time, he thought, I'll wear my right arm in a sling; they won't grin at me then. They'll see I couldn't possibly take the chains off myself. He kicked at the slush on the sidewalk. "Overshoes," he said to himself, and he began looking for a shoestore.

When he came out into the street again, with the overshoes in a box under his arm, Walter Mitty began to wonder what the other thing was his wife had told him to get. He hated these weekly trips to town—he was always getting something wrong. Kleenex, he thought, razor blades? No. Toothpaste, toothbrush, bicarbonate, carborundum, initiative and referendum? He gave it up. But she would remember. "Where's the what's-its-name?" she would ask. "Don't tell me you forgot the what's-its-name." A newsboy went by shouting something about the Waterbury trial.

. . . "Perhaps this will refresh your memory." The district attorney thrust a heavy automatic at the quiet figure on the witness stand. "Have you ever seen this before?" Walter Mitty took the gun and examined it expertly. "This is my Webley-Vickers 50.80," he said calmly. An excited buzz ran around the courtroom. The judge rapped for order. "You are a crack shot with any sort of firearm, I believe?" said the district attorney insinuatingly.

"Objection!" shouted Mitty's attorney. "We have shown that the defendant could not have fired the shot. We have shown that he wore his right arm in a sling on the night of the 14th of July." Walter Mitty raised his hand briefly, and the bickering attorneys were stilled. "With any known make of gun," he said evenly, "I could have killed Gregory Fitzhurst at 300 feet *with my left hand.*" Pandemonium broke loose in the courtroom. A woman's scream rose above the bedlam, and suddenly a lovely, dark-haired girl was in Walter Mitty's arms. The district attorney struck at her savagely. Without rising, Mitty let the man have it on the point of the chin. "You miserable cur!". . .

"Puppy biscuit," said Walter Mitty. The buildings of Waterbury rose up out of the misty courtroom and surrounded him again. A woman who was passing laughed. "He said 'puppy biscuit,'" she said to her companion. "That man said 'puppy biscuit' to himself." Walter Mitty hurried on. He went into an A&P. "I want some biscuits for small, young dogs," he said to the clerk. "Any special brand, sir?" The greatest pistol shot in the world thought a moment. "It says 'Puppies Bark for It' on the box," said Walter Mitty.

His wife would be through at the hairdresser's soon. She would want him to be waiting for her as usual in the hotel lobby. He found a big leather chair facing a window, and he put the overshoes and the puppy biscuit on the floor beside it. He picked up an old copy of *Liberty* and sank down into the chair. "Can Germany Conquer the World Through the Air?" Walter Mitty looked at the pictures of bombing planes and of ruined streets.

. . . "The cannonading has got the wind up in young Raleigh, sir," said the sergeant. Captain Mitty looked up at him through tousled hair. "Get him to bed," he said wearily. "With the others. I'll fly alone." "But you can't sir," said the sergeant anxiously. "It takes two men to handle that bomber, and Von Richtman's circus is between here and Saulier." "Somebody's got to get that ammunition dump," said Mitty. "I'm going over. Spot of brandy?" He poured a drink for the sergeant and one for himself.

War thundered and whined around the dugout and battered at the door. There was a rending explosion, and splinters flew through the room. "A bit of a near thing," said Captain Mitty carelessly. "The box barrage is closing in," said the sergeant. "We only live once, sergeant," said Mitty, with his faint, fleeting smile. "Or do we?" He poured another brandy, tossed it off, then stood up and strapped on his Webley-Vickers automatic. "It's 40 kilometers through hell, sir," said the sergeant. Mitty finished one last brandy. "After all," he said softly, "what isn't?" The pounding of the cannon increased; there was the rat-tat-tatting of machine guns, and from somewhere came the menacing pocketa-pocketa-pocketa of the new flame-throwers. Walter Mitty walked to the door of the dugout, humming *Auprès de ma blonde*. He turned and waved to the sergeant. "Cheerio!" he said. . . .

Something struck his shoulder. "I've been looking all over this hotel for you," said Mrs. Mitty. "Why do you have to hide in this old chair? How did you expect me to find you?" "Things close in," said Walter Mitty vaguely. "What?" Mrs. Mitty said. "Did you get the what's-its-name? The puppy biscuit? What's in that box?" "Overshoes," said Mitty. "Couldn't you have put them on in the store?" "I was thinking," said Walter Mitty. "Does it ever occur to you that I am sometimes thinking?" She looked at him. "I'm going to take your temperature when I get you home," she said.

They went out through the revolving doors that made a faintly derisive whistling sound when you pushed them. At the corner drugstore she said, "Wait here for me. I forgot something. I won't be a minute." She was more than a minute. Walter Mitty lighted a cigarette. It began to rain, rain with sleet in it. He stood up against the wall of the drugstore, smoking. . . .

He put his shoulders back and his heels together. "To hell with the handkerchief," said Walter Mitty scornfully. He took one last drag on his cigarette and snapped it away. Then, with that faint, fleeting smile playing about his lips, he faced the firing squad: erect and motionless, proud and disdainful, Walter Mitty, the Undefeated, inscrutable to the last.

———— • ————

At Mike Romanoff's restaurant in Hollywood, a stranger stopped Fred Astaire and said: "Well, well, Charlie Smith—what happened to you? You used to be fat, now you're skinny. You look shorter, too."

"I'm afraid you've made a mistake," Fred smiled amiably. "I'm not Charlie Smith at all. I'm Fred Astaire."

"So," sneered the other man, "you changed your name, too!"

———— • ————

On several occasions I had been checked out by the same cashier at our local supermarket. She surprised me one day by greeting me with: "Good-morning, Mr. Spiers." I said nothing, since this was not my name. But on subsequent trips she continued calling me Mr. Spiers so I told her my name was Foster. She was good-natured about her error, and I thought we had decided who I was. However, the next time I was in the store, she said to me, "You know, Mr. Spiers, there's a man who comes in here who looks exactly like you."

My grandfather came home from his daily walk in a rather agitated state. "I met Tom Jones," he told me, "and I said, 'How have you been, Jones?'

"And Jones replied, 'Fair to middling, thank you. How have you been, Smith?'

"'Smith!' I said. 'That's not my name!'

"'Nor is my name Jones,' said the other fellow. Then we looked each other over again, and true! It was neither of us!"

A very large man and a smaller one had been long enough at the bar to reach the confidential stage. "Do you know," remarked the large one, "I weighed only three and a half pounds when I was born?"

"No!" said the small man incredulously. "And did you live?"

"Did I live? Boy! You should see me now!"

An old lady dining alone asked the waiter about a gentleman at the next table. "That is Mr. Kreisler, madame," said the waiter.

Delighted, the old lady tripped over to the maestro's table. "May I have your autograph?" she begged. "I've always longed to meet you and tell you what wonderful pleasure you've given me and my husband. You see, we had one of the very first cars you ever made!"

Smiling, Fritz Kreisler wrote on the menu card and returned it to her. It read: "Gratefully yours, Walter P. Chrysler."

Survival of the Fittest

GOING OUT FOR A WALK
MAX BEERBOHM

NOT ONCE in all my life have I gone out for a walk. I have been taken for walks; but that is quite another matter. People seem to think there is something inherently noble and virtuous in the desire to go for a walk, and that they have a right to impose their will on whomever they see comfortably settled in an armchair, reading. "Come out for a walk!" they say in that imperative tone they wouldn't dream of using in any other connection; and you may as well go quietly.

Walking for walking's sake may be as highly laudable as it is held to be; my objection to it is that it stops the brain. Experience teaches me that whatever a fellow guest may have of power to instruct or amuse when he is sitting in a chair, or standing on a hearthrug, quickly leaves him when he takes one out for a walk. The man's face that was so mobile is now set; gone is the light from his fine eyes. He says that A. (our host) is a thoroughly good fellow. We tramp along another furlong or so, and he says that Mrs. A. is a charming woman. Presently he adds that she is the most charming woman he has ever known. We pass an inn. He reads vapidly aloud to me: "The King's Arms. Licensed to sell Ales and Spirits." I foresee that during the rest of the walk he will read aloud any inscription that occurs. We pass "Uxminster.

11 Miles"; and I see far ahead a small notice-board. He sees it too. He keeps his eye on it. And in due course, "Trespassers," he says, "Will Be Prosecuted." Poor man!—mentally a wreck. Luncheon at the A's, however, salves him. Behold him once more the life and soul of the party.

How comes it, this immediate deterioration in those who go walking for walking's sake? I take it that not by his reasoning faculties is a man urged to this enterprise, but by something in him that transcends reason—his soul, I presume.

"Quick march!" raps out the soul to the body.—"Halt! Stand at ease!" interposes the brain. "To what destination, and on what errand," it suavely asks the soul, "are you sending the body?"— "On no errand whatsoever," the soul makes answer, "and to no destination at all. The body is going out because the mere fact of its doing so is a sure indication of nobility, probity, and rugged grandeur of character."—"Very well," says the brain, "I flatly refuse to be mixed up in this tomfoolery. I shall go to sleep till it is over."

The brain then wraps itself up in its own convolutions, and falls into a slumber from which nothing can rouse it till the body has been safely deposited indoors again.

———————— • ————————

Robert Benchley heartily disliked the outdoors. He went to great pains to avoid fresh air. One sunny day in Hollywood a friend called on the humorist and found him under a sun lamp. "Why are you sitting under that?" demanded the friend. He pointed to the sun-drenched lawn. "Why don't you sit out there?"

Said Benchley, recoiling, "And get hit by a meteor?"

A Hollywood reporter asked William Powell how, despite his age, he managed to keep so physically fit.

"I have a swimming pool," the star replied. "Every day I give it a long, crucial look. I think a lot about tennis and I talk a good game of golf. After that I start to worry because I never get enough exercise. Worry makes me lean. Leanness is fitness. And there you have it."

———————— • ————————

Paunchy middle-aged man, perspiring profusely, to other man in businessmen's gym: "The trouble is I'm not in shape to keep fit."

———— • ————

Just before a series of women's physical-fitness classes was due to begin, notices were posted in the local newspaper giving the time and place of the meetings and instructing participants to wear gym shoes and loose-fitting clothes. On opening night, one woman appeared in a skimpy blouse and tight-fitting shorts. Another member commented, "You're probably going to have trouble doing the exercises in those clothes. Remember, we were told to wear loose clothing."

"If I had any clothing that was loose," the first woman retorted, "I wouldn't have joined this class."

———— • ————

FORD'S PHYSICAL UNFITNESS PROGRAM
COREY FORD

MAN I know pulled a muscle in his back on a rowing machine. Another man banged his chin on the floor when both arms collapsed while he was doing push-ups. Still another is hobbling around in a cast because he dropped a barbell on his toe.

This new physical-culture cult is piling up casualties across the country. Everybody's trying to be fit so his clothes will. All you hear these days is the creak of straining joints and crack of flexing knees, punctuated by the dull thud of another victim who lost his grip on the parallel bars. Groups of middle-aged health addicts assemble at dawn in sweat suits and sneakers, set to sally forth for a brisk jog around the park. All but me. When it comes to jogging. I sally a very poor fifth.

The trouble is that the fitness fanatics won't leave the rest of us alone. Don't take a taxi, they insist; walk to work each day. Ignore the elevator, climb those stairs. Spend your lunch hour playing handball or squash. Do your own chores when you get home at night. Spade that garden. Mow that lawn. Haul that barge; tote that bale. Quit drinking, cut out smoking, eat nothing but health foods like yogurt and yeast, and you'll live longer. At least, it will seem longer.

The fanatics have the facts and figures to prove it, too. They'll reel off statistics on the life expectancy of people who don't keep in condition, or whip out a chart showing the relationship between lack of exercise and hormone deficiency, which causes the knees to bend backward. A fitness program will not only increase your vitality, they argue, but will keep you from sagging in front or lagging behind. Try it for a month, and your friends won't know you. (What's more, they won't want to.)

I wouldn't mind so much if the fanatics weren't so smug. There's nobody more condescending than a biceps buff, virtuously sipping tomato juice at a cocktail party while assuring the other guests that he thinks nothing of starting off his day with a three-mile run. (Frankly, I don't think much of it myself.) He's always looking for a chance to demonstrate his prowess. I met one not long ago who proceeded to crush my fingers in an iron grip, and then Indian-wrestled me off balance onto the sofa. "No wonder you're panting," he said as I clambered to my feet. "Look at the shape you're in."

Well, I admit that the shape I am leaves something to be desired. My figure is not outstanding, except around the middle; I have a tendency to slump where I ought to bulge; and I haven't touched my toes since I was a baby. Maybe a program of conditioning would help, I conceded, if only to fasten my top pants button again.

My first problem was to decide which program to follow. One friend suggested that I start off with a series of setting-up exercises: 20 push-ups, ten sit-ups and one throw-up. Someone else urged me to buy a set of barbells. (By the way, whatever became of the old-fashioned dumbbell?) No sooner had I converted my bathroom into a home gymnasium, complete with wallpulls and vibrators and a sauna bath, than all my outdoor friends insisted that I should add a few hours of exercise in the open air. One expert advocated scuba diving; another claimed that the latest thing was mountain climbing.

After listening carefully to their advice, I tallied up the time I'd have to spend each day getting fit. Including 18 holes of golf and a steam bath and massage, which all the experts agreed on, I found that the total came to 23¾ hours, leaving me approximately 15 minutes to read my mail, say hello to the family, and catch a few winks of sleep before tomorrow's workout.

So, in self-defense, I've developed a health plan of my own, which I call Ford's Physical Unfitness Program. Instead of setting-up exercises, my plan, outlined here, substitutes a sitting-down exercise. The only requirements are a comfortable easy chair by the fireplace, a hassock and a pair of house slippers.

Step One: Stand erect with back to chair. Place each hand on an arm of chair behind you, palm downward. Take a deep breath, flex knees, and lower yourself until your rear is planted solidly on the seat cushion. Exhale.

Step Two: Extend both legs straight out before you, and elevate them onto the hassock. Do not use your hands to lift your feet unless absolutely necessary.

Step Three: Lean backward so that your head rests against rear of chair, close both eyes, and let your lower jaw sag until your mouth is hanging open. Breathe in and out gently. If someone in the room is talking, increase volume to a low but steady snore.

There are certain variations of this sitting-down exercise designed to benefit other parts of your body. For example, beckoning to your wife to fetch your house slippers will strengthen your forefinger. Holding a newspaper open before you will develop your upper arms. Tilting a highball glass to your lips now and then builds up your wrists.

Reverse the foregoing directions whenever you get up to mix another highball, or throw a log on the fire, or answer the phone. If you feel you've had enough workout for one day, let the phone ring. Probably it's just another health addict calling, anyway.

Liquor is Quicker

A drunk who had been wandering around Times Square finally went down into the subway at 42nd Street. About half an hour later he emerged at 44th Street and bumped into a friend who had been looking for him. "Where on earth have you been all this time?" the friend asked.

"Down in some guy's cellar," the drunk said. "And, boy, you should see the set of trains he has!"

A drunk walked into an open elevator shaft and fell three stories. Gingerly he stood up, brushed himself off, reseated his hat.

"Dammit," he exclaimed, "I said up!"

A regular customer at a certain bar always ordered two whiskeys, both of which he drank. At first, the bartender asked him why he didn't order a double whiskey. "You don't understand," was the reply. "One is for me and one's for my friend, who's out of town. We always drink together."

One day, the customer, looking very doleful, ordered a single whiskey. The bartender asked sympathetically, "Has your friend passed away?"

"No," the man sighed. "My doctor ordered me to give up drinking."

Wife to hung-over husband on New Year's morning: "How do you want your eggs—scrambled, fried or intravenous?"

Doctor to patient: "I'm switching you to the sober man's diet."

During a recent hot spell in New York, a panhandler collapsed on the street. Immediately a crowd gathered and began offering suggestions.

"Give the poor man a drink of whiskey" a little old lady said.

"Give him some air," said several men.

"Give him a drink of whiskey," said the old lady.

"Get him to a hospital," someone suggested.

"Give him a drink of whiskey," said the old lady.

The babble continued until all at once the victim sat up. "Will you all shut up and listen to the little old lady!" he hollered.

Man, gazing into liquor-store window, to companion: "Remember the fun it was fighting a cold before the anti-histamines?"

An intellectual type we know stopped in at a bar the other day and asked for a martinus. "Don't you mean a martini?" asked the bartender. "If I had wanted two," he replied, "I would have asked for them."

As the crowd of commuters thinned out, the bartender saw an old customer sitting alone at a table muttering to himself. At times he'd laugh heartily and at others cut the air with his hand in a gesture of disgust. As soon as he was free, the bartender went over to the table. "Mr. Benson, what are you doing?" he asked.

"Can't I just sit here and tell myself stories?" asked Mr. Benson.

"Surely," the barkeep soothed him. "But what does that gesture mean?"

"Oh, that," said Mr. Benson, beaming. "That's when I tell myself one I've heard before!"

A fellow still suffering from his adventures of the night before walked into his favorite pub the next day. "Two aspirin," he said to the bartender. "And don't slam the lid on the box."

Two drunks wandered into a zoo and stopped in front of a lion's cage. As they stood watching, the lion suddenly let out a roar.

"C'mon, let's go," said one of the men.

"Go ahead if you want to," the other replied. "I'm gonna stay for the movie."

A woman phoned a tavern and asked for the bartender. "Kindly tell my husband that you have told me that he has just left," she said, and hung up.

There's a bistro which has a shrunken head displayed over the bar. Underneath the head is this sign: "My, that *was* a dry martini."

This Too, Too Solid Flesh

YOU, TOO, CAN REDUCE— BUT WHY BOTHER?

JEAN KERR

FRED ALLEN used to talk about a man who was so thin he could be dropped through a piccolo without striking a single note. Well, I'm glad I never met *him;* I'd hate to have to hear about *his* diet.

When I was a girl—way back in Truman's Administration—it was fun to go to parties. The conversation used to crackle with wit and intelligence because we talked about *ideas*—Gary Cooper in Western movies, the superiority of beer over lotion as a wave-set. Go to a party now and the couple next to you won't talk about anything except their diets—the one they've just come off, the one they're on now, or the one they're going to have to start on Monday if they keep lapping it up like this.

I blame science for the whole business. Years ago when a man began to notice that if he stood up on the subway he was immediately replaced by *two* people, he figured he was getting too fat. So he went to his doctor and the doctor said, "Quit stuffing yourself, Joe." And Joe either stopped or he didn't stop, but at least he kept his big mouth shut. What was there to talk about?

Today, with the science of nutrition advancing so rapidly, there is plenty of food for conversation, if for nothing else. We have the Rockefeller diet, the Mayo diet, high protein diets, low-protein diets, "blitz" diets which feature cottage cheese and something that tastes like thin sandpaper, and so on and on.

Where do people get all these diets? Obviously not from the newspapers. For one thing, you can never catch the newspaper diet when it *starts*. It's always the fourth day of Ada May's Wonder Diet, and after a brief description of a simple slimming exercise that could be performed by anybody who has had five years' training with the ballet, Ada May gives you the menu for the day. One glass of skim milk, eight prunes and three lamb kidneys. This settles the matter for most people.

493

If you have formed the habit of checking on every new diet that comes along, you will find that, mercifully, they all blur together, leaving you with one definite piece of information: French-fried potatoes are out. But once in a great while a diet will stick in your mind.

The best diet I've heard about lately is the simplest. It was perfected by the actor Walter Slezak after years of careful experimentation. You eat as much as you want of everything you don't like. And if you should be in a hurry for any reason (let's say you're still wearing maternity clothes and the baby is eight months old), then you should confine yourself to food that you just plain hate.

Why is the American woman being hounded into starvation in order to duplicate an ideal figure which is neither practical nor possible for a person her age? I'll tell you.

First, it is presumed that when you're thinner you live longer. (In any case, when you live on a diet, it *seems* longer.) Second, it is felt that when you are skin and bones you have so much extra energy that you can climb up and shingle the roof. Third—and this is what the Beauty Editors are really getting at—when you're thin you are so tasty and desirable that strange men will pinch you at the A & P and your husband will not only follow you around the kitchen breathing heavily but will stop and smother you with kisses as you try to put the butter back in the icebox. This—and I hope those in the back of the room are listening—is hogwash.

Think of the happy marriages you know about. How many of the ladies are still wearing size 12? I've been giving this a lot of thought in the last 20 minutes, and what I have discovered is that the women who are being ditched in my own troubled circle are one and all willowy, wandlike and slim as a blade. In fact, six of them require rather extensive padding even to look flat-chested.

The reason, I believe, that men hang onto their well-endowed spouses is because they're comfy and nice to have around the house. In a marriage there is nothing that stales so fast as physical beauty—as we readers of the movie magazines have observed. What actually holds a husband through thick and thick is a girl who is fun to be with. And any girl who has nothing to eat since nine o'clock this morning but three hard-boiled eggs will be about as jolly and companionable as an income-tax inspector.

So I say, ladies, find out why women everywhere are switching from old-fashioned diets to the *modern* way: no exercise, no dangerous drugs, no weight loss. For that tired, run-down feeling, try eating three full meals a day with a candy bar after dinner and pizza at 11 o'clock. Don't be intimidated by pictures of Audrey Hepburn. Just sit there smiling on that size-20 backside and say, "Guess what we're having for dinner, dear? Your favorite —stuffed breast of veal and corn fritters."

———————— • ————————

Doctor to obese patient: "I've done all I can to get your weight down, Mr. Murphy—I suggest that you just learn to be jolly."

Overheard: "I've found this wonderful new diet doctor— he lets you eat anything you want, as long as you pay your bill."

Imbibing while reading *The Drinking Man's Diet,* husband to wife: "My head feels lighter already."

The glass that cheers isn't a full-length mirror.

Reducing-salon ad in the Louisville *Courier-Journal:* "Let us alter your birthday suit."

Stout matron to friend: "I only weigh myself on days when everything goes wrong. I figure those days are ruined anyway."

———————— • ————————

Doctor to stout patient: "You've been swallowing your food again."

Woman diner to friend: "I haven't lost weight since I've been counting calories and carbohydrates, but my arithmetic has improved."

Dowager to waiter, "May I order a little later—my 19-day diet ends in seven minutes."

A Hollywood producer, who had been telling everyone about his diet, was discovered in a restaurant eating a tremendous steak. "What's the idea?" demanded a friend. "I thought you were on a diet."

"I am," said the producer. "This is just to give me the strength to continue it!"

Plump woman on scales, to friend: "I'm afraid I've come to the destiny which ends our shapes!"

Leave It to the Ladies:
FEMININE VIEWPOINTS

THE MAJOR OR CENTRAL ADVANTAGE in the existence of two sexes rather than one needs no demonstration, even though it is frequently demonstrated. A minor advantage is that it is responsible for a never-ending stream of humor based on the absurdities either sex is alert to detect in the other. If there were only a single sex, or if the individual contained both sexes in him/her/self, the field of humor would be considerably restricted. It is hard to think of certain mollusks, for example, as capable of producing a molluscoidal Mark Twain or Robert Benchley.

I cannot conceive of the Deity as gloomy or vengeful. "Male and female created He them"—the very idea could have occurred only to Someone with a sense of humor. At any rate each sex has been hilariously identifying the other's weaknesses for so long that by rights complete mutual disillusionment should have set in. Happily this is not the case.

It is only fair to point out, however, that women may not be quite so funny as we think they are, because in most cases the "we" is masculine. That is to say, there being more male humorists than female humorists, the ladies tend to get the short end of the stick of laughter. That is why the editors deserve a pat on the back for including below the amusing piece by Elsie McCormick. She manages to make fun of her sex in such a way as to make clear their superiority—a typical female trick, as a male would say. But perhaps all of us, women or men, who are given to sage remarks about the more charming sex should keep in mind Bertrand Russell's warning: "For my part I distrust *all* generalizations about women, favorable and unfavorable, masculine and feminine, ancient and modern."

Equal Rites

The women's liberation movement has liberated some women from hats, shoes, stockings, slips and bras. The next thing you know they'll be complaining because they have nothing to wear.

---•---

Editor & Publisher revealed a clue to the extent of the inroads the women's liberation movement is making; "Reporters and copy readers on the Washington *Post* and the Washington *Star* have been told by their managing editors to watch their language when they write about women. They are not to use adjectives such as 'pert,' 'cute,' or 'dimpled'; in fact, they are adjured to avoid use of descriptive words which would not be used if men were involved."

As one newsman put it: "Well, there goes double-breasted."

Women's lib wants to change the rules of poker so four queens beat four kings.

---•---

HOW TO ENRAGE
THE NEW WOMAN
ART BUCHWALD

THE WOMEN'S liberation people take themselves very seriously, and well they might. It's very hard to say anything to them without getting them very mad. While I have no idea what you *should* say to someone in women's lib, here are some of the things you should *not* say:

"Well, now that you've got your college degree, I suppose you're going to find yourself a husband."

"Have you heard the latest one about the woman driver who. . . ."

"I suppose if you take this job, you'll probably become pregnant."

"For a woman, you play very well."

"There's a gal in our office who is as good at selling as any man."

"I beg your pardon, ma'am, is the head of the house home?"

"Don't feel bad, I even know men who don't understand it."

"No, sit down and join us. We have nothing important to say."

"I met this woman doctor the other day, at the hospital, and she really seemed to know what she was doing."

But if you really want to see her climb the wall, start singing: "You've come a long way, baby. . . ."

---∙---

If a woman ever makes the White House, will the presidential plane be called the Suffrajet?

I happened to be right behind two businessmen and one young woman—apparently a secretary—who arrived at the door of an office building simultaneously. One of the men passed through, but the second hesitated. Sensing his uncertainty, the young woman piped up, "You go ahead— I'm liberated."

During a social affair at a Navy base, the cocktail conversation turned to the current women's liberation movement. Someone repeated the story about the suffragettes during the early 1900s, in which an old campaigner heartened her young recruits with: "Just pray to God. She'll help you."

I discounted this tale as the sort of sexual chauvinism that went out as women's rights came in, 50 or more years ago, until I went to the base gas station the next day. Here the attendants are all women—wives and daughters of base personnel. A big strapping girl approached my car, put her head in the window and asked, "Fill him up?"

A girl confided to her friend at lunch that she had just joined women's lib. The other wanted to know what kind of liberation she was looking for. "I want to get married," she said, "and not have to work anymore."

It Figures

THE WOMAN'S WAY
DICK ASHBAUGH

When I build my better world, I know one thing that is going to be outlawed. That's woman's intuition.

Take the little matter of starting the car on a cold morning. I am standing in the garage, already 20 minutes late for work, glaring at this large hunk of inanimate metal. I have primed the carburetor, checked the plugs and filed the points. At this point my wife walks in. "The license plate looks loose to me," she says. "That's probably why it won't start." In icy silence I tighten the license plate and step on the starter. The car not only starts but the dashboard clock starts ticking and the dome light, which hasn't worked for four years, suddenly shines like a little star in the sky.

That's woman's intuition.

If the radio goes on the blink it is foolish to worry about the tubes or transformer. You slam the desk drawer three times and in comes N.B.C. If my electric shaver doesn't work, do I worry? No. I go down in the basement and kick a certain water pipe. Sometimes I fail to kick the right pipe and have to be led down again and shown, but it always works. If the furnace goes off suddenly, I just reach up and put a drop of cologne on the thermostat. "I discovered that last winter," my wife informs me calmly.

Occasionally I get a little confused. Yesterday, for instance, I was tinkering in my workshop, and the electric drill wouldn't work. "Dear," I sang out, "would you know why the electric drill isn't working?"

"Certainly," she called from some place overhead. "You'll have to change your shoes."

Reluctant to tramp all the way upstairs, I searched around until I found an old pair of tennis sneakers. I put them on but still the drill didn't work. Just then my wife came downstairs. "What," she said, "are you doing in those old tennis sneakers?"

"I changed them so the drill would work," I said, and then added triumphantly, "but it doesn't!"

"Of all the egg heads," she moaned. "I said change the fuse. It blew out yesterday morning. Who ever heard of making a drill work by changing your shoes!"

Of course nobody ever had.

---•---

Woman, shopping for wallpaper, to clerk: "Now we're getting somewhere—that's the exact opposite of what I want."

Woman, getting estimate for auto repairs, to mechanic: "Well, what would it cost *without* parts and labor?"

---•---

---•---

In a Chicago restaurant one woman was overheard saying to another: "Why don't you go to him in a perfectly straightforward way and lie about the whole thing?"

A friend of mine burst into my house one morning and stormed indignantly: "I'm so mad at Jim I don't know what to do!"

"Why?"

"Last night I dreamed that some blonde hussy was flirting with him, and he was purring like a kitten."

"Oh, Helen," I said, "it was only a dream."

"Well," she exploded, "if he acts like that in *my* dreams, what in the world do you suppose he does in his?"

Angry wife to husband: "No! Every time we discuss something sensibly, I lose!"

That famed intuition, the feminine hunch, never tells what a husband is having for lunch.

---•---

THOSE FEMININE FOIBLES
FRED SCHWED, JR.

THE chief charges commonly leveled against women are classic: they reach their decisions emotionally instead of logically; they are unpredictable; they usually don't like each other much; they have a genuine fondness for trouble and if there isn't any real trouble they will cook up some out of boredom. Finally, they must have the last word and a disproportionate percentage of the other words.

The amiable rejoinder to all this would seem to be—what's the matter with having a set of persons who are different from men? Also, most of them look nicer, smell nicer, sound nicer and feel nicer than men.

One must also admit that their illogical, feminine conclusions have a dizzy sort of charm about them. How drear a place this world would be if women brought to their problems the cold precision of certified public accountants. Then I would never have heard, as I once did, a pretty woman say to her husband: "I know you don't particularly care for artichokes, dear, but the grocer didn't have any."

That was long ago and far away, but I have never forgotten it. Whenever I am bored I can always wonder what she meant, or what she thought she meant.

Money seems to be the chief commodity about which otherwise intelligent women have the most whimsical notions—as when a wife has persuaded her family to move to a community which they can't afford to live in by a clear thousand a year. In all sincerity and hopefulness such wives will attempt to correct this calamitous miscalculation by trudging all over town to buy pork chops and moth balls several cents cheaper—in disregard of the prosy truisms of arithmetic. If a girl manages to save an average of three cents on a hundred different purchases it is clear that she has worked hard and should get a good mark for effort, but that is all. The ancient adage "Take care of the pennies and the dollars will take care of themselves" seems to have a strong appeal for women. Actually, the thing to take care of is the hundred dollars, or the thousand dollars or, preferably, the million dollars—then the pennies will take care of themselves.

Mom supplied me with my first glimpse of a woman's views on money when I was but a stripling. "Fred," she said earnestly, "you must get the habit of regular saving. Even if you set aside as little as two dollars a week, you'll be amazed at what it will add up to at the end of a year." I tried to explain that if it added up to anything else than $104 I should be so amazed that I would submit a detailed report to Professor Einstein for further study. I hope I did it gently.

I have touched thus far only on the foibles of women. It must also be noted that women's ideas, formulated as they are without the hampering shackles of logic, sometimes leap to brilliant solutions unobtainable by males.

The charming wife of one of my publishers once had a truly unusual publishing idea. It was to be a *Dictionary for Bad Spellers*. She explained that if she thought "philistine" began with an "f," she wasn't going to get far looking it up in an ordinary dictionary. It was the sort of idea that only a woman could dream up. It is also the sort of idea which will make a fortune someday.

And then there was the time my literary agent phoned and told me some fine news. I could hardly wait to phone my wife. "Listen," I blurted, "how would you like to be made love to by a man who has just sold *The Saturday Evening Post* an article for a staggering amount of money?"

Her reaction was far from what I expected. She seemed a little confused and uncertain, and finally said: "Well, uh, really, I don't know. Is he good-looking?"

Shop Talk

Knowing that a friend needed some new bedding, I had been pricing blankets. Suddenly I realized that the clerk must be getting tired of pulling them down from the shelf, where there was now only one left. "I'm terribly sorry," I said. "I'm really not buying today. I was only looking for a friend."

"Well, madam," replied the clerk wearily, "I'll take down the last one if you think he's in it."

Harassed butcher to fussy customer: "Anything else you'd like to know—perhaps the name of the cow?"

Woman customer to furrier: "Could you have the coat delivered with the price tag still on it to my neighbor, Mrs. Flegenheimer, by mistake?"

Housewife in supermarket: "I'm sorry, I can't remember the brand—but I can hum a few bars of the commercial."

When I was being fitted for a new girdle, the saleswoman asked, "Is Madam *quite* comfortable?" Madam was. "Can Madam breathe deeply with ease?" Madam could. "Does Madam feel she could wear this garment all day without discomfort?" Madam did.

"Then," said the clerk, "Madam obviously needs a smaller size."

Matron to greeting-card clerk: "Do you have a get-well card that hints she's not as sick as she thinks she is?"

An angry woman went into a Long Island store and sputtered, "It's about an electric iron I bought—"

"You wish to complain?" asked a clerk.

"Complain!" she retorted. "That I could do by mail. I have come here to *revile* someone!"

Sign in a women's lingerie shop: "Just like the government, we give aid to underdeveloped areas."

Wife to husband: "I'm going to do some shopping. I'll be back in about twenty dollars!"

Salesgirl to woman in fitting room: "On the other hand, Madame doesn't do anything for the dress either."

Shoe clerk to woman customer: "Let's start with the larger sizes and work down until we get that stab of pain we're looking for."

Complaint-department clerk to carping woman shopper: "Madam, it may interest you to know that 19 of our clerks have turned in complaints about *you!*"

Matronly customer to clerk showing her one of those small-model washing machines: "Young man, I want my clothes *agitated,* not just *irked.* "

Shopper trying on coat, to saleslady: "It looks too much like something I could afford."

Ladies' Daze

WOMEN'S SECRET LANGUAGE
ELSIE McCORMICK

THE MOST WIDELY used language in the world has neither name nor dictionary. If you are a woman you've been able to speak it almost since childhood. If you are a man you couldn't learn it if you studied it for 50 years.

I'm referring to the strange combination of words, intonations, faint eyebrow-liftings and well-placed pauses by which women contrive to do such things as carry on a lively little duel in tones so dulcet that a man thinks they are exchanging compliments; comment scorchingly on an unpopular female absentee while giving men the impression she is their bosom friend; make gracious, face-saving gestures—which they have little intention of following through—to ease awkward social situations.

For example, when it's time for guests to go home, the good hostess naturally prefers to give the heave-ho in a delicate manner. This has led to much male befuddlement. Many a man, sitting comfortably by another couple's fireside after a leisurely Sunday luncheon, has been dragged out suddenly by his wife despite the hostess's pleas to remain longer. Maybe the hostess said, "Can't I give you just another spot of coffee?" in a tone that left "before you go" hanging in the air. Being tuned in on the hostess's beam, his wife received a signal that it would be folly to ignore.

Many a male has come to grief through failing to note an allied sort of booby-trap. Picture, for instance, two couples walking home from an afternoon concert. As they are saying good-by outside Couple No. 1's house, Wife No. 1 pleasantly inquires, "Won't you come in for a cup of tea?"

If she had said heartily, "*Do* come in and have tea with us!" Wife No. 2 would probably have accepted. But, to a woman's ear, an overpolite, tentative tone indicates clearly the lay of the landscape.

Unfortunately, before she can give a good excuse for declining, Husband No. 2 may barge in with, "Why, sure! Edie and I haven't a thing to do until dinner." Thus, in a living room strewn with Sunday papers, Couple No. 2 find themselves eating soggy graham crackers served by a tight-lipped hostess, and wishing they were in Baffin Land.

In this field of awkward social situations, the pregnant pause is also extremely convenient. When Mrs. Jones telephones Mrs. Smith to say that her four spinster cousins have just arrived from Medicine Hat and that she'd like to bring them to the Smiths' cocktail party, Mrs. S. doesn't say, "Over my dead body!" Instead she replies cordially, "Oh, yes, bring them by all means"—but she pauses for several seconds before saying it. This lets Mrs. J. know that, unless she wants to be left out of Mrs. S.'s future social plans, she had better buy the cousins a bottle of blackberry cordial and let them have their own party at home.

Another technique which women sometimes use is the reversed-meaning statement. A man should realize that when his wife says, "I don't want a thing for my birthday," she is speaking not English but her ancient mother tongue. What she really means is, "I haven't noticed any packages being sneaked in, so I just want to be sure you don't forget." The number of doghouses occupied by gentlemen who took literally the statement "I don't want a thing . . ." would stretch from here to the Westminster Kennel Club.

If a woman makes a *habit* of expressing herself through opposites, her husband must be careful about agreeing too freely. It's a grave mistake to agree, for instance, when one's wife says of a lady to whom one might have been slightly attentive at a club dance, "That Miss Smith is quite handsome, isn't she?" A husband who says "Yes" to his wife's complimentary remarks about a feminine creature whose name she preceded with "that" does so only at his peril.

Realization of how hard it is even for intelligent men to comprehend what the other sex is really saying came to me soon after I was married. My husband and I attended a party at which two young women fought a round that had all the feminine guests on the edge of their chairs. As soon as we made our departure, I asked my bridegroom what he thought of the battle. He looked blank. "What battle?"

"Why, the one that started when Alice told the brunette who was trying to take over Alice's boy friend that she looked awfully sweet in that dress," I replied. "It was obvious that the brunette had spent a lot of money to make herself into a flaming siren. Telling her that she looked sweet was the same as saying that she was no more dangerous than Little Red Riding Hood, and that her outfit was a complete dud."

My husband, puzzlement in his brow, remarked that they seemed to be getting along all right afterward. "In fact," he said, "the brunette was even running herself down and paying Alice compliments."

"That's what *you* thought," I answered. "Here's one of those compliments. Alice was trying to show up the other girl by talking to her about the new book on Matisse. Then the brunette said, 'You're so brilliant and you've read so much. Poor little me —I just don't know anything. But maybe if I had more evenings at home, I'd do some reading, too.'"

"Well, well!" said my spouse.

Often the meaning of the language relies on intonation alone. Thus a woman can say, "I think she's very nice," and produce any of a dozen different meanings. For instance: (1) said brightly and with a ring of sincerity, it probably means that she really is very nice; (2) a faintly belligerent attitude, with emphasis on the first word, lets the audience know that the lady is so unpopular that only a courageous person would say anything in her favor; (3) a flat, expressionless tone conveys the idea that she's quite a bore; and (4) a slight, insidious drawling of "very nice" announces that the speaker could say a great deal more about her, and probably will when she gets a better chance.

An important rule is that the women participating must never give open sign that they understand what is really being said. Thus no girl would ever reply to an undercover buffet with, "Your dress isn't so much either!" But she may answer "Your dress is pretty, too. My aunt had one like it last year and just loved it."

While the hidden language does produce complications, it has its obvious advantages. But, men, if you think *you'd* like to learn it, I can only suggest that you take up Sanskrit instead. You'd find it much easier.

Two women on a bus tour of Mount Vernón, George Washington's beautiful house on the Potomac, were enthusiastically admiring the various rooms.

"And did you notice, Grace," commented one, "everything's furnished in Early American?"

Bride, gazing at new furniture: "And to think they made all this out of those crinkly little walnuts!"

A friend of mine, settling a relative's estate, had to go through all her belongings. She had been a thrifty soul who had saved everything, labeling each package. My friend thought he had hit a high of some sort when he discovered a package marked "Dress snaps that do not match." But shortly afterward he found a box labeled "String too short to use."

At a dance studio, an overanxious pupil frequently danced the steps without waiting for her tutor's lead. Finally he said, "Pardon me, but aren't you anticipating?"

"Why, Mr. Fowler," she said, "I'm not even married."

Woman to hairdresser: "Tint the gray hair black, color the black hair blond, then put a streak of gray through the center so it will look natural."

Spokesman for matronly threesome to cab driver: "Would you mind driving another ten cents' worth? Three just won't go into four dollars and ten cents evenly."

You Can't Win

She was sick in bed, and her husband, who was fixing her a cup of tea, called out that he couldn't find the tea. "I don't know what could be easier to find," she answered. "It's right in front on the pantry shelf in a cocoa tin marked 'matches'!"

WOMEN HAVE
NO SENSE OF HUMOR
ROBERT THOMAS ALLEN

WHEN I was six I said to a little girl who lived next door, "I bet I can stand two inches away from you and you can't touch me."

"How?" she asked.

"By standing behind a door." I laughed so hard that marbles rolled out of my pants pockets.

The little girl looked at me as if I were a frog. "What's so funny about that? *Nobody* could touch you if you were silly enough to stand behind a door."

In all the years since, I still haven't been able to figure out a woman's sense of humor.

Women either laugh at the wrong time or at the wrong joke or they don't laugh at all. I know one quaint woman who says, "Hmmmm—then what?" after the joke is over; and another who laughs all the way through the joke until the punch line, then sobers up and asks me where I'm living now.

The whole thing, of course, is that the humor in a joke doesn't come from the joke itself, but from a lot of mental pictures, feelings and associations that the joke suggests. A person whose mental pictures are made up of new living-room drapes, little spring suits and Gregory Peck is sure to see things differently from a person whose psyche revolves around main bearings, lake trout and eager-eyed little stenographers.

Women carry around with them a solid ballast of down-to-earth realism that won't let them bounce very high. This is one reason for the dismal way they react to shaggy-dog stories, which derive their humor from being contrary to reason.

One night I came home, and as soon as I got in the door I said, "You want to hear a funny joke, honey? Well, there was a guy, see, and every day he sat in a restaurant with a piece of celery behind his ear. Then one day he put an onion behind his ear, and a man who had been watching him every day couldn't stand it any longer so he went over and said, 'Say, Mac, why you got an onion behind your ear?' and the guy says, 'They didn't have any celery.'" The last words I just got out before I collapsed in helpless mirth.

My wife said, "Why didn't they have any celery?" Then she added absently, "That reminds me. We're having Bill and Grace over tonight. We need some cheese."

That night I told the joke to Bill and Grace. Bill let out a great belly laugh. Grace smiled amiably and said, "Celery is so expensive, too," then turned to my wife and said, "I said to myself just today that if food prices keep going up I'll have to get a husband who makes more money."

At this the two girls went into gales of laughter while Bill and I sat there solemnly sucking olives.

A woman doesn't give herself over to pure play as readily as a man. A man will hold up a business conference to tell a joke. A woman will listen to one only when the dishes are done and the kids are safe with a sitter and she's out for the evening. In between she gives only a fraction of her mind to it, which isn't enough.

I remember one time I said to my wife, "You hear the one about the two old guys sitting in an English club, and one says, 'Sorry to hear you buried your wife this morning, old boy,' and the other says, 'Yes. Had to. Dead, you know.'"

My wife looked at me with the same expression she'd started with. My smile felt as if it were falling off my face in chunks.

"What did she die of?" my wife asked.

"Look," I said, flushing. "One guy says, 'Sorry to hear you buried your wife—'"

"I got that part," my wife said. "And don't start shouting. If you're going to act that way, I don't want to hear the story."

Another reason that things often go flat when a man tries to make a woman laugh is the fact that a man is telling the joke. A woman thinks a man is funny most of the time, although she rarely lets him know. I've seen women go into hysterics telling one another how their husbands shop, or the way they pamper their cars, or behave with blondes. But to have a *man* start thinking he's funny spoils the joke.

I've found that it isn't just *my* wife's sense of humor I can't figure out. I run into the same trouble with other guys' wives. Occasionally at a party when things got rolling and one or two of the girls would tell a couple of jokes of a biological type, I used to dig up one of my own. The girls, including my wife, would all stop laughing. They'd look at their shoes, then one would turn to another and say brightly, "Your hair looks lovely since you let the ends grow."

Now I've learned to tread lightly when it comes to mixing humor with women. I save my jokes until the boys are out in the kitchen watching me measure the drinks, and let the women go on talking about the little summer dress they picked up for next to nothing. Then one drops her voice to a whisper, and soon the others burst into gales of laughter.

Someday, somehow, I'll find out what's so funny.

———— • ————

An architect was having a difficult time with a prospective home-builder. "But can't you give *some* idea," he pleaded, "of the general type of house you want to build?"

"Well—" replied the man hesitantly, "all I know is it must go with an antique doorknob my wife bought in Vermont."

Oh, darling," the wife said tearfully, "the woman next door has a hat exactly like my new one!"

"And I suppose," her husband responded, "that you want me to buy you another?"

"Well, dear," she pointed out, "it would be cheaper than moving."

The easiest way to change a woman's mind is to agree with her.

Women are never satisfied. They are trying either to put on weight, take it off or rearrange it.

———— • ————

Ruth," moaned her long-suffering husband, "you promised you wouldn't buy a new dress."

"I couldn't help it," said the modern Eve, thinking quickly. "The devil tempted me."

"Then why didn't you say, 'Get thee behind me, Satan'?" the husband asked.

"I did," his wife replied sweetly. "And then he whispered over my shoulder, 'My dear, it fits you just beautifully at the back.'"

One evening when I came home from work I found my wife sitting on the porch watching the children play. When I asked about dinner she said the electricity was shut off. "Well, I suppose we'll have to go out to dinner," I said, and she promptly started to phone a baby-sitter. Then it dawned on me that we have a gas stove. "But you don't need electricity to cook!" I exclaimed.

"No," she replied, "but I was going to vacuum before I started dinner."

Driven Crazy

Woman after head-on collision with man motorist: "You had no right to assume that I had made up my mind."

After hearing someone complain about the difficulty of parallel parking, a lady driver insisted there was nothing to it. "You back up," she said, "until you run into the car behind, then go forward until you run into the car ahead."

Harold Coffin: The sneakiest thing about "women drivers" is the way they turn out to be men, right after you've criticized their driving to your wife.

Woman driver to policeman giving her a ticket: "Gosh, I didn't even realize that there were that many miles *in* an hour."

In Milwaukee a man spotted a young woman futilely edging in and out of a tiny parking space. Ten minutes later, thanks to his directions, the car was neatly parked in the space.

"Thank you very much," the woman said. "This is very nice, but I was trying to get out."

Small boy to father: "I wish you'd let Mom drive. It's more exciting."

An uprooted palm tree suspended on chains from a boom truck suddenly swung around into the street and hit a parked car. The driver jumped out and looked over the damage. "You've got to come with me and explain this to my husband," she said to one of the men.

He assured her that his company would pay but the woman was adamant. "It isn't the money," she explained. "I want a witness along when I tell my husband I was hit by a tree."

Woman driver to companion after parking car: "That's close enough . . . we can walk to the curb!"

Husband to wife who's driving: "I don't know where you're going to park — I don't see any empty blocks."

On a Virginia turnpike a toll collector, walking back to his booth with a cup of coffee, stopped to let a car pass through — and watched in amazement as the woman driver smiled warmly at him and dropped her quarter into his coffee.

R. S. V. P.:
AMERICANS ENTERTAIN

O NE OF THE STAPLES of American humor springs from the sense we hypergregarious people have that there is a close association between boredom and partying. (See Leacock and Benchley below.) I think it was Ring Lardner who put this tersely. When asked whether a certain busy hostess was entertaining that evening, he replied, "Not very."

As we gradually move toward the homogenized, all-bugged, Big Brother society of the near future, some of the social friction producing the kind of humor that follows will tend to disappear. For example, the name-forgetter will no longer be embarrassed. In the interests of efficiency individual names will vanish and we will know each other by our Social Security numbers prominently tattooed on our persons. The guest list and duration of all social gatherings will be decided by the computer. The troubles Stephen Leacock talks about will be no more, for there will be a carefully prescribed list of safe topics (both questions and answers) that all of us will have memorized. Indeed each of us may be programmed for all possible conversational eventualities, so that there will be none of the talk-vacuum so feelingly described by Robert Benchley. And the result may be an improvement on cocktail parties.

Be My Guest

FROM HOST TO GUEST IN ONE GENERATION
J. P. McEVOY

IT STARTED back in the sixth grade. I liked the sixth grade, especially Rip Van Winkle and the fun he had up in the Catskill Mountains. Someday, I said to myself, I am going to live in the Catskills. . . .

It was the old spinning wheel that got me. I really bought it rather than the house. Later I found it was a prop. For many years after that I saw the same old spinning wheel in many houses for sale—a technique similar to salting a gold mine. But there was a grand smell of nuts and apples and old wood-smoke about the place. And more than that, I had a Catskill right in the backyard.

I was happy. At last I was away from it all. I will keep it a very small house, I said to myself. One bathroom, one guest room. I am 125 miles away from New York City, I said. I will have no visitors, no guests.

So I fixed up a little corncrib for a studio in which to write plays and novels—novels that would electrify the country. Only the sound of falling leaves to lull me, and a faint distant rumble of ninepins.

Now I know that you *can't* keep a country place from growing. As the children grew larger their room grew smaller. So that meant a wing and a bathroom and that meant more hot water, a larger water heater and a larger furnace, which meant enlarging the basement. And as long as you're enlarging the basement, why not make some storerooms? Also, while you are adding a wing it would be easy to enlarge the kitchen. The old oil stove was too small so we put in a gas stove, which meant a little house for the gas cylinders—and why not make it larger and use it for the pump house?

Now the house had a wing which unbalanced it, so it needed another wing, with a music room. Its windows opened up a view which made a terrace imperative. But a terrace needed a roof to keep off the sun and as long as you had a roof you might as well enclose it, for use in the winter. But not without more radiators, which meant a bigger furnace and a larger basement. Finally I learned to leave a gang of workmen in the basement permanently. They had a camp and lived down there, and the sound of their singing in the evening after a hard day's work was cheerful indeed.

I forgot the guest room we put in the children's wing for the children's guests. So now we had two guest rooms, and in some mysterious way that became known all over New York State. From there it spread rapidly west until in almost any town you went to you saw little groups of people gathered, saying, "You know the McEvoys up in the Catskills have some guest rooms. Why don't we drop in on them on our way east?"

The solution is a guest house, I said to no one in particular. But a builder heard me. There was always a builder standing around. And in no time at all I had a guest house. It had guest rooms and a living room, which I later learned was also a guest room because my guests brought guests and complained sometimes they had no room for them. Some of the guests fixed up a little kitchen in the guest house and lived there unmolested for weeks. They built their own path to the swimming pool. . . .

The swimming pool. While you're at it make it big enough, somebody said. Maybe it was I. So I ordered one sixty feet long and so much dirt came out of the hole I had to hire a gardener to make terraces out of it. After that I had to keep the gardener all year round to take care of the terraces. And then he got married and had a baby so I had to build him a house. The swimming pool was incomplete without a bathhouse and that meant more plumbing which, together with the guest house and the gardener's house, overtaxed the septic tank so we had to put in a bigger septic tank, which meant moving the garden, enlarging the terraces, hiring another gardener and putting a wing on the garage with a room in it for him and another bathroom—which meant more plumbing.

All this time I had no place for guests' cars and no rooms for their servants, so I enlarged the garage, adding more servants' rooms upstairs, which meant more plumbing and a still larger septic tank—so the garden grew larger, which called for more gardeners, more rooms for gardeners—and more plumbing.

The children and their guests had no place to play except a tennis court and a swimming pool, so why not fix up the old barn—very simple, you don't have to spend much money on it. The old barn wound up with a hardwood floor for dancing, a fireplace big enough to roast an ox, a billiard table and a system for amplifying dance records.

The indoor fireplace naturally suggested an outdoor one, so a large stone terrace was added with some ovens and a motor-driven rotisserie which could broil a dozen chickens at once. Since it could, it did. And that meant more guests because waste is a sin.

But what is a country place without horses? It's pretty nearly all right I can tell you now. But then I was young and didn't know, so I bought a horse. But all of us couldn't ride one horse, so soon it was a horse apiece. And you could hardly ask guests to bring their horses from New York. So as we added stalls for more horses we added rooms for more grooms. Sometimes I used to wonder how just one horse could have started that enormous development growing so rapidly in the lower orchard. But I didn't get a chance to do much wondering because I was too busy supporting all this. I built series of studios to work in but the development soon caught up with me and I had to move farther and farther out into the woods. The morning I used to devote to writing were now spent in overseeing this busy subdivision. The afternoons were spent in conferences with my contractors and engineers; the nights in poring over my books—checkbooks.

In the same artless fashion the guest list expanded. Now I had permanent guests, semipermanent guests, weekend guests, guests for the night, drop-in guests, guests on the American Plan, on the European Plan, guests for breakfast only, guests for swimming only, guests for tennis and tea. There were other classifications such as social guests, business guests, old pals, new friends, old teachers, cousins of the governess, shipboard acquaintances and distant relatives. There were guests who came up to see the tulips and were still there to help trim the Christmas tree.

It wasn't exactly a circle—it was a kind of a spiral, and I couldn't see where it was going because I never thought to look. One night I did pause, I remember, because there was a ten-acre parking field near the barn and I was having a party and the servants came in to say there was no more room for the cars. I wondered if maybe this whole thing was getting a little bit out of hand. I left the party several times and went to other parties, but when I came back it was still going with band blaring and lights blazing and the rollicking sound of laughter and screams and breaking glass, occasionally punctuated by the shrill sirens of the state troopers.

That was only one of many times the place was so full I had to go to New York to sleep. Gradually I found myself going there more and more for repose and meditation. And it was then I made a great discovery: that if you really want to be alone and get away from it all take the smallest room in the biggest hotel in the largest city in the world. I remember I woke up and the room was so quiet I was afraid—I wasn't used to this. I called room service and had my breakfast sent up, the waiter clucking over me like a mother hen. I read the morning paper through without one single interruption. There was no knock on the door—no ring on the phone. I was lost in the magic of it all and then I understood—and loved it. I was a guest!

I have stayed in a lot of other places since I became a guest. The hotel room was all right for a start, but I could hardly make a career out of it. Many friends had invited me to be their guest. But I had been too busy being a perfect host. Now I put the same time and energy into being a perfect guest. From host to guest in one generation—that was the complete cycle I had achieved.

When the evening starts to bore me,
My yawns I try to stifle.
I'm too polite to say, "Let's go!"
But how I hope my wife'll.

Tired host saying good night to evening callers at the door in wintry setting: "Yes, we must get together again soon. Have a nice summer."

Wife to husband: "If they don't leave by six, start talking about your fishing trip. If they stay on, give them your political views."

Robert Benchley was staying at the estate of a very boring elderly maiden aunt. She had planned to go strolling with him one afternoon, but he excused himself on account of bad weather. Shortly afterward she saw him sneaking out alone. "Oh, Robert," she cried, "has it cleared up?"
   "Just partly," said Benchley. "Enough for one, but not enough for two."

Husband to wife as they leave friends' house: "I didn't mind the movies of their baby and vacation so much, but those commercials sandwiched in for his insurance company!"

Yawning host, looking at wrist watch, to visiting couple: "Who pays attention to time when good friends are together —why, it's only twelve eighteen and a half."

The Party Line

The cocktail party was in full swing, when the host's small daughter pulled at her father's sleeve. "Daddy," asked the puzzled youngster, "haven't we had this party before?"

THE ART OF OPENING
A CONVERSATION
STEPHEN LEACOCK

O PENING a conversation is really the hardest part. Other communities solve it better than we do. In China, conversation between strangers after introduction is always opened by the question, "And how old are *you?*" This strikes me as singularly apt and sensible. Here is the one thing that is common ground between any two people, high or low, rich or poor—how far are *you* in your pilgrimage in life?

Compare with the Chinese method the grim, but very significant, formula that is employed in the exercise yards of our penitentiaries. "What have you brought?" asks the San Quentin or Sing Sing convict of the new arrival, meaning, "And how long is *your* sentence?" There is the same human touch about this, the same common ground of interest, as in the Chinese formula.

But in our polite society we have as yet found no better method than beginning with a sort of medical diagnosis—"How do you do?" This admits of no answer. Convention forbids us to reply in detail that we are feeling if anything slightly lower than last week, but that though our temperature has risen from 91.50 to 91.75, our respiration is still normal.

Still worse is the weather as an opening topic. For it either begins and ends as abruptly as the medical diagnosis or it leads the two talkers on into a long and miserable discussion of the weather of yesterday, of the day before yesterday, of last month, of last year and the last fifty years.

Let one beware, however, of a conversation that begins too easily. This can be seen at any evening reception, as when the 521 hostess introduces two people who are supposed to have some special link to unite them at once with an instantaneous snap— as when, for instance, they both come from the same town.

"Let me introduce Mr. Sedley," says the hostess. "I think you and Mr. Sedley are from the same town, Miss Smiles. Miss Smiles, Mr. Sedley."

Off they go at a gallop. "I'm so delighted to meet you," says Mr. Sedley. "It's good to find somebody who comes from our little town."

"Oh, yes," answers Miss Smiles. "I'm from Winnipeg, too. I was so anxious to meet you to ask you if you knew the McGowans. They're my greatest friends at home."

"The—who?" asks Mr. Sedley.

"The McGowans—on Selkirk Avenue."

"No-o, I don't think I do. I know the Prices on Selkirk Avenue. Of course you know them."

"The Prices? No. I don't believe I do. You don't mean the Pearsons?"

"No, I don't know the Pearsons. The Prices live near the park."

"No, then I'm sure I don't know them. The Pearsons live close to the college."

This is the way the conversation goes for ten minutes. Both Mr. Sedley and Miss Smiles are getting desperate. Their faces are fixed. Their sentences are reduced to—

"Do you know the Petersons?"

"No. Do you know the Applebys?"

"No."

Then at last comes a rift in the clouds. One of them happens to mention Beverly Dixon. The other is able to cry exultingly: "Beverly Dixon? Oh, yes, rather. At least, I don't *know* him, but I used often to hear the Applebys speak of him."

And the other exclaims with equal delight—"I don't know him very well, either, but I used to hear the Willie Johnsons talk about him all the time."

They are saved. Half an hour later they are still standing there talking of Beverly Dixon.

———————— • ————————

Man to young thing at cocktail party: "I don't fly anywhere, Miss Briggs. I'm space man in an advertising agency."

———————— • ————————

At a cocktail party an enthusiastic rocket scientist was explaining what tremendous advances science had made. "Why, only this year," he said, "we sent several mice into outer space."

A bejeweled dowager, obviously unimpressed, remarked, "Isn't that an awfully expensive way to get rid of them?"

Wife to husband at party: "Ray, tell them that story I always finish for you."

Cocktail-party hostess to new arrivals: "This group is discussing Vietnam. The bunch by the window is on politics. And the ones by the mantel are attacking the school system. Take your pick!"

Wife to husband: "Well, you certainly made a fool of yourself—I can only hope that no one at the party realized you were sober."

An actor, discussing the previous night's party, asked his wife: "Was that you I kissed, out in the patio?"

She thought for a moment, then countered: "About what time, dear?"

Woman, at cocktail party, to clergyman: "What's your calling—civil rights, poverty or peace?"

Man's infinite capacity for inflicting suffering upon himself and his fellows needed an art form through which the emotions attendant to that fact could find amateur expression. Thus the party was invented.

A celebrity hound approached Groucho Marx at a party. "You remember me, Mr. Marx. We met at the Glynthwaites' some months ago."

"I never forget a face," Groucho replied, "but I'll make an exception in your case."

Frowning wife to husband at cocktail party: "I wish you'd stop introducing me to people as your roommate."

Open-house host to arriving guests: "Mighty glad you folks could come. I didn't even know we were obligated to you."

Tactical Errors

Amid the black-tie crowd in the theater-lobby crush of a posh opening night, humorist Bennett Cerf came across a man he knew. He could see that the man knew him, too. The face was familiar but unfamiliar, friendly but out of place, demanding recognition but denying it.

Cerf quickly calculated the probabilities of the man's identity, brushed up his brightest grin and chanced an opening. "For heaven's sake!" he exclaimed. "When did you get into town? Can't we have lunch?"

"Don't be silly," the man replied. "I'm your dentist."

My memory for names is notably bad, and at public gatherings I always rely on my wife to help me. But on one occasion we became separated, and I beheld a matron bearing down upon me whom I felt that I should recognize. I was greeting her with a warm handclasp when a man I knew rather well came along. Still clasping the lady's hand, I waved my other hand in greeting. "Hello, Fred," I called. "How is your lovely wife these days?"

"You ought to know," replied Fred. "You're holding hands with her!"

At a New York college the faculty arranged a get-acquainted bridge party at which all those with matching favors started the evening as partners. A new art instructor, fresh from Holland, drew a Kewpie, as did one of the faculty wives. The next evening he found himself being introduced to the same lady at another reception. He electrified all within earshot when he protested, "Oh, no, do not introduce *us*. We haf babies together last efening."

Comedian Alan King was told that after a command performance in London he would meet Queen Elizabeth. For two days he carefully practiced his greeting. "How do you do, Your Majesty. How do you do, Your Majesty. How do you do, Your Majesty." Hour after hour, he articulated the words in anticipation of meeting the Queen.

Came the big night and he was introduced to Her Majesty. "How do you do, Mr. King," she said.

"How do you do, Mrs. Queen," he answered.

A tactless guest cornered her host and babbled, "Who is that old lady chattering over there in the corner?"

"That," said the host with frigid dignity, "is my eldest daughter."

"Oh, dear," exclaimed the embarrassed guest, "she's lots older than you are, isn't she?"

Theodore Roosevelt was enormously proud of his reputation for remembering names, and he left nothing undone that would enhance it. I sometimes suspected him of looking into people's hats to get their initials. And I am sure he read both minds and lips. A caller would begin with, "I'm Mr. Jo—" and before he knew what had happened to him, he had been affectionately called "Jonesy" and shoved out into the hall. But the usual system failed to work in the case of a New York haberdasher named Kaskel who thought he would help out the colonel with a little personal history.

"Mr. President," he said, "I made your shirts—"

"Major Schurtz," interrupted the President, "I'd have known you anywhere."

EXCUSE MY BOO-BOO
COREY FORD

I CAN REMEMBER names if I don't have to. It's when the pressure is on that my mind sits on its hands. I was engaged to a girl once, but our nuptial plans were called off because she got tired of being introduced as Miss Uh. Nice girl, too. I could tell you her name right now if you hadn't asked me.

I suppose it's due to nervous tension (they say there's a lot of that around these days). It happens every time I act as host. Let me enter a room with a newly arrived couple, to present them to my other guests, and I can feel my mental gears grinding together and the transmission locking tight. I stare at the sea of faces, but not a name comes to me. Obviously I knew who everybody was when I invited them here, but now all I can do is murmur lamely, "Well, I guess you probably all know each other already," and beat a hasty retreat to the kitchen, on the pretext of getting more ice.

When it comes to a mental block, I live in the big white house on the corner. Ask me a direct question, and the answer goes and hides under the rug. I know my telephone number perfectly well, but when someone requests it in a hurry I have to look in my address book under "Ford." During the war I used to worry about what would happen if my plane were forced down behind enemy lines. Had an interrogator shone a light in my face and demanded my name, rank and serial number, I'd have been shot for a spy.

Even if I *can* think of a name, it isn't necessarily the right one. This is because I read in some book (the title is right on the tip of my tongue) that you can recollect a person's name by associating it with something it reminds you of. As a result, Mr. Crooker becomes fixed in my mind as Mr. Swindler, Miss Finch is greeted as Miss Birdseed, and Mrs. Burpee turns out to be Mrs. Belch. There's a neighbor in Vermont, a rock-ribbed Republican named Charlie Truman, who has quit speaking to me because I invariably address him as "Harry."

I can (and do) carry these lapses to even more distressing extremes. The harder I try to avoid a subject, the more it dominates my conversation. If an acquaintance is sensitive about his balding pate, for example, I'm sure to make some allusion to billiard balls.

Not long ago I was invited to spend the weekend with an old

friend at his country place. On our drive out, he confided happily that his wife thought she was pregnant. "Don't say anything about it, though," he added. "The doctor isn't sure yet."

From the moment I arrived, everything I said was loaded. "I'm sorry to barge in on you like this," I told the wife. "You probably weren't expecting a stranger." Feeling my forehead growing warm, I suggested that we take a stroll around the grounds. "You live a long way out of town," I remarked to her. "Do you have any trouble with deliveries?"

Some carpenters were working on a wing to the house, and I observed, "Well, I see you're going to have a new addition shortly." I admired the babies'-breath in the garden, I inquired about her shrubs—"Is there a good nursery handy?" Later as we sat on the terrace I commented sentimentally on how nice it was to be together like this in a family way.

This is known as the progressive boo-boo (it gets worse as the consternation grows), and probably the best example is the predicament of a young man I knew whose fiancée brought him home to meet her parents. "Dad's still pretty violent about the New Deal," she cautioned him, "so don't mention F.D.R." This weighed on his mind so heavily that when his prospective father-in-law asked him how he liked his job, he replied, "Well, to be perfectly franklin. . . ." His fiancée suggested hurriedly that they might like their after-dinner coffee in front of the hearth, whereupon the rattled young man assured the father eagerly, "I'd certainly enjoy a little fireside chat!"

Realizing that her husband was turning purple, the girl's mother tried to change the subject by asking the young man where his home was—at which point he rose abruptly, left the house and never saw the girl again. "How could I explain that I lived in Roosevelt, Long Island?" he asked me later.

The insidious thing about mental lapses is that they become a habit. Once I've started twisting sentences around, I'll do it every time. When I shake hands with someone, for instance, I'm apt to say, "I'm so nice to meet you." The other afternoon I failed to recognize a lady acquaintance in a hotel lobby, and to cover my confusion I explained flatteringly, "You look so pretty that I didn't know you."

This foot-in-mouth disease seems to be contagious. I realized that I am not alone in my cerebral derailments when I read about the banquet chairman whose guest of honor had delivered a somewhat lengthy harangue. "Thank you, Professor," he said into the microphone. "You would have been welcome here tonight if you had said nothing at all."

And I cannot help feeling a sympathetic twinge for the Brooklyn lady who asked a visiting author when his personal letters would be published. "Posthumously," he replied. "Oh, I do hope it will be soon!" she gushed.

Which brings to mind a postcard from a friend at home sent me while I was traveling abroad recently. "We miss you as much as if you were here," she wrote. I'm still trying to figure that out.

Dinner at Eight

FILLING THAT HIATUS
ROBERT BENCHLEY

THERE is one detail of behavior at dinner parties which I have never seen touched upon in etiquette books, and which has given me some little embarrassment: What to do when you find that both your right-hand and your left-hand partner are busily engaged in conversation with somebody else.

You have perhaps turned from your right-hand partner to snap away a rose bug which was charging on your butter from the table decorations, and when you turn back to her to continue your monologue, you find that she is already vivaciously engaged on the other side—a shift made with suspicious alacrity, when you come to think it over. So you wheel about to your left, only to find yourself confronted by an expanse of sun-browned back. This leaves you looking more or less straight in front of you, with a roll in your hand and not very much to do with your face. Should you sit and cry softly to yourself, or launch forth into a bawdy solo, beating time with your knife and fork?

Of course, the main thing is not to let your hostess notice that you are disengaged. If she spots you dawdling or looking into space, she will either think that you have insulted both your partners or she will feel responsible for you herself and start a long-distance conversation which has no real basis except that of emergency. You must spend the hiatus acting as if you really were doing something.

You can always make believe that you are talking to the person opposite, making little conversational faces and sounds into thin air, nodding your head "Yes" or "No," and laughing politely every now and again. This may fool your hostess in case her glance happens to fall your way, and it surely will confuse the person sitting opposite you if he happens to catch your act. He is naturally going to think that he had better not take any more to drink, or that he had better not go to any more parties until some good specialist has gone over him thoroughly. It is this danger of being misjudged which makes the imitation conversation inadvisable.

You can always get busily at work on the nuts in front of your plate, arranging them in fancy patterns with simulated intensity which will make it look as if you were performing for somebody's benefit, especially if you keep looking up at an imaginary audience and smiling "See?" Even if you are caught at this, there is no way of checking up, for any of the dinner guests might possibly be looking at you while talking to somebody else. It isn't much fun, however, after the first five minutes.

If you have thought to bring along a bit of charcoal, you can draw little pictures on the back on either side of you, or lacking charcoal and the ability to draw, you might start smothering the nicer-looking back with kisses. This would, at least, get one of your partners to turn around—unless she happened to like it. As time wears on, you can start juggling your cutlery, beginning with a knife, fork and spoon and working up to two of each, with a flower thrown in to make it harder. This ought to attract *some* attention.

Of course, there is always one last resort, and that is to slide quietly under the table, where you can either crawl about collecting slippers which have been kicked off, growling like a dog and frightening the more timid guests, or crawl out from the other side and go home. Perhaps this last would be best.

A young lady with a touch of hay fever took with her to a dinner party two handkerchiefs, one of which she stuck in her bosom. At dinner she began rummaging to right and left in her bosom for the fresh handkerchief. Engrossed in her search, she suddenly realized that conversation had ceased and people were watching her, fascinated.

In confusion she murmured, "I *know* I had two when I came."

At a formal dinner the hostess, who was seated at the far end of the table from Leonora Corbett, wrote a note to the actress and had the butler deliver it. Miss Corbett couldn't read without her glasses, so she asked the man at her left to read it to her. "It says," he began, "'Leonora, dear, do me a favor and please don't neglect the man at your left. I know he's a bore, but talk to him.'"

The Most Rev. R. C. Trench, who many years ago was Protestant Archbishop of Dublin, had a morbid fear of becoming paralyzed. One evening at a party, the lady he sat next to at dinner heard him muttering mournfully to himself, "It's happened at last—total insensibility of the right limb."

"Your Grace," said the lady, "it may comfort you to learn that it is my leg you are pinching."

At a dinner party a shy young man had been trying to think of something nice to say to his hostess. At last he saw his chance when she turned to him and remarked, "What a small appetite you have, Mr. Jones."

"To sit next to you," he replied gallantly, "would cause any man to lose his appetite."

Sitting next to a taciturn man at a dinner party, a young woman made valiant efforts to get him to talk. She tried sports, current events, books, travel, food, theater, weather —all to no avail.

Finally he leaned toward her and said, "Try me on leather."

Latitudes
and
Attitudes:

LOCAL COLOR

O NE OF THE INTERESTING THINGS about our regional
jokes is their standardization. We enjoy them partly
because they're what we expect. Boston jokes generally turn on local pride or social snobbery, Maine jokes on
taciturnity, Dixie jokes on the Civil War or funny speech
habits, hillbilly jokes on either the smartness or the dumb-
ness of the natives, and Texas jokes on three of the dullest
things in the world—mere money, mere size, and mere   *531*

murder. Even foreigners long ago knew the kind of cracks they were expected to make: W. E. Gladstone (attributing it, the coward, to an unnamed Bostonian) reminded us that "there are not ten men in Boston equal to Shakespeare." As for Los Angeles, the jokes are always the same. The type of them all is the remark attributed to Frank Lloyd Wright: "If you tilt the country sideways, Los Angeles is the place where everything loose will fall." For terseness it is hard to beat Oliver Herford's "In the midst of life we are in Brooklyn." But the fact that each region makes fun of all the others somehow seems to unify rather than divide us. That is why we should rise up and call the humorist blessed.

New England Flavor

A friend who was visiting in Maine wanted to order 1500 lobsters for an office picnic. Seeing a door with the sign "McGregor & Daggett—Lobsters Wholesale," he went in. He found a weathered Yankee fisherman in rubber overalls, woolen shirt and rain hat working on a lobster pot.

"Mr. McGregor or Mr. Daggett?" my friend asked.

"Don't make much difference," the Down Easter said, "seein's how one of us is dead."

Approaching the grilled window of a tiny post office in a small New England town, I called out to the stern-faced woman on the other side of the grille, "Good morning, are you the postmistress?"

"No," she replied testily. "I'm the postmaster. Uncle Sam doesn't pay me enough to be anyone's mistress!"

The editor of a Vermont weekly sent to one Hiram Sparks a notice that his subscription had expired. The notice came back with the laconic scrawl: "So's Hiram."

An exchange student from Africa, dressed in colorful native robes, entered a bank in a Maine coastal town, stepped up to the teller's window and told the elderly man in charge that he would like to cash a check. The teller eyed the student critically, then remarked, "You're from outta town, ain'tcha?"

While vacationing on Cape Cod we stopped at a small wayside stand and bought some tomatoes. When I commented that they were small, the proprietor's reply was, "Ay-up."

Returning a day or two later, I mentioned that the tomatoes had not been very flavorful. The old gentleman nodded and said, "Lucky they was small, ain't it?"

A Bostonian, after meeting a Vermont farmer and being impressed with his common sense, suggested a game. "We'll ask each other questions," he said, "and the person who can't answer pays a dollar."

The Vermonter considered the idea, then pointed out that the Boston man was more educated and experienced than he. The odds would be evened if the Bostonian paid $1 and he paid only 50 cents. The Bostonian agreed.

"What has three legs and flies?" asked the Vermonter. Minutes passed while the Bostonian pondered.

"I don't know," he finally admitted. "Here's your dollar."

Then he asked the same question: "What has three legs and flies?"

"Darned if I know," said the Vermonter. "Here's your 50 cents."

Two middle-aged schoolteachers who rented sight-unseen a camp in New Hampshire were dismayed by its isolation. After a few frightening nights, they offered the old fellow who supplied them with ice and firewood a small sum weekly if he would sleep on a cot on their screened porch every night. He agreed, and my friends enjoyed the summer so much that they took the camp the following summer. They immediately looked up old Joe, but were stopped in their tracks by the sign above his door:

JOE JIMPSON

ICE   WOOD   BAIT   ODD JOBS

NARVUS WIMMEN SLEPT WITH

25 CENTS A NITE

On a recent trip to Vermont, I did some research on agricultural statistics and noticed that the cow population of the state was larger than the human population. "How do you account for that?" I asked a native son.

"We prefer 'em," he replied.

Trying to determine why production had declined in a plant in Maine, an efficiency expert asked the company's personnel director, "How many of your employes are approaching retirement age?"

"Well," replied the personnel director, "we haven't got any going the other way."

Boston Bred

A Boston lady, finding a stranger next to her at dinner, asked him politely where he lived.

"Out West," he replied. "It's two nights on the sleeper from Boston."

"Oh," she said, "a sleeper, how interesting. I have always wondered what they were like.

"Have you never been on one?" he asked.

"No—you see, I was here already."

The Hotel Wentworth in Portsmouth, New Hampshire, has long been a favorite vacation spot for the elite of Boston. The last time I was there I overheard a conversation between a 90-year-old Beacon Hill aristocrat and a woman guest from New York. "I don't see why Bostonians are considered cold and stand-offish," the New Yorker said. "The ones I've met have been perfectly lovely and more than ready to go halfway in making friends."

"It is obvious," said the proper Bostonian stiffly, "that you have not met the right people."

In any other city it would say "No Exit." But in Boston, graven in the marble over the door of the Ritz-Carlton Hotel, is: "Not An Accredited Egress."

When Bishop Phillips Brooks was preaching in Trinity Church in Boston, he made a plea for more kindness toward strangers who sat uninvited in the family pew. This was a good deal to ask of Bostonians, but one woman was moved by it nonetheless. After services she told the bishop so.

"Do put one in my pew next Sunday," she said graciously. "Thin, and no perfume."

The morning commuter train to Boston was almost empty when I got on board. I took a seat and was quartering my newspaper when I realized that an umbrella was being tapped on the floor beside me.

There stood a Proper Bostonian, bowler, pince-nez and all. "Pardon me, young man," he whispered discreetly. "You must be new here—you're sitting in *my* seat."

An elderly Boston newspaperman interviewing playwright John Patrick apologized for cutting the interview short. He had to cover a show at the planetarium, he explained. "They're reproducing the sky exactly as it was the night Christ was born."

"Over Bethlehem?" Patrick asked.

"Of course not," the reporter answered indignantly. "Over *Boston.*"

We had just landed at Chicago's Midway Airport when the No. 3 engine of our DC-7 caught fire. There was danger of an explosion, and my fellow stewardess and I began emergency evacuation procedures. She directed some of our 73 passengers down an emergency slide which was hooked into position at the main cabin door while I opened exits over the left wing, hopped out, helped people through these exits and directed them down the ditching rope.

In the midst of the desperate disciplined hurry, I looked inside the cabin to find an elderly couple still seated, quietly observing the frenzied proceedings. As people flew out of windows, down ropes and slides, they calmly asked, "Do you want the Boston passengers off, too?"

One Saturday morning a young doctor was summoned to the Beacon Hill home of a Boston matron whose regular physician was out of town. She explained that the night before she had fallen at Symphony Hall and injured her leg.

"You know those two steps going down to the left from the orchestra?" she asked.

"No," replied the doctor, "I'm afraid I don't."

"Were you at the symphony Friday night?" she asked.

"No, I wasn't."

"Have you been to the symphony this season?"

"No, I haven't."

"Well, have you *ever* been to the symphony?" she persisted.

"I'm afraid I never have," the doctor said.

"In that case," she said, "you are obviously not the type of doctor I want."

Dixie Cracks

On a visit to Richmond, a man who wanted to see the Edgar Allan Poe home, now a museum, hailed a taxi and told the driver to take him to the Poe House. After a long drive, the cab pulled up before a weather-beaten structure on the outskirts of town—the County Home for the Indigent.

A woman was arguing with an elderly Southerner about the effects of alcohol.

"Statistics prove," she announced, "that people who don't drink live much longer than those who use alcohol."

"My dear madam," said the Southerner, "why should I sell my birthright for a mess of dotage?"

The secretary of a machinists' union in Pennsylvania wrote to an Atlanta, Georgia, firm requesting a miniature Civil War pup tent that the firm was giving away as a promotion item. On the coupon, he identified his occupation as "union officer."

The Atlanta company wrote back: "We regret to inform you that we have only five of the miniature tents left. We have decided to reserve these for Confederate officers. We believe you will understand our position."

One of the two girls remarked, "Men are all alike."

The other girl, from the Deep South, replied, "Men are all Ah like, too."

At a party, one of the men approached a couple who had recently moved to Pittsburgh from the South. Addressing the wife, he asked, "Are you one of those Southerners who are still fighting the Civil War?"

We all silently applauded her answer. With an amused twinkle she replied, "Not unless fired upon, suh."

A proud citizen of Charleston, South Carolina, attending the University of Wisconsin, was dilating upon the splendors of his home town when a Yankee, thinking to put him in his place, asked, "Where *is* Charleston?"

Turning slowly toward the enemy, the orator replied with quiet dignity, "Charleston, sir, is that untarnished jewel shining regally at that sacred spot where the Ashley and the Cooper join their majestic waters to form the Atlantic Ocean."

A British acquaintance of mine has studied the accents used in the South and come up with these definitions of words:

Abode: Wooden plank.
Balks: A container, such as "match balks."
Beckon: Meat from a pig, usually eaten at breakfast with eggs.
Coat: A place of justice. "Coat's in session."
Faints: A barricade of wood or brick.
Frustrate: Tops. The best.
Lack: To enjoy, as in "I lack fried chicken."
Tarred: Weary. "I'm awfully tarred."
Tin Sin Stow: Woolworth's.

Westward Ho

When his doctor advised a change of climate, the eastern city-dweller went looking for a healthy place to live in the Southwest. In one small Arizona town he approached an old-timer sitting on the steps of the general store.

"Say," he asked, "what's the death rate around here?"

"Same as it is back East, bub," came the answer, "one to a person."

A sign in a public laundry in Phoenix testifies that the Old West isn't entirely dead. It reads: "Do Not Wash Horse Blankets."

A shrewd businessman was on a trip through the Southwest and was looking for presents to bring home to his friends. He spotted an Indian with a pile of blankets for sale and asked how much he wanted for the lot.

"A hundred dollars," the Indian said.

"Nothing doing," replied the businessman. "I'll give you twenty-four."

The Indian picked up his blankets and started to walk away. "Listen, mister," he said, "bargains like Manhattan Island you're not going to get anymore."

An old-time judge in the Northwest had a great fondness for assessing fines. Once he sat both as judge and coroner over the body of a stranger found dead in the woods with $40 in gold and a six-shooter in his pockets. The judge fined the corpse $40 for carrying a concealed weapon.

Frontier coroner's verdict: "We find that the deceased came to his death by an act of suicide. At a distance of a hundred yards he opened fire with a six-shooter upon a man armed with a rifle."

Sign at a cattle guard at the entrance to a ranch near Mullen, Nebraska: "Drive Carefully. The Life You Save May Be Next Year's T-Bone."

A King Ranch ad in *Western Livestock Journal* features a photograph of a Santa Gertrudis prize bull with the caption: "There is money in his genes."

And did you hear about the poor but honest cowboy who called his horse "Hi Ho Stainless"?

Backwoods Banter

The doctor in a Black Mountain, North Carolina, clinic asked the weather-beaten mountaineer how he was feeling. "It's like this," drawled the man from the hills after a few seconds of silence. "I'm still kickin', but I ain't raisin' any dust."

Hey, there!" a passing motorist called to a hillbilly who was reclining under a tree. "Your house is on fire!"

"Know it," the hillbilly replied without moving.

"Well, why don't you do something about it?"

"Doin' it now," the hillbilly replied. "Bin a-prayin' fer rain ever since she started."

A Yankee judge, visiting in Kentucky, attended a local picnic where a mass quarrel developed. The dispute became so violent that the judge sought out the local constable and demanded: "You're an officer of the law. Why don't you put a stop to all this warfare? These men are committing a flagrant breach of the peace!"

The constable stared at the judge in amazement. "Them fellers ain't committin' no breach of the law," he declared. "They're just fightin' among themselves."

A West Virginian worked at a factory in a neighboring state. Telling his co-workers about a forthcoming trip back to his native state, he said, "Martha and me are repairin' to go on a little vacation back to West Virginny."

A fellow worker interrupted, "You mean you're 'preparing' to go on a trip, not 'repairing.' To 'repair' means to fix something."

"That's what I said," retorted the mountaineer. "We're fixin' to go."

A few summers ago I visited Hannibal, Missouri, the sleepy little river town where Mark Twain spent his boyhood. Stopping at a roadside stand one day, I asked the white-bearded old proprietor if he had known Mark Twain. The reply was prompt, long-suffering and a little indignant.

"Sure I did," he replied. "And I know just as many stories as he did, too. Only difference is, he writ 'em down."

As the porter of the little West Virginia hotel showed us to our room he informed us that the spry old gentleman at the desk was 98 years old. Much impressed, we stopped later and struck up a conversation. "You certainly have a lot of pep for a man nearly 100 years old," I said. "How do you keep that way?"

The old fellow scratched his head thoughtfully. "I ain't decided yet, ma'am. I'm dickerin' right now with two or three cereal companies over my endorsement."

A Kentucky judge told of a memorable case in which the defendant was accused of kicking another citizen in the stomach. The defense lawyer argued that there was no real evil intent. When the defendant took the stand, the prosecutor shouted at him, "How can you possibly say that you delivered this terrific kick in the stomach without intending to?"

The defendant studied a while. "He must have turned around too quick," he said.

Lone Star Stoppers

Near the town of Raymondville in the Rio Grande valley of Texas, a fugitive barricaded himself in a small house and threatened to shoot anyone who came within range. Local officers called in a Texas Ranger, and in the gun battle that followed, the fugitive was killed. The justice of the peace, acting as coroner, returned the verdict: "Suicide. Failing to coöperate with a Texas Ranger."

Traveling on a train near Wichita Falls, Boyce House, the humorist, struck up a friendship with a hard-bitten Texas rancher. The train stopped at a little tank town, and the two went to get a bite to eat. When they boarded the train again, a "city feller" was sprawled on their seats. The rancher politely asked the interloper to move. He paid no attention.

At that the rancher pulled out his six-shooter and bounced it a few times across the man's skull. "Now I'll give you exactly four and one half seconds to get out of our seat," the rancher growled. The stranger vamoosed.

The rancher shoved his gun into his belt and said sorrowfully to House: "It's fellers like that who give Texas a bad name."

There's a new Texas yarn—about the woman who called her hubby and said, "Will you please get the car out, Tex, and drive the kids to the back yard so they can play?"

It was a little boy from Texas who marched up to Santa Claus and asked, "What can I do for you?"

An Easterner was being driven by a rancher over a blistering and almost barren stretch of West Texas when a strange bird scurried in front of them. Asked what it was, the rancher replied, "That's a bird of paradise."

The stranger from the East rode on in silence for a moment, then said, "Long way from home, isn't it?"

A Texan was dictating his will to his lawyer: "To my son I leave three million dollars—and he's lucky I didn't cut him off entirely."

After a wealthy Texas oilman had cashed a huge personal check, it came back from the bank stamped "Insufficient Funds." Beneath these words appeared the handwritten notation: "Not you—us."

An ardent fisherman from Dallas made a trip to Bull Shoals Lake in Arkansas. After pulling in a 6½-pound largemouth bass, the Texan boasted to his native guide, "Why, heck, in Texas we use that size for bait.

The Arkansan smiled, nodded appreciatively—and dropped the fish back into the lake.

A Bostonian visited San Antonio and asked a native, "What is that dilapidated-looking ruin over there?"

"That, suh, is the Alamo. In that building, suh, 136 immortal Texans held off an army of 15,000 of Santa Anna's regulars for four days."

"Um-m-m," said the Bostonian, "and who was that man on horseback on that hill over there?"

"That, suh, is a statue of a Texas Ranger. He killed 46 Apaches in single-handed combat and broke up 27 riots in his lifetime. Where you from, stranger?"

"I'm from Boston. We have our heroes there, too. Paul Revere, for instance—"

"Paul Revere!" snorted the Texan. "You mean that man who had to ride for help?"

I was attending a convention in San Antonio and a professor of economics from the University of Texas was speaking. The group included a large number of Oklahomans. When he generously mentioned the neighboring state as an "outlying province of Texas," a husky Oklahoman jumped to his feet and shouted back, "Brother, there ain't no state that can out-lie Texas!"

A Texas woman whose husband had recently struck oil was holding forth at a dinner party about her furs, jewels, cars and fabulous new house. One of the guests inquired how many bathrooms the new place had, and she replied loftily, "I can seat seven."

On a visit to tiny Israel, a Texan boasted: "Why, in Texas you can get on a train, ride for days and still be in Texas."

His Israeli companion nodded sympathetically. "We have the same trouble with our trains," he said.

Ice Breakers

Eskimo girl to Eskimo boy: "It's not that I don't like you—it's just that you have such a cold nose."

A friend of mine who was visiting in Alaska met a man and married him after a very brief acquaintance. When she got home she explained why their courtship had been so short. "When it was dark enough to park, it was too cold," she said. "And when it was warm enough, it was too light."

During our first long winter in Alaska I called a repairman to work on our stove. "Just exactly how long *does* winter last up here?" I asked him.

"Lady," he said, "the first year I was up here it lasted 13 months."

Senator E. L. Bartlett of Alaska was twitting House Speaker Sam Rayburn of Texas about the fact that Alaskan statehood had reduced Texas to second rank in size.

"If you don't keep quiet," Rayburn warned, "a few Texans will come to your state and throw a cocktail party. When they get through using your ice, you'll be smaller than Rhode Island."

In the dining room of the Hotel Juneau in Juneau, Alaska, the featured dessert is "Baked Texas."

At Eskimo trial: "Where were you the night of October 11 to April 3?"

British Accent

English nanny to children, at Madame Tussaud's Wax Museum in London: "And that is George Washington, the founder of America. Some say, of course, that he should not have done it."

AMERICA, FROM A SAFE DISTANCE

ALEX ATKINSON

ENTERED the United States by way of New York, a thriving
city largely situated on a small island off the coast of New
Jersey. I had decided that this would be a convenient jump-
ing-off place for a tour of the country, since it is connected to
the mainland by ferry and several bridges, each of which is the
longest in the world. From here, across the picturesque Harlem
River, it was but a stone's throw to Hartford and the grim wastes
of the Appalachian Mountains, dotted with lonely commuters'
shacks.

Here, as down the entire right-hand side of the U.S.A., the
sense of urgency seizes you like a fever, so that you frequently
find yourself halfway through tomorrow's schedule before you've
digested yesterday's tranquilizer. In the office of one well-to-do
businessman whom I met, there was a sign which read: "It's
Too Late Already."

New England is up in the top right-hand corner—about as far
away from wicked Las Vegas as it can get without actually putting
out to sea. It is very old and slightly more historic than Stratford-
on-Avon.

Maine is bigger than any other New England state, and has
more sardines. Its inhabitants vote two months earlier than anybody else—not because they are impatient but because the whole
world knows they're going to vote Republican, so they figure they
might as well get it over with and go on planting potatoes.

In the quieter parts of New Hampshire, where the true New
England atmosphere prevails, I was often reminded of home:
thatched cottages, soft-drink ads, leafy lanes and bubble-gum
machines. But there the resemblance ends, for the people are
starchy, secretive and unbending. How I missed the familiar
sound of laughing British crowds—the readiness to exchange
confidences with total strangers, the brilliant flashes of color
from the women's beige overcoats, the lighthearted bowlers of
the men! Here I found only silent groups all dressed in gray
and black, who stood in the streets and stared at me suspiciously,
holding pitchforks and Nonconformist hymnbooks.

It was much the same in Vermont. When I asked the way in a

town there, the village green emptied in an instant. Shutters banged across all the windows, and I was aware of beady eyes watching me through chinks. Here, I discovered, they use only one word at a time, like Gary Cooper, and it usually means No. If it doesn't mean No, it means Why.

When I asked them what they thought of Britain, they narrowed their eyes and began collecting jagged stones. Appropriately enough, it was Emerson who said there should always be a minority unconvinced. It lives in Vermont.

On my way from New England to the Middle West I stopped off in Pennsylvania, which turned out to be a mixed-up state altogether. For instance, one day you might run into a crowd of Amish people walking about without any buttons, and the next you might find yourself in a country-club district, where everybody knows everybody else and can't understand how in the world they can afford to keep two convertibles *and* a British car. These are mostly commuters, of the same type as those to be found in parts of New York. One night they have a party of their own, and the next they go to a party up the street, and so on. In this way they manage to see the same people every night, but against a different décor. It makes them feel that they *belong*.

Dust-stained, smelling of hot rubber and sheep-dip after driving along a highway for three weeks in a dead-straight line, I reached the Middle West. It is a region of contrasts: in one Main Street you might see a boy wearing baseball boots and a space helmet, while in another you might not.

Although to many Midwesterners the outside world remains an enigma, I found that a number of them knew about England. England is where the British live. The British roam around constantly in gunboats, colonizing defenseless people. They are chiefly remarkable in that they flatly refuse to pay their War Debts.

A Missourian told me that a good many Midwesterners wouldn't have picked the Middle West as a place to live if they'd had a choice. "The way I figure it," he said, "it all came about by accident. In the old days most everybody from the East was heading out to California, and it just so happened that round about halfway they hit the Middle West, and a lot of wagons broke down. So some folks said 'The hell with it, we ain't in no fit condition to do a repair job—we might as well stay right here.' And they did."

In Chicago I saw very little of the underworld gangs (or Trade Unions, as they are now called), but there was some sporadic shooting as I drove along State Street; and in the burlesque houses, honky-tonks and other dens of iniquity which abound to ensnare the gullible traveler (I must have visited at least 30) I thought I caught sight of some hatchet men, footpads and politicians from time to time. I couldn't be sure, though, because Chicago citizens tend to look alike.

It was Chicago, by the way, that had the fire—not San Francisco.

Off I went to the West, starting with Oregon, which is such a lonely place that parts of it haven't even been found yet. But on the Columbia River there is a dam (I forget its name) which is the biggest thing anyone has ever made since the world began. It is used for making electricity, I was told, and weighs three times as much as the Great Pyramid of Cheops. "And how much electricity," asked my guide with a faint sneer, "have they got in Cheops?"

"I don't know," I said defensively, "but who weighed that pyramid for you?" For the rest of my visit I was pointed out as the mad Englishman.

Westerners are less complicated than Easterners. They will shoot you down like a dog one day and invite you round for flapjacks and molasses the next. They live mostly in ghost towns, fighting posses, claim jumpers, train robbers and the Flathead Indians. So many are descended from participants in the Battle of Little Bighorn River that General Custer's gallant little band must have amounted to over a division, and I can't see why he didn't drive those Sioux clear up into Saskatchewan.

The U.S. passion for exaggeration is especially noticeable in the Western parts. In Colorado they served me a steak which lasted my entire stay—one week. Each night when I got back to my hotel I'd have it sent up to my room and hack another five inches off it. On the last evening, admitting defeat, I hid the remaining three quarters of a pound in the wardrobe. Then I checked out. When I got to Dallas it was waiting for me, with a note from the management: "Sir—you never finished your chop."

Swinging through the South, I entered Kentucky by way of the Cumberland Gap, like Daniel Boone before me, and made immediately for the country of the Mountain Men. Here the women are distinguishable from the men by the fact that they take their pipes out of their mouths to spit.

I asked a mountaineer named Zeke, who was 103 years old, how he passed his time. He told me that in winter he mostly sleeps, in the spring he chases some likely female cousin about the rocks, in the summer he makes moonshine whiskey out of potato peelings and coffee grounds, and in the fall he mostly drinks it.

Virginia, apart from tobacco auctions and its plucky refusal to abolish the chain gang, is chiefly noted for history. All U.S. history happened in Virginia, so that as I drove through the state I was able to piece together the nation's entire past. It goes like this:

After Raleigh discovered the Indians in Virginia, including Pocahontas, a lot of English came to Jamestown. They soon became obstreperous and refused to pay taxes to the king. Jefferson (a Virginian) having written the Declaration of Independence, Virginia proceeded to supply most of the Presidents from George Washington right through to Wilson. In 1861, as soon as "Dixie" was composed, Virginia seceded, and there followed the Civil War, fought entirely in Virginia. That was really the end of American history, if I understood my guide correctly. Geronimo surrendered in 1886, John Scopes was fined $100 for teaching Evolution in 1925, and the FBI shot Dillinger dead outside a cinema in 1934, but all these things were simply signs of the times, and did not count as history. Not a single one of them happened in Virginia.

As I drove through Georgia, where the wheels of my car squelched deliciously through the peaches that kept falling from the trees in sackfuls, I learned that it was someone in Atlanta who uncovered the secret of how to make Coca-Cola, thus ushering in a way of life that has survived two world wars. I also learned that I had been misinformed: the Civil War apparently did *not* take place entirely in Virginia.

It seemed only fitting to conclude my journey in Washington, D.C., where I asked a man to give me a brief outline of the political system. He explained that there are two parties: the Republicans, who stand for prosperity, peace and a gradual emergence from the chaos left by the New Deal; and the Democrats, who stand for peace, prosperity and a gradual emergence from the chaos left by President Hoover. The Presidency is a difficult job, and every four years the country is overrun with people declaring loudly that they have not the slightest intention of standing for the office. This is called campaigning.

As my homeward-bound ship nosed into the gray wastes of the Atlantic, a wave of memories overwhelmed me. How to sum it all up? And then it came to me: the words of the wise old man I met on the beach at Ocean City, Maryland.

"Son," he said, gazing across the calm waters of Sinepuxent Bay, "a country that has invented the cash register and the bifocal lens, the submarine and barbed wire, the Mason jar and the lawn mower, evaporated milk and the split-phase induction motor, is going to find an answer to it all *one* of these days—you just see if it don't."

I nodded approvingly as I stood at the rail looking out over the restless ocean, until the last trace of the Statue of Liberty had sunk below the horizon.

———— • ————

A British general, newly arrived in Washington to serve in the combined Chiefs of Staff setup, was touring the War College with an American colonel. They came upon some colorful prints depicting the War of 1812. "War of 1812? Whom were we fighting?" asked the Britisher.

"We were fighting you, sir," mumbled the embarrassed colonel. "Don't you remember, the British burned Washington?"

"Burned Washington!" The general was thunderstruck. "We burned Joan of Arc, I know—but never Washington!"

On a train during a tour of the United States an Englishman fell into conversation with a Texan, who embarked on a long recitation of the wonders of the Lone Star State. "Maybe you didn't realize it while you were going through my state," the Texan wound up, "but all of Great Britain could fit into one corner of it."

"I dare say it could," said the Englishman dryly. "And wouldn't it do wonders for the place!"

The daughter of an Englishman who was traveling in South Africa under circumstances of considerable discomfort was advised by her mother to say over to herself, on first awakening, these three comforting considerations: "I'm an Englishwoman, I was born in wedlock, I'm on dry land."

———— • ————

An old lady was taking a pet tortoise by train from London to Edinburgh and wanted to know whether she ought to buy a dog ticket for it—as one has to do in England when taking a cat by train, because cats officially count as dogs.

"No, mum," said the ticket inspector. "Cats is dogs, and dogs is dogs, and squirrels in cages is parrots; but this here turkle is a hinsect, and we won't charge you nothing."

In England, a young man wanting to talk to a friend in Ealing went to the telephone and said to the operator: "Ealing 6000, please."

"What number did you say, sir?"

"I said 'Ealing 6000.'"

"Spell it, please."

"All right. E for 'erbert, A for what 'orses heat, L for where you are going, I for me, N for what lays the heggs, and G for Jesus."

He was promptly connected with the right number.

When an American importer approached Twining, the famous London tea merchants, to negotiate for the American distribution rights for their brand, an elderly Twining was not too friendly about it. He harrumphed and said, "You know, we had quite a lot of trouble over there."

"Trouble?" said the importer.

"Yes," said Mr. Twining, "they dumped a shipment of our tea into Boston Harbor."

Children's Hour:
THE YOUNGER SET

OF THE *Treasury*'s thirty sections, this is my favorite.
I would like to think my pleasure in these stories is
not rooted in any sense of superiority to children—
but, being a dumb adult, I can't be sure. The humor of children springs less from the fact that we know more than they
do (though sometimes it seems that way) and more from the

fact that they look at the world *freshly,* almost like poets, and we don't. And because we don't, because imagination in us is half dead, the reactions of children to life seem to us hilariously odd. Take that wonderful exclamation of the little girl looking down into the Grand Canyon: "Golly, Dad, what happened?" That is *exactly* right. It sums up the Grand Canyon in a way that would never occur to grownups. It is vivid, true—and, of course to us, very funny. In that shrewd masterpiece called "A Handy Guide to Grownups" young Miss Owsley has us down pat: "They think differently because they have been in this world longer and have had more time to learn about everything and get used to it. So they aren't so surprised about the world any more."

The Mouths of Babes

The two young daughters of a friend of mine had been given parts in a Christmas play at school. At dinner that night they got into an argument as to who had the most important role. Judy, aged 11, was very superior.

"Why, of course mine's the biggest part," she told five-year-old Lucy. "Anybody'll tell you it's much harder to be a virgin than an angel."

An eight-year-old came home full of praise for her new swimming instructor. Asked by her mother how old he was, she thought a moment, then replied, "I don't know, but I'd say he is either a late teen-ager or an early man."

Small fry to gushing matron: "You're getting big yourself!"

A sixth-grade girl, assigned to write her autobiography, included in her paper: "I have a brother 13 years old. He plays on the school football team and is an offensive throwback."

A cold drizzle darkened the streets. To keep her tiny dog warm, a woman put him under her coat, letting only his alert little head protrude from the opening between two buttons near her waistline.

While they were waiting at a bus stop, a small boy, who had been looking her over for some time, finally went up to the woman and asked, "Are you a kangaroo?"

On a crowded cross-country bus, a youngster occupied one section of the seat just ahead of his father and mother. When the space beside him was pounced upon by a lady of gargantuan proportions, the boy turned to his mother and announced discreetly, "F-A-T, huh, Ma?"

Before Thanksgiving a Minnesota first-grade teacher asked her pupils to tell her what they had to be thankful for. "I am thankful," said one small boy, "that I am not a turkey."

A Junior Miss, exposed for the first time to the musical life of the Berkshires, wrote home: "Of all the musical compositions I have heard the one I like best is 'The Damn Nation of Faust' by Berlioz."

My English class was reading from the Journals of Louisa M. Alcott. We came to the section where Miss Alcott wrote, "I keep busy writing short stories which I hope to sell for $5 or $10 to keep the wolf from the door." I asked the boy reading, "What do you think Louisa Alcott meant by saying she was trying to keep the wolf from the door?"

"I suppose she just didn't want the guy bothering her," he replied promptly.

A little Mexican boy in an American school, told to write the first verse of "The Star-Spangled Banner," began: "José, can you see?"

A Boston mother was pleased but puzzled with the Christmas card her son brought home from kindergarten. It showed a scraggly-looking tree with presents dangling from it, and in the center something that looked strangely like a bullet. Explained the youngster, "It's not a Christmas tree—it's a cartridge in a pear tree."

I was telling my nine-year-old granddaughter the story of the princess and the frog. "When the little frog rescued her golden ball from the well, the princess was so grateful she let him spend the night in her room," I said. "And the next morning when she woke up he had turned into a handsome prince and they were married and lived happily ever after."

My granddaughter looked at me dubiously.

"Don't you believe the story?" I asked.

"No," she replied, "I don't. And I'll bet her mother didn't either."

A few days ago I overheard my small grandson doing his arithmetic homework. "Three plus one, the son of a bitch is four," he was saying. "Three plus two, the son of a bitch is five. Three plus three, the son of a bitch is six." And so on. Horrified, I went to see his teacher and asked her about it. At first she was equally horrified, then, "I get it!" she cried. "We teach the children to say 'Three plus one, the sum of which is four. Three plus two, the sum of which is five.'"

A first-grader in a Kirkland, Washington, school volunteered to recite a nursery rhyme. "Little Miss Muffet sat on a tuffet," he intoned, "eating her curves away."

Pajama-clad tot calling out to parents: "I'm going to say my prayers. Anyone want anything?"

Young lad on knee of department-store Santa: "Notice one thing—I'm adequately clothed."

Birds and Bees

Small boy to friend: "My mother tried to tell me the stork doesn't bring babies. What a wild story *she* gave me!"

At a military wedding, the groom, only recently back from the Solomons, had hardly glimpsed his bride before the ceremony. Therefore when time came for the kiss, it was a long one, lasting on and on until a child's voice rang out in the silence of the church:
"Mummy, is he spreading the pollen on her now?"

The modern child quizzed her mother as to her own origin, and was given the traditional answer: "God sent you."
"And how did you get here, Mother, did God send you, too?"
"Yes, dear."
"And grandma?"
"Yes, dear."
"And great-grandma?"
"Yes, dear."
"Do you mean to say, Mother, that there have been no sex relations in this family for over 200 years?"

Small boy to small girl: "Are you the opposite sex, or am I?"

Small boy to friend: "Well, I know all the facts of life, but I don't know if they're true."

At a Rotary Club luncheon, a friend of mine heard a speaker explain how to tell children the facts of life. That night, deciding to put the advice into practice, he called his older son into his study. During the detailed—and nervous—explanation about the bees and the flowers, the boy listened dutifully, making no comment. To avoid the ordeal a second time, the father suggested that the boy pass along his knowledge to his eight-year-old brother. The boy agreed, and went off to their room.

"Want to know something?" the father heard the older boy ask.

"What?"

"You know what married people do when they want to have kids? Well, Pop says that bees and flowers do the same thing!"

Small boy to playmate, as pretty little girl passes by: "Boy! If I ever stop hating girls, she's the one I'll stop hating first!"

My eight-year-old nephew and I had been talking about breeding the family poodle when he asked, "How did I start?"

Not knowing what would be acceptable to both child and parents, I hesitated, "Oh, you started as a seed or an egg," I replied.

"Which?" he countered.

"Does it really matter?" I asked.

With a disdainful look he said, "I'd just like to know whether I'm a flower or a bird!"

Child arriving home from school: "We learned all about sex today. Big deal!"

Husband to wife as they start out to dinner, leaving sitter with young son: "I say when they begin asking for a blonde instead of a brunette they're old enough to stay alone!"

It's a Small World

Hearing bells of ice-cream wagon, one small fry to another: "Listen! They're playing our song."

A small boy debunked the talk about a painless dentist in his neighborhood. "He's not painless at all," said the youngster. "He put his finger in my mouth and I bit it and he yelled just like anybody else."

A salesman called a prospective customer the other day and the phone was answered by what was obviously a small boy. "Is your mother or father home?" the salesman asked. The child said no. "Well, is there anyone else there I can speak to?"

"My sister," the youngster piped. There was a rather long period of silence, then the salesman heard the boy's voice again.

"I can't lift her out of the play pen," he said.

A friend of mine took her small son to visit a department-store Santa Claus. "And what would *you* like for Christmas?" asked the jolly old saint.

The child stared at him horrified. "Didn't you get my *letter?*" he asked.

Rudolph had heard a great deal about his little cousin Peter, but had never met him. So when he learned Peter was coming for a visit, the youngster was overjoyed. But when his cousin arrived, he took one look at him and burst into tears. "I thought," he wailed, "that Peter was a rabbit!"

———— • ————

$\mathbf{A}$ lecturer at London University, just appointed to a new post in the United States, informed his three-year-old daughter that she would soon be making her home in America. That night the child ended her evening prayers: "Good-bye, dear God. I'm going to America."

$\mathbf{A}$ctor Dan Duryea's son, Dickie, aged four, answered the telephone when Dan was sleeping. Trying to be grown-up, he asked the caller, "Would you like to leave a message?"

"Yes," said the caller. "Tell him Mr. Brown called."

Dickie got a pencil and paper and said, "Mr. Brown? How do you spell it?"

"B-R-O-W-N."

A moment of silence, then a very small voice asked plaintively, "How do you make a 'B'?"

$\mathbf{H}$olding tightly to her father's hand, a little girl peeked cautiously from the rim of Grand Canyon into the mile-deep abyss with its tumbling peaks and gorges. Recoiling, the youngster gasped: "Golly, Daddy, what happened?"

$\mathbf{A}$ housewife answered the doorbell to find a little girl of five and her younger brother, relatively new at walking, standing on the step. The little girl was all dolled up in an old formal of her mother's and a grown-up hat. Her little brother was wearing one of his father's hats that wobbled on his head and an older brother's coat that hung almost to the walk. "I am Mrs. Smith," said the little girl in a very formal tone, "and this is my husband, Mr. Smith. We've come to call."

The woman who had answered the call fell in with their act and invited "Mr. and Mrs. Smith" in for tea. The kids walked in and sat down and the hostess went immediately to the kitchen for some cookies and milk. When she returned the callers were already headed for the front door. "Must you go so soon?" asked the hostess. "I hoped you could stay for tea."

The little girl tossed back an artificial smile. "We can't, thank you," she said pleasantly. "Mr. Smith just wet his pants."

Young lad at dancing school: "I'd like to challenge you to the next dance."

My neighbor's two youngsters built a clubhouse in their yard. On the wall in childish lettering was a list of club rules. No. 1 reads: "Nobody act big, nobody act small, everybody act medium."

When the librarian questioned the little boy's book choice, *Advice to Young Mothers,* he explained, "I'm collecting moths."

My small neighbor's Sunday-school class had drawn names for a Valentine party at which each boy was to bring a box of candy to share with a girl as part of the refreshments. "I wanted Sue's name," Timmy complained. "But Billy got it."

"Oh, I wouldn't let it get me down," I said. "Surely Sue isn't the only pretty girl in your class."

"Course not," he said disgustedly. "But she's the only one who can't eat candy."

A friend has a son named after him. He reports that when his wife answered the telephone the other day a childish voice said, "May I please speak to Harry?"

"Do you want big Harry or little Harry?" she asked.

"Why—uh—big Harry, I guess," answered the voice. "The one in the fourth grade."

Looking Up

When I asked my class to write out the Ten Commandments, one boy put down, for the Fifth Commandment, "Humor thy father and thy mother."

A HANDY GUIDE
TO GROWNUPS*
JENNIFER OWSLEY

DEAR KIDS:
    This book is written for the purpose of helping you to understand adults and get along with them better.

I think there are too many books for adults about understanding children. Adults have been children before, so they should know something about children. But we have never been adults and don't know anything about them except what we can notice.

The world belongs to adults. They make it the way it is and run it. If you want to know about the world, you have to know about adults. That is why I have decided to try the brain-breaking job of writing this book for you.

I hope you will like it.

The more adults you get to know, the more you will realize each one is different. If you think they are all like your mother, you will get fooled.

Adults are not just big children. They think and act differently.

One of the reasons for this is that when you grow up you get larger and can reach higher places, and so you can do different things. For instance, when you were four you probably couldn't see over the edge of the kitchen sink. When you get bigger you can see right down into it. So you know what washing dishes is like. This is fun at first.

If you were twice as high as you are, elevators would not fright-

---

*According to the publishers, the author was almost 11 years old when she started this manuscript. Investigation established beyond a doubt her claim to authorship.

en you because you would not have your head pressed between people's stomachs. The furniture would fit you, and it wouldn't get you anywhere to climb up on it. Probably that's why adults don't climb. Besides, they are too stiff.

They think differently because they have been in this world longer and have had more time to learn about everything and get used to it. So they aren't so surprised about the world any more.

I think probably there are other reasons why they are different which I don't know about.

Every child knows a lot more about his own parents than anyone else, so I will not try to tell you about any parents except mine.

My parents do not seem to be the ordinary kind. You never can tell what my mother is going to say until she says it. She is likely all of a sudden on Sunday afternoon to start painting the living room pink. When she stays up after midnight she might be having a party or she might be doing the washing. This is partly because she works, but some mothers who work are not like that at all. When she is tired she gets cross and wants everyone to rush around doing housework, but she doesn't seem to think housework is important when she is rested.

She doesn't tell me what to do, which some of my friends' mothers are always doing. This is all right, but we have to do more thinking for ourselves than children whose mothers are willing to do it for them.

My father does not live with us so I can't write much about fathers. When there are fathers it is very nice. They are strong and can carry you, they aren't so interested in bedtime and what is good for you, and they have a good smell different from women.

Several of my best friends don't have fathers at home either, but all of them have mothers. I guess family life is more interesting to mothers than it is to fathers, or maybe women are tougher.

Most grandmothers think your mother is spoiling you, but nearly all grandmothers spoil you more than your mother does. That is because they are even older than parents. Most grandmothers think you need more food, washing and sleep than you are getting. Parents are more likely to realize that you have other interests besides these, but if you can stand the sleep, grandparents are more fun to be with than anybody.

Grandparents are even stiffer than parents and don't like being bounced at. They are more tired than parents and dislike noise more. They have more time, though, than parents, and they are always on your side and are the best grown-up friends you have.

If your mother and your relations disagree about the best rules for children, stay out of the argument and don't worry. Your mother will go right on doing how her habits are.

Teachers are the most important adults to know about of all. They know the things you want to know and are supposed to help you get to know them, too.

The worst kind of teachers are the kind that like some children and don't like others. They like children who do not make trouble and who are bright enough to learn by themselves, and they do not like the ones who can't learn unless the teacher helps them. If you get a teacher like this, all you can do is try to like them as much as possible. It helps to remember that you only have to like them for one year.

If you are the pet of one of these teachers, you have to make the other kids know you don't want to be, even if you are scared to do anything bad and really like your schoolwork. I am not very brave about teachers myself, but I am telling you, anyway, it is more important to have other kids be your friends than teachers like this.

Luckily more teachers are the best kind. They like all of the kids at least a little. You do not have to worry about getting along with them because they already know how to get along with you.

Adults like to talk more than children do. The longest hours in life are when your mother has you by the hand and stops to talk to some friend of hers on the street.

Or maybe when she is telephoning is worse. Her friends always get her on the phone when she is cooking your dinner or reading to you. Hardly any mothers will stop talking until you bother them quite a lot. I think it is perfectly fair to bother them as much as you have to. After all, they can call their friends back after you have to be in bed. Some of the ways to bother them are going upstairs and calling them, starting outdoors without any coat on, turning on the radio real loud, and so on. You can tell better than I can how much it takes and what you can get away with.

When your parents' friends come to dinner it is much pleasanter because then you can be there, too, and there is no question whether you still ought to be up or not. These guests are always nice to children no matter how bratty they act, because grown-up friends are more polite than honest, not like children who are the other way around.

Parents also like to visit their friends and go to shows and things that happen after bedtime. There is nothing you can do about this. If you raise a big enough fuss you can make them stay at home with you, but you can't make them like it.

Some mothers go to parties in the afternoon. These are mostly for ladies doing good of some kind. If the party is at your house there is a lot of work included. Washing curtains and slipcovers, scrubbing floors, dusting, polishing, cooking food—and finally a lot of big ladies come and gurgle at you, breathe on you and take hold of you. You have to bear it. The food is wonderful, though.

Parties in the evening are different. There are men there and the ladies are thinner. Some parents let you come down for the first part of the party. All the adults laugh a lot. The house only has to be ordinary clean at this kind of party.

You have to watch out how you tell the neighbor ladies about parties at night. Some people grow up and go right on thinking going to bed early is important. I do not see any sense in growing up to be this kind of an adult.

Money is more important to adults than it is to children. To understand adults you need to understand a little about the way they think about money.

Some parents give their children an allowance. The advantage of this is that you can count on it regular ahead of time. If you get an allowance it is best to make sure it is enough to cover what you have to buy with it. Allowance parents are likely to be grim about extras.

Other parents give children spending money whenever they feel like it. They give more if you baby them along.

Some think children should earn all the money they get. This is to teach children the value of money. It seems to me buying things teaches it to you better. Others think children have too much money to spend nowadays and ought to do everything cheaper than someone bigger would do the same thing.

The older people get, the more they think you can buy with less money. When old ladies give you a nickel for working all Saturday, washing dishes, going to the store and running around, it is because either they think you really can buy something with a nickel or else they think time isn't worth anything to a child, even Saturday. There is no use to explain to them. If you want to be kind to them and like helping, then look pleased and tell them thank you.

Getting to be a woman or a man I should think is the most important thing that happens to children and very interesting to talk about. Some parents think so, too, and do not care how much you find out as long as what you find out is so. Others think it is bad even to think about it.

My mother says you should not tell what you know about growing up to other children because all parents want their children to learn about it in the way they think best, not your way. This is probably true, but if you know something your friend wants to know, you have to decide whether your friends or their mothers are most important. I have to tell you that if you decide against the mothers you will probably get into trouble and will have to take the consequences.

One adult told me it is so wonderful to be grown-up that you can't understand about it ahead of time, and they want to keep it for a secret surprise. I do not believe this, because if it makes them so happy to be grown-up then I should think they would go on being happy as long as being grown-up lasts. But I do not think adults are so very much happier than children, even though they know all the secrets.

Religion is what adults have when they get together and agree about God. Religions mostly have churches, so they can meet and take up collections, and so on.

Some people think about God the way they do about Santa Claus. They know Santa Claus is magic, but they want their children to think he is real, and they are mad if you tell their children he is magic. The kind of adults that I think are the easiest to talk to are the kind that do not think it will bother God any for the children to think their own thoughts, but this kind is scarcer than the others. You had better keep your mouth shut until you know what kind of adult you are talking to, until you understand more about religion than I do.

Writing this book was fun, but I seem to have gotten more mixed up as I went on. This is probably because I kept growing up myself all the time. Sometimes I hate being so young, and sometimes I act childish on purpose. Maybe when I am grown-up I will still have some childish feelings underneath. Maybe growing up doesn't ever get quite finished.

Small boy to librarian: "Do you have anything on the parent from 30 to 35?"

Six-year-old Jerry came downstairs bellowing lustily. "What's the matter?" asked his mother.

"Papa was hanging pictures and he just hit his thumb with a hammer," said Jerry.

"That's not so serious," soothed his mother. "A big boy like you shouldn't cry at a trifle like that. Why didn't you just laugh?"

"I did," sobbed Jerry.

In a school essay on parents a small girl wrote: "We get our parents when they are so old it is very hard to change their habits."

A child's comment on piggy banks: "They teach children to become misers and parents to become bank robbers."

Small boy to father laden down with tennis rackets, fishing rods, baseball bats: "But I've already got lots of pals—can't you just be my *father?*"

A couple of Little Leaguers were asked how the big game had gone.

"Oh, it was a very good game until the third inning," one replied. "Then they had to call it because the parents were rioting all over the field."

Scholars All

A third-grader, asked if he knew what a person in charge of a library is called, replied promptly, "Sure, a bookie."

A youngster, being called down for a poor report card, asked: "What do you think the trouble with me is, Dad—heredity or environment?"

Teacher, commenting on little boy's poem: "Since your poem is about flowers, Russell, I think the word 'smell' would be more appropriate. You can still have it rhyme by substituting 'bluebell' for 'mountain pink.'"

Little boy to friend in school bus: "I woke up with chills and fever and headache and sore throat and earache and upset stomach—but it didn't work.

Ricky had reached school age, and his mother managed with a blast of propaganda to make him enthusiastic about the idea. She bought him new clothes, told him about the other children he would meet and got him so sold on the project that he eagerly went off the first day, and came back with excellent reports of school.

Next morning his mother went into his bedroom and said he had to get up.

"What for?"

"You have to go to school."

"What, again?" asked Ricky.

A boy brought home his report card and explained to his father why his marks were so poor: "Remember, Dad, I'm just an ordinary son of ordinary parents, and this is an ordinary report card."

Will you please stand as I call your names?" our school principal asked the mothers at a PTA tea. "I'm sure the teachers would like to tie you up with your children."

A teacher tells us she was a little startled by this note she received from the mother of one of her pupils: "Dear teacher. Please excuse Paul for being. It was his father's fault."

---•---

Father to mother: "At least this report card proves he isn't taking any mind-expanding drugs."

Small boy to father: "Here's my report card and one of yours I found in the attic."

As part of a test in my ninth-grade English class, the students were to write a letter that some well-known person might have written during his life. Time was limited, but I was hardly prepared for Don's brief note: "Dear Josephine, I am sorry to inform you that I did not make out so well at Waterloo. Yours truly, Napoleon."

---•---

CLASSROOM CLASSICS
EDITED BY ALEXANDER ABINGDON

Definitions

Acrimony, sometimes called holy, is another name for marriage.

Filet Mignon is an opera by Puccini.

A hamlet is a little pig.

A polygon is a man with more than one wife, preferably living.

Teetotalers are boys who carry golf clubs. They are generally paid, except in Scotland.

Sinister means a woman who isn't married.

Politics

The President has the power to appoint and disappoint the members of his Cabinet.

A Conservative is a kind of greenhouse where you look at the moon.

Geography

The climate of Bombay is such that its inhabitants have to live elsewhere.

The equator is a menagerie lion running around the earth and through Africa.

Denver is just below the "o" in Colorado.

567

History

In preparation for the channel crossing, Caesar built 18 new vesuls vessils vesles botes.

1066 is in the ninth century because centuries always for some reason or other fall back one.

Henry VIII had an abbess on his knee, which made walking difficult.

Queen Elizabeth was the "Virgin Queen." As a queen she was a success.

Hygiene

For fainting: rub the person's chest, or if a lady, rub her arm above the hand.

There are four symptoms of a cold. Two I forget and the other two are too well known to mention.

Doctors today say that fatal diseases are the worst.

False doctrine means giving people the wrong medicine.

Penned In

Our neighbor was worried because she had not heard for several weeks from her son at boarding school. Eventually she received this letter:

"Dear Mother: They are making us write our parents. Love, Jack."

Then there was the small boy who wrote: "Dear Aunt Ruth, I want to thank you for all the gifts you have sent me in the past, and all you intend to send me in the future. Love, Eugene."

An independent five-year-old, given to keeping his own counsel, wanted to write his uncle in California. Although he had already mastered "Uncle Jack," he had no idea how to spell the necessary "Dear." But his frequent visits to the zoo offered a solution. He searched the dictionary until he found a certain picture, with the delightful result that his letter started: "Caribou Uncle Jack."

When her favorite radio thriller, broadcast from Minneapolis, urged listeners to write in for a "mystery gift," our neighbors' eight-year-old daughter painstakingly addressed the envelope to the program at "Many Apples, Many Soda."

One of the prettiest and most popular of our young teachers recently announced her engagement. Fellow teachers and pupils naturally heaped good wishes upon her but she was hardly prepared for a note from one eight-year-old, which read:

Dear Miss Smith,

    I hope you have a happy and sexfull married life.

Your friend,
Mary

Thank-you note from a nine-year-old: "I love the book you sent me at Christmas. I have been reading it day and night and am now on page ten."

To all essayists, we would like to commend the clarity, brevity and general interest of the following from the pen of eight-year-old John Morrison of Rochester, New York, who wrote on "What My Dog Means to Me": "My dog means somebody nice and quiet to be with. He does not say 'Do' like my mother, or 'Don't' like my father, or 'Stop' like my big brother. My dog Spot and I sit together quietly and I like him and he likes me."

Hundreds of children sent in letters for the Milwaukee *Sentinel's* "My Pop's Tops" contest. Here are quotations from some of the entries:

"We have such good fun with my daddy that I wisht I had knew him sooner."

"My Pop's Tops because he always takes good care of us children when my mother is in the hospital getting another. I have eight brothers and four sisters and know from experience."

"He taked me fishin he taked me hunting, once he even taked me to the burlest show. It was wonderful."

"I don't have no real father because he went away when I was young, but now I have got two fathers, both very good."

"He wants me to learn. Once he took me to Fence Lake and thrun me in to see if I could swim and I couldn't. He saved me, too."

"I think all Pops are tops because if we didn't have Pops where would we be?"

"He is a farmer. He smells like a cow and when I smell that cow in the house I know Pop is home and I am glad."

"My Pop is tops because every time I ast him for a knickel he will start preeching that when he was a boy he had to earn his kenickls and at the same time he is putting his hand in his pocket and pulls out a kinckel, saying this is the last kinkel I have."

"My Pop's tops because he was a brave soldier. He didn't see me until I was three years old yet he is just as good to me as if he knew me all my life."

For his high-school graduation, I sent my nephew a check. Several weeks went by without a thank-you note. But when my next bank statement arrived, I found on the back of his canceled check, scrawled above his endorsement: "Dear Aunt Virginia—You know how I hate to write, but thanks a lot!"

A little girl's thank-you note: "Thank you for your nice present. I always wanted a pin cushion, although not very much."

A nine-year-old won his first literary prize for a school composition on manners. "I have good manners," he wrote. "I say good-night and good-morning and hello and good-bye, and when I see dead things lying around the house I bury them."

A San Francisco man gave his nine-year-old daughter $10 for her birthday so that she could open her first bank account. She was filling out the bank application when she came to the line asking the name of her former bank. In big bold letters, she wrote: "PIGGY."

Scout's Honor

One Boy Scout to another: "Do you ever have days when you feel just a little untrustworthy, disloyal, unhelpful, unfriendly, discourteous, unkind, grumpy, wasteful, cowardly, dirty and irreverent?"

A scoutmaster, noticing that his recruit scouts were having difficulty getting organized at their first cook-out, asked whether they had forgotten any essential equipment. "Yes," one boy replied. "My mother."

Soon after my son joined the Boy Scouts he was excitedly preparing for his first overnight hike. It was March and still chilly, but they were planning to use sleeping bags. A few nights before the big event, as he got into bed, he said seriously: "Would you please put my electric blanket on three tonight, Mum? I've got to start toughening up for roughing it."

During a first-aid course for Girl Scouts, the question was asked, "What would you do if a child swallowed a house key?"
One girl's reply: "I'd climb in through the window."

Two Boy Scouts appearing before the troop committee to be examined for advancement from tenderfoot to second class were asked to explain the mouth-to-mouth method of artificial respiration. One of them began his explanation: "You take one hand and hold the victim's nose. And with your other hand you open his mouth and remove his bubble gum. . . ."

During the preliminary inspection at a Boy Scout camp near Hazelton, Pennsylvania, the director found a large umbrella hidden in the bedroll of a tiny scouter. As it was obviously not one of the items of equipment listed, the director asked the lad to explain. The tenderfoot did so neatly by asking: "Sir, did you ever have a mother?"

One Cub Scout to another: "The best way to make a fire with two sticks is to be sure one of them is a match."

The latest revised edition of the *Boy Scout Handbook* contains an interesting change in the section on how to make pancakes over an open fire. It begins: "Make the pancake batter according to instructions on the box. . . ."

Two Cub Scouts whose younger brother had fallen into a shallow pond rushed home to Mother with tears in their eyes. "We're trying to give him artificial respiration," one of them sobbed. "But he keeps getting up and walking away."

Camping It Up

Some youngsters at summer camp write very little but say a great deal. For instance, a 10-year-old New York lad wrote his parents from Vermont: "This camp has everything and they don't need me."

Our neighbors were able to send their son to a camp for two weeks for the very reasonable fee of $65. It was his first vacation away from home. More than a week had gone by before the anxious parents received their first card. It read: "Dear Mom. Tell Dad that I know how he can save $65 next year."

A father's letter to his daughter at summer camp:

"Highland Park is fine. The food is good, and I like my wife. Yesterday we went on a trip to the golf course. The golf pro is nice and let me ride in a golf cart. I fed it some gasoline. Can I have a golf cart when I get home?

"We camped in last night, and I slept in a bed. My roommate froze her fingers fixing my dinner, but she will be okay when the maid gets back Tuesday. Today we are having competition to see who can make money the fastest. I came in last. Your mother won the spending contest. When you have a chance, please send me a CARE package. Love, Dad."

Our 11-year-old came bustling home from summer camp with the air of a young John D. Rockefeller. It seems he had gotten permission to use the camp mimeograph and had printed 100 copies of the following letter which he sold to his busy fellow campers at a nickel a copy:

Dear Mom and Dad,

I am having fun here at camp. We are playing baseball and swimming a lot. We sit around a campfire every night and sing songs and play games. The meals are fine and I feel very good. I hope that you are both feeling good. I will see you soon. Love——"

A neighbor's young son, back from two weeks at his first camp, was excited about badges awarded him for the greatest improvement in swimming skill and for naming the most birds. His mother saw that there was another ribbon. "Aw," he said, "I just got that for havin' my bag packed neatest when we started home."

"Why, that's fine," she told him. "I'm proud of you!"

"Aw, I hadn't never unpacked it," he explained.

Letter from a nine-year-old camper: "Dear Mom and Pop: Camp is O.K. The food is wonderful and they don't make you eat it. Love, Allen."

Then there was the eight-year-old girl who wrote her parents: "We are having a lot of fun; we play games, weave and string beads and take hikes and every night we all cry ourselves to sleep."

Attention, All Camp Counselors: Many new campers are with us this year and parents are anxious to know how their youngsters adjusted to camp life. We urge you to use the following guide in writing parents our customary end-of-season reports:

If—
The boy wouldn't go near the water . . .
He was a fussy eater . . .

Write—
Although swimming was not Bobby's favorite sport . . .
He never made a glutton of himself . . .

If—
He couldn't get along with his fellow campers . . .
His tent was always messy . . .

Write—
He made a real effort to find new friends . . .
Of course, boys of his age aren't always neat . . .

If—
He's without doubt the worst camper we've ever had . . .
We wouldn't have him back on a bet . . .

Write—
He's outstanding in certain respects . . .
Although our rates are doubling next year, we hope . . .

A youngster's first card from camp read: "Dear Mom, I told you if you made me go to camp something terrible would happen. Well, it did. Love, Bonnie."

Guess what!" a camper wrote her father. "There is a foot-long catfish under our cabin, two other catfish and a lot of baby ones. We are feeding them so they will trust us.

"P.S. Could you send me a hook and line?"

A woman whose son was attending summer camp received an ecstatic letter from the director. "Robert is one of the most promising youngsters we have ever had here," he rhapsodized. "He is a fine athlete, has a world of vitality and enthusiasm and his sportsmanship and leadership leave nothing to be desired. If every boy we had were such a splendid example of American youth as Robert, we would feel we had succeeded far beyond our fondest expectations."

The mother wrote back: "I am happy to hear that Robert is doing so well. He seems to be an excellent camper. I have a son there, too—named George. How is he doing?"

A father reports that he received two alarming postcards from his boy in camp. The first one read: "They say the flood probably won't reach our tent." The second: "We've been taking some pretty long hikes. Please send my other sneaker."

Teen Time

As a junior-high-school teacher distributed the first report cards of the year, she noticed that one blond teenager was scowling. "What's the matter? Aren't you satisfied with your marks?" she asked.

"I certainly am not," said the girl. "You gave me an F in Sex and I didn't even know I was taking it!"

The fact that our 12th-grade English textbook is a generation behind the times became obvious in a recent classroom incident. I was instructing the class in adverbial clauses, and my face turned beet-red as I read this sentence to a room full of giggling seniors: "After I had taken the pill, I was ready for bed."

Father describing his adolescent daughter: "She's fourteen, going on twenty."

Father to daughter's suitor: "My daughter says you have that certain something, but I wish you had something certain!"

Wife to husband, as son chatters on the telephone: "Junior's just at the awkward age, dear . . . too old to say anything cute and too young to say anything intelligent."

Discouraged teen-age girl to friend: "The label says it's a 30-day guaranteed beauty treatment. Maybe it all happens at once on the last day!"

Adolescence: That period when a boy refuses to believe that someday he'll be as dumb as his father.

A gawky lad from New England came to New York with his girl, and took her to nearby Playland Amusement Park. They had heard a lot about the Tunnel of Love and were especially anxious to try it out. But when they got home, the kids expressed disappointment.

"Shucks," the boy said, "it was dark and damp and uncomfortable. Besides, we got soaking wet."

"How come?" asked a friend. "Did the boat leak?"

The kid looked amazed. "There's a *boat*?"

Teen-age girl on telephone: "If that click on the extension is you, Mother, remember that wiretap evidence is inadmissible."

High-school boy to girl friend: "My dad wants me to have everything he didn't have when he was a boy—like all A's on my report card!"

A friend of mine reports that his 15-year-old son, after only six dates, has bought a little black book for telephone numbers. On the cover the boy has confidently written "Vol. I."

A tall, thin teen-ager had been sent to the principal's office for fighting. Asked why she was always getting in fights, she said, "As long as they call me 'Turnpike,' I'll fight."
   "But why do they call you that?" exclaimed the principal.
   "Not a curve in sight," said the girl sadly.

Teen-age girl to boy friend: "I would never realize by dating you, Sheldon, that the American teen-ager spends 14 billion dollars a year!"

Teen-ager coming home from dance to mother: "Roger was the life of the party—that gives you an idea of how dull it was."

My teen-age nephew had approached his father for an increase in his allowance. After delivering a lecture on the virtues of economy, the father added plaintively, "Don't you realize, son, that there are more important things than money?"
   "Of course," the boy replied. "That's the trouble."
   "What trouble?" the father asked.
   "Those important things cost money to date."

INVITATION TO THE DANCE

I T IS easy to forget, with age, that asking a girl to a dance is not, at 16, a simple business. The thought that a lad nearly six feet tall might be too bashful to ask a young lady to go to a dance never enters one's head.

That is, until the end of the school year approaches and with it, school dances. One gathers, listening to feminine talk at dinner, that the youngest lady of the house desires very much indeed to go to a certain dance but that she has not been asked. One regards as scientifically as possible this young lady. She is very young, a bit angular, not beautiful perhaps, but not unattractive, either. Is she doomed to an adolescence during which she will be the girl who isn't asked to dances? One is reassured by news that few of her contemporaries have been, as yet, asked to this dance.

Day follows day with no sign that a boy—one boy in particular —is going to ask this young lady to this dance. The only hopeful note is that he has asked no one else. Each day the youngest lady of the house arrives home with a news bulletin—so-and-so has been invited to the dance.

The youngest lady of the house begins to look forlorn. She discovers, through a third party, that this particular young man really wants to ask her to the dance but that he has not been able to summon the courage. One has seen this lad—big, for just-turned 16, weighing about 160 pounds—and one is puzzled.

Working in the garden one sees the young man driving his father's car slowly by the house, and one is seen in return. The car jerks forward and speeds away. Had one not been in sight, would he have come in and delivered the golden invitation? The telephone rings, but before the youngest lady can reach it the ring stops. One knows—one is sure—it was he, and that nerve failed at the final minute. The youngest lady of the house, four days before the dance, begins to fret. She has a new dress and an appointment with the hairdresser; are these for nought?

One comes home next day and opens the front door. The lady of the house, looking ten years younger, cries, "He asked her!" One grumbles that it is about time, secretly breathing a little sigh of relief—not only that the youngest lady has been asked, but also that one is fortyish and need not relive those terrible, terrible teens.

Sibling Sentiments

Little boy, who has just let in young man, calls to sister: "The bird-in-hand's here!"

Kid-brother to sister's suitor: "She's upstairs working on her acceptance speech."

Three-year-old Linda watched her aunt unpack with much excitement, waiting for her present. At last two bean bags were produced, one red and one blue. "Which one would you like, Linda?" asked the visitor. "One is for you and the other is for Skippy."

Without hesitation, Linda replied: "I want Skippy's."

Little boy to friend about baby brother: "He has some teeth, but his words haven't come in yet."

Girl answering telephone: "Marie isn't in just now. This is her 111-pound, five-foot-three, blonde, blue-eyed sister."

I went into a toy shop to order some hobby supplies. I noticed a tiny girl standing with her mother. The clerk was showing the girl an elaborate doll. "Now, this model walks, talks, cries and drinks," she explained.

"I have a baby sister who does that," the tot replied scornfully. "I just want a doll."

$\text{———} \bullet \text{———}$

A friend of ours brought the cheerful news home to his six-year-old son that the stork had delivered a lovely baby sister. "Aw," said the lad, "I was hoping for an older brother!"

Small girl, showing her older sister's bedroom to playmate: "My sister's 19. I thought I'd have her room someday, but she never married."

$\text{———} \bullet \text{———}$

Zoo Story:
ANIMAL
KINGDOM

I N COMMUNIST CHINA, we are told, pets have been abolished, thus saving a lot of money, a lot of time, and a lot of street-cleaning. The rational thing is for us to follow their example. We could convert New York City into a livable place with the money we expend annually on pets. But we won't do it. Americans of all sizes and both sexes are suckers for pets. And surely one of the reasons is that they're so diverting, especially when they're being, from their own point of view, most sensible and businesslike. But also when they're being consciously playful. Samuel Butler puts it this way: "The great pleasure of a dog is that you may make a fool of yourself with him and not only will he not scold you, but he will make a fool of himself too." As for cats, they are extraordinary creatures, so extraordinary that there's a whole literature about them. (See, for instance, "What Every Young Cat Ought to Know.") Cats seem at first glance enigmatic. But actually they are more diverse, richer in character than most other pets. One can think of dozens of adjectives applicable to one or another of the cats we may have known: sly, polite, superior, crazy, wise, playful, baleful, elusive, dainty, reserved, neat, sleepy. . . .

A Dog's Life

THE DOG THAT WOULDN'T COME HOME
JAMES THURBER

JEANNIE was a small Scottish terrier. Her jaw was skimpy, her haunches frail, her forelegs slightly bowed. She thought dimly and her coordination was only fair. Even in repose she had the strained, uncomfortable appearance of a woman on a bicycle.

Jeannie did everything the hard way, digging with one paw at a time, shoving out of screen doors sideways, delivering pups on the floor of a closet completely covered with shoes. She developed a persistent troubled frown which gave her the expression of some-one trying to repair a watch with gloves on.

Jeannie spent the first two years of her life in the city. When she was taken to the country to live, she clung to the hearth for weeks, poking her nose out now and then for a dismaying glimpse of what she conceived to be God's great Scottie trap. But finally the scent of moles in the lawn and the scurry of squirrels brought her out for tentative explorations.

Within a few months Jeannie took to leaving the house when the sun came up and returning when it began to get dark. She began to look sleek, fat, smug, and at the same time pleasantly puzzled, like a woman who finds more money in her handbag than she thought was there. I decided to follow her discreetly one day, and she led me a difficult four-mile chase to a group of summer cottages. Jeannie, it came out, was the camp mascot. She had muzzled in, and was shaking down the cottagers for ham-burgers, fried potatoes, cake and marshmallows. Jeannie had won them over with her only trick. She could sit up, not easily but with amusing effort, placing her right forefoot on a log or stone, and pushing. Her sitting-up stance was precarious, but if she fell over, she was rewarded just the same. She couldn't lose. The camp was a pushover.

Little old One Trick gradually figured out that the long trip home after her orgies was a waste of time. There all she got was a plain wholesome meal once a day—no pay-off for a terrier who had struck it rich over the hills. She took to staying away for days at a time. I would have to go and bring her back in the car.

One day the summer people brought her home themselves, and Jeannie realized the game was up. The next time I drove to the camp to get her she wasn't there. I found out finally from the mailman where she was. "Your little dog is stayin' with a school-teacher in a cottage the other side of the lake," he said.

The schoolteacher, I found out, had opened her door one morn-ing to discover a small Scottie sitting up in the front yard, begging. The cute little visitor had proceeded to take her new hostess for three meals a day, topped off now and then with chocolates. But I had located Jeannie's hiding place, so she moved on to fresh fields. "Your little dog's stayin' with some folks over near Dan-bury," the mailman told me a week later.

I found her, and opened the door of the car. She climbed slowly up onto the seat beside me. We both stared straight ahead all the way home.

Jeannie was a lost dog. There wasn't anything to do about it. After all, I had my own life to live. Before long I would have had to follow her as far as Stamford or Darien or wherever the gravy happened to be thickest. "Your little dog—" the mailman began a few days later. "I know," I said, "thanks," and went back into the house. She came home of her own accord about three weeks later and I think she actually made an effort to adjust herself to her real home. It was too late, though.

When Jeannie died, at the age of nine, possibly of a surfeit of chocolates, I got a very nice letter from the people she was living with at the time.

———— • ————

A dog teaches a boy fidelity, perseverance, and to turn around three times before lying down.

Small boy looking at great Dane: "Is he for me or am I for him?"

A sportsman went to a hunting lodge and bagged a record number of birds, aided by a dog named Salesman. Next year he returned and asked for Salesman again. "Hound ain't no durn good now," the handler said.

"What happened!" cried the sportsman. "Was he injured?"

"No. Some fool came down here and called him 'Sales Manager' all week. Now all he does is sit on his tail and bark."

A woman came into the classified-ad department of the New York *Times* with a dog in her arms, dictated a dog-for-sale ad and left. A few minutes later she telephoned the office to say that the ad should not be run. She was merely throwing a scare into the dog because he had been naughty. Having heard the ad dictated, the dog became properly penitent and mannerly.

Youngster in pet shop: "I want the puppy with the happy ending."

———— • ————

During our show-and-tell period in the third grade, Mike mentioned that his pet beagle was expecting puppies. From then on, the class eagerly awaited the news of their birth. When the day arrived, Mike announced glumly, "Well, they're here."

It was obvious that he was disappointed, but because of the intense interest of the class, I asked, "What's wrong, Mike? Tell us more."

"Well," he said, "I wanted a collie, and my sister wanted a poodle, and all we got were beagles—and we already have a beagle."

The dog is man's best friend; this alone is depressing.

In Levelland, Texas, John Yates got his lost dog back after he put this ad in the paper: "Lost or strayed, Chihuahua dog answering to name of Chico. Brilliant dog, acutely aware of national and world politics—he shakes all the time."

In Philadelphia one of the city's small-fry clubs put on a dog show for its young members. One six-year-old entered the family basset hound. When he returned home his father wanted to know how the dog had fared. "He would have won best of breed," the little boy said. "But another basset hound showed up."

Husband arriving home with enormous dog to indignant wife who is surrounded by small children: "But I *did* consult you—you said last night a Great Dane was all we needed around here!"

Sign over dog in pet-shop window: "Reduced! Obedience School Dropout."

Small boy showing dog to father: "She's a bargain for 50 cents. She's going to have puppies."

A woman with a fuzzy poodle under her arm swished into a cocktail lounge. Then, ignoring the waiter who came up, she fussed over her fidgeting animal, cooing baby-talk: "There, there. Nobody's going to hurt mamma's itsy-bitsy baby."

Finally the dog settled down and the woman turned to the waiter. Without batting an eye he asked courteously — if somewhat coldly — "Your first dog, madam?"

A small manufacturing company has a stray dog as an honorary vice president. A spokesman explains: "His ability to get along with anyone, his prompt response to a pat on the back, his interest in watching others work, his great knack for looking wise and saying nothing, make him a natural."

A woman went into an exclusive pet shop to buy a dog. After inspecting every purebred in the place, she told the proprietor that they were all priced far too high. "Madam," he retorted, drawing himself up haughtily. "Perhaps you had better go to a used cur dealer."

Sticker on a Hollywood sports car: "Help Stamp Out Tall Dogs."

DOWN, BOY, DOWN, BLAST YOU!
CHARLTON OGBURN, JR.

WOULD you like to carry a perpetual load of guilt, to know that no matter how much you give of yourself it will never be enough, and to take on a load of chronic harassments? You would? Then I have just the thing for you: a dog!

A devoted dog. One that will sit in front of you all evening while you are trying to read, looking at you with anxious, supplicating eyes until you feel like a brute for ignoring him. Did someone say that bestowing a few pats and affectionate words will reassure your loyal friend and enable you to go on with your reading? Only a dedicated and mindless propagandist for man's most insatiable dependent—and the country is full of just such propagandists—would venture so preposterous a claim.

A dog's need for reassurance is a bottomless well. You could devote an entire day to ministering to a dog's need to feel wanted —stroking it, romping with it, crooning over it—and the instant you desisted, the rejected creature, with an imploring whimper, would nose under your arm to confront you with an expression of bewilderment and hurt. Don't you love me any more? its eyes would ask. Am I hateful to you? Do you wish I were dead?

One way or another, a dog is a full-time proposition. Questions must be constantly in your mind. If the dog is outdoors, is it getting lost or run over, upsetting a neighbor's garbage can, mauling or being mauled by a neighbor's dog? If indoors, is it chewing up your wife's kid gloves, lying on the sofa rubbing into the fabric the stench of the decayed fish it rolled in ecstatically the day before or, seized by a sudden need, is it forgetting its housebreaking or throwing up on the rug?

To know that the dog is prevented from getting into mischief by being shut up in the cellar or tied up in the yard relieves your mind of one set of distracting concerns only to afflict it with another. The dog has nothing to do. The dog is a prisoner. You have taken on a dog and now are failing it in companionship. Here you sit and there the dog languishes, an innocent, loving creature condemned to the same punishment that would be visited upon a human criminal.

The condition of being a dog-owner is that you are continually in a state either of exasperation over the dog's misdemeanors or of self-recrimination because you have let the dog down. None of this you would discover from the effervescent manuals written for prospective dog-buyers. These books make much of the dog's intelligence, its desire to please its master, its responsiveness to training. Humbug! The dog is certainly intelligent, up to a point, but its intelligence is devoted to getting what *it* wants. Anyone who thinks that a dog has its master's happiness uppermost in its mind has never eaten his meals with his devoted pet covetously watching every single forkful.

As for that longing to be trained that the books would have you believe burns in a dog's breast, that is the greatest hoax of all. To begin with, most of what you wish a dog to do, or more often not to do, is uncommunicable. "Don't wag your tail when passing the Dieffenbachia; it whacks the leaves off. Don't dig holes in the flower bed. When there are guests within hearing, don't lap water out of the toilet." How to get these ideas across, the books don't say. "Living with a dog," observed a friend of mine with a great, clumsy golden retriever, "is like having an idiot relative in the house."

Nothing is more foreign to a dog's nature than obedience. True, there are dog-owners whose charges obey their commands, but those persons are all of a special sort—leathery-complexioned outdoorsmen who go around talking of bloodlines and who live more with dogs than with people. The dog knows that they will never give up until it does obey.

With you and me, it knows just the opposite. "Here, Shaughnessy!" you cry. But you know that Shaughnessy, racing madly, his face transfigured with rapture, ears flapping in the breeze, will pay no attention. Shaughnessy has got your number.

It is not as if our requirements of the dog were exorbitant. If our dog just wouldn't jump up on everybody, if he'd just obey when we say "Down!" that would be enough. But let a guest arrive—especially a woman—and up he goes, eager and possessive. If it is a small dog, he snags a woman's stockings; if a Great Dane, he licks off her makeup. Of course, you can always shut the dog up when there are guests coming, if you do not mind their being greeted by the howls of a soul in purgatory.

Leo Rosten once said of W. C. Fields that no man who dislikes dogs can be wholly bad. But outspoken honesty on this subject is rare. Dogs enjoy an idolatrous press. Have you ever heard of a dog story in which the dog was the villain? The prevailing view is that any man without a warm spot in his heart for dogs lacks the very attributes that make a dog admirable—loyalty, genuineness, capacity for unquestioning love, steadfastness.

The iconoclast might quite reasonably disagree. "Look, I've had a dog," he might plead. "There were scratch marks on our new car the first week. Every time my wife cleaned house, the dog would celebrate by galumphing through a mudhole. He would sleep unperturbed when a stranger drove up, but wake the baby by barking every time our best friends came over. You couldn't reach down to tie your shoelaces without your hand closing on a cold, wet nose. Besides that, he'd want to be let in or out of the house 50 times a day."

But how often do you hear anyone talk like that? Total indoctrination—that describes the conditioning of the American mind toward dogs. It begins early in life. No boy can grow up in our country without having it borne upon him that unless he is a boy with a dog, he does not really count. And, of course, the combination does seem a natural one. Boys and dogs are much alike, similarly the creatures of impulse, equally irresponsible, alike possessed of sources of energy that are never long exhausted and also can never be harnessed to any useful end. They are equally indiscriminate in diet and devoid of any sense of hygiene, each abetting the other in his most socially deplorable proclivities.

But what about the 30- or 40- or 50-year-old boy with a dog? Can a grown man put up with a dog? Obviously, grown men do. The reason they can is not only that they have been brainwashed but that, here again, the human and canine partners minister to each other's weaknesses. The man, buffeted by the world, consistently defeated and humiliated, as we all are, has the crutch of the dog's worshipful esteem. The most hopeless incompetent can be a god to a dog.

As may have been suspected, I did not become so over-familiar with canine nature by observing my friends' pets. In fact, there is even now a dog in our family. We took one on at the behest of our young daughters. I was rather surprised when, some time after we had assumed the burden, my wife remarked that I'd probably be much less bothered by the dog's tagging after me if I did not make so much of her. "Leave it to the girls to pat her and rub her chest and talk baby talk to her," she counseled. "After all, she's supposed to be *their* dog."

Which, of course, is true. But the creature does show a certain attachment to me which is difficult entirely to disregard. She is a pure-blooded Dalmatian of a very distinguished line. She has— as I should be less than candid not to admit—a certain nobility. Much as you might wish to be free of her and be able to call your time your own, you do not treat such a dog unfeelingly. And another thing: I do not pretend to have those qualities that cause a person to stand out among his fellow men and command their respect and allegiance; the very idea is laughable. Still, when another living being perceives in you such qualities, it cloaks you with a certain responsibility. She may be the biggest pest in the world, but you have to show her some consideration. Don't you?

Cat Nips

WHAT EVERY YOUNG CAT OUGHT TO KNOW
PAUL W. GALLICO
AND SUZANNE SZASZ

WHEN I was a very young kitten my mother had an unfortunate encounter with a motorcar and I found myself alone in the world. I was not unduly disturbed, since I was intelligent and resourceful, but after a week in the country living on a revolting diet of grubs and insects, I determined to take over a family and become a house cat.

I have often discussed with friends the manner in which I attained success, and since I am not affected with vanity, I was able to point out clearly the extraordinary perception and outstanding cleverness behind each move on my part. So impressed were they that they begged me to write my story down and codify my experiences with human beings in a set of regulations for the young.

This I have done. But first a brief account of the manner in which I took over my own family, who shall be nameless, since it is not my purpose to embarrass them.

The Take-Over. I emerged from the woods, hungry and disgusted, to see, standing in a clearing, a small, pleasant-looking white house with green shutters. The grounds were neat and well-kept and obviously belonged to persons of some affluence. An expensive car in the garage confirmed this. If you want to take over a poor family, that's your business. It wasn't going to be mine.

At the back door I reconnoitered. A man and his wife were having breakfast inside. They looked exactly like the people I wanted, so I jumped onto the screen door, hung there and cried piteously. I knew exactly how I appeared to them. Irresistible!

"The poor little thing," the woman cried. "It wants to come in. Maybe it's hungry. I'll give it some milk."

Just as I expected! I already had her. All I needed was to get one paw inside the door and—

However, it wasn't going to be that simple. The man! He began to bellow that he hated cats and wouldn't have one in the house. "Nix! Nothing doing!" he yelled. "If you've got to feed it, give it some milk in the barn and then get rid of it. It doesn't come in here."

Here was a challenge. If there's anything that's fun to work over, it's a man who thinks he is a real cat-hater. While he roared, I kept crying heartbreakingly. Finally, the woman opened the door and picked me off, saying to him, "Oh, don't make such a fuss, darling. I'll just give her some milk and we'll put her out afterward."

It didn't work that way of course, and we had a lovely day together while he was at work. Then just before evening she took me in her arms, kissed me and said, "Now, Kitty, I'm afraid you must go. He'll be coming back."

I stayed out until I saw them eating their supper in the dining room. Then I went to the screen door again and just cried and cried and cried. At last the man shouted, "For heaven's sake, why don't you get it and feed it? I can't hear myself eat with that yelling going on."

So the woman fetched me, and I had another good meal, and later slept in the barn.

After that it didn't take long. The very next night I was sitting on the woman's lap interfering with her sewing, and the man was reading his newspaper. I got off her lap, had a good stretch and went over and sat looking up at him. At first he pretended he didn't notice, but finally he said, "What is it you want, Kitty?"

I gave him the full treatment—the big "hello," with the rub around the ankles. As I expected, the man came all apart. He said, "Why, Kitty, do you want to sit in *my* lap?" With that he picked me up and began to stroke and chuck me under the chin. I turned on the purr and the charm, cuddling up and giving his hand a couple of licks, spreading on the butter so thick you could slice it.

Just then there was a flash of lightning, a crash of thunder, and it began to pour. They went around closing windows, the man carrying me with him, saying, "Nothing to be frightened of, Kitty old girl. Just a little thunderstorm, that's all."

Later the lightning stopped, but it kept on raining. "I guess we can go to bed now," the woman said. "Will you put the cat out?"

The man looked at her as though she were out of her mind. "Put her out on a night like this? Are you crazy?"

"But I thought you said you didn't want a cat in the house."

The man was furious. "Well, I *don't* want a cat in the house, but that doesn't mean putting her out in a cloudburst. Look, she's trembling like a leaf! Haven't you got any heart?"

Trembling was right. I was trying to keep from laughing out loud.

Attitudes. One of the most important things for any cat to master for the proper and thorough subjugation of a household is a set of "attitudes." Poses, expressions, play of body and features, all are lumped into the manner in which you remain at all times alluring, fascinating, charming, pleasing, lovely and sweet.

For instance, I cannot begin to tell you how effective the "silent miaow" can be for breaking down human resistance. The technique is ridiculously simple. You look up at the subject, open your mouth as you would for a fully articulated miaow, but you permit no sound to issue. The effect is simply staggering. The man or woman appears to be shaken to the core, and will give you practically anything, for it creates a picture of helplessness that pierces directly to the human heart. I usually confine its use to begging at the dinner table, but it can be used to good effect at other times when you want something they are not inclined to give you.

Actually, any appeal to their vanity as the godlike givers of things to small, so-called helpless creatures may get you larger portions and nicer tidbits. And it helps to keep them from thinking of the situation between them and you in its true light, namely, the extent to which you have taken them over.

Property Rights. The morning following my take-over I went upstairs, got onto my people's bed and slept next to the man, where it was nice and warm. Later I woke him up by walking on his face. He sat up, took hold of me and said, "Why you little cutie! Who asked you up here? Come on, let's have a look at you." And he began to play with me.

"Darling," his wife said, "do you think she ought to be on the bed?"

He threw her a dirty look. "Why? What's wrong with that? he said. "Look, she's nuts about me."

The bed was mine from then on.

Motherhood—Yes or No? Kittens can happen to anyone. I've had mine and I wouldn't have missed the fun for anything. I am all for it—provided someone else has the next batch.

It happened, of course, when I was very young. I had my house running smoothly, the man and his wife nicely subjugated, when I fell in love, with never a thought to the consequences.

He was pure white, a veritable White Knight, and an absolutely fascinating devil. I lost my head. The things he told me and the promises he made! I was this; I was that; I was unique; I was the center of his universe. I have always known I was unique but, you know, it's different when you hear someone else say it. We went for long walks together.

I was a good mother. I am sure I made a charming picture with my brood about me, nursing or cuddled close, but that doesn't alter the fact that they nearly resulted in breaking up our formerly quiet, happy household.

The man became insanely jealous of me because of the attention I lavished on my kittens. Whenever *he* wanted to play with me I was busy washing them or feeding them. Before long he was making himself unpleasant to his wife as well because *she* was paying too much attention to the kittens. Later *my* nose was put out of joint when he began to make more fuss over the kittens than he did over *me*.

Then the question of homes for them arose. That's when the idea is likely to come to your people that as long as they are cleaning out a batch of kittens, why not do a 100-percent job, get rid of you, too, and start all over again with some peace in the house. I don't say it will always happen, but a smart cat plays the percentages. Next time that White Knight shows up, go play with your catnip mouse and forget about him.

They Need Us. It's not the easiest thing in the world, this taking over of a house and family. Humans, you'll find, can be selfish, inconsiderate and stubborn. Yet, with all these handicaps they have this strong and wonderful thing they call love and when they love you and *you* love them, nothing else seems to matter.

593

Although you will never solve the mystery of this human love, you will no doubt discover, as I did, something that is part of it. Male or female, young or old, good or bad, they are all lonely but, unlike us, they are not self-sufficient enough to bear it. The fact is: *they need us.* Often, when I think of how I can ease this condition simply by sitting on their laps, or just being about, it gives me the pleasantest feeling in my stomach and starts me purring.

And you need not be ashamed if this happens to you, too.

———————— • ————————

A woman telephoned a veterinarian and asked him to come examine her cat. "I don't know what's wrong with her," the woman told him. "She looks as if she's going to have kittens, but that's impossible. She's never been out of the house except when I had her on a leash."

The vet examined the cat and said there was no doubt of her pregnancy. "But she can't be," protested her mistress. "It's impossible."

At that point a large tomcat emerged from under the sofa.

"How about him?" the vet asked.

"Don't be silly," said the woman. "That's her brother!"

Man, watching departing figure, to wife holding basket of kittens: "I don't think he represents the Welcome Wagon at all."

In her apartment one evening, a woman who likes all animals heard a cat meowing, and playfully meowed back. She couldn't see the cat, for a building abutment cut off her view. But the cat meowed back and she repeated the call, this time putting plenty of oomph in it. Thus the calls went back and forth for some time, loaded with quavers, innuendo and passion. The lady was exultant. "Isn't it wonderful," she said to her husband, "I can speak cat language!" But her triumph was deflated when the neighbor who rides to town with her husband dropped in the next morning. "The funniest thing happened last night," he said. "I meowed at a cat and he meowed back—we must have kept it up for 20 minutes."

———————— • ————————

Boy patting kitten: "He must be talking to somebody—I can hear the busy signal."

Then there was the clever cat that ate cheese and breathed down the rathole with baited breath.

Driving past a farmhouse, we saw a sign on the fence:
"FREE CUTE KITTENS"
Two weeks later the sign read:
"FREE ~~CUTE~~ KITTENS"
A month passed and the sign changed to:
"FREE ~~CUTE KITTENS~~
CATS"
On our last trip past the farm, we found a new sign:
"FREE CATS AND CUTE KITTENS."

Husband as wife shows him cat surrounded by new kittens: "She did all right for a cat that didn't know a soul in the neighborhood three months ago."

Horsing Around

Not long ago, the Toledo, Ohio, Junior League attempted to raise money by putting on a horse show. The socialite who was in charge of the affair fell ill the day before it was to open, and another girl, new to the ways of horseflesh, was put in command. Shortly before the event, she received an anxious telephone call from a man who had several horses entered. "I know this is for charity," he said apologetically, "and I'm sorry to have to ask you to do this, but can you scratch one of my horses for me?"

"Surely," said the Leaguer pleasantly. "Where?"

After her first horseback ride, a young lady was heard to comment: "I never imagined anything filled with hay could ride so hard!"

---•---

Notice on a community bulletin board in San Francisco: "Ten-year-old boy would like garden work and odd jobs after school and on Saturdays to help support a dependent who eats like a horse. P.S. It *is* a horse."

At a track in England some years ago a mounted policeman was helping to get the race horses into starting position. At the cry, "They're off!" the policeman's horse broke with the field and the astonished bobby found himself desperately trying to pull in his mount. The best he could do, however, was to slow him down to third place. On the stretch the horse began to fight it out with one of the official entries, and despite the policeman's efforts to pull out of the race, he came in second, a scant neck behind a horse ridden by Freddy Archer, one of England's greatest jockeys.

When my husband and I, city born and bred, first moved to an isolated part of Wyoming, a neighboring rancher gave generously of his time and experience in helping us get started. We noticed that he invariably hopped on his horse to do even the shortest errand. One day, when he mounted to ride no more than 30 feet, my husband said, "Don't you *ever* walk?"

"Son," the rancher replied seriously, "if the good Lord had wanted me to walk, He'd have given me four legs."

A man trying to buy a horse from a Vermont farmer was startled when he named $1000 as his price. Nonetheless the prospective buyer countered with a reasonable $100 offer. "That's a helluva discount," mused the farmer, "but I'll take it."

As the buyer counted out the money he couldn't resist asking why the farmer had accepted $100 after first naming ten times that sum. "Well," he drawled, "I thought mebbe you'd like to own a thousand-dollar hoss."

---•---

I HATE HORSES

BIL GILBERT

URING the course of a misspent life as a naturalist, I
have, without regret, lavished time, money and affection
on raccoons, foxes, ferrets, llamas, cheetahs, bears,
hawks, crows, snakes, turtles, dogs, cats, and certain even more
improbable beasts. I have also, either voluntarily or involuntarily,
been burdened with horses off and on since childhood, invariably
to my deep regret. To be perfectly frank, I find horses about as
personable as crows, more delicate than hummingbirds, less
efficient than bicycles, and more expensive than floozies.

A horse is an animal who, left in front of an oat bin, will eat
himself to death. A hot horse will drink water until his hoofs
fall off. Horses are very good at poisoning themselves; they have
a fine instinct for finding, and an insatiable appetite for eating,
toxic herbs that brighter animals avoid.

Horses also have weak nerves; they are the most hysterical of
all domestic animals. They will not only stay in a burning barn,
but if led out will break away and go back to be broiled alive.
Mice, bits of paper blowing about, a flapping leather strap,
oddly shaped rocks, wheelbarrows, beer cans or simply reflected
light will give a horse the screaming meemies. However, the
same enormous, cowering beastie that rears at a gum wrapper
will, in a savage fit of paranoia, turn on a man and bite or stomp
on him.

Besides the afflictions that they bring on themselves out of
sheer stupidity or cowardice, horses are prone to a really spec-
tacular number of diseases. A few of these troubles are Ringbone,
Spavin, Corns, Seedy Toe, Thrush, Colic, Constipation, Azotemia,
Heaves, Coughs, Colds, Hives, Fever, Wolf Teeth, Sleeping
Sickness, Boils, Poll Evil, Capped Hocks—and, neither last nor
least, Fistula of the Withers. I have designated some of these
afflictions in horsey parlance. If you get a horse, any veterinarian can translate them into common English and a common
$25 medical bill.

So far as I know, horses also are the only animals who catch
madness the way other creatures catch cold. For example,
there are "weavers"—animals who sway from side to side in
their stall, hour after hour, day after day. Weavers, because
they are weavers, have prodigious appetites but are seldom

597

fit for riding—their energy having been expended in pursuit of their mania. And weaving is contagious. If one horse in a barn is a weaver, soon every other horse will pick up the habit, and the stable will resemble the rehearsal hall of the Bolshoi Ballet.

There also are "cribbers"—horses who suck, chew and mouth endlessly on the edges of stall doors, mangers or other pieces of wood. Cribbers grind down their teeth and fill up their stomachs with slivers. And there are "wind suckers." They repeatedly throw back their foolish heads and swallow great gulps of air, which gives them colic and ulcers.

Finally, there are a great many horses whose difficulties are individual and bizarre. Some will fly into a tantrum if, when being curried, the right side is not brushed before the left. There are horses who detest women. There is a horse I know who *must* have a duck in his stable, another who will drink only if the handle of the bucket is turned toward him. Krafft-Ebing would have had a lot more fun with horses than with people.

In view of what can and usually does go wrong with a horse, it is not surprising that the first consideration in buying one is to find a "sound" animal. This is not easy because (1) horses are, as indicated above, naturally unsound, and (2) horse sellers have as many ways of camouflaging horse defects as horses have defects. The tricks of the horse-selling trade are many. Some are new, as, for example, the use of tranquilizers to improve, temporarily, the manners of manic horses. Some are old. One quack remedy says that heaves—equine emphysema—can be suppressed for a day or two by pouring coal oil into a horse's left ear. Some horse peddlers can still be identified by the telltale whiff of kerosene about them, while alert horse buyers can be spotted by their habit of sniffing in a nags left ear.

Of the three nags with which I now share my property, income and time, one is a little white-faced gelding of vaguely Morgan antecedents, called Governor. He will, of course, as almost all horses will, blow up his stomach when being saddled, the better to be able later to slip his girth. However, he never kicks, seldom bites, and if the person riding him has strong arms and strong will, Governor moves along very nicely for an hour or so.

We also have a pair of Tennessee Walker mares, a mother-and-daughter combo. When we bought them, the only obvious blemish was on the older mare, Rosie—a long scar on the inside of one leg. The scar was the result of an old injury, a common, run-of-the-mill horse accident. Rosie had stuck her foot through a barbed-wire fence. Being a horse rather than something smarter, she had, instead of withdrawing her leg, tried to pull the fence down—in the process, cutting through an artery.

Both mares, like Governor, were said to be "broke the best," which means that with some caution, persistence and guile, the animal can be ridden with fair safety and comfort. This proved to be the case. It is true, too, that Rosie, unless cross-tied, will bite hell out of you while you are trying to saddle her. Becky, the daughter, is a little difficult to catch in the field, and she is inclined to lounge around, eating clover and sniffing the breeze. Also, she is terrified of snowdrifts, gas meters, spotted dogs and *one* nearby yellow highway sign marked "CURVE."

But we're satisfied. When we think what horses *can* be, these failings seem hardly worth mentioning.

Animal Crackers

One owl to another: "How many times must I tell you—it's whooo, not whommm!"

Two monkeys discussing evolution: "You mean to tell me that I'm my keeper's brother?"

Turtle to turtle: "Don't you love the sound of rain on your roof?"

Male elephant as female passes: "Wow! A perfect 258-297-314!"

Exasperated dragon: "Mother said there would be knights like this."

One caterpillar to another, as they watch butterfly: "You'll never get me up in one of those things."

In London's Trafalgar Square there lived a boy pigeon; at St. Paul's, a girl pigeon. One day, they almost flew into each other over the Law Courts. They looked. They fell in love.

They courted very happily. They met every day, alternately on the dome of St. Paul's and on Nelson's Column.

One glorious morning in early May, when hearts as well as birds were singing, the rendezvous was set for 11 o'clock in Trafalgar Square. Usually so prompt, the girl pigeon had not arrived by 11:05, and the boy pigeon began to feel anxious. At 11:15, he was pacing a balustrade. Just when he was about to phone the police and ask whether any serious accident had been reported, he saw his friend strolling gaily down the steps of the National Gallery. He hastened to meet her.

"Darling," she said, "I'm so sorry, but it was such a lovely morning, I thought I'd walk."

Chicken to turkey: "Only Thanksgiving and Christmas? You're lucky—with us it's every Sunday."

Mouse to mouse: "I've got three sisters in psychological testing and an uncle in heart research."

Sheep, getting sheared: "The usual."

Mama Bear to Papa Bear: "You call it hibernating—I call it goofing off!"

Lamb, serenading another: "It had to be ewe. . . ."

Shivering polar bear cub to his mother: "I don't care *who* my ancestors were—I'm cold!"

One cow to another: "I have no idea how it tastes. Personally I never touch the stuff!"

One circus elephant to the other: "I'm getting sick and tired of working for peanuts."

One very angry skunk to another skunk: "So do you!"

Mother rabbit to her small child: "A magician pulled you out of a hat—now stop asking questions!"

Fish to swordfish: "The transatlantic cable? Oh, you *didn't*."

One firefly to another: "Give me a push—my battery's dead."

Mama bear to papa bear: "This is positively my last year as den mother."

Male crane to female: "Look, baby, we either whoop it up or face extinction."

Kindred Spirits

LOOK WHO'S GONE BANANAS OVER TV!
NEIL HICKEY

AMONG the primates at the Yerkes Primate Research Center, on the campus of Emory University in Georgia, are 15 gorillas, 35 orangutans, 85 chimpanzees and 125 human beings. The gorillas, orangutans and chimpanzees all love television. They spend hours totally involved in it. In brief, they've gone bananas over the tube.

At least that was the ominous rumor that filtered north to New York. Arriving at the Yerkes Center only hours after hearing the report, I burst breathlessly into the office of the director, Dr. Geoffrey H. Bourne, and demanded to know the truth. "What kind of simian silliness is this, anyway?" I inquired. "Apes aren't smart enough to watch television. Television is for *people!*"

"Now, now," said the doctor, raising his arms. "No offense intended. But we *do* have television sets here for the animals, and it is a fact that they *do* enjoy TV as a pastime."

I slumped into a chair next to an especially ugly gorilla skull. "Then it's true," I muttered.

The doctor patted my shoulder. "Cheer up," he said "They don't like *all* kinds of programs. Mostly the ones with lots of action. And sometimes a documentary."

"Sometimes a documentary!" I shouted, leaping up. "Where does that leave *us?* Television is the most important entertainment and communication form ever invented. Millions of human beings absolutely love it. They watch it maybe six hours a day. And now a bunch of apes are grooving on the same programs that *we* are!" I leaned closer to him. "Do you know what this could do to the national morale if the news got out? How long has this been going on?"

"Only a few months. I first got the idea when I heard about a chimpanzee in Santa Barbara named Bobby who was very fond of television, especially programs with a lot of violence. One of his favorite scenes was the barroom brawl in Westerns. He'd always scream with excitement, jump up and down, and throw things at the set whenever a fistfight broke out. He learned to recognize the 'bad guy' and loved to see him come on the screen.

"It occurred to me that if Bobby liked TV that much, maybe it was just what we needed here at the Center to keep the other apes entertained. So I made a public appeal for old television sets, and now we have 15. Come on, I'll show you.

"It's not remarkable that apes like television, you know. They have extremely acute eyesight, and have no trouble discerning figures on the screen. We once had a chimp who could sort photographs of apes and human beings into two piles. Apes on one pile, humans on the other. The only trouble was, every time she got to her own picture, she put it on the pile with the human beings.

"We have probably the most valuable and extensive collection of nonhuman primates anywhere in the world," the doctor continued. "Because of their similarities to man, the 'great apes'—gorillas, orangutans, chimpanzees and gibbons—are considered the ultimate in research animals. They get bored and neurotic, you know, with nothing to do—even more so than human beings."

We went past a long row of cages, each of which houses a pair of apes, their faces pressed against the wire mesh. And there, arrayed before them in neat alignment, were television sets, their tubes flickering with the action of an Errol Flynn pirate movie.

Dr. Bourne walked down the row, greeting the apes by name. "Good morning, Wendy. Good morning, Soda." A few of the animals gave a perfunctory show of recognition to the doctor, and returned to their watching. He pointed to a pair of chimps. "Those two were deeply involved in soap operas yesterday . . . scarcely budged for more than an hour and a half. I'm not saying they follow the story line, but they do enjoy watching the actors move about. We tried giving them toys to keep them entertained, but they dismantle almost anything. TV has been just right for them to pass the time."

In the nursery—yes, the nursery—a cluster of tiny apes (some of them in diapers) were sitting on the floor, bemused by the TV images. "Just like children," said Dr. Bourne, with a smile.

It was all too unreal. For more than an hour we observed the animals as they clustered around the sets. Some sat cross-legged, their jaws agape; others watched while hanging from overhead bars.

"Better stand back," said the doctor. "Sometimes an ape will secrete some water in his cheek, wait until a stranger comes close—then let him have it right in the eye. They love to watch your reaction."

I retreated quickly out of range. So *this* was the level of humor these beasts enjoyed.

"What we really need around here," said Dr. Bourne, "is a video-tape setup so that we could structure our own programs. We could set it up with colored buttons: red for a Western, blue for a soap opera, yellow for a game show. You know, give them a free choice and see how they react."

Yes, of course. That was the next inexorable step. A rating system for apes. Just tell us what you want to see, Jocko, and we'll pipe it to you.

"What you're seeing is in no sense serious experimentation," 603

Dr. Bourne said. "It's purely a pastime for the animals during periods when they're not, you know, *working* with the doctors and technicians here. It's nothing more, really, than an antidote to boredom for them. They sit, have a snack, and watch a program."

"And how, pray tell, does that make them different from the rest of us?" I asked as Dr. Bourne led the way past cages of apes who were now staring—rather idiotically, I thought—at a soap opera.

Strolling away from the Yerkes Primate Research Center that day, I wondered if the world should, in fact, know what is going on there. Anyway, I pondered, it will be *years* before the apes become a real target audience for TV programmers, before gorillas start writing to the networks demanding to see *King Kong* every five minutes, before advertisers see the potential of the ape market, before. . . .

A white rat, recently returned from the laboratory to his cage, ran up to a fellow rat in great excitement. "You know what?" he exclaimed. "I've got Dr. Zilch conditioned!"

"How so?" asked his buddy.

"Well," said the first rat, "every time I go through the maze he gives me food!"

An ape was used to assist in tests on a high-speed rocket track at Edwards Air Force Base, California. Objecting to being strapped onto the rocket sled, he was quieted by a technician who gave him a banana. No sooner had the ape begun to eat the banana, however, than he found himself a half-mile down the desert, with the fruit smashed over his face. But the ape got his revenge. Next time he was used for a similar experiment, the technician gave him a second banana. Result? The ape hit him over the head with it.

A famous biologist, having unsuccessfully tried to teach a monkey to play ball, decided as a last resort to leave the little creature alone in a room with a bat and ball. He closed the door and waited a few moments. Then, very quietly, he stooped and peered through the keyhole.

He found himself staring into an intent brown eye.

A friend of mine with a new cocker spaniel puppy wanted to train him to "speak" for his meals. He would hold the dog's food just out of reach and then bark a few times before giving it to him. The pup, he hoped, would associate barking with food, and begin to "speak" for himself.

After a week or so of this, he again held the food just out of reach, and waited for the dog to bark. The puppy failed to take his cue, but the owner put the dish before him anyway. Then my friend got a real shock. The puppy refused to eat—until his master barked.

University of Nebraska psychologists testing the ingenuity of rats have found some rats that test the ingenuity of psychologists. One rat, for instance, was supposed to be running inside an "activity wheel" while an automatic counter kept track of the wheel's revolutions. But the rat was found lying in his cage calmly spinning the wheel with his paw.

Be a Sport:

SPORTSMANSHIP

RUSSELL MALONEY once said: "Most males who don't care about big-league baseball conceal their indifference as carefully as they would conceal a laughable physical deficiency." Well, I'm no hero but I'm willing to admit that I do not care about the carefully manipulated business called baseball (or football). Considered as *games* they seem to me about on a par with the commercial transactions of the Mafia; they should be reported on by financial writers. That's why I've never been able to respond properly to the humor of sport, except when it is handled by a rare master such as Ring Lardner. The defect is mine, and I take no pride in it. So I hope the sketches and jokes that follow will send our readers into gales of laughter. I *do* like a couple of remarks by one of my favorite though now antiquated humorists, Kin Hubbard. About boxing he said, "I'll bet the hardest thing about prize fightin' is pickin' up yer teeth with a boxin' glove on." As for competitive exercise in general Mr. Hubbard reported with his usual realism, "Luther Motts, founder an' president o' the 'Fit-at-Fifty Club,' dropped dead with his skates on."

Diamonds in the Rough

On an October Sunday, an important eastern newspaper made the following listing in its radio schedule:
"1:00—Back to God. (If no World Series game.)"

Dr. Bobby Brown, brilliant third baseman of the New York Yankees, got his medical degree and served his internship while still a member of the team. He was asked by umpire Red Jones what branch of medicine he intended to specialize in. Always a ballplayer at heart, Dr. Bobby immediately replied: "Vivisection of umpires."

A British visitor to Yankee Stadium, unable to understand the game, left as the scoreboard read:
1 0 0 0 0 0 0 0 0
1 0 0 0 0 0 0 0 0
When asked by a kid outside the gate, "What's the score?" the Briton shrugged, "Oh, it's up in the millions."

While watching a ball game in Boston's Fenway Park, my attention was distracted by the conversation of a couple behind me. The husband, who had been explaining the complexities of the game to his wife, suddenly remarked excitedly, "Look, we've got a man on every base!"

"But, dear, so has the other team," his wife countered.

One sweet young thing arrived at her first ball game during the fifth inning. "The score is nothing to nothing," she heard a fan say.

"Oh, good," she cooed to her escort. "Then we haven't missed a thing."

A baseball manager who had an ulcer was in his physician's office for a checkup. "Remember," the doctor said, "don't get excited, don't get mad, and forget about baseball when you're off the field." Then he added, "By the way, how come you let the pitcher bat yesterday with the tying run on second and two out in the ninth?"

In the early days of World War II everyone in baseball was much concerned over whether the game could be continued. Bucky Harris, who had just accepted the managerial job in Philadelphia, encountered Umpire Bill McGowan and asked anxiously: "Do you think there will be any baseball this year, Bill?"

"Gosh, Bucky," answered the umpire, "I dunno. Your guess is as good as mine."

"I know that," said Bucky. "But this is the first time you ever admitted it."

A Baltimore fan once asked Umpire Eddie Rommel why he threw manager Paul Richards out of a ball game.

"Richards wasn't feeling well," said Rommel.

"Oh, come on now. Was that reason enough to throw him out of the ball park?"

"It certainly was. He said he was sick of my decisions."

Dizzy Dean, former star pitcher for the St. Louis Cardinals, was a huge success as a television broadcaster of baseball games, partly because of the innovations he has made in our language. "He slud into third" was the first much-publicized departure. Later he varied "slud" with "slood," and then one afternoon came up with, "The trouble with them boys is they ain't got enough spart." Pressed for an explanation of this, he obliged: "Spart is pretty much the same as fight or pep or gumption. Like the *Spart of St. Louis,* that plane Lindbergh flowed to Europe in."

When Joe DiMaggio made his major league debut, he struck terror in the hearts of American league pitchers with his lusty bat. One hurler who did not frighten easily, however, was Bobo Newsom. One afternoon, when he was scheduled to face the Yankee Clipper, his manager said to him: "Watch that fellow DiMaggio, Bobo. He's a terror."

"Nuts," said Bobo. "The guy must have a weakness, and I'll find out soon enough what it is."

DiMag came to bat three times and hit three stinging doubles. When Bobo shuffled into the locker room at the end of the game, his manager asked: "Well, Bobo, did you find his weakness?"

"Yep," replied the pitcher. "He has a weakness for doubles."

Woman on telephone, at the same time watching baseball game on television: "Yes . . . with some woman. Would you mind swinging your camera along the third-base box again?"

Jabs and Crosses

On the eve of the Dempsey-Tunney fight they sent Mike Trent, an old timer who was in Dempsey's stable, over to scout the Tunney training camp and bring back information of value to Dempsey, on Tunney's style and hitting power. Mike came back with face all beaming. "It's a setup," says he. "I seen him readin' a book."

Asked why he decided to retire from the prize ring, Rocky Graziano said: "I looked in the mirror after my last fight and saw my beaten-up face and decided there must be an easier way to meet congenial people of my own age."

Newspapermen like to tell about the time a sports editor we'll call Bunny McBride was making up the paper, when a fight manager came in with his fighter to try to sell Bunny a column.

"Bunny," he said, "meet the champion of South Africa."

"Who let you in?" Bunny wanted to know. "Sorry, can't talk now. I'm busy. Some other time."

"But, Bunny, really, this is the champion of South Africa. Make you a good story."

McBride still waved him away. "Sorry, too busy."

The manager was insistent. "Bunny, you oughta meet this kid. He's champion of South Africa!"

McBride really got mad. Looking up for the first time, he lifted as beautiful a wallop as was ever seen, in or out of the ring, and caught the champion of South Africa smack on the kisser. He went down in a heap, without a sound.

"Now I'm the champion of South Africa," muttered McBride, and went on with his work.

After retaining his heavyweight crown by knocking out challenger Joe Walcott, Joe Louis was taken to see movies of the fight. Asked how he liked the picture, Louis commented laconically, "It had a real nice ending."

An editor once assigned Michael Arlen, the fastidious author of *The Green Hat,* to cover the Carpentier-Joe Beckett fight. Arlen, who had never seen a fight before, came dressed in bowler, stiff collar and cuffs, carrying a cane and wearing a flower in his lapel. When the fight was over he sent in this report: "Mr. Beckett reached the center of the ring. He bowed to me and I bowed back. But then I discovered that Mr. Beckett's bow was not due to any recognition of me, but was the result of a severe blow to the stomach rendered by Mr. Carpentier."

In 35 years of hobnobbing with fight managers and lesser figures of the pugilistic trade, Sports Editor Dan Parker of the New York *Daily Mirror* had developed a fine ear for Manhattan's ringside speech. Once Parker gave a health report on Armand Weill, manager of Heavyweight Champion Rocky Marciano, as told by "Al" himself: "My blood pressure is poifick. It was 150 vitriolic and 98 diabolic. The doctor said I had a coupla minor ailments and I says, 'That's funny. I never woiked in the mines.' So he told me I had fallen archeries. Since I went on that diet I ain't got no ulsters or no abominable trouble. I had to practickly fast for a coupla days—jest a large cup of demitasse in the mornin' and a little brought at night—lamb brought. He said I didn't have no sign of kodiak trouble around the heart or no coroner's trombone disease. Everythin' was okey dokel wit' my gold bladder too."

Concluded Columnist Parker: "As I looked at the healthy specimen, I impulsively exclaimed: 'What a built!'"

A fight broadcaster, trying to interest women in boxing, wanted to make the girls feel that this was their sport too; so he started off with these immortal words: "Hi there, fight fans and fannies."

Grin, Place, and Show

Some years ago, the owner of a stable signed famous jockey Eddie Arcaro to ride his entry in a stakes race at the Arlington Park track in Illinois. Before the horses went to the post, the owner gave Arcaro detailed instructions: "Break fast. Get into fourth position at the first turn. Hang there until the clubhouse turn. Then make your move as you head into the stretch, and you'll win going away."

Arcaro nodded confidently—and proceeded to finish last. The owner came storming up to him after the race. "I told you exactly what to do!" he spluttered. "You were supposed to stay in fourth position until the last turn and then take the lead as you came into the stretch."

"What?" demanded Arcaro. "And leave the horse?"

Sir Gordon Richards, England's most famous jockey, is the first man of his profession to have a knighthood conferred on him. When Sir Gordon, who is just five feet tall, was first told of the honor, he quipped, "Mother always told me my day was coming, but I never realized that I'd end up being the shortest knight of the year."

Of the system-players at the Tijuana track, Jack Dempsey remembers a lady who bet on gray horses only. This was his mother, Mrs. Cecilia Dempsey. One day, Dempsey recalls, his mother was still cheering when all the other cheers had faded away. "What are you cheering for?" he asked. "The race is over."

"Yes, I know," she said. "But my horse is not in yet."

Jimmy Durante bet on a horse at Santa Anita, and the nag lost by inches. "What that horse needed," bragged an ex-jockey, "was my riding."

"What he needed," corrected Durante, "was my nose."

Eddie Arcaro tells of a Westerner who entered an eight-year-old horse in a race at an Eastern track. Since the horse had had no previous races, he went off at odds of 80 to 1. But he galloped home first by several lengths. The stewards, naturally suspicious, called the owner in for questioning.

"How come you never raced this horse before?" they demanded. "After all, you've had him for eight years."

"Well, to tell the truth," the Westerner said sheepishly, "we couldn't catch him until he was seven."

Every evening on a race-track hotel porch, a group of trainers gathered to exchange tales about their horses. A small and graying stranger used to listen silently but intently. Finally one night he said, "I've been listening to you fellows for two weeks, hearing you talk about horses, and you haven't mentioned a horse with *class* yet."

"What do *you* call a horse with class?" someone demanded.

"Let me tell you about a mare I used to race out in Montana. Annie G. was her name. At the end of the meeting there was a $5000 stake. It was a mile and a quarter and she didn't want to go that far, but it was a lot of money, so I put her in.

"The racing secretary had a feud on with me, so though she was a little thing that couldn't carry much weight he put 160 pounds on her. All the good jockeys had engagements, so all I could get was an apprentice boy.

"She liked to run on the rail, but she drew No. 16 post position. She wanted a dry track too, but on the day of the race it came up deep mud. She hated for anything to touch her, but when the break came, the outside horse slammed her and knocked her off stride.

"Just the same she looked the leader eye-to-eye around the first turn and into the backstretch. Halfway down, the apprentice boy felt his saddle slip, and with that big field behind him he got scared and pulled to the outside fence.

"That mare stopped over there and she had a foal. Well, gentlemen, Annie G. won that race by three open lengths. And the foal ran second.

"That's what I call a horse with class."

HORSEPLAY

PRISCILLA D. WILLIS

IN FLORIDA one day a friend of mine who owns horses invited me to go to the races with him. His trainer, Barney Weener, and another trainer joined us in his clubhouse box right above the finish line. For an amateur like myself, the day augured well. I could hardly fail to make a hatful if I bet the way these pros did.

I placed the *Morning Telegraph,* my scratch sheet, a program and Madame Pearl's Selections, clipped hastily from the noon paper, on the vacant chair in the box. The others had nothing, not even a program.

"Jack's colt's going a little dinky," Barney Weener observed, watching the horses for the first race canter by on their way to the post.

"That's the Amberglo Jack bought at Saratoga," the other trainer commented. "He nearly bowed in the slop at Aqueduct last fall. Jack had to stop with him and turn him out."

"He could still be a good one, though," Barney insisted.

"Not if they run him on an off track. His mother backed up ten lengths in the mud—couldn't handle it at all—and this colt's just like her. He likes to hear his feet rattle."

"I caught him in fourteen and change away from the gate the other morning," Barney declared. "He seems to grab holt of this track real good."

"Horses for courses," my friend opined, and the others nodded.

The horses were at the post. Nobody had gone out to make a bet. Number 5 was 15-to-1 on the tote board, and Madame Pearl had him as the best bet of the day, but I hadn't felt like crawling over these experts and running to the two-dollar window. So I sat there and watched Number 5 win with consummate ease. My good manners had cost me $28.00.

"The way the race was ran," Barney explained, "Jack's horse never had a chance. First thing, the ground broke out from under him at the start, and when he finally got himself untracked he had no place to go. He was in a blind switch the whole trip."

I was beginning to feel as if I were in Zurich, where everybody speaks Suisse-Deutsch and you're lucky if you catch every eighth word.

Four races went by, and no one had made a bet. Madame Pearl, especially bright today, had two other long-priced winners. By not betting I was losing money fast. Before the fifth race, in which my friend had a horse entered, Barney's friend hissed, "How d'you like your chances?"

Without moving his lips or turning his head, Barney hissed back, "I think we got a mortal lock."

The men left the box, my friend and the second trainer fanning out through the crowd toward the betting windows while I followed Barney down to the saddling enclosure. There I listened to the instructions he gave his rider.

"This colt breaks real fast," he said. "Take him back off the lead and lay about third or fourth going down the back side. Let him move on the elbow. If you can't get through on the rail at the head of the stretch, circle the others; he'll have plenty left." Turning on his heel, the horse trainer dived into the crowd. I trotted along. He didn't stop until he reached the $50 window. He pushed two bills through the wicket.

"You gonna bet?" he asked me. "He's 6-to-1 now, but he'd ought to go off closer to 8."

In the pressure of this moment all reason failed me. I watched my fingers fumble in my wallet, slowly extracting its entire contents. "Here," I heard myself say to the face in the window, a blur of nostrils and eyeglasses, and the face pumped out a ticket that was a different color from any I'd ever seen. Once the ticket was in my hand, however, my composure returned. I felt suddenly wealthy. Striding confidently away, I noticed two somber-faced men carefully observing Barney.

"Beards," he replied to my unspoken question. "Beards hang around the big windows to see how much a trainer bets on his horse. If he loads, they figure he thinks he has a real chance."

Back in the box I tried to focus my glazed eyes on the field going postward. I must have looked pale, because my friend leaned over and patted my arm. "You haven't a worry in the world," he reassured me. "There's a saying that the only two times a man shows all his teeth is in the dentist's chair and in front of the camera in the winner's circle. You'll be right there with us!"

"Really?" I said stupidly, and looked at the ticket stuck to the palm of my wet hand.

Then the horses were in the gate, tossing their heads and stamping. One of them reared up and threw his rider. The horse's number, I noted, was 4. Barney Weener jumped to his feet and exploded. "That son of a gun done the same thing last time! He almost come down on my horse! The stewarts shouldn't let him start till he learns how to come out of a gate!"

An instant later the gate opened. A wall of horses plunged forward. Our horse, No. 8, outbroke the field, just as Barney Weener had told the jockey he would. The boy steadied him, taking him back until he was lying third according to instructions. Rounding the turn out of the backstretch, the horse made his move. He was shut off by the two leaders drifting in close to the rail, but the jockey circled them and found a path in the middle of the track. He drew off by three lengths.

I computed the return on my ticket. A new roof, a trip to Nassau, that rose garden I wanted—all danced like sugarplums through my befuddled head. I regarded almost scornfully the men leaning out over a row of petunias in front of the box, waving their arms, and roaring like the zoo lions at feeding time: "Go on with him, Johnny!" "All the way, boy!" "That's carrying the mail, kid!" All at once they stopped.

Wedging myself between their shoulders, I saw a horse come blazing out of the pack, ears pinned, head low, gaining on ours with every desperate stride. It was No. 4—the one that had thrown his rider in the gate. A jump from the wire he caught my friend's horse to win by a long chestnut neck.

Growling that his horse had spit the bit out at the eighth hole, Mr. Weener scrambled out of the box to meet him when he came back to be unsaddled. The other trainer evaporated into the crowd.

"Well," said my friend, with a smile that showed only two front teeth, "it's always a horse race, isn't it?" He tore up his tickets and hurled the pieces into the petunias.

As I picked up my papers to leave, my eyes fell on the clipping of Madame Pearl's Selections. In the fifth race it was No. 4, a horse with the insinuating name of The Boob. He paid $68.20.

Par for the Course

When miracles happen on the golf course, it is important to know how to respond to them. At Pebble Beach, California, songwriter Hoagy Carmichael, who is an avid golfer, teed up on a par-three hole, picked up a club and hit the ball. It bounced once on the green, went right to the pin, dropped in for a hole in one. Hoagy didn't say a word, but reached in his pocket, pulled out another ball, teed up, then observed, "I think I've got the idea now."

Now," said the golf pro, "suppose you just go through the motions without driving the ball."

"But that's precisely the difficulty I'm trying to overcome," said his pupil.

A complacent golfer teed his ball, looked away to the next green, and declared confidently, "That's good for one long drive and a putt." He swung the driver, tore up the sod, and managed to move the ball a few feet off the tee. Stepping forward, the caddie handed him the putter and suggested, "Now for a hell of a putt."

Well, you said I had to choose, didn't you?" demanded the husband, in bed with his golf clubs.

One golfer to another: "First it was my marriage. Now the magic has gone out of my nine iron."

A San Diego man returned home from a Saturday round of golf and was greeted by his two youngsters asking, "Daddy, did you win?"

"Well, children," he replied, "in golf it doesn't matter so much if you win. But your father got to hit the ball more times than anyone else."

A well-adjusted person is one who can play golf and bridge as if they were games.

If you think it's hard to meet new people, pick up the wrong golf ball.

One golfer, in golfmobile, to another: "Since I've straightened out my drives, I've been shooting this course consistently in less than two pints of gas!"

Like most beginners, he managed to hit one magnificent, long drive during the 18 holes. When the round was over, he couldn't stop boasting about that particular shot. "Wasn't that drive marvelous?" he asked a friend for the tenth time.

"Yes," was the reply. "It's a shame you can't have it stuffed!"

A golfer who had made a spectacularly bad shot and torn up a large piece of turf took the sod in his hand and, looking wildly about, asked: "What shall I do with this?"

"If I were you," said the caddie, "I'd take it home to practice on."

Golfer to golfer: "Speaking of the credibility gap—what's your handicap?"

Posted in a British golf club in Africa: "If the ball comes to rest in dangerous proximity to a crocodile or a hippopotamus, another ball may be dropped."

A golfer sliced his drive, and the ball went through the windshield of a passing car. The startled motorist lost control and quickly hit two other cars. Soon a policeman arrived, surveyed the accident scene and found the golfer standing by his ball on the road.

"What are you going to do about this?" demanded the policeman.

"First thing," replied the golfer, "change my grip."

A young broker, after a particularly brutal session in a sand-trap, sought to relieve the uncomfortable silence by cheerily declaring to his caddie: "Funny game, golf." "'Tain't meant to be," replied the boy.

Out at his golf club alone one day, my cousin got up a match with a stranger. Thinking it might make it more fun to play for money, he asked his companion what he went around in. "Seventy-two," was the reply. My cousin, who plays in the middle 90s, quickly decided against any bets. But they had not played many holes before he realized that something was wrong. The other man took stroke after stroke on each hole. And when they reached the 12th hole, he picked up his clubs and started back toward the clubhouse. "Hey, where're you going?" yelled my cousin.

"In," said the other firmly.

"But how come? We've only played 11 holes," protested my cousin.

"I know," was the answer. "But I only allow myself 72 strokes. *Some* day I may get all the way around."

For several years, a minister and a professor had regularly played golf together. They were evenly matched and there was a keen rivalry. Then one spring the professor's game suddenly improved so much that the minister was regularly beaten. The preacher's efforts to improve his own game were unsuccessful, but finally he came up with an idea. He went to the bookstore, picked out three how-to-play-golf texts, and had them sent to the professor for a birthday present. It wasn't long before they were evenly matched again.

Woman golfer, teeing off, to husband: "Now tell me if you notice anything I'm doing right."

Wife to golfer in sandtrap: "And how is Lawrence of Arabia doing on this hole?"

Cutting the Deck

Overheard during a bridge game: "I'd like a review of the bidding with the original inflections."

A favorite bridge story concerns the bride who came home to mother on her wedding night crying. "All he did was talk about the duplicate tournament you and he played in last night," she wailed. "He started by explaining how he played the first hand, and when he got to hand No. 25 I ran out and came home to you."

"That's too bad," answered the mother. "The 25th hand was the most interesting of the night."

At the conclusion of one of my lectures on point-count bidding," says Charles H. Goren, "an old lady approached me and announced, 'My partner and I have decided to adopt your system, Mr. Goren. Why, it's even better than cheating!'"

A reluctant husband found himself drafted as a fourth at bridge, but managed to extricate himself rather swiftly by looking at his hand and muttering, "Let's see, what have I got here? A ten of valentines, an A of clovers, a nine of arrowheads, and a. . . ."

A woman who plays cards one night a month with a group of friends was concerned that she always woke up her husband when she came home around 11:30. One night she decided to try not to rouse him. She undressed in the living room and, purse over arm, tiptoed nude into the bedroom —only to find her husband sitting up in bed reading.

"My gosh!" he exclaimed. "Did you lose everything?"

An ardent bridge player, when informed by her obstetrician that she had delivered twins rather than the one child she had expected, remarked, "It's just like Harry to double me when I was vulnerable."

All evening long four card players had been pestered by a kibitzer. When he went out of the room for a moment, they hit on a plan to silence him. "Let's make up a game no one ever heard of," one of them said. "Then he'll have to shut up."

The kibitzer returned. The dealer tore two cards in half and gave them to the man on his left. He tore the corners off three cards and spread them out in front of the man opposite him. Then he tore five cards in quarters, gave 15 pieces to the man on his right and kept five himself. "I have a mingle," he said. "I'll bet a dollar."

"I have a snazzle," the next man announced. "I'll raise you a dollar."

The third man folded without betting and the fourth, after due deliberation, said, "I've got a farfle. I'll raise you two dollars."

The kibitzer shook his head vehemently. "You're crazy," he said. "You're never going to beat a mingle and a snazzle with a lousy farfle!"

Going from San Francisco to Chicago by air, I was engrossed in a book on bridge when the stewardess stopped and looked over my shoulder. "That must be a fascinating love story you are reading," she said.

Startled, I looked at the chapter heading with fresh eyes—"Free Responses After an Original Pass."

Field and Stream

Sign on a Michigan farm: "Attention Hunters—Please Don't Shoot Anything on My Place That Isn't Moving. It May Be My Hired Man!"

AN ALL-PURPOSE PREFABRICATED YARN, APPLICABLE TO ANY FISH, OF ANY SIZE, ANYWHERE

CHARLES W. MORTON

ERTAIN SIMPLE rules govern all fishing stories. The narrator hooks a fish and (a) catches it or (b) loses it. The only variables are the species of fish—hence its size and habitat—and the kind of tackle used in his wisdom (or folly) by the narrator. Much time-consuming thought will be saved, therefore, if writers merely fill in a few blanks as the facts warrant.

The story must begin with a modest statement of the author's credentials: "I've fished for the mighty _____ off Acapulco and the battling _____ along the Florida Keys. I've seen a maddened _____ swamp a dory off Wedgeport. But for sheer power and gameness I've seen nothing that can equal, pound for pound, a _____."

That's a perfectly workable opening, even when applied to some notoriously inert species. The narrator uses the same fill-in for a rock cod, which behaves much like a boot full of water, as he would for a 50-pound muskellunge.

The narrator then introduces his guide, always a terse, monosyllabic man; this saves the writing of much improbable dialogue. The narrator assumes at this point the disarming role of chump and leaves the high strategy to the guide. ("We never did learn Joe's last name, but he taught us all there was to know about _____ s.")

And so to that mysterious locality, known only to Joe, where the narrator will have a chance to pit his cunning against the great-granddaddy of all _____ s. It makes no difference whether Joe is a Kanaka or a Canadien, whether they travel by express cruiser, mule or pirogue; their destination always disappoints the narrator: "It looked like the last place in the world to try for _____ s. But Joe merely grunted. '_____ here,' he said. 'Big one.'"

Joe of course is right. The author's first lure, a _____ (spinner, fly, minnow, or grapnel baited with a small shoat—it's all the same), has hardly touched the water when down goes the rod, out screams the line! It is all the author can do to keep his footing against that first wild rush of the _____.

The next two hours are crammed with action, while the author brings in one gigantic _____ after another, the biggest he has ever seen, one looking as if it would go for at least _____ pounds on the scales. But hold on. Joe seems contemptuous. Bored stiff. "Big _____ still here," Joe grunts, gesturing at the water.

Comes the final cast. Nothing. No _____ of any size seems interested. Suddenly, a few yards beyond the lure, the waters swirl. "Some vast invisible force was causing a submarine upheaval. Spellbound, I watched a great tail appear for an instant as the monster lazily rolled over and submerged again. I turned to Joe. 'Don't tell me that was a _____! They don't *get* that big.' But Joe only grunted. *'Big _____!'*"

The author's tackle is far too light for a _____ of this size, but it's too late now. So *down* goes that rod again. *Out* screams the line. Even with a _-pound drag, the _____'s rush carries all before it. The leviathan hurls himself far out of the water and comes down with an echoing splash. The author vainly tries to reel in precious line.

"My rod bent almost double. Pandemonium reigned." More leaps, lunges—a page or so of them. Then, "Suddenly my line went ominously slack. I began frantically reeling in.

"'_____ gone,' Joe grunted."

Remains only the unbelievable circumstance of the leader when the narrator finally winds it to the surface. Gut, wire, or ⅜-inch log chain, its condition never varies: "Bitten *clean through!* Mute evidence that the _____ had met man's challenge—and won!"

They prepare to leave. "But suddenly the waters were convulsed again, as the mighty _____ broke the surface in all his majesty and, with a final derisive smack of his great tail, disappeared—still the monarch of _____ (Spectacle Pond, the Upper Orinoco, Hillsboro Inlet, etc., etc.)."

———— • ————

Wife, returning from fishing trip with husband, to neighbor: "I did everything all wrong again today—I talked too loud, I used the wrong bait, I reeled in too soon and I caught more than he did!"

———— • ————

A few helpful tips for anyone who wants to catch a porcupine were offered recently by the Lands and Forests Department of Ontario, Canada, in a bulletin reading in part as follows: "The best way to effect his capture is to wait until he's in the open. Then, watching for his slapping tail, rush in quickly and pop a large washtub over him. Thus you have something to sit on while you figure out the next move."

We were talking about the fish we catch in Florida. One of the fishermen, a Northerner, came back with this story about the enormous catfish he had landed in his home state.

"To give you an idea," he related, "it took a power winch to land it and a crane to get it up on the beach. There weren't any scales around large enough to weigh the fish so I got my little Brownie camera out and photographed it as a matter of record.

"The picture," he concluded, "weighed 11 pounds."

The old-timer sat on the riverbank, obviously awaiting a nibble, though the fishing season had not officially opened. I stood behind him quietly for several minutes. "You a game warden?" he finally inquired.

"Yep," I lied, figuring to scare him a little.

Apparently unruffled, the old man began to move the fishing pole vigorously from side to side. Finally he lifted the line out of water.

"Just teaching him how to swim," he explained, pointing to a minnow wiggling on the end of the line.

Wife to husband fishing from boat: "It seemed to me the overshoe put up a better fight than the tire."

Wife to returning fisherman: "Gesundheit! What else did you catch?"

Shivering wife in rowboat to duck-hunting husband: "Tell me again how much fun we're having—I keep forgetting!"

Woman hunter, about to fire, to husband: "Of course I heard it moo—why shouldn't a moose moo?"

Wife to sportsman husband: "Couldn't you go fishing instead of hunting? All we have is white wine."

Like No Business I Know:

STAGE AND SCREEN

S HOW BIZ is rich in wit, usually of a devastating sort. This is because the wit of insult is a useful weapon in a business where the competition is deadly. Also it's because it attracts, on the one hand, genuinely brilliant satirists like George Kaufman and Fred Allen, and on the other hand, predestined figures of fun (no examples supplied); and the latter are designed by nature to arouse the laughter of the former. There are thousands of classic, well-remembered instances that illustrate both situations (and others) that crop up continually in the world of make-believe. Take Howard Dietz's "A day away from Tallulah is like a month in the country." Or Kaufman's "Massey won't be satisfied until he's assassinated." Or Fred Allen's "Hollywood is a great place if you're an orange." Or John Steinbeck's six-word review of Cecil B. DeMille's *The Ten Commandments:* "Saw the movie. Loved the Book." Or Yul Brynner's self-description: "I am just a nice, clean-cut Mongolian boy." Or Ethel Merman's delightful summary of Mary Martin: "She's O.K. if you like talent."

The examples given below are as good, or better, but I miss some instances of the wit that flashes out again and again in the context of grand opera and classical music. There is something especially endearing in Arturo Toscanini's blast at an orchestra whose performance dissatisfied him: "After I die I shall return to earth as the doorkeeper of a bordello and I won't let a one of you in."

Hurray for Hollywood

A Hollywood star was being a bore about her next role. "I was made for the part," she gushed.

"Shhh," said a listener, "do you have to tell everybody?"

Heard in Hollywood: "He's a character actor: when he shows any character, he's acting."

Two Hollywood children of oft-divorced parents got into an argument. As it became more heated, one said, "My father can lick your father."

"Are you kidding?" cried the other. "Your father *is* my father!"

One woman to another in a Hollywood night spot: "She's so kind to animals—why, she'd do anything for a mink."

A New York show girl decided to try for a Hollywood career. She had been told that the key to success in Hollywood was to create a grand impression. So she traveled with a maid.

At the hotel she registered: "Mary Doe and made."

Told that a famous mind reader was planning to locate in Hollywood, Monty Woolley snapped: "It is my prediction that he will starve to death."

Screen Gems' fan mail department received a letter from what they believe is the most respectful child in America. The letter, addressed to Rin Tin Tin, began: "My Dear Mr. Tin."

A Hollywood mogul who had never learned to read or write managed nicely by signing his checks with two crosses. His banker called him recently. "How about this check, here, it's got three crosses?"

"My wife has social ambitions," explained the mogul. "She thinks I should have a middle name."

A publicity director of 20th Century-Fox was asked how he obtained the true ages of his contract screen actresses. "We use the half-and-half method," he explained. "The exact age of any woman is obtained by adding half the years she acknowledges to half the years her best friend gives her."

An aspiring actor who was getting nowhere in Hollywood decided to see if a little publicity might help. Going to an office near one of the studios, he inquired of the receptionist about the different kinds of publicity. "We got two kinds, son," she replied. "Piety and notoriety. Which do you want?"

Ernest Truex defined a Hollywood contact man as "all con and no tact."

Nearly every Hollywood actor, writer and director has an agent, whose ten-percent fee is a fact of life as inevitable as death and taxes. Consider the writer who was giving blood to the Red Cross. As the blood flowed into the tube, he automatically thought of his agent, H. N. Swanson. "Don't fill it all the way up!" he exclaimed. "Ten percent belongs to Swanson."

A film salesman was trying to sell the latest Clark Gable picture to a cinema proprietor in the wilds of Venezuela. "Clark Gable is dead," he was told. "You recall the film *Parnell?*"

"Yes. A box-office winner."

"*Si, señor,* but the Gable he died in that."

"Look here, I don't. . . ."

"I tried to show another Gable film after that," went on the Venezuelan. "And what happen? Hell broke loose. *Señor,* my clients see the Gable die in one picture. Cannot one believe one's own eyes? So far as this village is concerned, Gable is dead."

In Hollywood the eternal triangle consists of an actor, his wife and himself.

Girl to friend in a Hollywood night spot: "All I'm looking for is a man who's kind and understanding. Is that too much to expect of a millionaire?"

Trying to eclipse his brother's gift of a Cadillac, a Hollywood producer paid $10,000 for an amazing mynah bird to give his mother on her birthday. The bird spoke 11 languages and sang grand opera.

On the night of her birthday he called her long distance. "What did you think of the bird, Mama?" he asked.

"Delicious!" she said.

Prime Time

An African woman, viewing her first TV program, asked, "After all the good men killed all the bad ones, why are they told to brush their teeth?"

TV serviceman to customer after completing repairs: "Well, there she is—all set to insult your intelligence again."

Producer Mike Todd, Jr., told how one African head-hunter explained his glimpse of a TV set to another: "It's a wonderful machine where they shrink the whole body."

Woman to husband at breakfast table: "Funny you don't like that cereal—six dancing chipmunks and a purple baby elephant on TV spoke rather highly of it."

There's a lot of talk about television being a great asset in the intellectual development of today's children. My three-year-old nephew, for example, is an avid TV viewer, and even the commercials command his interest. One day, when visiting relatives, he opened their cat's mouth and after careful inspection remarked, "What small dentures you have!"

My suspicions that the children were watching too much television were confirmed one day when my seven-year-old son was trying to put on his freshly washed and dried tennis shoes. "These shoes," he said, "sure don't stretch like a Playtex Living Bra."

A visitor from abroad, preparing to return to her home-land, bought a television set to take back to her family.

"Can't you buy a TV set in your own country?" she was asked.

"Oh, yes, but American programs are so much better than ours."

Wife to husband, as TV master of ceremonies winds up program: "He certainly *ought* to thank us for watching!"

A TV comedian consulted a psychiatrist because of his frightening dreams. "Every day I take a nap," he said, "and I dream that I'm telling fabulous jokes that keep the audiences hysterical for a whole hour without a stop."

"I don't see anything so terrifying about that dream," said the psychiatrist.

"You don't?" shouted the comedian. "A whole hour without a stop? That means I'm unsponsored!"

Radio and TV boners from the book by Kermit Schafer:

"At Heitman's you will find a variety of fine foods, expertly served by experienced waitresses in appetizing forms."

"Before our next recorded selection, here's an item of interest. Last night at the Municipal Hospital there were 42 babies born. And now, 'Don't Blame Me.'"

On a TV commercial Betty Furness gave out with this advice: "Try your Westinghoush waser with a full load on."

"And now, Nelson Eddy sings 'While My Lady Sleeps' with the men's chorus."

"You'll hear about these wonderful cupcakes during the curse of the next commercial!"

On the radio quiz "Share the Wealth," contestants were asked to name several events in history associated with animals. When the quizmaster came to Lady Godiva, a young lady contestant unhesitatingly answered, "Bear!"

Wife at TV set to husband: "Shall we watch the six o'clock news and get indigestion, or wait for the 11 o'clock and have insomnia?"

Little boy to pal, as they leave movie: "I like television better. It's not so far to the bathroom."

VIEWER'S LAMENT
JOHN STEINBECK

I NEVER see the great or even the good television shows. People telephone and say, "Did you see the great show last night at 11 o'clock?" And I didn't. I was reading or talking or had gone to the theater or perhaps was just sitting staring into silent space.

Then again I have a call: "Be sure to look at television at 9:30 on Friday." I really set my mind to it, but, sure as shooting, I either forget or look at the clock to find it is ten o'clock and I have missed it.

Occasionally my kids see a great television show by never turning the set off and I have even tried this. I have sat through a whole day of cartoons and old Western pictures and Lassie, right through the sad comedians and the song stylists. This turns out to be the day when there are no great shows. This so exhausts me that for three days I never turn on the set and during those three days it is reported to me that the screen was lousy with great shows. I guess I am just unfortunate.

I don't know how to participate in the great richness I feel is going on around me. I see the forests of antennas, the darkened rooms from which conversation, reading and even one level of consciousness have disappeared, and I am angry that I can't seem to take part in it.

Our kids are going to be all right because they can't remember how it was before. To them television is a way of life, as natural as breathing, albeit a little asthmatically. Sometimes I wish I could share it with them—or do I?

Star-Spangled Banter

A lady of ample girth once attended a rehearsal with W. S. Gilbert. Sir William was summoned backstage, and when he returned his guest was missing. He asked a nearby stagehand where the friend had gone. "Oh," answered the stagehand pointing backstage, "she's round behind."

"I asked you," retorted Gilbert, "for her geography, not her description!"

In reviewing his long career, actor Ernest Thesiger said that the saddest moment for him was when he was approached by a lady who had last seen him as a handsome young matinee idol, and she asked: "Weren't you Ernest Thesiger?"

Casting director to starlet: "Your voice is okay, sweetie, but we'll have to dub in your acting."

Cary Grant, on an actor's problems in speaking a line while drinking iced tea: "If I bring the glass up too soon, I sound like a man hollering in a barrel. If I hold it up in front of my mouth, I spoil my expression. If I put it down too hard, I kill a couple of words on the sound track; if I don't, I make it seem unreal. I have to hold the glass at a slight angle to keep the reflections out of the lens. It has to be absolutely still to keep the ice from tinkling. And, finally, I have to remember to keep my head up because I have a double chin."

Johnny Carson was once asked, "What made you a star?" He answered, "I started out in a gaseous state, and then I cooled."

Cameramen from *National Geographic* filmed Broadway star Carol Channing at an after-theater party for her latest hit show.

"National Geographic!" she exclaimed. "Which part of me do you want—north, south, east or west?"

Mae West, who wrote her own screen plays, handed her producer the script for a picture co-starring Victor McLaglen and herself. The producer read it and went screaming to the telephone.

"Mae!" he wailed. "You've killed off your co-star in the second reel! You can't do that!"

"Why not?" asked Mae in deadly calm.

"He's your co-star!" he shouted again. "All great authors let their principals live longer than that. Why even in *Romeo and Juliet* Shakespeare let Romeo live until the last act."

"Yeah?" drawled Mae. "Well, Shakespeare had his technique and I have mine."

The title of Mae West's autobiography, *Goodness Had Nothing to Do With It,* comes from an episode in one of her movies. A cloakroom attendant, on seeing Mae's jewels, commented, "Goodness, what beautiful diamonds!"

To which Mae retorted, "Goodness, dearie, had nothing to do with it!"

A prospective starlet, just off the jet, to her manager: "Do I buy a sweater too small and become a star, or a sweater too large and become a folk singer?"

Two Hollywood stars ran into each other at the door of their psychiatrist's office. "Hello, there," said one. "Are you coming or going?"

"If I knew *that,*" said the other, "I wouldn't be here."

Zsa Zsa Gabor was asked which of the Gabors is the oldest. "Well," replied Zsa Zsa, "she would never admit it—but it's Mama."

You know, Jimmy," the late John Barrymore reportedly remarked to Jimmy Durante, "someday you should play Hamlet."

"The hell with them small towns," replied Durante. "New York is the only place for me."

Charlie Chaplin once had a battle with a fly that kept buzzing around him during a picture conference. After slapping at it several times, Charlie became exasperated and called for a swatter. As the discussion continued, he sat with the swatter poised and a menacing eye on the elusive fly. Three times he swung at it; three times he missed. At last the fly settled on a table directly in front of him, and Charlie raised the swatter. But just as he was ready to deliver the death blow, he deliberately lowered his weapon and allowed the fly to escape.

"For heaven's sake!" someone blurted out. "Why didn't you swat it?"

Charlie shrugged—"It wasn't the same fly."

Reviewing her early Brooklyn years, Broadway star Barbra Streisand said, "We were awfully poor. But we had a lot of things that money can't buy—like unpaid bills."

Walter Pidgeon's Aunt Nan was one woman who was not impressed by the actor's charms. She had always wanted Walter to become a lawyer, or at least something more respectable than an actor. So when she read in the papers that he had been ranked second to President Conant of Harvard among "The Ten Best-Dressed Men in America," she wrote: "Dear Nephew: I am glad to see you finally associated with an intellectual. Kindly thank your tailor for me."

When Herb Stein remarked that Jane Russell's success was due to her having a big studio behind her, Mack Sennett snapped, "Son, it isn't what Miss Russell has behind her."

Production Lines

Hollywood producer Bryan Foy told some friends, "I've had actors make all kinds of pitches at me for a job, but the topper came from a guy who called me up one day and said, 'Brynie, I'm not calling for a job. But I'm writing a letter to my mother—and I thought you could tell me how to spell *malnutrition.*'"

Darryl Selznick hadn't found the story that suited him for six years and had reached a point where he was ready to listen to all comers. An unknown aspirant was ushered into his august presence one day. "They tell me you have a play," said Selznick. "Go ahead and read it to me."

This was more than the author, a victim of severe stuttering, had expected. The chance was too good to miss, however, so he sat down and read his whole play. When he had finished, Darryl Selznick called his secretary.

"Sign this guy up at once!" he cried. "He's got a new twist that'll have them rolling in the aisles. Every character in his play stutters."

In response to the question on a movie preview card, "Which scene did you enjoy most?" one patron wrote: "The scene in the lobby after the show, between the producer and the director."

Producer: a man who stands in the back of the theater on opening night and wishes he were dead.

One of the biggest production shots in Cecil B. DeMille's epic *The Ten Commandments* was about to take place next to one of the Pyramids. It was a battle scene requiring 10,000 extras and costing $50,000 and, naturally, DeMille was anxious for it to come off all right. He set up one camera close to the scene, a second on a platform overlooking the battle and a third on a hill overlooking the entire countryside.

When everything was set he fired a pistol and the action began. All the extras played their parts to perfection and slew and were slain in heroic fashion. Finally the happy director shouted, "Cut!"

"How was it?" he asked the cameraman on the close-up.

"Too much dust," he replied. "I didn't get anything."

"What about you?" DeMille shouted to the man on the platform.

"My motor broke," the man shouted back.

Almost in tears, DeMille took a megaphone and screamed to the man on the hill. "HOW WAS IT, HARRY?"

Waving his hand, the man on the hill called out, "ANY TIME YOU'RE READY, MR. DE MILLE!"

When I want your opinion," a producer snapped at his assistant, "I'll give it to you."

Two Hollywood producers were watching the star of a Las Vegas show. "I wonder who made her dress," said one of them admiringly.

"It's hard to say," said the other. "Probably the police."

Meow, Meow

At a Hollywood party an actress said cattily to Greer Garson when the tea arrived, "You pour, Greer dear, because you're so used to playing ladies."

"No, you pour, dear," Miss Garson replied, "because you might need the experience some day."

After Tallulah Bankhead saw the movie based on Tennessee Williams' *Orpheus Descending,* she told Williams, "Darling, how awful for you. They've absolutely ruined your perfectly dreadful play."

Joan Crawford, about an actress, "That feather in her hat—it's sticking out of her brain."

David Niven served as an officer in the British army before he went to Hollywood and became a movie star. Then, when World War II broke out, he returned to England and rejoined his regiment. An old colonel, seeing him when he reappeared in the officers' mess, said to him, "Ah there, Niven, where have you been?"

"I've been doing pictures," Niven said.

"Really?" said the colonel. "Water colors?"

Oscar Levant: "My doctor won't allow me to watch Dinah Shore. I'm a diabetic."

Tom Jenks' comment about a starlet who just became engaged: "They're made for each other. He owns oil wells, and she's always gushing."

A story is told of Noel Coward and Lady Diana Manners, who met at a dinner party in England at a time when they entertained no great liking for each other.

"Did you see my last play, *Private Lives?*" asked Mr. Coward.

"Yes," replied the actress.

"What did you think of it?"

"Not very amusing."

There was a pause.

"Mr. Coward, did you see me play the role of the Virgin in the *Miracle?*"

"Yes."

"And what did you think of it?"

"Very amusing," answered the playwright.

One Sunday night, doing a stint as mistress of ceremonies, Tallulah Bankhead was asked about Bette Davis's obvious impersonation of her in the movie *All About Eve*.

"Bette and I are very good friends," Tallulah remarked sweetly, "There's nothing I wouldn't say to her face— both of them."

One actress to another: "Darling, I sometimes wonder if you don't play too large a part in your life."

Cast a Cold Eye

During his vaudeville days, comedian Fred Allen was playing to a Cleveland audience that sat on its hands throughout his act.

When he returned to his dressing room a fellow performer asked: "How did it go, Fred? Did you kill them?"

"No," said Allen. "They were dead when I got there."

Playing to an indifferent Boston audience, comedian Jackie Leonard told them, "If I were Paul Revere, I wouldn't have warned *you*."

Goodman Ace's capsule criticism of the play *I Am a Camera:* "No Leica!"

The late Professor Barrett Wendell, after seeing a performance of the opera *L'Enfant Prodigue:* "The only signs of a Biblical source were the fatted calves."

From a movie review by Judith Crist: *"The Leopard* is, at best, spotty."

Heywood Broun, while serving the New York *Tribune* as drama critic, was once sued for libel by an actor whose performance, he wrote, was the worst he'd ever seen. The actor lost his suit. Shortly Broun sat in judgment on the unfortunate again. His comment? "Mr. Doe's performance was not up to his usual standard."

At a dull Broadway premiere, singer Margaret Whiting yawned: "I've seen more excitement at the opening of an umbrella."

I can't tell you how many weeks I have labored on this manuscript," the writer told the producer, "polishing a scene here, adding a line there, eliminating scenes, adding new characters."

"What a pity," said the producer, handing it back to him. "All work—and no play."

Matron at box office: "Is this one of those plays the critics all raved about, or is it a good one?"

When an American comedy opened in London, an English critic confined his review to a single sentence. "Last night's play simply didn't come off," he stated, "but it will."

The critic of a London evening paper, reviewing a play entitled *Dreadful Night,* wrote just one word: "Exactly."

Gene Fowler, then a major writer at MGM, was taken into the projection room to see a rough cut of an inferior movie. It was a spy saga of the Civil War. When the showing was over, he was asked, "Mr. Fowler, do you think this picture will offend the South?"

"Yes," answered Fowler. "And the North, too."

Of a poor play, Heywood Broun once wrote: "It opened at 8:40 sharp and closed at 10:40 dull."

George S. Kaufman wrote in a review of a bad Broadway comedy: "Judging by the laughter in the rear of the house, someone must have been telling jokes back there."

One of the briefest musical criticisms on record appeared in a Detroit paper: "An amateur string quartet played Brahms here last evening. Brahms lost."

I have knocked everything except the knees of the chorus girls, and God anticipated me there.

Pianist Artur Schnabel took bad reviews to heart. Once, after a concert, he was panned by a leading critic for his rendition of Beethoven's "Moonlight Sonata." It was 2 a.m. when Schnabel read the review. Stung, he phoned the critic and shouted: "Who are *you* to say that Schnabel played the Moonlight poorly? I say he was superb."

"Who is this?" demanded the critic, half asleep.

"This is Beethoven," snapped Schnabel and hung up.

Curtain Calls and Pratfalls

Even when she was a relative newcomer to Broadway, English actress Gertrude Lawrence was the high priestess of the art of upstaging. Once, playing a scene with Bert Lytell, then president of Actors' Equity, she ate a bunch of violets while he was telling her he loved her.

A midwestern theater was at the height of its season, with Basil Rathbone in *The Heiress* slated to be followed by Boris Karloff in *Arsenic and Old Lace*. During a tense scene of *The Heiress* a bat swooped down from the top of the theater across the footlights. Without a pause Rathbone turned, waved his arms and said in a loud stage whisper: "No, no! Next week, next week!"

Opera soprano Phyllis Curtin has sung the role of Salome all over the world. On one occasion she had no opportunity to rehearse with or even to meet the baritone who sang John the Baptist. When the head of John the Baptist was brought out on a silver platter, it was accompanied by the baritone's card, which read: "Madame, it is a pleasure to make your acquaintance."

As a spellbound audience left the theater after watching the pantomime artist Marcel Marceau, one chap observed: "You know, if that guy could talk he'd be sensational!"

At a performance of Archibald MacLeish's play *J.B.*, I fell into conversation with a couple next to me. "I'm enjoying the play," the woman said, "but I wish I understood it better."

"Have you read the Book of Job, on which it's based?" I asked.

"No," she said, "I haven't." She turned to her husband. "Darling, we *must* get it!"

Pianist Artur Schnabel played a concert in a hall noted for its weird acoustics. Afterward he asked, "How did it sound out front?"

"I'm not sure," replied a friend. "The acoustics were so poor, I heard only half of what you played." Then, noting the look of dejection on Schnabel's face, he quickly added, "But I heard that half twice, Artur!"

What do you have to know to play the cymbals?" someone asked conductor Sir Malcolm Sargent. "Nothing," was his reply. "Except when."

While Oscar Levant was playing an especially brilliant passage of Gershwin's "Piano Concerto in F" in a college auditorium, a telephone began ringing in a nearby office. Levant ignored the persistent ringing, but the audience began squirming. Finally, without interrupting his playing, Levant looked out toward the audience and said, "If that's for me, tell them I'm busy."

During a performance at the California Laguna Beach Playhouse, a sweet little old lady, obviously unaccustomed to legitimate theater, started to leave the theater immediately after the first act. "My, but I did enjoy the play," she told the hostess.

"Can't you stay to see the rest?"

The little lady smiled sadly. "There wouldn't be much use. Look," she pointed to the program, "it says here—Act II, same as Act I."

In the dazzling white armor of Lohengrin, Lauritz Melchior once sang his sad farewell to Elsa, moving step by step with the surging music toward the swan boat which would carry him away. But something happened off stage, and the mechanics pulled the swan into the wings before Melchior could step into it. Finishing his song, in a *sotto voce* plainly audible in the fifth row, he asked, "What time does the next swan leave?"

Vocal affectations always distressed Jerome Kern. Once he was directing an actress who stressed her *r*'s so outrageously that Kern could bear it no longer. When the actress drawled, in her stagy accent, "Tell me, Mr. Kern —you want me to c-r-r-ross the stage, but I'm behind a table. How shall I get ac-r-r-ross?"

Kern, gazing at her like an amiable macaw, countered, "Why, my dear, just r-r-rroll over on your *r*'s."